Management Control Systems

Management Control Systems

Text and Cases

Abhijit Dutta

Dean & Professor (Finance & Control)
Mahendra Institute of Management and Technical Studies, Bhubaneswar

JAICO PUBLISHING HOUSE

Ahmedabad Bangalore Bhopal Chennai
Delhi Hyderabad Kolkata Lucknow Mumbai

Published by Jaico Publishing House
A-2 Jash Chambers, 7-A Sir Phirozshah Mehta Road
Fort, Mumbai - 400 001
jaicopub@jaicobooks.com
www.jaicobooks.com

MANAGEMENT CONTROL SYSTEMS
ISBN 978-81-8495-233-9

First Jaico Impression: 2011

Printed by Pashupati Printers (P) Ltd., Delhi-95

This book is dedicated to
the Lotus Feet of
SRI SRI RAMAKRISHNA PARAHANSA DEV
and
SRI SRI MAA SARADA DEVI

Foreword

With increasing globalisation and the advancement of technology, business organisations have become more complex and more competitive. Though organisations have become more flat in terms of reporting, the emergence of various integrating mechanisms, like committees, matrix structures and cross functionalities, has shown that the traditional simple structures are no longer sufficient to meet contemporary challenges. Management planning and control have also changed considerably to keep pace with these changes. Particularly, in the case of management control systems, the trend of change has been from periodic control to more frequent control, from overall control to multiplicity of control, from subjective understanding of performance to greater quantification and from key performance indicators to balanced score cards comprising all indicators.

In keeping with these changes over the years, the practice of management control systems has also evolved. Externalities have become an important factor in designing these systems. New topics such as advanced methods of valuation, control related audit, enterprise-wide applications, benchmarking, ethical and moral issues in control, exposure to multinationals issues etc., have been added to enrich the subject. This book by Dr. Abhijit Dutta covers these topics in great detail and clearly presents the normally accepted management control topics.

The basic topics of management control such as the concepts of a responsibility centre, key variables, types of cost from the control perspective, an open and closed system, budget and target setting, diagnostic process and decision making, are very crisply presented in the book. The chapters on budgeting, standard costing, variance analysis and transfer pricing expose the reader to the topic of cost accounting which is essential as a building block for understanding any management control system. Further, control systems for functional areas such as production control, marketing control, control of operational processes and control of projects have also been discussed in the book to give a comprehensive picture of the functional areas.

The book has been written, primarily keeping in mind the needs of postgraduate students in management. The learning objectives at the beginning of the chapter and a set of review questions at the end of the chapter keep the reader well focused in the learning process. The texts are very lucidly written. Well written cases on Indian situations can be useful in case discussion sessions and supplement the concepts. Executives working in the area of monitoring and control will find this book useful as conceptual reading and also as a handbook while designing their own control systems and processes. Innovative examples given in various boxes in the book are befitting in the context of the text. The marginal highlights and quotes help in quick recapitulation of the essential concepts and ideas. These new features make this book different from other books on management control and the book is likely to be a very popular text book.

—B. Mohanty

Professor & Former Dean, Xavier Institute of Management, Bhubaneswar

Preface

Management control system is an area of management discipline which brings together several areas and disciplines in order to understand how a business organisation works and how strategy is implemented.

Essentially drawing its ideas from a mechanical system, management control system has come a long way and now incorporates thoughts such as cybernetics and financial control. It is now a widely read subject, which is delivered both in the specialised courses of finance and as a core course in many business schools.

The present book has been developed to cater to the needs of Indian students in general and those who would like to use the Indian aspect of the subject in other parts of the world.

The large number of illustrations and examples help in an easy understanding of the subject. The book cites a large number of Indian case studies, which can be used for class room discussions as well as syndicate learning.

The author will be very happy to receive constructive comment on the book.

—Abhijit Dutta

Acknowledgements

The author gratefully acknowledges the support of Jaico Publishing House, the printer, the writers of the case studies, the students who have passed through his classes in management control and who have helped sharpen his faculties.

The author would also like to thank everybody in his family who gave so much time while he was busy composing the book.

Contents

PART—A

INTRODUCTION TO MANAGEMENT CONTROL SYSTEM

CHAPTER 1

Management Control System: An Introduction

LEARNING OBJECTIVES OF THE CHAPTER

- Management control system: An introduction
- Scope of management control system
- Need of a management control system
- Functions of a management control system
- Organisational context of a management control system
- The design and purpose of a formal and informal management control system
- Management control system and subsystems that affect it
- Processes of accounting and management control
- Complex industrial dynamics, disaster and management control system
- Cybernetics and system approach to a management control system

1.1 INTRODUCTION

The business scenario today is rapidly changing due to geo-political environmental factors. The onset of global business is creating multi layer businesses both in the small and large sector. It is very interesting to observe that all these organisations are adapting to similar processes due to the changed economic environment.

The onset of global business is creating multi layer businesses both in the small and large sector.

This is driven by the fact that organisations are losing business competence if they operate from one location or by using one set of guiding principles. The consistency and effectiveness of performance solely lay in the management of the business. In simple terms the function of management is to plan, organise, integrate and inter-relate organisational activities to achieve its objectives. This is facilitated through management control systems.

In simple terms the function of management is to plan, organise, integrate and inter-relate organisational activities to achieve its objectives. This is facilitated through management control systems.

A control system is a set of formal and informal systems to assist the management in moving forward to realise organisational goals. Control helps in guiding employees effectively towards the accomplishment of the organisation's goals. Since, a management control system is a set of interrelated structures that facilitates the processing of information for the purpose of assisting managers in coordinating the

A control system is a set of formal and informal systems to assist the management in moving forward to realise organisational goals.

parts, and attaining the purpose, of an organisation on a continuous basis, it is difficult to establish a control system in an environment of distributed accountability, reengineered processes and empowered work structure. Control systems are integral to all organisations. They deal with coordination, resource allocation, motivation and performance measurement.

The development of a management control system started with the development of the theory and practice of modern management theory.

The development of a management control system started with the development of the theory and practice of modern management theory. In fact F.W. Taylor had suggested a control system in the theories he propounded. The idea of management control system originated at the end of the First World War. The resource crunch and the heavy demand pushed industrial processes to the brink. At that time, the focus of the control system was on the performance of physical production. Later, during the final days of colonial rule of the British Empire, the focus shifted to production control, but by and large still directly controlled physical activities. It was in the late 1950s and early 1960s that the new science of cost accounting revolutionised the system of control process. For the first time it was felt that by controlling costs, a significant amount of business could be achieved. However, by the 1980s the focus had shifted to activity based control with the predominant focus on human resource management. From the late 1990s to date the focus has been on system-sub system management.

Figure 1.1 gives an idea as to how the management control paradigm has shifted and changed with time.

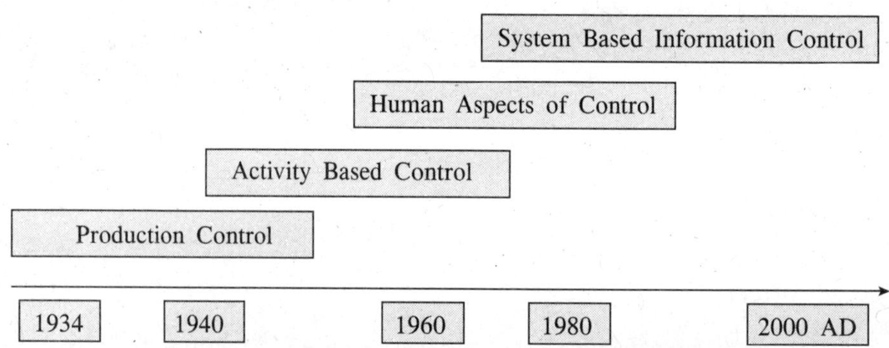

Fig. 1.1 : Historical perspective of development of management control system (A. Dutta, Management Control System, 1st Ed Kalyani, New Delhi 2008)

1.2 SCOPE OF MANAGEMENT CONTROL SYSTEM

Management control system is basically a system of information processes which validates and verifies the physical processes in the organisation.

All businesses have a common goal. In order to achieve that goal, several business processes work in tandem with each other, despite being diverse in nature. The scope of management control system comes into the picture because of this. In this context management control system is basically a system of information processes which validates and verifies the physical processes in the organisation.

Depending on its nature, management control system can be divided into two categories as given below:

1.2.1 The Closed End Management Control System

A closed management system is a system in which the information flows through the activity, the result, the matching of the standard preset, analysis of the variation if any and taking corrective steps to mitigate the mistake. Closed end control mechanics uses a receptor and a corrector mode of operation.

A closed management system is a system in which the information flows through the activity, the result, the matching of the standard pre set, analysis of the variation if any and taking corrective steps to mitigate the mistake.

In an organisation where there is an annual budget with preset goals and performance parameters, the implementation, collection of performance information, measurement of variance and thereafter taking corrective action on any negative variance across a preset standard is an example of a closed end control system.

1.2.2 The Open End Management Control System

An open management control system is a system in which the feedback mechanism is continuous in every step of the activity and follows a matrix system where several receptors interact with several correctors in the system.

An open management control system is a system in which the feedback mechanism is continuous in every step of the activity and follows a matrix system where several receptors interact with several correctors in the system.

A corporate system in which there is a continuous internal audit parallel to the general accounting and budgeting process enables an open end control system as it provides multiple feedbacks which are supportive of each other and work towards a common objective – say cost control.

Components of a Management Control System

A management control system essentially has the following four components:

1. **A detector or sensor:** This part detects the change or deviation.
2. **An assessor (actual vs. standard measurer):** This part measures the change in relation to a set standard.
3. **An effecter (feedback and alternator):** This part begins the control process by taking in the feedback and altering the process to what is deemed to be normal.
4. **A communicating network:** This is the backbone of the control system, as all the above mentioned three parts actually work with the help of this network by transferring information through it.

Figure 1.2 below gives a schematic picture of the relationship between the various components of the management control system in a business.

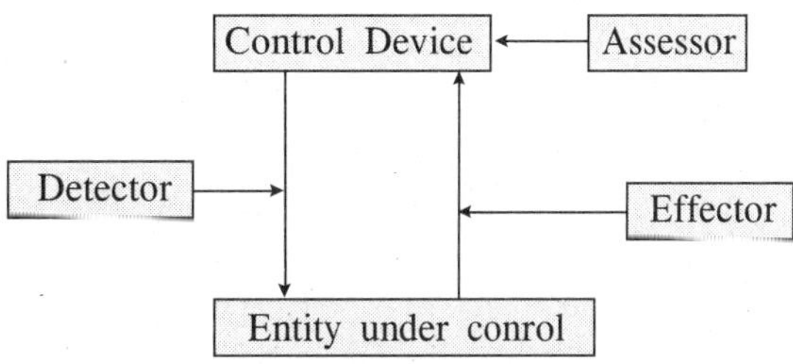

Fig. 1.2: Various components of management control system (A. Dutta, Management Control System, 1st Ed, Kalyani, New Delhi, 2008)

1.3 NEED OF MANAGEMENT CONTROL SYSTEMS

The management control system needs to provide a direction to the overall process of the business and steer the organisation towards the realisation of such goals that the business has set for itself. The management control system runs like a thread through the system and acts as a backbone which supports the organisational systems.

The need of the control system is to maintain that desired state of activity in the business. Information about the actual state of the organisation is compared with the desired state, and if there is a major deviation, corrective actions are taken.

The need of the control system is to maintain that desired state of activity in the business.

In an organisation, the control system involves the following functions:

1. Analysing and planning the activities of an organisation.
2. Coordinating the activities of the organisation.
3. Communicating information to different levels of the hierarchical structure.
4. Evaluating information and deciding the action to be taken.
5. Influencing employees of the organisation to change and accommodate to the new system.

In the planning stage, the management of an organisation decides what the organisation should do. The control process compares actual accomplishments with the set plans. Another important purpose of the control system is to ensure that the work of each part of the organisation is in harmony with that of the other. Control systems are designed to bring about unity of purpose in an organisation through the efforts of individuals.

The purpose of management control is to ensure that the right strategies are carried out to attain the organisation's goals. Management control systems anticipate future conditions. They are not self-regulating in nature. Managers usually operate in situations of uncertainty and the control systems ensure that proper actions are taken whenever they are needed, in spite of the uncertainty.

Management control systems help the management in decision-making. In the management control process, decisions are made according to procedures and timetables.

Management control systems help the management in decision-making.

It may be remembered here that management control system is an interdisciplinary subject. It uses the knowledge of all branches of management as it gives a direction to the business and helps the business to run effectively. This interrelating part of the management control system makes it an integral part of the business strategy. It is believed that the management control system provides for the implementation of the strategy and measurement of any deviation.

Management control system is an interdisciplinary subject.

1.4 FUNCTIONS OF MANAGEMENT CONTROL

The domain of the management control system is to accelerate the productivity and improve the quality of the end product of a business. The basic functions of the management control system are therefore to:

1. **Enable strategic planning**: Management control begins with the enablement of strategic planning of a business. The process of alignment with the vision, mission and goals of the business ensures an effective path for the business.
2. **Establish management control:** Thereafter, the process of control becomes important in the business as it helps in taking corrective steps in every managerial process whenever it goes wrong.
3. **Enable task control:** Task control is the root to all control as it enables the business tasks at all levels of the business to become one with the goals of the business.
4. **Lay the road map for the control of the strategy:** One major role of the control system is to lay a road map to strategy so that it can easily be employed.
5. **Ensure control of the operation.** The last, but not the least, function of the management control system is to ensure the operations of the business are controlled in such a way that the overall strategy, functions and tasks are carried out in the right direction.

1.5 ORGANISATIONAL CONTEXT OF MANAGEMENT CONTROL SYSTEMS

An organisation consists of many functions and the control system must ensure that the multiple functions of the organisation run in tandem. The control systems are designed to assist the management to run the business in orderly way with a realistic description of the goals of the organisation.

The control systems are designed to assist the management to run the business in orderly way with a realistic description of the goals of the organisation.

The roles of the management control system in helping the organisation to run effectively are given below.

1.5.1 Organisations

1. **Subunits:** Organisations are divided into subunits. Subunits comprise individuals who perform certain activities to fulfil the purpose of the organisation. The subunits are based on the principles of division of labour. Division of labour enables monitors to specialise in certain tasks which improve the efficiency of the subunits. For example, all the activities that are concerned with marketing may be combined with a marketing department which can be termed as a subunit.

   The control system plays a major role in coordinating the efforts of these subunits. The cost of coordinating these subunits may be referred to as transaction cost.

   Control system designers try to design systems which help in minimising the transaction costs. Inefficient coordination of errors in subunits results in excess transaction costs. Each subunit should have the objective of reducing transaction costs so that the overall performance of the organisation is improved.

   Control system designers try to design systems which help in minimising the transaction costs.

2. **Effectiveness and efficiency of an organisational subunit:** An organisational subunit is said to be effective when it meets the overall purpose of the organisation and it is said to be efficient when it meets the needs of the constituents of the organisation.

   Effectiveness relates to the organisation's ability to meet the social purpose whereas the efficiency relates to the realisation of the business objectives by the organisation for its stakeholders.

   Effectiveness relates to the organisation's ability to meet the social purpose whereas the efficiency relates to the realisation of the business objectives by the organisation for its stakeholders.

   If the subunits become effective and efficient the organisation also becomes effective and efficient. An effective and efficient organisation meets its social demands and in the process consolidates and strengthens its constituents within the business.

3. **Executive function and management control system:** Securing essential efforts from the employees, providing a perfect system of communication and establishing the goals and objectives of the business and thereby delegating it are the three essential managerial functions, which were established by Chester Barnard.

   However, these functions are not confined to an executive. It is the role of the entire management team to delegate responsibility of the right people and ensure that the management control system is put into place.

4. **Response to internal and external stakeholders:** The management has to be interactive and take various decisions regarding the business, keeping in mind both the internal and external stakeholders. The management control system helps in striking a balance between the internal efforts and the external activities. It enables the business to absorb any changes that can occur in the market.

   The management control system helps in striking a balance between the internal efforts and the external activities.

5. **Organisational survival and control systems:** The market conditions are highly dynamic in today's modern world. The rapid changes in customer needs and the major stakeholders' needs necessitate that the business adopts innovative business methods. As a result of this the traditional control systems are becoming redundant. Optimum utilisation of resources makes it necessary for a business to look for adaptive control systems. Unless the internal control and information systems are as efficient as the outside ones in the market, the business will not be able to survive. This will be the only key to success in the changing business scenario.

6. **Control system and human behaviour:** In order to design and deliver a good management control system, it is essential to note that it is going to operate in a human system. Hence the basic qualities of a human being such as rationality, creativity and morality should be kept in mind. In addition, the desire of a human being to control others makes the system loaded with individual's perceptions of control which often makes an organisational system to fail.

1.6 THE DESIGN AND PURPOSE OF FORMAL AND INFORMAL CONTROL SYSTEMS

1.6.1 Formal Control System

A management control system generally follows two paths; the formal and the informal system. The formal control systems are laid down according to the need and goals of the organisation, which have to be realised through the control mechanics. The informal management control system originates out of the general socio-cultural milieu.

A formal control system consists of the following sub systems:

1. Management style and culture of the organisation
2. Infrastructure
3. Rewards
4. Coordination and integration
5. Control tools and process

Figure 1.3 shows the relationship between these subsystems effectively.

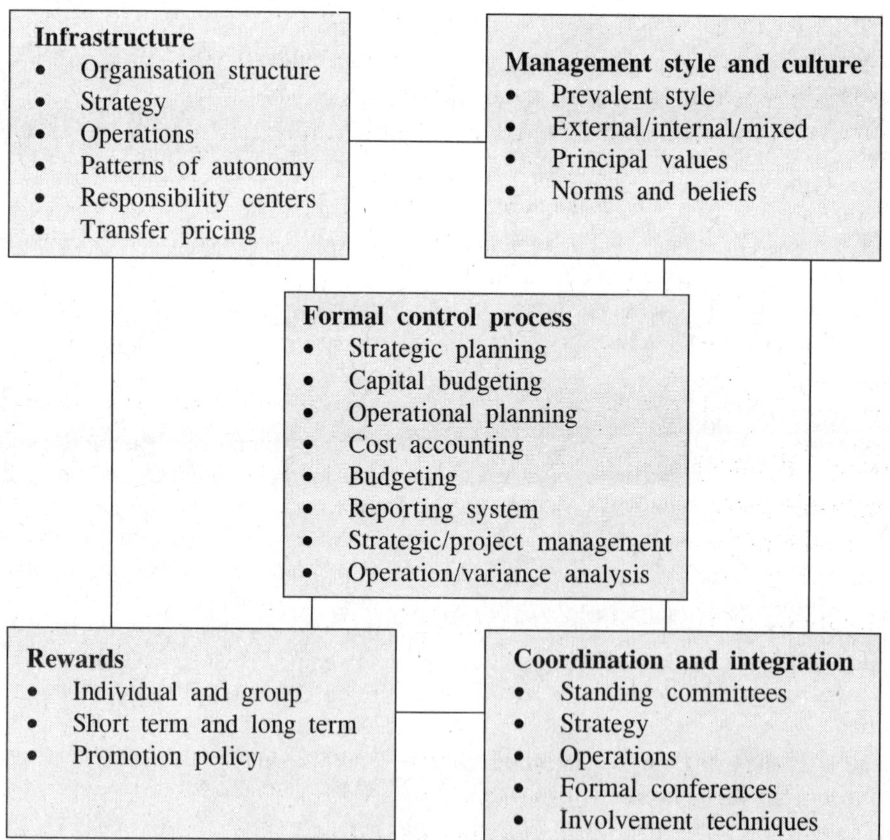

Fig. 1.3: Formal control system (Source: J.A. Maciarello, C.J. Kirby, Management Control System, PHI, 2nd Ed, 1997)

The formal control system focuses on the need of both the internal and external stakeholders. It is based on the information system established by the organisation. It is highly dynamic in nature since it takes the basic forces of the market into consideration.

It is observed that the informal management control system uses the same backbone as the formal control system in its operation.

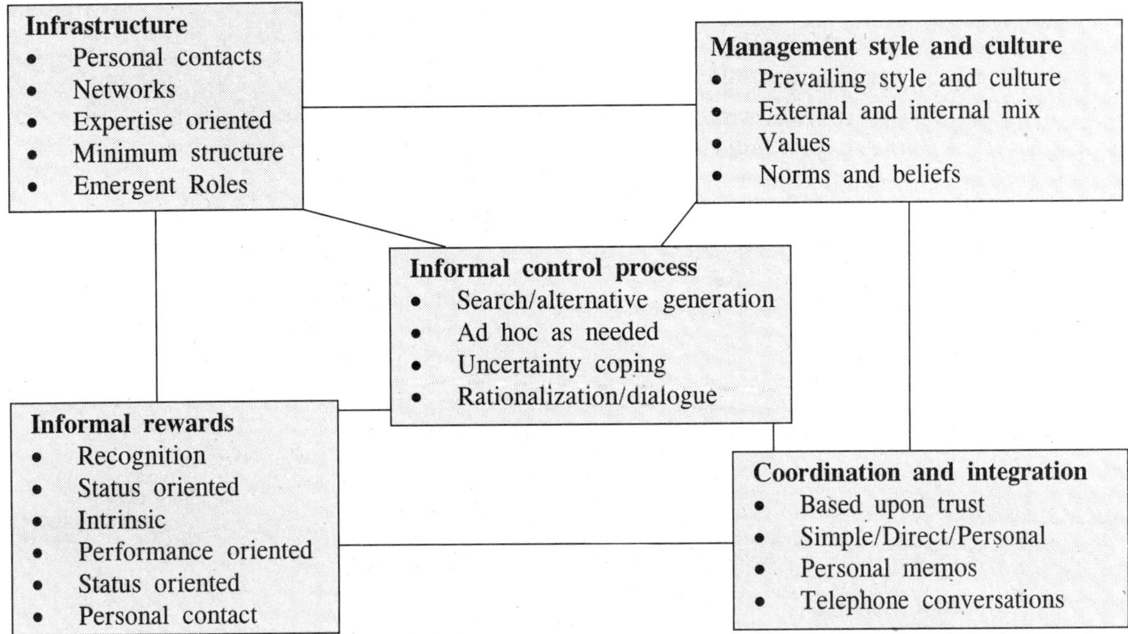

***Fig. 1.4** Informal control systems (Source: J.A. Maciarello, C.J. Kirby, Management Control System, PHI, 2nd Ed, 1997)*

1.6.2 Informal Control Systems

Organisations have their own informal systems in place. These consist of interaction between individuals and groups. These informal systems do not show up on the organisational chart of the business. However, such informal systems help to make the organisation more conducive to work and enhances the employees' willingness to work for the organisation. Figure 1.4 above shows the relationship that exists in an informal control system within the paradigm of the formal control system.

The informal control system is dependent on the expertise, experience and trust amongst the people working in the organisation and the stakeholders. The availability recognition based on informal coordination makes the mechanism sound. Such informal control systems are highly dependent on the style and culture of individuals and the group.

The informal control system emerges from informal interaction and socialisation between people in the organisation, and thus makes the organisation adaptable to changes. Since in an informal system, there is free flow of information cutting across hierarchical levels, it makes the organisation more open and responsive to the environment for technical innovations and change.

1.7 MANAGEMENT CONTROL SYSTEM AND SUBSYSTEMS THAT AFFECT IT

The management control system is affected by several subsystems which are given in the following sections.

1.7.1 Organisational Style and Culture

A control system should be such that it coordinates the management's culture and helps in blending the styles of work of the top level management. A good control system should serve as a continuum from highly autocratic to highly participative function of management.

1. **Organisational culture:** Corporate culture depends primarily on the shared values and common perception in an organisation. The larger the premise of a shared value the greater is the strength of the corporate culture.
2. **Organisational culture as a control mechanism:** The better the corporate culture, the lower is the dissonance in the organisation. This facilitates the adaptation of the control system. A corporate culture must be consistent with the requirements of the organisation and the environment of the business. A process of self control through acceptance of shared values boosts the organisation's performance.
3. **Coaching people for skill and common values:** In order to increase the acceptability of the control process the management should enable processes that lead to the understanding of common values, procedures and policies. This enables the people within the organisation to appreciate the system and rise to the cause of the organisation.

1.7.2 Processes of Formal Control

The formal control process has two dimensions as given below.

1. **Formal planning process:** The formal planning is dependent upon strategic planning and operational planning. These are supported by the strategic budget and operational budget. In common terms, the strategic budgets are long term capital budgets. The formal planning process supports the formal control system internally.
2. **Formal reporting process:** The formal reporting system is designed to guide an organisation using the relevant information collected continuously from the organisation. It forms the backbone of the corrective actions that need to be taken. Formal reports serve as background material on which the strategic planning is carried out. In fact, the strategic planning substantially depends on the current business occurrence. Hence, strategic planning needs to be changed and should accommodate the current operational plan.

1.7.3 Infrastructure

The infrastructure refers to the relationship that exists between the subsystems and their autonomy. The patterns of autonomy relate to the delegation of responsibility to the subunits. When both operational and strategic autonomy are given to the subunits, the subunit is termed as a Strategic Business Unit (SBU). Such SBUs increase customer responsiveness and entrepreneurial skills and garner more profit by integrating the goals of the organisation. A key issue in designing the management control system is to locate the SBUs at the right point in the organisational chart.

1.7.4 Rewards

One of the essential functions of an executive is to induce individuals to participate in the various activities of the organisation. The best method of doing this is to use an appropriate incentive program. Incentives may be monetary or non-monetary. Non-monetary compensations include acceptance, status, desired associations, pride of workmanship and desirable physical conditions.

Rewards may be individual rewards or group rewards. Individual rewards include compensation based on individual performance. Group rewards are tied to the overall performance of the organisation. Group rewards may be based on short-term or long-term performance.

1.7.5 Coordination and Integration Mechanism

Organisations need specific vehicles for communication to help in coordination, decision-making, conflict resolution and development of commitment and trust amongst the employees. In order to achieve this it is essential that there are committees that look after such issues. Such committees should have formal meetings and conferences to discuss issue based agendas and also for general development in areas of their interest. The larger the shared value through such committees and conferences the greater is the chance of successful implementation of the formal control system.

1.7.6 Informal Control Process

Management decisions are based upon experience, intuition and feeling.

Informal control processes are formed as a result of interaction between people based on such experience, intuition and feeling.

Informal groups help in resolving a problem at the root level by forming ad hoc teams. Such an informal process helps in improving the productivity of the organisation. Besides, informal control processes uphold the values of the organisation. It has been observed that informal reward systems also help in developing a strong morale in the employees of the organisation. The respect that the individuals enjoy in an organisation also develops a strong bond in the organisation.

1.8 PROCESSES OF ACCOUNTING AND MANAGEMENT CONTROL

It is an established fact that the accounting system provides the most data in a business. This is partly because of the fact that accounting is quasi legal in nature and hence mandatory for the business.

Accounting collects critical information about the business over a regular period of time in several forms and thus facilitates the control process.

An accounting system can be broadly classified into financial accounting, cost accounting and management accounting. The financial accounting and cost accounting collects the critical data about the business. The data are diverse since financial data are more or less based on transactions and the cost data are based on activities. The management accounting in turn helps in making meaningful reports about the business, such as the health of the business and strength of the business. We will see later, that management accounting, along with the other two systems, is a vital system of control tools in the business.

1.9 COMPLEX INDUSTRIAL DYNAMICS, DISASTER AND MANAGEMENT CONTROL SYSTEM

Until now we have discussed the control system for a business under normal circumstances. We need to understand that a business is a set of complex processes which work as an interlocking system of information network. This network emerges at various points of the control and affects the physical processes of the business. A well managed management control system identifies the flow of information through the physical activities of the organisation. By facilitating such an identification of the interlocking network of information, the management control system enables right decisions to be taken.

A good management control system should be enabled with a system so that a disaster has the least effect on the business processes.

A business may often encounter a disastrous situation. A disaster is an abnormal situation, and hence calls for diversion of all resources to mitigate its effect. It is desirable to incorporate an appropriate built in system in the management control process, which can identify a disaster, prepare for it and deal with it correctly, so that the post disaster effect is low. A good management control system should be enabled with a system so that a disaster has the least effect on the business processes. It is a well known fact that the modern day information technology organisation has a separate cell to keep it in readiness to face any disaster. These include physical location preparedness and system level preparedness.

1.10 CYBERNETICS AND SYSTEMS APPROACH TO MANAGEMENT CONTROL SYSTEM

Cybernetics has its origin in the Greek word 'Kybernetcs' which mean the person who steers a boat.

The word cybernetics has its origin in the Greek word 'Kybernetcs' which mean the person who steers a boat. Thus cybernetics is the science of control which steers the activity of a system by coordinating all the sub-systems and leads to the desired result. Norbert Weiner coined the term in the 1940s and defined it as "The entire field of control and communication theory, whether in the machine or in animal".

"The entire field of control and communication theory, whether in the machine or in animal".

Cybernetics deals with the self regulatory principles in a variety of systems, which range from human and biological systems to mechanical systems. Cybernetics processes view a complete system as a collection of many subsystems which are unique in nature but work in tandem and depend upon each other to deliver the ultimate function or result of the system. Cybernetics is greatly dependent on complex information and a feedback network, which act as a reference to improve the initial actions and results. The science of cybernetics has been used in various fields such as radar technology, human genetics and artificial intelligence, to name a few.

In a management control system, cybernetics is used as a tool to set up norms or targets for a decision making information system. The actions are taken pursuant to the goals set. Cybernetics is used to establish the fact that in a business organisation there are subsystems which influence the greater system and which themselves are influenced by the environment and by each other. These complex relationships being influenced by each other and the environment and the corrective actions, which are mostly self regulated, answer some of the complex questions of the control mechanism of an organisation, which is almost like a living organism.

In a management control system, cybernetics is used as a tool to set up norms or targets for a decision making information system.

SUMMARY

A business organisation pursues diverse activities aimed at meeting a common goal which is ultimately reflected as the nature of the business. Since these activities are drivers they need to be controlled to get the desired results. A management control system serves this purpose and integrates and coordinates the various activities of the business to a common goal. Each management system works in the context of the organisational structure it functions in. The design and purpose of the management control system varies from business to business. A business organisation can opt for an open end control or a close end control depending on what it desires to achieve. Within an organisation, both formal and informal control systems are established. The formal control systems are established keeping in mind the business need and are accompanied by a suitable reward system. On the other hand informal systems are more or less created from the interaction of individuals and the system in the organisation. Both these control systems help in development of the organisation. It may be noted that the business actually operates through complex industrial dynamics and it is necessary to be prepared for any disaster that may occur in the business. A good control system should be prepared for a disaster and post disaster recovery. Since, business organisations are seen as an interaction between a system and subsystem, cybernetics come into the picture to enable the process of control. The control mechanism is strengthened by the use of accounting processes, which primarily provide the information and the data base for processing the control mechanics.

Review Questions

1. Why is management control important to a business?
2. Give a detailed historical perspective of the management control system. How did the management control system evolve?
3. What is the scope of the management control system?
4. What are the close and open control systems of management control?
5. What are the components of the management control system? Describe them in detail.
6. What are the needs of the management control system?

7. What are the functions of the management control system?
8. How is the effectiveness of an organisation different from its efficiency?
9. What are formal and informal control systems?
10. What are the subsystems that affect the management control system?

Analytical Questions

1. A European bank wants to start operations in India. What are the various factors that it has to keep in mind in order to ensure an effective control system?
2. A manager was newly appointed to supervise the floor work in a factory. He found that the workers reported only to the works head of the factory for all their needs and factory related problems, which included the production process. He thereafter segregated the work and factory related problems and identified various persons to which each kind of problem was related. The workers were confused and this slowed down the process of work.

   Do you think that the approach was correct? Would it yield results in the short term or long term and how?

CHAPTER 2

Key Variables in Management Control Process

LEARNING OBJECTIVES OF THE CHAPTER

- Introduction to key variables
- Processes of identification of key variables
- Classification of key variables
- The key variables for the business: Ensuring across the board control
- Key control indicators and control mechanics
- Techniques to identify the key variables of a business
- Limitations of key variables

2.1 INTRODUCTION

Key variables are those indicators or variables that influence the business in a big way. They are sometimes called the "**key budgeting factors**". These factors, variables or indicators are so crucial that a small change in them will affect the business in a big way.

Key variables are those indicators or variables that influence the business in a big way.

Key variables can be external factors or internal ones. Some of the external key variables are technology, environment and competitive status of the business in relation to the other businesses. The internal ones may range from tasks to strategy set in the business. A good control system tries to understand these indicators since they can be the locus of control in an organisation. For example if a business has a key variable or indicator such as skilled labour, the control function should try to strengthen the sourcing and retention of such skilled labour in the organisation.

Key variables can be external factors or internal ones. Some of the external key variables are technology, environment and competitive status of the business in relation to the other businesses.

Figure 2.1 shows the relationship between internal and external key variables in a business.

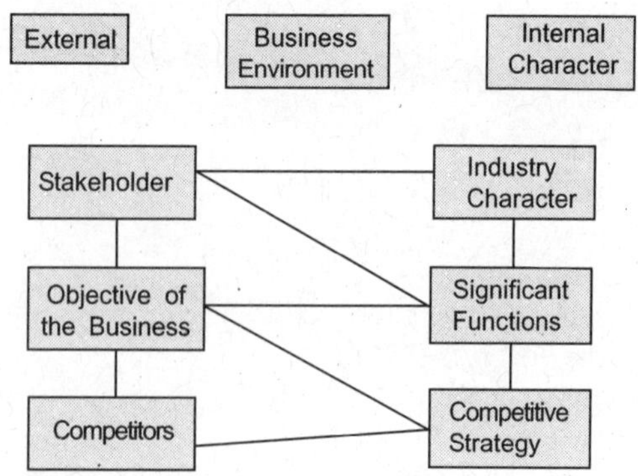

Fig. 2.1: Interrelation between the internal and external key factors

2.2 KEY VARIABLES AND THEIR SOURCES

The external key variables mostly come from the nature of the business, the types of the stakeholders and the competitors the business faces. The internal key factors come from the task, industry character, significant function and the strategy adapted. One may observe here, that since the business functions in a common environment, there are common minimum requirements and performance benchmarks for both the external and internal key factors. Some of these are elaborated in the sections below.

The external key variables mostly come from the nature of the business, the types of the stakeholders and the competitors the business faces. The internal key factors come from the task, industry character, significant function and the strategy adapted.

2.2.1 Nature of Business

The degree to which the business is sensitive to its immediate environment greatly depends upon the nature of business. For example, if an industry is the primary processor of the raw material, any change in the price or availability of the raw materials will affect the business. However, if the business is only remotely associated with the same kind of raw material, but still uses it, the business may not be immediately affected by any change in price or availability. Hence, the nature of the business significantly influences the way a business is conducted.

2.2.2 Type of Stakeholder in the Business

A (business) stakeholder is an individual or a group of individuals who share some minimum requirement with a business organisation. By the type of stakeholder, is meant the degree to which the stakeholders participate in the business and the extent to which they are risk accepters.

The lower the involvement and risk taking ability of the various stakeholders in the business the lower will be the growth in the business.

The lower the involvement and risk taking ability of the various stakeholders in the business the lower will be the growth in the business. Conversely, an increase in both participation and risk taking ability of the stakeholders will mean a larger degree of influence on the day to day activity of the business though it might mean a higher return for the business.

There is a need to be balanced in such a situation and the controls system should be able to deal with the complexities arising out of the involvement of the stakeholders in the business.

2.2.3 Competitors of the Business

Each business has its own kind of competitors for the business. Generally there are two kinds of competitors: The substitutes and the complements. The substitutes are those who can eventually take up the market share of the business. The complements cannot take over the market, but they can club with the substitutes and sooner or later eliminate the business in this context. Hence the competitors hold a key position in identification of the deciding factor in the business.

2.2.4 Objective of the Business

The objective of the business is stated in the mission and vision statement of the business. This in turn is the key to the competitive strategy of the business. The strategy generally identifies the key variables that need to be identified and monitored in order for the business to grow.

2.2.5 Industry Character

The character of the business is primarily derived from the industry in which it thrives. The industry in turn is the collective expression of expectations of the business comprising it. Therefore, to a great extent the key variable is imbedded in the industry character.

2.3 PROCESS OF IDENTIFICATION OF KEY VARIABLES

The process of identification of the key variables is done through input–output analysis. This analysis helps in understanding the modus operandi through which the input is processed to become the output and the linkages in between. The idea behind this is to enable the control process to identify the points in which the controlling action should be taken. For this purpose, the variables in the business are divided into the following categories:

- Inputs
- Production
- Marketing and selling
- Liability management
- Asset management

We will deal with the various issues one by one in order to understand the input–output classification.

2.3.1 Inputs

In a typical production oriented business the input generally rotates around the raw martial. The concerned area in the raw material is the availability, the quality and the cost. Typically it can be referred to as the '**Q**uality – **T**ime – **C**ost' or QTC factor. It may be noted here that QTC is critical to the business since the market leadership of the product (which may also include service as a part of it) is largely dependent on it. Hence, when an input analysis is carried out, it is essential that the QTC analysis is also carried out to establish the leadership of the product in the market. The QTC of the raw material needs to be monitored at all points of time if the business has to achieve the desired result as set by the business strategy. Therefore, it serves as the corner stone of key variables in the control mechanics of the business.

2.3.2 Production

Production is essentially dependent on four basic issues, namely the production process, the technology, the cost and the ability to meet the time schedule.

2.3.3 Production Processes

Production processes are in turn dependent on the capacity utilisation and quality control. It may be noted here that production systems which are always trying to be rational on cost are often cost ineffective. In this, poor quality of work might lead to substantial losses over a period of time. It has been observed that the poorer the quality, the larger is the rework time required, which includes loss of man-hours and loss in post sales processes. Hence, a close watch on the production process must be in place to run an output – input function.

2.3.4 Technology

A correctly chosen technology can give the business a lead in the market.

Technology plays a vital role in deciding the output of the business. A correctly chosen technology can give the business a lead in the market. It is appropriate to point out here that the research and development of technology often may not take place in the same country where it is put to use. The above factor is often a component of the technology transfer. One of the greatest difficulties of technology transfer is the adaptation of the technology to the new environment which may not be the same as the one in which it was developed. An output input analysis, should essentially keep this issue in mind when identifying the technology.

Another point to consider is the quality and durability of the technology. Good technology should be able to provide support for a reasonably long period of time as set by the standards of the business it is meant for. High maintenance and a lot of rework means the technology being used is not very good. This not only increases the cost but also diverts money and attention from the main focus of the business.

2.3.5 Cost of Production

Cost of production plays an important role in determining the fate of the business.

Cost of production plays an important role in determining the fate of the business. In an exercise conducted by the General Electrical Company (GEC), the cost of the business was divided into three components: The **infrastructure cost**, the **engineering cost** and the **discretionary cost**. It was found that the infrastructure and the discretionary costs are high, whereas the engineering costs are low.

The infrastructure costs – as the name indicates – are the cost of the basic infrastructure of the business. The engineering costs are the costs where a relationship between the input and the output can be established. The discretionary costs are those which cannot be classified under the above two costs. However, it may be noted that the engineering costs are the ones that can be easily identified and controlled. An increase in the other two costs essentially means indiscriminate and unplanned wastage of cash, unless there are strong reasons to back up such increases in costs.

2.3.6 Time Schedule and Delivery

These are critically important in most businesses. Delays in the delivery system need the special attention of the management. This is more applicable in an industry where there are chances of products being spoiled due to time lapse.

2.3.7 Marketing and Selling

Information on marketing and selling is critical to the business for the following reasons:

1. **Selling information:**
   a. **Ordering position:** The number of orders placed by the customers/retailer/wholesaler per order size undertaken is critical to the business. Such information helps in deciding the batch size and production schedule.
   b. **Maturity schedule of credit sales:** The maturity schedule of the credit sales is important information for the business because it helps in cash planning and management of the overall working capital of the business.
2. **Marketing information**
   a. **Market share** of the business in terms of sales available is critical information since, the complete business planning and revenue modelling is dependent on such information.
   b. **Budget information of the promotional and advertising expenses** of the competitors is equally critical to the business since, there are a number of decisions which will ultimately be taken based on such information and will mean cash position of the business.

2.3.8 Liability Management

Liabilities as is well known are the source of funds for business today. Hence appropriate information about the liabilities will automatically influence the business decisions. Stated below are some of the key concern areas and information critical to a business in terms of liabilities.

1. Cost of borrowing: The cost of borrowing the capital sources of a business is very critical to the business. This is essentially due to the fact that the overall profitability is dependent on the cost of the sources of the capital in the long run. The concept of Economic Value Added (EVA) which shows the operating profit in excess of the cost of capital is becoming one of the most used concepts of modern day business in order to ascertain the actual wealth generated in the business.

2. Nature of capital: The nature of the capital depending on the participation in the business will decide the degree of risk associated with each borrowing. The greater the involvement, the greater is the risk. Hence, in planning the overall budget the nature of capital is critical.

2.3.9 Asset Management

The management of assets is critical to a business. The higher the turnover of assets, both fixed and current assets, the better it is for a business. In fact the financial analysis necessary to interpret the health of the business is primarily based on the turnover of assets. It may be pertinent here to observe that the key issue which needs to be identified in the control system is the working capital turnover ratio (which shows how good the net current asset has performed in terms of net sales) and the total asset turnover ratio.

2.4 CLASSIFICATION OF KEY VARIABLES

Key variables or variables can be classified into four categories which affect the performance of the business. They are detailed below.

2.4.1 Environmental Variables

As discussed earlier, the business is conducted in an environment which to a great extent decides what exactly will be conducted by the business house. It decides the scope, diversity and uncertainty that are associated with a business.

2.4.2 Strategy Variables

The variables which affect the long term goals and values of the business are known as strategic variables. The more elaborate the strategy variables are in their definition the greater is the scope to control them.

2.4.3 Process Variables

Process variables refer to the processes that are laid out in the business. They define the interaction between the system and the employees of the organisation.

2.4.4 Structure Variables

They represent the way the organisation is represented. Broadly, the structure of the organisation is divided into two, centralised structure and decentralised structure. Centralised structure ensures a single point reporting which is distinctly different from the point of operation of the business. The decentralised structure on the other hand ensures different points of reporting, accountability and control at various points and levels depending on the requirement of the business. The effectiveness of the structure variables are gauged on the basis of the process variables.

2.5 THE KEY VARIABLES FOR THE BUSINESS: ENSURING ACROSS THE BOARD CONTROL

Depending on the issues discussed earlier, each organisation should be able to identify some comprehensive and across the board key variables for the business so that they can adopt a management control system with ease.

Each organisation should be able to identify some comprehensive and across the board key variables for the business so that they can adopt a management control system with ease.

It is often found that the key variables that are identified are the ones that are easy to measure or for which some data are already available. This may ultimately defeat the purpose of the control mechanism at large.

An easy way out of this problem is to use a multivariate technique such as factor or cluster analysis to boil down to a few indicators which are the key to the business[1].

The key variables so found need to be all inclusive and should be able to touch upon the key issues in the management of the business.

2.6 KEY CONTROL INDICATORS AND CONTROL MECHANISM

The ability of an organisation to implement a control process is largely dependent on how the key variables have been chosen. The key variables interact with each other in all areas of the business. The ability of a control system is indicated by the efficiency and effectiveness of the key variables that have been used. Efficiency here means the ability to do things correctly and effectiveness means the ability to do the correct things at the right time and situation.

The ability of a control system is indicated by the efficiency and effectiveness of the key variables that have been used.

The control mechanism is affected by the problems of coordination in the business. If a business has identified the key variables properly but fails to coordinate its activities, then, despite all the efforts, the control mechanism will fail to work.

In an organisation which has various profit or responsibility centres, it is of utmost importance that the key issues or indicators are representative in nature to all of these centres.

2.7 TECHNIQUES TO IDENTIFY THE KEY VARIABLES OF A BUSINESS

The techniques to identify the key variables are divided into two groups, namely traditional

[1] Refer to any book on advanced statistical methods for a clear understanding of data reduction techniques, such as cluster and factor analysis. Today, most of the standard statistical packages can deal with such data reduction techniques.

techniques and modern techniques. The classification is done on the basis of sophisticated tools which were earlier known but were not possible to use due to their complexity. With the availability of sophisticated computers and computation facilities the task of using the modern tools and techniques has become quite easy.

2.7.1 The Traditional Techniques

The traditional techniques were mostly dependent on verification using the naked eye or on the basic observations made of day to day activities of the business. The traditional techniques can be broadly divided into two commonly used tools, namely, (a) the observation of deviation (b) mean reduction method.

1. **The observation of deviation method:** In this method the budgeted and actual performances of some of the processes of a business are observed and are related to the overall profit and profitability of the business. If it is observed that a negative or positive deviation is adversely affecting the profit and profitability of the business, then it is identified as a key variable. Thereafter processes are identified with this system and control mechanics is established to monitor and guide the business along the line of these key factors.
2. **Mean reduction techniques:** Although it is called the mean reduction method, in principle however it is used as the modal value. The techniques comprise calculation of the central tendency of time series data of a given key factor (a large number of factors can also be used). The central tendency used here generally comprises the mean or mode (mostly mode as mentioned earlier). Then quartiles are extracted from the series. Observed concentrations of the modal value along with the quartile values are identified. The zone of concentration along with the range of values is noted. The larger the concentration and closer the value, the greater is the chance of a factor being identified as the key variable.

2.7.2 The Modern Techniques

The modern techniques use statistics as a tool to identify the key variables. The sources of data are still the accounting information and cost accounting information. Now a days, other data maintained by a business, such as human resources data, are also used. The most common techniques used under this head are (a) regression analysis and (b) cluster and factor analysis.

1. **Regression analysis:** This is a very well established statistical tool and finds the strength of dependence by using the least square of the mean deviation. The coefficient extracted from the linier equation establishes the relationship between the dependent and independent factors in the equation. Ideally, the profitability sets the dependent factor and the regression is run against multiple independent factors which the business believes affect the profitability. The coefficient of correlation shows the strength of the interdependency. The higher the inter-dependency, the greater is the chance of a factor being included in the list of key variables and vice versa.
2. **Factor and cluster analysis:** The factor and cluster analysis also uses regression analysis. Here a large number of indicators are identified for a business. Multiple regressions are run to replace each of the indicators as dependent factors and the others as independent factors. In the process the strength of dependency of each factor against the other is tested. Then by using the least square methods the Eigenvalue (dependency) is extracted. The indicator(s) which have the largest bonding are taken as factors. Each factor is then taken as a key variable for the business.

2.8 LIMITATION OF USAGE OF KEY VARIABLES

The key variables have a number of problems and limitations. Foremost amongst them is the absence of consensus amongst the managers. Besides, the absence of a proper scale to measure them and lack of clarity also hampers the process of identification of key variables and using them for the purpose of the management control system.

Another major problem faced by the process of identification is the tendency to depend on numerical data and ignore the qualitative information which might actually influence the business.

To overcome this limitation, the business processes should be thoroughly checked and the reduction techniques should use statistical processes.

SUMMARY

The chapter primary dealt with the key variables that are essential to be identified for the successful implementation of the management control system and to obtain the best out of the business. The key variables are dependent on the external and internal factors, which in turn affect the key strategic issues in a business. The key variables are generally dependent on the production system, technology, the input, the liability sources and the asset sources of the business. A good management control system generally does what is called an input output analysis. The most effective way of identification of key variable is statistical analysis. However, heavy bias towards numerical sources and managerial subjective bias is a limitation of the identified key variables in the business.

ANNEXURE 2.1

EXAMPLES OF KEY VARIABLES IN SOME INDUSTRIES

Hospital

- Cost of treatment for a particular ailment
- Recovery percentage per patient admitted

Hotel

- Room occupancy
- Number of complaints received per customer
- Revenue contribution by the restaurant

Insurance

- Numbers of claims settled
- Time taken to settle claims
- Number of early claims settlements

Electric Bulb Manufacturing Company

- Number of defects per batch
- Number of demurrages per shipment
- Number of production days lost
- Number of man hours spent on training

Some general key success variables

- Profitability
- Employees' work satisfaction
- Market share

Review Questions

1. What are key variables?
2. What are the sources of key variables? Identify some key variable sources for any industry of your choice.
3. What is the process of identification of key variables?
4. What are the various ways in which key variables can be classified?
5. How does one ensure across the board control?
6. What are the techniques of identifying key variables? Enumerate one of them in detail.

Analytical Questions

1. Identify the key variables in a manufacturing industry. Thereafter, explain how they can be used to develop a good management control system.
2. In order to upgrade into a "STAR" hotel a small size local hotel wants to identify its key variables so that it can focus on its growth. State the steps it should follow to identify the key variables so that it can upgrade itself.

CHAPTER 3

Designing Management Control Systems

LEARNING OBJECTIVES OF THE CHAPTER

- Process of designing a control system
- Identifying the organisation's hierarchy
- Understanding the process of the business
- Establishing the linkages between the various stakeholders towards goal congruence
- Establishing goals for a business
- Designing the control system
- Implementing techniques of the control system

3.1 INTRODUCTION

While designing a management control system it is necessary to understand the environment in which the control system will operate.

A management control system is an overall process. Hence, while designing a management control system it is necessary to understand the environment in which the control system will operate. Furthermore, the hierarchy through which the control will flow and the concerned parties for whom the control system is designed is to be appreciated. The management control system should be designed in such a way that it leads to goal congruence[1] of the business. In order for this to occur the parties involved in the management control (system) should be able to appreciate and internalize the goals of the organisation or business.

3.2 PROCESS OF DESIGNING A CONTROL SYSTEM

In order to design a management control system it is necessary to carry out six essential steps as noted below:

1. Identify the organisational hierarchy.
2. Understand the process of the business.
3. Establish the linkages between the various stakeholders towards goal congruence.
4. Establish a formal information flow between various departments and subunits of the business.
5. Design the control system.
6. Implement the control system.

3.3 IDENTIFYING THE ORGANISATION'S HIERARCHY

In order to establish a management control system it is essential to identify the organisational

[1] The goals of any business are realisable propositions which a business wants to achieve in the short as well as the long run. Hence goal congruence refers to the process in which all the business activities are aligned to the set goals of the business.

hierarchy. The organisation's hierarchy supports the control system in a business organisation. The flow of authority in the organisation through the business hierarchy enables this. It may be noted here that the hierarchy is grossly dependent on the organisational structure. The other factor which influences the hierarchy is handing down authority and responsibility.

It may be noted here that the hierarchy is grossly dependent on the organizational structure.

The organisational hierarchy influences the business in many ways. An example of this would be the establishment of a budget in an organisation. The budget is generally passed down with the objectives set down by the top management to the lower rung of management. The lower management substantiates it and ratifies it for functionality until it is sent up again for approval. In the process, as is clearly visible, the backbone is established by the hierarchy.

The budget is generally passed down with the objectives set down by the top management to the lower rung of management.

3.3.1 Existing Hierarchy

It may be noted that a management control system may be established for a new or an existing business. It may be contextual to say that besides the hierarchy of the business organisation, there is a common pattern of hierarchy in the industry also. Therefore, it is essential to study both the organisational and industry hierarchy.

The following example will illustrate this point more clearly. In the software industry, the organisations are predominantly flat and are interlinks of projects. So to establish a new management control system for a software business (firm) the organisation hierarchy should be kept in mind. This will ensure two things. First, the new workers, who come from the same industry, will not experience a cultural shock and second, there is no time lost in acclimatising to the control system.

3.3.2 Changes Needed or Anticipated

If there is a need to change the organisational hierarchy, it should be done keeping in mind the following questions.

1. What is the nature of the industry in which the current business is established?
2. Does the business have a well laid out goal and does the business hierarchy support it?
3. What is the least modification that can facilitate and accommodate the new management control system?
4. Is the current reporting system helping in goal congruence for the business?
5. Can the new system be implemented in such a way that it will not disturb the existing information system or at least lead to the least disturbance?

On answering the questions the business will be able to support the control mechanism which is being designed for it.

3.4 UNDERSTANDING THE PROCESS OF THE BUSINESS

In order to establish an appropriate control system for the business, it is essential to appreciate and understand the processes of the business for which the control system is being designed. The business processes are the underlying and guiding factors of the business. Links between the various subsystems and their effectiveness depends on the business processes. The business processes can grossly be divided into three categories,

In order to establish an appropriate control system for the business, it is essential to appreciate and understand the processes of the business for which the control system is being designed.

1. Centralised business process
2. Decentralised business process
3. Matrix process

These are elaborated below.

3.4.1 Centralised Business Process

In a centralised business process the decisions and financial resources rest at the top of the business hierarchy. In a centralised system, the subunits of business are function oriented and do not take any decisions at their level.

These organisational forms mostly follow top down information flow and the control flows from top to the bottom of the organisation. Generally, in such a business, the operational data flow upwards and the decision and business information relating to the business flow downward.

These organisational forms mostly follow top down information flow and the control flows from top to the bottom of the organisation.

Often it has been observed that this style of operation is what is called "do what you are told or else..." type.

The control mechanisms are autocratic or at the least, bureaucratic in nature. It is generally observed that the inherent process in such an organisation is sometimes mistaken as a management control system. Whereas there is no conflict in the idea of an organisation being centrally organised and the management control system as such, it should be clearly understood that a management control system is a process through which the direction and dimensions of the business are kept in the right direction and it is not a "*carrot and stick policy*".

3.4.2 Decentralised Business Process

Decentralised systems are diametrically opposite to the centrally organised business process. Here, as the name indicates the functional subunits enjoy a substantial amount of freedom and decision making powers.

Decentralised systems are diametrically opposite to the centrally organised business process. Here, as the name indicates the functional subunits enjoy a substantial amount of freedom and decision making powers.

The difference between the centralised process and the de-centralised process is that in the latter, both data and information critical to the business can move in either direction that is; top to bottom and bottom to top. This enables the system to become vibrant, by accepting the right information and assimilating the correct decision through the feedback at the ground level of the business. Establishing a control system in such an organisation requires projecting the spirit of participation and individuality that is inherent to the organisation.

3.4.3 Matrix Form of Business Process

Matrix organisations lie between the centralised and the decentralised systems. Here, the functionality is cross dependent and the organisations do not follow a single line of information. A typical matrix organisation is cross functional in nature at the business sub unit level. Matrix organisations facilitate upward, downward and diagonal flow of information and data in an organisation.

Matrix organisations facilitate upward, downward and diagonal flow of information and data in an organisation.

These organisations are lean in nature, generally facilitate quick decisions and are highly adaptive in nature. Designing a control function for such an organisation requires appreciation of the cross functional nature and interdependency of the business subunits and their criticality to the business.

3.5 ESTABLISHING THE LINKAGES BETWEEN THE VARIOUS STAKEHOLDERS TOWARDS GOAL CONGRUENCE

A business should strive towards goal congruence. This text would not be complete if business goals are not discussed. Business goals are of two types: General goals and specific goals.

The general goals of business deal with the normal business needs, such as profit, profitability and wealth creation. They are the broader goals which decide the purpose of the business.

The specific goals are the ones which are specific to the business and determine the character of the business. The specific goals decide the course of action of a particular business. For example, while the business may have the greater goal to be the market leader by keeping itself ahead of the price competition, a specific goal could be to maintain ethical standards while the general goal is sought.

To enable a proper control system it is essential that the goal and methods of goal congruence should be explained to all the employees in the organisation. The process of internalisation is crucial since this will enable the employees to be a part of the greater mission of the business.

To enable a proper control system it is essential that the goal and methods of goal congruence should be explained to all the employees in the organisation.

Since, the goals are set at the task level and are assimilated at the strategy level, it is important that the internal and the external stakeholders be taken into confidence while doing so. For example, the shareholders of a company should be made aware by the employees or management of the company of the strategic choices before the company and the road map to success in the business. Unless such clear processes are set before the stakeholders, the confusion might lead to a catastrophic situation and chaos in the organisation due to cross talk and cross purpose debate.

3.5.1 Establishment of Goals for Business

Establishing goals for the business involves three stage strategies:

Stage A: ***Establishing the general purpose of the business.***

Example: Setting up a software company to develop a package for a single retail company.

Stage B: ***Establishing the specific modalities through which the specific objective could be achieved.***

Example: Choosing the right front end, back end and the right kind of professional for the job.

Stage C: ***Identifying the exact goal which needs to be achieved to deliver the above two.***

Example: Identifying the exact price range, packaging and the parties with whom the deal can be struck; establishing a quality benchmark in the market. Setting down the ethics and conduct of the business.

Once the goals of the business have been established, they should be appropriately communicated to all who have to comply and accomplish them.

3.5.2 Enabling Goal Congruence

To enable goal congruence, the organisation must set down a clear task or job description. Besides, as noted earlier, clear communication regarding the goals of the business, to all the concerned persons, is necessary. If need be, training should be imparted to the employees and other parties in the business to establish a common belief in the goal and attaining it.

Organisation must set down a clear task or job description.

It has been often found that a little bit of hand holding is needed in an organisation if new goals are established. This overcomes the initial resistance that a new process faces in the organisation.

3.6 ESTABLISHING A FORMAL INFORMATION SYSTEM FLOW BETWEEN VARIOUS DEPARTMENTS AND SUB UNITS OF THE BUSINESS

The crux of the control system lies in the proper flow of information within the sub units of the business in the right form and at the right time. Such a process requires designing the information system, designing the form of reporting and establishing a collection process to be precise.

The crux of the control system lies in the proper flow of information within the sub units of the business in the right form and at the right time.

3.6.1 Designing an Information System

In order to facilitate and develop a management control system, it is essential that a proper information system is designed. The importance of an information system is crucial to the process since the control system in an organisation will use it to implement the control mechanics.

In order to facilitate and develop a management control system, it is essential that a proper information system is designed.

Generally, the design of a control system is a four stage process as given below:

1. Requirement study
2. Analysis of the above data
3. Designing the information system and developing it
4. Testing the information system
5. Implementation

3.6.2 Form Design

Once the information system is in place, the reporting form which will be used to carry the information across the system or the organisation needs to be developed. The forms may be physical forms or electronic forms, depending on the availability of resources. The design of the form requires the following steps:

1. Understanding the purpose for which the information is sought
2. Compressing data to fit in a single form.
3. Delivering a form which is self explanatory
4. Enabling a tabulation facility to be used later

3.7 DESIGNING THE CONTROL SYSTEM

The control system is generally of two kinds: (a) open control system and (b) closed control system.

Generally any control system has an input device (virtual system), an assessor (one which understands or detects the problem), the correcting system and the feedback system.

1. **Open end control system:** Such a system enables and interacts with the input and output at several levels. Generally any control system has an input device (virtual system), an assessor (one which understands or detects the problem), the correcting system and the feedback system. The whole system is placed in a loop in an organisation. In an open system they are placed in such a way that information flows between the subsystems, especially the assessor and the feedback system. Figure 3.1 shows how the system works.

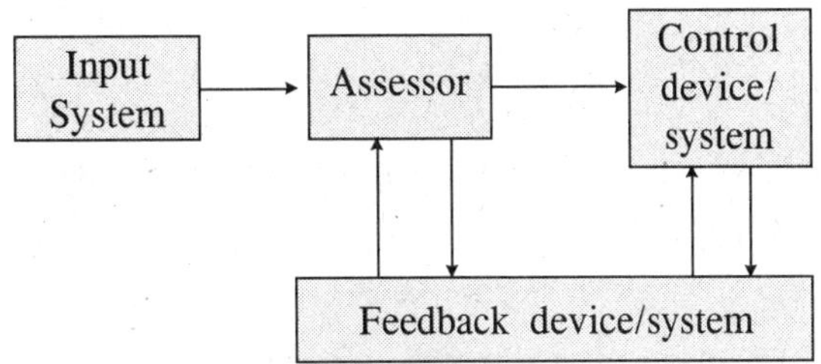

Fig 3.1 Open control system in an organisation (A. Dutta, Management Control System, 1st Ed, Kalyani, New Delhi, 2008)

2. **Closed control system:** In a closed feedback system the correction process is only in one direction and hence there is no chance of any interaction between the feedback system and assessor system independently. Figure 3.2 shows how the system works.

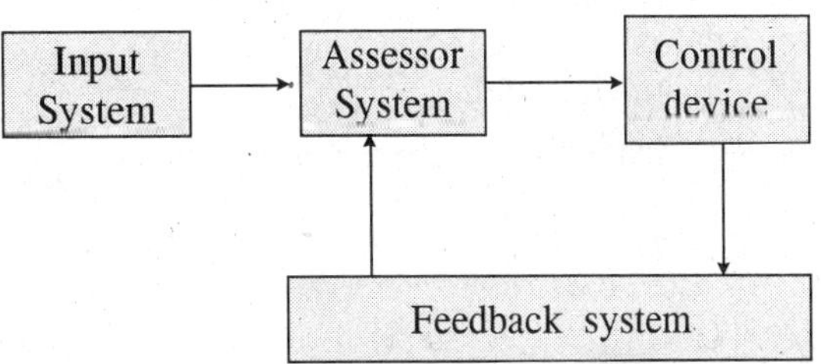

Fig.3.2 Closed control system in an organisation (A. Dutta, Management Control System, 1st Ed, Kalyani, New Delhi, 2008)

3.8 IMPLEMENTING THE CONTROL SYSTEM

There is always a default control mechanics which is inherited by any business organisation since the control factor is largely environmental in nature.

The implementation of a control system faces a number of dynamic challenges. To start with, there is always a default control mechanics which is inherited by any business organisation since the control factor is largely environmental in nature. The next biggest challenge which is faced by the designer of the control system is the resistance to change. In normal circumstances, the implementation of the control system follows any one of the methods stated below. It may be useful to know that, these implementation systems can be mixed and matched to form hybrid processes to ease the process of implementation of the designed control system.

3.8.1 Implementation Techniques

The three most commonly used implementation techniques are as follows:

1. Sharp cut off method
2. Parallel run method
3. Phased implementation method

1. **Sharp cut off method:** This method as the name indicates uses a definite date or time frame where the old control system is withdrawn and the new control system takes its place. This process requires foolproof design of control keeping in mind all the systems and subsystems of the business. Generally, this system requires a lot of consensus before and at the point of implementation of the control system.

   This method as the name indicates uses a definite date or time frame where the old control system is withdrawn and the new control system takes its place.

   The disadvantage of the system is that, it gives no scope to revert to the old system, if the new system is found to be inadequate despite all the precautions taken to develop it.

   One good way to deal with this problem is to include as many components of the old system, which can logically be accommodated, in the new control system.

2. **Parallel run method:** This method of implementation takes the prudent course of testing the new system while the old one exists. The idea behind this is to make a comparative analysis of the system in the actual work place. The process is slightly cumbersome, since there are a number of forms generated to support both the systems in parallel. Besides, it might be time consuming to generate and analyze so much information at any point of time. There is also the fear of becoming confused about the source of the information and using it for the wrong system. However, such difficulties can be overcome by exercising caution and some amount of hand holding.

   This method of implementation takes the prudent course of testing the new system while the old one exists.

   In this process, the new system gets to learn the old processes and the resistance to change is much less as the advantages of the new system become clear to the users.

3. **Phased implementation method:** The phased implementation method is a hybrid of the above two processes. Here, several phases of organisation control are identified. Then an old system is phased out and a new system is inducted. The implications of the new system replacing the old system are noted and corrected until the next phase is taken up. This process is completed until the whole of the system is replaced.

   Phased implementation method is a hybrid of the above two processes.

3.8.2 Implementation Process

The implementation process passes through a feedback module. The system is first developed taking into consideration all the required items. Later, the system is put to use until the verification of its dependability is carried out. If it fails the validation, then it is sent back for reconstruction by taking in the feedback. Figure 3.3 shows the process of implementation of the control system.

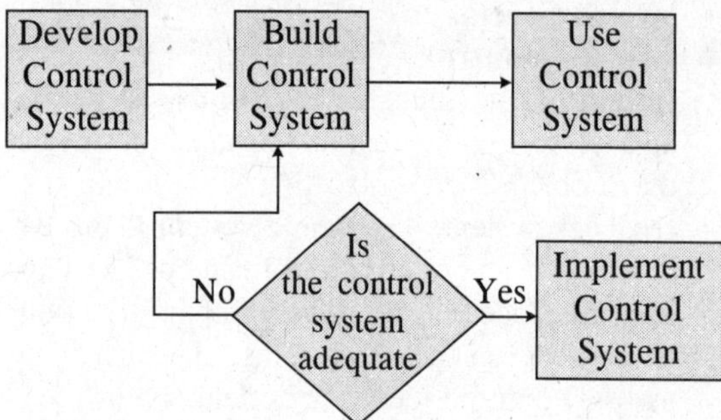

Fig.3.3 Process of implementation of control system in a business organisation (Source: A. Dutta, Management Control System, 1st ed, Kalyani, New Delhi, 2008)

SUMMARY

In this chapter we have tried to understand the essentials of designing a control system, which may be either a closed or open control system. The process of implementation and the factors which influence the design of the control process were also discussed. As we understand there are several ways to implement a control system and one or more of them can be used by the organisation. The pros and cons of implementation techniques were also established.

Review Questions

1. Describe the stages of designing a control system for an organisation?
2. What are the processes of implementing a management control system?
3. What do you think are the difficulties of designing and implementing a control system?

Analytical Questions

1. How will you design a management control system for a business school?
2. If you are a newly recruited financial manager of a business, and are given the duty of implementing a computer based accounting system by replacing the old manual system, what are the problems you might face? How will you go about implementing the same?

PART—B

ENVIRONMENT OF MANAGEMENT CONTROL SYSTEM

CHAPTER 4

Organisation, Strategy and Control

LEARNING OBJECTIVES OF THE CHAPTER

- Goals and objectives as corner stone of control
- Strategy as a pathway for a control system
- Behaviour as a pathway for a control system
- Responsibility centre
- Engineering cost, infrastructure cost and discretionary cost
- Benchmarking

4.1 INTRODUCTION

A control system is implemented in order to establish goal congruence in a business. The control system does not directly establish a strategy but rather enables the implementation of the strategy system as and when the business progresses. It is important that the control system is established in such a way that it does not contradict the strategies of the business.

4.2 GOALS AND OBJECTIVES AS BOUNDARY CONSTRAINTS

Goals are broader statements of the business and define where the business wants to go in the long run whereas the objectives are the means to achieve these goals.

Goals and objectives are established as a part of the business strategy building. Goals are broader statements of the business and define where the business wants to go in the long run whereas the objectives are the means to achieve these goals. Goals and objectives together form the boundaries of control mechanics for a business.

Both goals and objectives may change due to expansion of the business or due to changed realties of the business. Most goals and objectives as we understand them are a reflection of both the current needs and the long term needs of a business. Hence, while designing a control system, the goals and objectives of the business should be clear to the designer of the control system.

For example, a designer of a control system for a public interest program should keep in mind the focus of the program as well as the necessity of balancing the needs of the pressure groups. Or a typical business goal of achieving a certain quantifiable profit needs to be used as basic information for the design of the control system.

Goals and the objectives may translate into operational problems in the business.

We need to understand that the goals and the objectives may translate into operational problems in the business. Hence caution needs to be exercised in the way goals and objectives are used to design the control process.

4.3 STRATEGIES AS A PATHWAY FOR CONTROL SYSTEMS

Strategies are the processes through which a business deals with change in the internal and external environment of the business.

Strategies are the processes through which a business deals with change in the internal and external environment of the business. A strategy starts with the vision statement and finishes at task establishing which is translated to a realisable mission. Each mission is broken down into tasks which are accomplished through operational strategies that enable achievement of short term goals. While such translation takes places from the mission through vision to process, policy and goals and reaches the task, the control system forms the backbone for the transmission and transformation process in a business.

The control process uses the fundamental organisational hierarchy and the original memorandum of the business activity. The strategy provides the pathway for the control to work. The links between the sub units of the business are provided by the purpose established by the business strategy.

A well established strategy therefore constitutes half the work done in a business.

A well established strategy therefore constitutes half the work done in a business. The criteria for evaluating a business strategy are given below.

4.3.1 Criteria to Evaluate a Strategy

The key to evaluate a strategy depends on the issues listed below:

1. Internal consistency
2. External and environmental consistency
3. Applicability of the strategy in view of the resources available
4. Risk content of the strategy
5. Time frame of implementation and result orientation
6. Usefulness of the strategy

4.4 BEHAVIOURAL ASPECTS OF MANAGEMENT AND CONTROL PROCESS

The businesses are divided into responsibility centres which form the controlling units in the long run. Such responsibility centres are essentially strategic business units or sub units where the reward and evaluation of performance are carried out. The interaction of these responsibility centres with the business is based on goals and objectives laid down by the business. Since, the responsibility centres are headed by individual managers whose behavioural aspect largely influences the control system and since the control system is largely behavioural in nature, it is necessary to understand the pathways through which the control system and the business are linked. The key behavioural concepts which influence the management control system are perception, attitude, motivation, goal congruence, sub unit conflicts and their resolution, managerial style, resistance to change, force field analysis, compromising and sacrificing and socio cultural factors.

The key behavioural concepts which influence the management control system are perception, attitude, motivation, goal congruence, sub unit conflicts and their resolution, managerial style, resistance to change, force field analysis, compromising and sacrificing and socio cultural factors.

4.4.1 Perception

The interaction of the managers and personnel with the control system at various points determines the perception generated about the objectives of business. The seriousness of the management to implement the control process is gauged through the development of the control process.

4.4.2 Attitudes and Beliefs

Both attitude and beliefs are the result of the culture and background of the managers in the organisation.

Both attitude and beliefs are the result of the culture and background of the managers in the organisation. These in turn are influenced by the socio-economic background of the employees of the organisation. Such attitudes and beliefs serve as a good reference point and benchmark in the long run.

4.4.3 Motivation

The management's desire to attain the goals set by the business largely depends on the motivational dimension of the managers. The motivation comes from two sources, (a) the personal factors as laid down by Maslow and (b) the power centric needs of the individuals. In both the cases, the individuals working in an organisation seek positive affirmation for their performance and the calculated risks they take. A control system will be effective only if the motivational drives are directed towards the achievement of the control. An appropriate reward for the conformation will always have to be in place if the control system needs to work.

A control system will be effective only if the motivational drives are directed towards the achievement of the control.

4.4.4 Goal Congruence

In an organisation, individuals work with the purpose of fulfilling their personal goals. The organisation works toward the fulfilment of the organisational goal. In order to achieve the appropriate and desired result the two processes need to be synergised in one common code. Enabling the managers to overcome self interest and act towards the greater goal of the organisation requires strong motivation and a clear road map in the organisation. The closer the individual goals are to those of the organisation, the greater will be the success of the control system.

Enabling the managers to overcome self interest and act towards the greater goal of the organisation requires strong motivation and a clear road map in the organisation.

4.4.5 Sub Unit Conflict and Resolution

The business sub units have inherent conflicts. This is due to the fact that the sub units often have conflicting goals. In addition, there is the problem of optimisation of resource utilisation by the sub units. This leads to overt competition and sometimes cannibalisation of the market by the sub units. In order to resolve such conflicts, the management at the top resorts to tools such as transfer pricing and ERP solutions which mitigates the problem of cannibalization. However, sometimes, healthy compaction is encouraged by the top management in the business; for this coordination committees are established so that the overall effectiveness of the process can be established.

4.4.6 Managerial Styles

In principle management control can be established either through an autocratic style or through a participative and democratic style. We can for the purpose of clarity, refer to them as theory X and theory Y. In practice however, it is not really possible to use one style at a time. Hence a blend of the two is utilised, wherein thc stricture process is used for setting and implementing the policy and the participative process is used to create and internalise them. It is however the prerogative of the business to decide the level and blend of usage of the two managerial styles.

4.4.7 Force Field Analysis

Kurt Lewin used the force theories of physical science to develop a conflict theory in an individual. According to him, there are two forces which cause all conflict in an individual. The first force is a facilitating force which enables the individual and the other force, which he called the inhibiting force (friction or resistance), opposes the facilitating force. In a management control system, the forces are identified in review meetings of the sub units by the top management and the forces are classified so that the factors can be controlled either centrally or at the sub unit level.

4.4.8 Resistance to Change

Organisational inertia occurs due to the fact that a large organisation does not like to change, because it is apprehensive of such change. While designing a control system, the designer

Organisational inertia occurs due to the fact that a large organisation does not like to change, because it is apprehensive of such change.

has to be aware of such inertia. The lower the inertia the better is the chance that the control system works effectively.

4.4.9 Entrapment

Entrapment refers to a situation where one is trapped due to one's own decision. Often, the management takes up decisions which are not conducive to the business and to its stakeholders. However, they do not like to back track since it reveals the fact that the decision was wrong to start with. So often new decisions are taken to cover up the situation and as a result of this, resources which would otherwise have yielded good results are wasted. A well designed control system enables the system to correct itself through a multiple feedback and correction mechanism. A multiple feedback mechanism will enable the system/organisation to understand both the good and bad side of the system and keep a balanced view.

Entrapment refers to a situation where one is trapped due to one's own decision.

4.4.10 Compromising and Sacrificing

Complaisance is a situation where the most satisfying decisions are taken at the cost of the most effective and optimal decisions. Such a situation may occur if the accountability is less or due to the excess use of the pressure group. Such a satisfying decision sometimes compromises at the cost of the business.

Complaisance is a situation where the most satisfying decisions are taken at the cost of the most effective and optimal decisions.

However, at times a sacrificing attitude is adopted in order to change the course of action in a business or even to develop the business. Such an attitude is much more acceptable and often helps to smoothen out the rough edge of the control process.

4.4.11 Socio-cultural Influences

Human behaviour is profoundly affected by the culture embedded in the society. It has been found that tasks are often performed, keeping in mind the social and cultural values. For example a Hindu, may be influenced by the great philosophical work '*The Bhagavad Gita,*' which states that one should work without asking for the result that might come at the end of the task. The designer of a control system may find that the system is implemented without putting in place a formal control system. For example, the fact that a staunch follower of the Catholic Church believes in keeping high moral standards and flinching away from any kind of dishonesty, can in itself automatically enable the control system, if this religion group has a high representation in the work force. To sum up, it is interesting to note that a certain amount of moral control which comes from the social and cultural factors actually gets reflected in the business control process in a subtle manner.

4.5 THE PROCESS OF SETTING JOINT GOALS THROUGH CREATION OF RESPONSIBILITY CENTRES

One of the major exercises that is carried out in modern business is the creation of objectives for the business and setting goals jointly by the top management and the work force. The idea of Management By Objectives (MBO) plays a vital role in determining the pathways for success for a modern business. The core to such MBO is establishing business centres that are the responsibility of individual managers. Such centres are called responsibility centres and are generally classified as follows:

1. **Revenue centres:** They are business sub units where revenue is generated. They generally exist at the end of the value chain. Managers here have the responsibility of increasing the revenue and giving information of what is in the best interest of the business.
2. **Expense centres:** The expenses centres have inputs which are measured in monetary terms but due to the difficulty of assessing the outputs' monetary value, they are expressed in non monetary terms resulting in the common belief that the sub business unit is only engaged in expenses. The accounting

department and the rework department are typical examples of expenses centres. Generally the managers in charge are given the goal of reducing cost variance by comparing costs with the standard values.

3. **Profit centres:** These are sub units of the business where both the input and output are ascribed in terms of monetary value. The goals set here are to increase the numerical difference between the input cost and the output cost so that a greater profit can be garnered.
4. **Investment centres:** These are business sub units where assets are created and there is a control on the input output flow. An R&D centre is a typical example of this. The managers here are expected to use their discretion in order to reduce the incidental risks and costs arising out of the activities in such units.

The use of a responsibility centre follows cost patterns which can be described as follows:

1. **Discretionary costs:** These are management related costs of the business which are purely at the discretion of the business and the managers. They tend to reflect in terms of investment and expenses in the organisation. A productivity study conducted in Europe in the mid 1980s showed that 40 to 60 per cent of the total cost of a business tends to be discretionary in nature.
2. **Engineered costs:** These are the costs in which there is a perfect relationship between output and input and both of these can be measured. They are generally referred to as profit centres in responsibility accounting. About 30 per cent are reflected as engineered costs as per the study discussed above.
3. **Infrastructure costs:** These are costs which have a concrete out come in the long run. Generally about 10 per cent of the organisational costs are reflected as infrastructural costs. They are represented either as expenses centres or investment centres.

A schematic diagram of the cost centres is given in Figure 4.1.

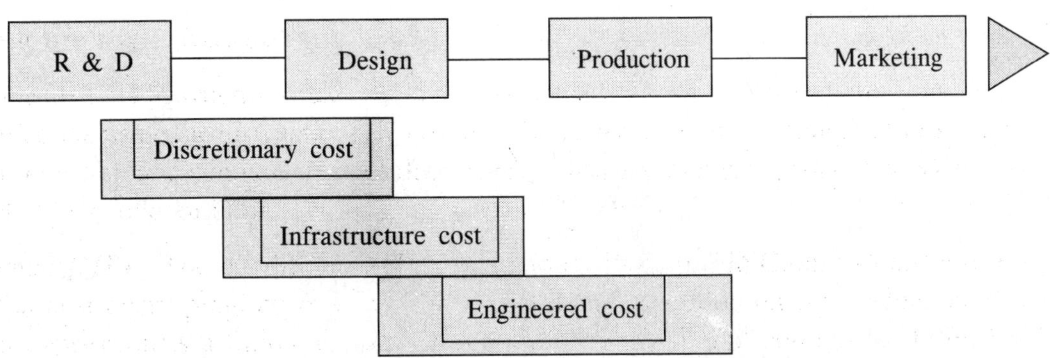

Fig 4.1: Establishment of costs across the value line

4.6 BENCHMARKING

Benchmarking (also "best practice benchmarking" or "process benchmarking") is a process used in management, particularly strategic management, in which organisations evaluate various aspects of their processes in relation to best practice, usually within their own sector. This allows organisations to develop plans on how to adopt such a best practice, usually with the aim of increasing some aspect of performance. Benchmarking may be a one-off event, but is often treated as a continuous process in which organisations continually seek to challenge their practices.

Benchmarking (also "best practice benchmarking" or "process benchmarking") is a process used in management, particularly strategic management, in which organisations evaluate various aspects of their processes in relation to best practice, usually within their own sector.

4.6.1 Advantages of Benchmarking

Benchmarking is a powerful management tool because it overcomes "paradigm blindness". Paradigm blindness can be summed up as the mode of thinking in which, "The way we do it is the best because this is the way we have always done it." Benchmarking opens organisations to new methods, ideas and tools to improve their effectiveness. It helps to break through any resistance to change by demonstrating other methods of solving problems than the one currently employed, and demonstrating that they work, because they are being used by others. The advantages of benchmarking are as follows:

Benchmarking opens organisations to new methods, ideas and tools to improve their effectiveness.

1. It gives a ***better understanding of the wants (expectations) of the customer*** because it is based on the reality of the market estimated in an objectivist way.
2. It leads to ***better economic planning of the purposes*** and the objectives to be achieved in the company because the objectives are based on what takes place outside, and then controlled and mastered.
3. Leads to ***an increase in productivity,*** by resolution of the real problems, understanding the processes and what they produce.
4. It leads to ***better current practices and a search for change.***
5. Leads to ***better competitiveness*** due to a solid knowledge of the competition and firm implication of practices and tried techniques by the staff.

Benchmarking has consequences which are beyond the process itself. It reforms all levels of the company, modifies the process of manufacture of the product leads (drives) and also reforms the hierarchical organisation of the company, the product itself and the state of mind of the employees.

Benchmarking has consequences which are beyond the process itself.

4.6.2 Collaborative Benchmarking

Benchmarking, originally invented as a formal process by ***Rank Xerox,*** is usually carried out by individual companies. Sometimes it may be carried out collaboratively by groups of companies (e.g., subsidiaries of a multinational in different countries). One example is that of the Dutch municipality-owned water supply companies, which have carried out a voluntary collaborative benchmarking process since 1997 through their industry association.

Procedure for benchmarking

1. **Identify your problem areas:** Because benchmarking can be applied to any business process or function, a range of research techniques may be required. They include: informal conversations with customers, employees or suppliers; exploratory research techniques such as focus groups; in-depth marketing research, quantitative research, surveys, questionnaires, reengineering analysis, process mapping, quality control variance reports or financial ratio analysis.
2. **Identify other industries that have similar processes:** For instance if one were interested

in improving handoffs in addiction treatment s/he would try to identify other fields that also have handoff challenges. These could include air traffic control, cell phone switching between towers, transfer of patients from surgery to recovery rooms.

3. **Identify organisations that are leaders in these areas:** Look for the very best in any industry and in any country. Consult customers, suppliers, financial analysts, trade associations and magazines to determine which companies are worthy of study.
4. **Survey companies for measures and practices:** Companies target specific business processes using detailed surveys of measures and practices used to identify business process alternatives and leading companies. Surveys are typically masked to protect confidential data by neutral associations and consultants.
5. **Visit the "best practice" companies to identify leading edge practices:** Companies typically agree to mutually exchange information beneficial to all parties in a benchmarking group and share the results within the group.
6. **Implement new and improved business practices:** Take the leading edge practices and develop implementation plans, which include identification of specific opportunities, funding the project and selling the ideas to the organisation for the purpose of gaining demonstrated value from the process.

4.6.3 Cost of Benchmarking

Benchmarking is a moderately expensive process, but most organisations find that it more than pays for itself. The three main types of costs are:

1. **Visit costs:** These include hotel rooms, travel costs, meals, a token gift, and lost labour time.
2. **Time costs:** Members of the benchmarking team invest time in researching problems, finding exceptional companies to study, visits and implementation. This will take them away from their regular tasks for part of each day, so additional staff might be required.
3. **Benchmarking database costs:** Organisations that institutionalise benchmarking into their daily procedures find it is useful to create and maintain a database of best practices and the companies presently associated with each best practice.

The term benchmarking also has a statistical definition. It is a method of using auxiliary information to adjust the sampling weights used in an estimation process, in order to yield more accurate estimates of totals.

Suppose we have a population where each unit k has a 'value' $Y(k)$ associated with it. For example, $Y(k)$ could be the wage of an employee k or the cost of an item k. Suppose we want to estimate the sum Y of all $Y(k)$. To do this we take a sample of the k, get a sampling weight $W(k)$ for all the sampled k, and then sum up $W(k) \times Y(k)$ for all sampled k.

One property usually common to the weights $W(k)$ described here is that if we sum them over all sampled k, then this sum is an estimate of the total number of units k in the population (for example, the total employment, or the total number of items). Because we have a sample, this estimate of the total number of units in the population will differ from the true population total. Similarly, the estimate of the total Y (where we sum $W(k) \times Y(k)$ for all sampled k) will also differ from the true population total.

We do not know what the true population total Y value is (if we did, there would be no point in sampling!). Yet often we do know what the sum of the $W(k)$ is over all units in the population. For example, we may not know the total earnings of the population or the total cost of the population, but we often know the total employment or total volume of sales. And even if we do not know these values exactly, surveys are often carried out by other organisations or at earlier times, with very accurate estimates of these auxiliary quantities.

The benchmarking procedure begins by first breaking the population into benchmarking cells. Cells are formed by grouping together units that share common characteristics, for example, similar

$Y(k)$, yet any variable that enhances the accuracy of the final estimates can be used. For each cell C, we let $W(C)$ be the sum of all $W(k)$, where the sum is taken over all sampled k in the cell C. For each cell C, let $T(C)$ be the auxiliary value for cell C, which is commonly called the "benchmark target" for cell C. Next, we compute a benchmark factor $F(C) = T(C)/W(C)$, then we adjust all the weights $W(k)$ by multiplying each weight by its benchmark factor $F(C)$, for its cell C. The net result is that the estimated W (formed by summing $F(C) \times W(k)$) will now equal the benchmark target total T. However, the more important benefit is that the estimate of the total of Y (formed by summing $F(C) \times F(k) \times Y(k)$) will tend to be more accurate.

SUMMARY

In this chapter the role of goal setting and the boundaries in which control is enabled in a business was explained. The influence of the various factors which create the control mechanics was studied. An attempt was made to understand the process of goal setting in defining the management control process. In order to overcome the management myopia and paradigm blindness it is essential that an organisation carries out joint goal setting and uses benchmarking as a method to attract the best practices in the management. This will enable the management to create the best goal congruence as it will be free from internal biases.

Review Questions

1. How does a goal set for the business act as a corner stone to the management control process? Explain with a suitable example.
2. What are the criteria for evaluating a strategy?
3. How does the behavioural aspect of the management influence the control system? Explain one of the behavioural aspects in detail.
4. What is entrapment? How does it become a deterrent to the control process?
5. Explain the field force theory with an example.
6. What is benchmarking? How does one set up a benchmark for an organisation?
7. What is the process of setting up a benchmark?

Analytical Question

A company uses a certain quality control process which was designed and delivered by a group of individuals working within the organisation. Later it was found that this method was slowing down the production of the organisation, leading to loss. This led to the team of individuals losing their jobs, since they could not justify the loss.

A few years later the organisation was rewarded by a group of industry experts for carrying out the best quality control process. Incidentally, this was for the same quality control which had earlier led to the group of individuals losing their jobs. The company wasted no time in taking advantage of the same to procure more orders from the market and subsequently made a huge profit. It soon became a benchmark in the industry.

Questions for discussion

1. Do you think the management was getting into entrapment?
2. Can you explain how field force theory worked here?

CHAPTER 5

Organisational Infrastructure, Organisational Design and Control System

LEARNING OBJECTIVES OF THE CHAPTER

- Decentralisation vs centralisation
- Control factors in an organisation
- Adaptive organisation
- Divisional autonomy
- Responsibility structure
- Inter profit centre relations

5.1 INTRODUCTION

In order to reach goal congruence in an organisation through an effective control, the design, infrastructure and the processes need to be aligned. The control system which is directed towards smooth implementation of the strategy needs to be oriented towards such a process by creating facilities which direct the system towards this implementation process.

This chapter discusses the modality of organisation design and the debate over implementation of such organisational design. In addition we will also try to understand the processes of an adaptive organisation.

The chapter begins with the organisational design which is in place, namely, centralised, decentralised or matrix system of organisation.

The centralised system is a system where the authority of the function of the organisation flows from the top management. As against this, decentralisation works bottom up, where the divisional heads are responsible for all the business decisions and carry out such responsibility within the ambit of the strategy laid down by the top management.

The centralised system is a system where the authority of the function of the organisation flows from the top management.

The matrix structure on the other hand uses a cross functional reporting system, where the strategic heads are connected to the different functional heads through the functions laid down by the business.

The matrix structure on the other hand uses a cross functional reporting system, where the strategic heads are connected to the different functional heads through the functions laid down by the business.

5.2 DEBATE ON DECENTRALISATION AND CENTRALISATION

Whether an organisation should go in for a decentralised system of organisation or a centralised version of organisation solely depends on two basic fundamentals; the size of the organisation and the span of control.

Whether an organisation should go in for a decentralised system of organisation or a centralised version of organisation solely depends on two basic fundamentals; the size of the organisation and the span of control.

With the growth in the organisation, the decentralisation of the business processes becomes inevitable, due to the fact that in most large business houses, the indent of control and the locus of control are in different locations. Hence, asserting control becomes difficult.

The span of control refers to the spread of control in the organisation. The spread of the business has always led the top management to think that control cannot be exercised once the power of managing the functional aspect of business is passed on to the decentralised business units.

The span of control refers to the spread of control in the organisation.

Contrary to the above arguments, it has been found that a decentralised organisation always performs better in terms of goal congruence since it allows a closer and more structured supervision of the subordinates in the organisation. In addition the subordinates also feel more empowered and contribute to the organisation. It may be noted here that with the right kind of environment, a manager operating under the decentralised form operates better since this system provides a continuous learning and improvement forum.

However, it should be kept in mind, that, a decentralised system should be used only when there is a certain degree of maturity within the organisation.

5.3 CONTROL FACTORS IN ORGANISATIONAL DESIGN

An organisation has to develop and adapt a design based on the effectiveness and efficiency of coordination. The best form will be the one which operates at the least cost per output. In choosing between the three designs of organisation that are available i.e., centralised, decentralised and the matrix form, the three critical points which decide the control mechanics are coordination, cost effectiveness and communication.

5.3.1 Coordination

Coordination is the crux of adopting an organisational design. It is well established that a centralised system gives better coordination since the decisions are taken centrally by the top management. As against this, the decentralised system requires the organisation to spend more resources so as to move in the right direction and obtain the optimum quantum of control. Switching from a decentralised system to a centralised system just for the purpose of coordination is costly since, in a decentralised system, the extra costs and any bottlenecks are taken into account by the functional manager, which substantially brings down the cost of running the organisation. The matrix system reduces this problem, as in this case the total charge of running the business is in the hands of the functional managers, allowing them to develop their own coordination plan across the organisation taking into account the functionality and the flexibility allowed within the system.

Switching from a decentralized system to a centralised system just for the purpose of coordination is costly since, in a decentralised system, the extra costs and any bottlenecks are taken into account by the functional manager, which substantially brings down the cost of running the organisation.

5.3.2 Cost Effectiveness

The decentralised system has been looked upon by many as a cost ineffective design because it uses multiple channels to operate the organisational control. This however, is not correct, since making use of multiple channels actually increases the organisational efficiency and offsets the cost that arises. In fact the centralised method, though apparently appearing to be cost effective, increases costs, due to rework and making decisions again and again. The matrix system however, decreases cost through motivation and coordination and making the organisation more flat and less hierarchical.

5.3.3 Communication

Communication is the backbone of control. It works best in the matrix form of organisation since, the communication works across the organisation. In the decentralised system communication mostly flows from the bottom up, and thus it is loaded with the market reality and devoid of any basic strategy. The centralised system promotes a top down communication and is often devoid of market realities. However, it may be noted that it is necessary for an organisation to adopt a control system in view of a particular organisational design. Therefore, the organisational design adopted depends on the nature of the business, the environmental concerns and the demands of the industry.

5.4 ADAPTIVE CONTROL AND THE ADAPTIVE ORGANISATION

Modern businesses function in a dynamic and changing environment. A business which cannot adapt to the changes in the environment will soon become redundant.

A business which cannot adapt to the changes in the environment will soon become redundant.

The organisation faces four major challenges from the environment namely, (a) environmental uncertainty, (b) environmental complexity, (c) environmental diversity and (d) environmental hostility.

Environmental uncertainty: The dynamic business function makes the environment more and more uncertain. In response to this, organisations become highly informal and encourage informal communication in place of formal communication. Such organisations adopt this style since, stricture and structure takes time to develop and the organisation may not have enough time to respond to the changing business needs.

Environmental complexity: Due to constant change in the business requirement, the demand and supply position changes and the change in the global factors such as geo political relationships and the environment in which the business operates become very complex. Such environmental complexity may lead the business to re-look at the niche segments where it would like to refocus its strength. Sometimes, decentralisation is a result and response to such complexity as it helps if the business concentrates its energy in a specific segment of the market by designing its system as a decentralised mode.

Environmental complexity may lead the business to re-look at the niche segments where it would like to refocus its strength.

Environmental diversity: As the business grows it is faced by diverse business which includes a wide range of customers, competitors and markets. The business should be able to respond to such diversity. Organisations generally respond to such a process by upgrading their abilities and changing their organisational design.

Environmental hostility: A hostile environment refers to the extreme changes that occur in the environment due to sudden changes in the political setup, the competitors' patterns or any other key variables. The response to such change depends on how fast such information can be gathered by the business. The changes are carried out within the organisation so that the business is not affected.

In an adaptive organisation, the following factors, which make it proactive to the environment, are observed:

1. **Implicit control system:** An implicit control system runs with the value system of the organisation and functions as a support for all informal activity which is taken up in response to the changing environment.

2. **Training and development facility:** Good training and development facilities which upgrade the skills of the employees and enable the implementation of changed processes easily.
3. **Integrity of the individual and the organisation:** A high level of integrity is quintessential for an organisational control.
4. **Global standards:** The standards of the organisation should be on par with global standards, as this leads to less uncertainty of the market and creates peer pressure.

5.5 DIVISIONAL AUTONOMY

Business organisations are increasingly requiring flexibility of operations, innovations in operations and creativity in execution. All these are possible only when the level of autonomy that is passed on to the divisions is aligned to the requirements of such autonomy by the subordinates. The degree and dimension of the autonomy is decided by the style of management and the processes that the organisation adopts. To a greater extent, the involvement of the functional managers and the level of trust and confidence that exist within the organisation decide the divisional autonomy.

To a greater extent, the involvement of the functional managers and the level of trust and confidence that exist within the organisation decide the divisional autonomy.

The responsibility that is entrusted to a division in terms of the financial autonomy also plays a very vital role. The greater the financial autonomy, the larger is the trust of the business autonomy in terms of business functions. In other words, the divisional autonomy serves as a second line of control by inducting autonomy in the system.

The greater the financial autonomy, the larger is the trust of the business autonomy in terms of business functions.

Rewarding managers on the basis of their performance, creates a basis for evaluation and passing on judgment by the top manager to the divisional manager. Thus, both tangible and intangible rewards act as a third line of control on the line managers by the top management.

5.6 RESPONSIBILITY CENTRES AND THE RELATED PERFORMANCE MEASUREMENT OF AN ORGANISATION

Responsibility centres are established to achieve goal congruence by providing space for hierarchical sequence and accountability in the organisation. The interlinking in the four responsibility centres namely, profit, revenue, investment and cost centres is possible by establishing an accounting system which can measure the efficiency of the process and the effectiveness of the process. The former is associated with the input-output measurement, whereas the latter is more directed to gauging output in terms of its goals and objectives. To explain the difference, we need to understand that measuring efficiency is akin to the measurement of productivity whereas measuring effectiveness is trying to achieve and measure the target set about the quality and quantity of the output in the market.

we need to understand that measuring efficiency is akin to the measurement of productivity whereas measuring effectiveness is trying to achieve and measure the target set about the quality and quantity of the output in the market.

It may be noted that measurement is the key to success in a control process. The often heard objective statement "**what cannot be measured cannot be controlled**" is perhaps more than true in this context.

5.6.1 Measuring the Efficiency by Return on Investment

While discussing the need of measurement, it is pertinent to talk about a measure that would be indicative in such a case. The most common measure in this case is the Return On Investment (ROI) which is essentially a turnover implication of asset on the total earning. It should be noted here that, to calculate the ROI, the responsibility centres' output measurement should be in place. The control paradigm helps in understanding the use of ROI as a measurement. When an organisational subdivision is able to reach its goal by attaining a certain return on its total investment, then the manager in charge of the investment centre needs to be made responsible for achieving the ROI for that division.

5.6.2 Establishing an Inter-profit Centre Relationship

In their quest to maximise the profit and returns, responsibility centres often face conflicts. The key reason for conflict, as discussed earlier, is the conflicting goals set by the management.

The responsibility centres function as a complete business in themselves.

This apart, the responsibility centres function as a complete business in themselves. As a result they have ample opportunity to interact with external customers and earn a profit, instead of subscribing to the internal interest of the organisation.

In the greater interest of the business it is required that all the energy of all the responsibility centres is aimed towards the goal congruence of the business. The measurement of the price, or rather setting the price for transferring the goods and services within an organisation from one division to another, may be a major problem.

Transfer pricing solves this problem to a great degree. Transfer pricing is a technique where the value of services and products are determined by two or more divisions. The basis of these are either total cost, incremental marginal cost or market prices, whichever optimises the value of transfer and leads to a higher return for the organisation as a whole.

Transfer pricing enables goal congruence by decreasing conflict between two divisions and enables a negotiated price for the transfer of goods and services, keeping in mind both the division and the organisation as a whole.

The autonomy of the division is established because there is fairness in setting the price with the help of transfer pricing mechanism. The choice of goals available for the divisional managers acts as an enabler of the control system under this system. The degree to which transfer pricing is adaptable depends upon the degree to which the control system is available for flexible upgrading of negotiation within the system.

SUMMARY

In this chapter we looked at the control system in designing the infrastructure and process for an organisation. We could briefly state that it sets the right kind of divisional autonomy that an effective control system needs. The process of effectively orienting the organisation towards a divisional autonomy depends on the measurement of the responsibility centres. The conflict of this system can largely be resolved through a properly designed transfer pricing mechanism.

Review Questions

1. An organisation adapts to the environment - Why do you think this is true?
2. What are the environmental factors which affect the business?
3. Explain the concept of "adaptive control" with an example.
4. How can ROI play an important role in measurement of the responsibility centres? Explain.
5. What is role of transfer pricing in reducing the conflict amongst the divisional managers? Explain.

Analytical Question

A petroleum company has three divisions, namely a refining division, a transportation division and an exploration division. Each division has a separate market and is free to negotiate the price in the market with the customers. It was found, through analysis, that the ROI of selling and purchasing for all divisions is higher on a stand alone basis but fails to increase the ROI of the organisation. What, according to you, could be a feasible solution to resolve the goal congruence conflict in the above case? Explain.

CHAPTER 6

Approaches to Management Control Systems

LEARNING OBJECTIVES OF THE CHAPTER

- Contingency approach to control
- Strategy and control systems
- Corporate strategy
- Business unit strategy

6.1 INTRODUCTION

Organisations are subjected to many environmental requirements. This requires them to adapt to several changes. Hence organisations are dynamic structures and managers are required to understand the way in which they can be controlled. Organisations are subjected to several factors which include environment, technology and business systems which in turn decide the way the business will operate.

The operation of the business depends on the competency and capacity within the organisation in the business. This gives the direction in which the business needs to move, that is to say, towards core competency or towards diversification. Depending on such a need, control models are also developed.

6.2 THEORY OF CONTINGENCY VERSUS THE THEORY OF UNIVERSALISM: DIRECTING TOWARDS A BETTER CONTROL SYSTEM

The contingency theory and the universalism theory revolve around the responsiveness of the business towards the environment, technology and its own organisational structure. The theories are an extension of the scientific management theory. The universalism theory puts forth the argument that there is a universal way in which the business responds to the change in environment, technology and organisation structure. The contingency theory opines that each business is a unique experience and each of them responds to the change it faces in terms of environment, technology and organisational structure in a unique way based upon a contingent approach.

The contingency theory and the universalism theory revolve around the responsiveness of the business towards the environment, technology and its own organisational structure.

Thus, the core of using these theories for the purpose of control is to ascertain how the business reacts to the three aforesaid factors

The core of using these theories for the purpose of control is to ascertain how the business reacts to the three aforesaid factors and in what ways the control approaches can be streamlined to create better results for the business.

and in what ways the control approaches can be streamlined to create better results for the business.

Before entering into a discussion as to how the framework of strategy can be used to implement a control we will examine the three crucial factors which change in a business.

6.2.1 Technology

Technology is one of the essential components in exerting the right kind of control. New technology entails better response to change since new technologies are designed for a newer environment. Therefore, technology helps managers to use resources in a better way and take decisions in line with the strategy laid down.

6.2.2 Organisational Structure

Organisational structures are set in such a way that the business should be able to respond to the uncertainties with ease. With an increase in the size of a business, the uncertainties of the business increase and so does the need for a more complex business organisation to cope with the change. The relational response of the management control system for such an organisation is also more complex.

6.2.3 Environment

Adapting to a change in the environment requires an organisation to be both prepared and adaptable. The approach of the contingency theory is to develop a highly sophisticated management control system within the organisation. The idea behind the theory is to develop a better fit for each organisation on a case to case basis, depending on the requirements it faces. Some factors such as uncertainty, independence and mission are not visible, whereas factors such as technology, organisational structure and function relation of the business are visible and hence more controllable.

6.3 STRATEGY AND CONTROL SYSTEMS

In general there are two kinds of businesses: those which have strategic plans, and those which do not have strategic plans. In the first case all the strategic options faced by the business are incorporated into the business, whereas in the latter case only some options are included in the budget of the business. Figure 6.1 describes the two kinds of businesses mentioned here.

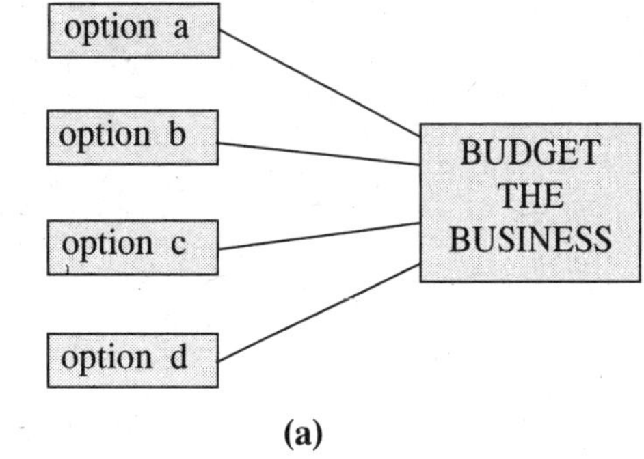

(a)

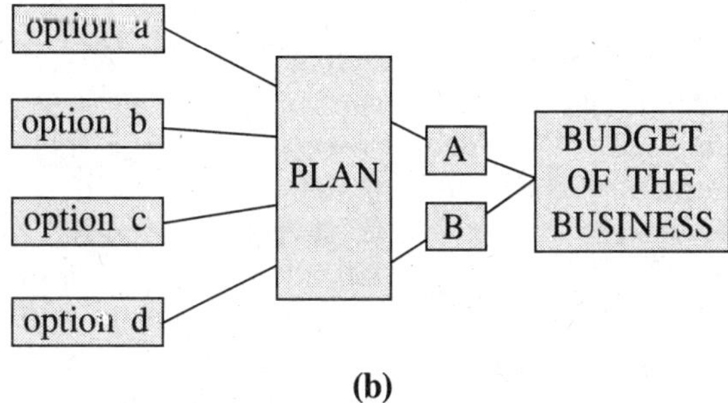

(b)

Fig. 6.1: Organisation (a) without and (b) with a strategic plan

Figure 6.2 gives an idea as to how strategy is placed side by side in an organisation for effective control.

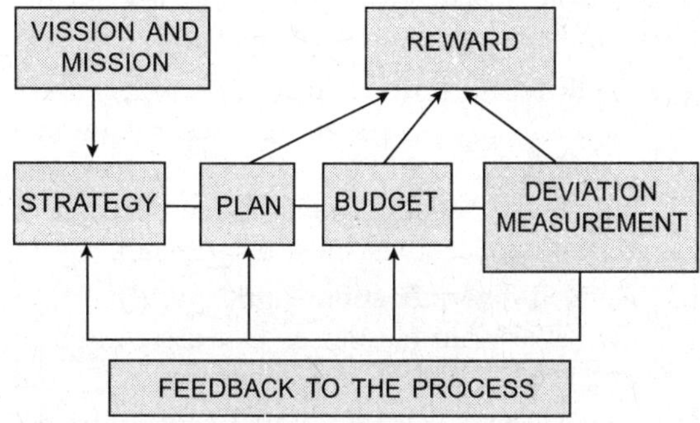

Fig. 6.2: Strategy and Control

6.4 CORPORATE STRATEGY AND DIVERSIFICATION

Corporate strategy refers to the business in its totality. As we have seen earlier, corporate strategy involves the integration of the business strategy in the plan of action for the business.

Designing the control system requires an understanding of the corporate strategy as a whole.

Designing the control system requires an understanding of the corporate strategy as a whole.

The degree of capacity building in a competence area is almost inversely proportional to the business diversification.

Each business has its own strategy, which is a response to the environmental factors mentioned earlier (see Chapter 2). It may be remembered that, the business response to the environment depends on the degree to which it is related to its core competence and the extent of diversification it has strategically adopted. The degree of capacity building in a competence area is almost inversely proportional to the business diversification. It has been observed that the greater the capacity of the core business the greater is the tendency of business to run single business units which are not diversified.

The control response to the three different business systems i.e., single business firm, related diversified firm and unrelated diversified firm, is therefore different. To understand the control system response we need to understand the three corporate strategies that a business commonly has in a generic business set up in the context of the three business systems stated above.

a. Single business firm: Such a firm concentrates on a single business and generally has high competency and high capacity to run the business. A good example is the decision of IBM to concentrate on a single chip.

b. Related diversification: In this case the firm diversifies into businesses that are related to one another and have a common set of core competencies. The development of a product line of soap and toiletries by HLL is an example of such related diversification.

c. Unrelated diversification: The firm operates in different areas of business which are unrelated to one another. The only common link is that they are managed and funded by one single business concern.

Figure 6.3 gives an idea as to how corporate strategy takes place in relation to competence and capacity.

capacity \ competence	high	low
high	single business	related diversification
low	unrelated diversification	question mark

Fig. 6.3: Corporate strategy in response to competence and capacity (Source: Jaworski, B.J. and Stakeholder, V., "Control Combinations in Marketing – Conceptual Framework and Empirical Evidence", Journal of Marketing, Jan 93, Vol. 57, No. 1)

6.5 RESPONSE OF THE CONTROL SYSTEM TO CORPORATE STRATEGY

The response of the control system to corporate strategy will depend on the diversification needed. The more the diversification in unrelated areas, the more is the need for the business to go in for decentralisation and adopt measures of capacity building by training personnel and developing the organisation.

When the diversification is in related areas of the business, then the competence of the business needs to be controlled. An ideal situation in this case would be to control the deviation in the production process and adopt a control system which ensures high quality of the product and prompt delivery.

In the case of single business, where both the competence and the capacity are high, the business tends to become a centralised business in order to serve the purpose of control.

In the case of the first two systems an appropriate incentive and reward system will help considerably in making the control system functional. An incentive and the reward system will help in the development of both the capacity and competence in the organisation.

In the case of a single business core competence needs to be highlighted through adoption of a very high level of competency mapping and creating a permanent niche area for development in the future. Microsoft's success of adopting "DOS" and building upon its strength and developing the "Windows" is a good example in this category.

In the case of a single business core competence needs to be highlighted through adoption of a very high level of competency mapping and creating a permanent niche area for development in the future.

6.6 STRATEGIES AVAILABLE FOR A BUSINESS UNIT

The strategic options available to a business depend on three core issues which in turn decide the mission of the business units and the business as a whole. The core issues which are available to the business are as follows.

a. Assessing the market opportunities and deciding the competence level of the business by understanding the internal and external strengths.

b. Understanding the fact that the competitive strength of one business unit will vary from another business unit. Therefore, allocating separate resources should be allocated for each business unit to get the best performance out of it.

c. The level of attractiveness in which the business unit exists in the market.

The approach to understanding these three core issues is a trade off between short and long run objectives of the business. The approach to the issues is mostly dealt with in the two most popular business solutions of the Boston Consultancy Group (BCG), namely 2×2 matrices of growth and market share and the GE 3×3 matrix which deals with industry attractiveness and business strength. Though these models differ in their approaches, they both lay down common course of action for the business in a specific business situation. The set of choices that are laid down for the business are as follows.

a. Build: The business unit that has high market potential needs to be given priority so that it can increase its own market share. This is done, even at the cost of the short run profit and sales revenue. Such decisions, generally lead to heavy investment in the business unit at the beginning and act as an investment centre.

b. Hold: This business strategy aims at protecting the market share of high market share business units. The cash inflow and the cash outflow in such businesses are almost equal. The idea is to retain the market share even at the cost of the business only breaking even.

c. Divest: A business which has a low market share and growth should withdraw from such a business unit.

d. Harvest: Such a business gives the maximum short run earnings and therefore the business should focus on them to reap the benefits in the short run.

The design of the control system is focused by deciding the business units' locus standing in view of the above points. The designer of the management control system has to align the choices available for the business units and the strategic planning process in the business.

The designer of the management control system has to align the choices available for the business units and the strategic planning process in the business.

The choice of a business strategy lies in asking the key question "Are we in the right mix of business?" The answer to the question is decided depending on whether the business is going to develop core competence or go for diversification. The second more pertinent question that the business should answer is "What businesses/ industries should

The choice of a business strategy lies in asking the key question "Are we in the right mix of business?"

The second more pertinent question that the business should answer is "What businesses/industries should we be in?" The decision to hold, build, harvest or divest depends on the answer to these questions.

we be in?" The decision to hold, build, harvest or divest depends on the answer to these questions.

The budgeting decision for all the four strategic options available will be different. While divest and hold are the two extreme decisions that a business can take, build and harvest are more moderate options. Revisions in the budget are more in the case of units that go in for the build option, followed by units that opt for the harvest option and are lowest in the case of units that go in for the divest option. Since, the input for the divest units is the least, the control information required from such business levels are also the least.

The strategic options available to the business decide the reward system that is available for the business. The build option has higher rewards in the organisation than the divest option. However, linking the rewards to the market share and innovation accelerates the control system since it has a long term perspective.

6.7 PORTER'S FIVE FORCES THEORY AND COMPETITIVE ADVANTAGE OF THE BUSINESS UNIT

Porter's five forces theory states that the intensity of rivalry between competitors, the bargaining power of the customers, bargaining power of the suppliers, the threat from substitutes and the threat of new entrants decide the course of action business has to take will shape up its business units. The generic structure of the control is derived from the above mentioned forces.

In the view of this, a business tends to gain cost advantage in the market by scaling up its production. It uses the models of the learning curve and quality control to take advantage of the cost in the market.

Differentiating the product and refocusing the basic product are two other commonly used processes that help the business to gain control of the market. In both cases, the idea is to relate the product to the needs of the customer, and shift the locus of control to the product rather than the externalities of the business.

SUMMARY

In this chapter we saw the response of a business in terms of the control strategies that exist for a business. The key to success is the correct alignment of the business to the strategy and control that is available to the business. The accomplishment of the business in terms of the set objectives and mission require understanding of the business units and their performance. The greater the accomplishment in terms of growth and a market share, the better is the business. Therefore, the management control of a business is greatly influenced by the competition faced by the business unit.

Review Questions

1. Fire fighting is the only way in which day to day business can be carried out. This leads to adhocness. Do you agree? Give reasons for your answer.
2. Why is it necessary for a business to understand the requirements of diversification?
3. What are the strategic options available to a business to reposition its business units?
4. How will the control be different under the four strategic options, i.e., hold, invest, divest and build?
5. What are the core issues that the business has to address to change its strategy?

Analytical Question

1. A national soap manufacturing company finds that a major multinational level player has entered the market for almost all of its product range. It undertook a study, where it found that the major player had a cost advantage in three toilet soaps targeted at the female population, in terms of marginal cost. However, the local company had an advantage in three basic products, namely health soap, dish washing detergent and medicated soap to fight dandruff. In the case of the latter three products, the market share of the local company was high because they had a cost advantage and a tie up with a known foreign toilet soap of international repute. However, the multinational company has also declared a tie-up with a highly reputed brand of international fame in the dish washing detergent segment.

   Decide the strategic options available to the local company and how it should go about them in its control process.

PART—C

TOOLS OF MANAGEMENT CONTROL SYSTEM

CHAPTER 7

Strategic Planning as a Tool to Management Control System

LEARNING OBJECTIVES OF THE CHAPTER

- Characteristics of strategic planning
- Significance of strategic planning
- Benefits of strategic planning
- Strategic planning process
- The allocation of resources
- Bower's model of the investment decision-making process

7.1 INTRODUCTION

Strategic planning is a long term process which involves decisions of the top level management. Strategic planning becomes effective only when there is an appropriate organisational structure to accompany it. At the end, the strategic planning will decide the physical and financial effectiveness of the management. This chapter examines the strategic planning processes and establishes a link as to how it is used as a tool for control.

7.2 CHARACTERISTICS OF STRATEGIC PLANNING

Strategic planning fundamentally consists of two processes, (a) setting goals and (b) strategy formation.

Strategic planning takes a long term perspective and thus is characterised by the following basic features:

1. Strategic planning is a complex process which involves deciding several variables.
2. Strategic planning is not process that is carried out on a regular basis but is carried out whenever there is a need to do so.
3. Strategic planning uses both external and internal data for creating the plan.
4. Strategic planning involves setting goals by communicating the process, policy and objective down the line of the organisation.
5. Strategic planning is a creative process.
6. Strategic planning is end result oriented.
7. At the topmost level of the organisation, strategic planning has no measurement standards, as they are largely conceptual.

7.3 BENEFITS OF STRATEGIC PLANNING

Strategic planning ensures that success comes from within the organisation. Capitalising on the knowledge and skill of the organisation is a key tool in this regard. The strategic process enables the organisation to document what it should do and what it should not do in the long run. Strategic planning is carried out through team building, improved personalised skills and more effective organisational communication.

Strategic planning ensures that success comes from within the organisation.

Strategic planning is ideally targeted at the top management. Hence it is devised by a group of two or three key responsible persons in an organisation.

The end results and the benefits of a strategic planning process is that the participants will be able to collectively develop their skills and be able to:

1. Understand the importance of the strategic planning process.
2. Reap personal benefits from strategic planning.
3. Create a vision statement for the organisation and the stakeholders.
4. Develop an organisational mission.
5. Identify critical success factors for the organisation.
6. Define the organisational goals.
7. Identify the barriers to success.
8. Translate goals into business plans.
9. Define organisational goals for the upcoming operating period.
10. Translate goals and barriers into action plans with assigned responsibilities and accountability norms.
11. Define the feedback and update process.
12. Become a stakeholder driven, enduring organisation.
13. Use team building, interpersonal and communication skills as a means to individual and organisational success.

7.4 SIGNIFICANCE OF STRATEGIC PLANNING

Strategic planning helps the organisation to internalize the strategic processes of the business. It prevents the manager from getting unpleasant surprises since the goals and the processes of the business undergo a strong scrutiny while the plan is inducted. Strategic planning takes into account the environmental changes, which are the corner stone for taking decisions in a business. When the strategic planning is inducted, the corporate culture is taken into consideration. Thus, it helps as a frame work of reference for budgeting and other financial allocations in the business. Strategic planning is as an integration of the various activities of the business into one comprehensive policy. It therefore, helps in coordinating the internal activities of the business.

Strategic planning helps the organisation to internalize the strategic processes of the business. It prevents the manager from getting unpleasant surprises since the goals and the processes of the business undergo a strong scrutiny while the plan is inducted.

7.5 THE PROCESS OF STRATEGIC PLANNING

Strategic planning is akin to setting up action plans for the business. Strategic planning extends the exclusive focus of the business in such a way that it includes all the decisions of the business including the short range plans and revenue generation. Generally six steps are followed in the process of strategic planning. These are discussed in the subsequent sections.

***First Step*: Reviewing and Updating the Strategic Plan**

Since strategic planning is a continuous process, the first step in setting up a strategic plan is generally reviewing the plan of the previous year. While reviewing the earlier plan, it is essential to incorporate the necessary changes which include any environmental and internal changes that the business is contemplating. The process of planning does not have any fixed time frame and hence can be started at any point of time depending on the urgency of the business. Usually, reviewing is done only when it is necessary to cope with the uncertainties in the business.

***Second Step*: Deciding on Assumptions and Guidelines**

In this step, the business has to decide how to incorporate necessary strategic elements in the plan. For this data regarding the current business situation are analysed by the business so that revenue implications are generally more or less stable. In this process, the goals and objectives are aligned to the business needs. Short range planning is synchronised with the long range plans and decisions regarding the discontinuation or addition of a line of business is taken care of. Guidelines regarding labour, salary and wages are also taken into consideration.

***Third Step*: First Iteration of the Strategic Plans**

After assuming the guidelines of the plan a business plan is formulated for implementation. The validity of data and initial analysis is carried out by the members of the business unit and is then passed on to the unit managers. The top up management is also consulted to see whether the plans are in agreement with the organisational requirements. Details of income statements and balance sheet items are scrutinised and justification carried out item-wise.

***Fourth Step*: Analysis of the Plans**

In this stage the top management integrates the business process by implementing the iterated strategic plan in the main course of action of the business. Several rounds of talks are held between the business units and the top management, so that the gap in planning can be understood. The gaps are then addressed by identifying business plans which can be improved by standalone decisions or by business acquisitions and mergers. The whole corporate objective is reviewed in this light. The strength and integration of the current business units for overall effectiveness is also carried out. The total internal strength of the business is estimated.

***Fifth Step*: Second Iteration of the Strategic Plan**

Once the above steps are over, it is generally, necessary to change some of the plans established earlier in view of recent developments. The necessary changes are therefore incorporated in the appropriate plans. These changes are generally a short term adjustment, which arise due to new technologies and other changes in the environment.

***Sixth Step*: Final Review and Approval**

The final stage is carried out by integrating the plan in the business and taking the approval of the top management including the board of directors. The approval process should be completed before the budgeting is done, which is a key to the implementation of the strategic plan.

7.6 THE ALLOCATION OF RESOURCES AND STRATEGIC PLANNING PROCESS

The strategic planning process reaches its critical stage when resources are allocated in the plan. There will always be some uncertainty in the allocation of resources in a long range plan. Hence, the organisation has to establish linkages with the strategic plans. The line of involvement of managers and their accountability needs to be set up so that the details of the allocation of the plan can be worked out. The responsibilities of each head need to be worked out in this connection so that a check can be maintained on the expenses of the organisation. The business should be able to identify its opportunity cost so that appropriate discounts can be made for all forecasted cash inflow and outflows.

It should be kept in mind that the number of approval steps and endorsement processes should be kept minimal so that the process does not slow down.

In order to have a proper allocation of resources for the successful implementation of the plan, the personnel of the organisation should be trained and educated regarding the strategic business processes which are being enabled through the plan.

7.7 BOWER'S MODEL OF THE INVESTMENT DECISION MAKING PROCESS

Bower's model of investment decision is based on the discrepancies between the plan and the actual process of implementation. The model states that any discrepancies of the plan should be realised by putting it into actual practice. The discrepancies here relate to the objectives laid down in the plan and the actual results which are observed after the implementation. Later, based on the discrepancies found, the key variables for a project are determined and moderated. The project is now set to be accepted at a functional level and depending on the competency of the task level managers and the reward of performances the project is accepted at the grass roots level of the business. Generally, higher risk projects are given higher rewards and lower risk projects are given lower rewards. Depending on the competency of the managers, the projects are chosen and implemented.

Bower's model of investment decision is based on the discrepancies between the plan and the actual process of implementation.

The Bower's model suggests a three level functioning of the strategic planning process. The lower level provides the basic data; the middle level manager synchronises it and the top level managers design the plan of action. The rewards and line of authority is set up by the top level management in mutual consultation with the various levels of the business.

The Bower's model suggests a three level functioning of the strategic planning process. The lower level provides the basic data; the middle level manager synchronizes it and the top level managers design the plan of action. The rewards and line of authority is set up by the top level management in mutual consultation with the various levels of the business.

SUMMARY

This chapter dealt with the strategic planning process as a tool to the management control system. It was observed that strategic planning essentially brings together the various dimensions of external changes and internal strengths to achieve the best results in the business. In doing so it consciously aims to remove the undesirable elements by focussing on the strength of the business and the environmental changes.

The new plans of strategy are streamlined by adjusting them to the rules, procedures, objectives and goals of the business. The long range financial allocation is done keeping in view the degree of the autonomy and need of allocation that percolates down the organisational line in the business.

In this regard the Bower's process is based on identifying the key discrepancies in the planning process. The process ensures that the management is thoroughly involved in designing the plan by inculcating the ideas upwards and the planning downwards in the business.

Review Questions

1. How does a strategic plan in an organisation act as a tool for the management control process?
2. What is the process of laying down a strategic planning process? Explain the various steps involved.
3. What is Bower's process? How does it help in understanding the strategic planning process?
4. How will an organisation which faces changes in the environment and technology design a strategic plan? What are the essential things it should take into consideration to do so?

Analytical Question

A printing press which uses high-end technology suddenly found that there was a complete change in the product they offered due to the entry of an absolutely new technology. In a bid to retain the market, it reviewed its financial plan and decreased the cost of the product in order to gain the market. This however, was wrongly interpreted by the customers. They believed that since the technology was becoming obsolete the company was trying to offload the product by bringing down the price; this led to a further fall in the market share of the company.

Where do you think the strategic planning went wrong?

CHAPTER

8

The Budget as a Tool of Control

LEARNING OBJECTIVES OF THE CHAPTER

- Concepts of budgeting
- Budget as a process to control
- Various budgets that enable management control
- Limitation of various budgets as a tool of control

8.1 INTRODUCTION

A budget is the translation of these business plans in quantifiable terms more so in monetary terms for a defined period of time.

Strategies are created by an organisation to achieve success in the business. To make the strategy work, the business makes plans which set the direction of the business. A budget is the translation of these business plans in quantifiable terms more so in monetary terms for a defined period of time. A budget is therefore a guiding path for the organisation to realise and implement its strategy in the long run and its plans in the short run. In short, a budget is an expression of the business strategy in terms of money for an executable period of time.

A budget is an expression of the business strategy in terms of money for an executable period of time.

8.2 BUDGETARY CONTROL

Budgetary control refers to the usage of organisational budgets, which are set for short and long term, to control and guide the business activity. The process of budgetary control follows a set rule of setting the budget, recording the actual results, comparing the results with the budgeted guidelines, calculating the variance and taking corrective results in case the variance is not favourable. Budgetary control therefore requires that appropriate authority, responsibility and accountability be given to the managers so that they can create goal congruence through realisation of plans and policies.

The process of budgetary control follows a set rule of setting the budget, recording the actual results, comparing the results with the budgeted guidelines, calculating the variance and taking corrective results in case the variance is not favourable.

8.2.1 Advantages of Budgetary Control

Budgetary control has several advantages, some of which are listed below.

1. Budgetary control uses several kinds of budgets which may be long term or short term in nature. These budgets are expressions of the corporate strategy in measurable monetary terms over a period of time. Hence, budgetary control helps in realisation of the organisational

strategy and helps the business to move on the right track both in the long and short run.

2. It bridges the gap between the planning and actual performance by constantly monitoring the processes of the business.
3. Since a budget is divided on the basis of function and cost allocation, it promotes specialisation and focusses the business activity.
4. Budget creation requires integration of ali the business functions and therefore it promotes the co-ordination and integration amongst the business policies.
5. Budgetary control brings objectivity to the business by establishing monetary value to the business.

> *Budget creation requires integration of all the business functions and therefore it promotes the coordination and integration amongst the business policies.*

8.3 NEED FOR BUDGETARY CONTROL

Why budget at all? This may be a pertinent question but, looking at the uncertainty and resource crunch that a business in the modern world goes through, there is no alternative to budgeting. Besides, a budget as we see it today is a very sophisticated tool of management control and strategy implementation. The need for budgetary control is felt because it helps in:

1. Reducing uncertainty
2. Increasing coordination amongst the various strategic business units in an organisation
3. Identifying the weakness of the business and focussing on the strength of the business
4. Keeping expenses under check
5. Identifying any deviation in the business

8.4 OBJECTIVES OF BUDGETARY CONTROL

The objectives of a budget are three-fold.

1. It establishes and ensures that the strategy is implemented
2. It creates measurable standards and comparable criteria
3. It provides a common thread of coordination within the organisation

8.5 ORGANISATIONAL SET UP FOR BUDGETARY CONTROL

A budget itself is an activity of the business. Besides streamlining the activities of the business it provides a platform for coordination. In most of the corporate forms of business, a budget is a set up in itself and acts as a business subsystem.

8.5.1 Organisational Set Up

The implementation of a budget requires that the basic structure on which the budget will operate be created so that it gives the desired results.

In order to do so, the following becomes absolutely essential for a budget.

1. **Budget centre**

   The budget centre is an activity area of a business which enables the development of the various budgets and acts as a coordination centre for the budget to be implemented. It is a responsibility centre in itself and is a facility centre for the appropriate implementation of the budget.

2. **Budget manual**

   A budget manual is a written document which facilitates the creation and implementation of a budget. A budget manual establishes the responsibilities for the managers who are entrusted with various kinds of budgets. In addition it provides clear instructions as how to establish a budget and how to coordinate with the other functions to establish a budget. It also gives the schedule of implementation of the budget in the business. The reports and the documents that are needed for the creation of the budget and the enabling process are also a part of budgetary control.

3. **Personnel and operational set up**

   Setting up a budget requires several processes and persons to be in place so that the creation and implementation of the budget is smooth. The activities of the important personnel and processes are listed below.

a. **Controller of the budget:** A budget controller is a person who oversees the creation, integration, management and revision of the organisational budget. The controller is a key person who integrates the thoughts and aspirations of the various departments of the organisation to the strategies of the business.

b. **Budget committees:** A budget committee consists of the functional heads of the various departments of the organisation such as finance, marketing, production, accounts etc. They work under the guidance of the budget controller to create the budget by analysing its facts and figures and help in implementation of the budget.

c. **Budget period:** The budget is generally set for one financial year. In many cases, the budget period is extended depending upon the needs and requirements of the business. For example a capital budget is generally set for more than one year and sometimes for a period as long as 5 to 10 years.

> *The budget is generally set for one financial year. In many cases, the budget period is extended depending upon the needs and requirements of the business.*

d. **Determination of key budgeting factors:** Key budgeting factors are those factors that have a great impact on the budget. It has been observed that if the key factors are changed or are moderated, the functioning of the business is greatly affected. The key factors may be external or internal to the business. They are sensitised in the budget so that the key result is achieved.

e. **Budget reports:** Budget reports provide crucial information on the variance of actual figures against the budgeted figures. The reports are designed to enable easy understanding. Sometimes, it is stated that the success of a budget depends on the nature and kind of report it is supported by.

8.6 FORMATION OF A BUDGET

A budget is created based on critical information in the business. The formation of the budget therefore depends on the nature and volume of information flow in the organisation. The budget controller provides a platform for the information flow and assimilation in consultation with the various departments of the organisation.

Generally, a budget is prepared through the instruction of the top management. Information thus flows up the organisational hierarchy. The managerial input and the accounting inputs provide the direction and helps in understanding the past financial performance of the business.

> *Generally, a budget is prepared through the instruction of the top management. Information thus flows up the organisational hierarchy.*

8.6.1 Budget Department

The budget department helps in coordinating the budget. It acts as link to establish and communicate the budget throughout the organisation. It helps in administration of the budget and revision of the budget while coordinating the work of the business as a whole.

8.6.2 Guidelines

Budget guidelines help to implement a budget. Guidelines are given to the responsibility centres so that there is uniformity in the business process while the budget is being implemented. The guidelines may consist of operational issues like wages, promotion, rewards etc., or strategic issues like creation of goals and procedures. Since all quarters of the business are taken into consideration for setting up guidelines, they are generally an expression of the unity of the organisation.

8.6.3 Budget Proposal

The budget proposals are the business' response to the external and internal environment. The external environment generally reflects the changes in levels of business activities and advantages the competitors gain in terms of cost. The internal environment consists of changes in the market share and the product mix of the company. Any change in response to cost cuts of the products and changes in the discretionary costs are also factors in the creation of a budget proposal.

8.6.4 Negotiation

A budget is prepared to improve the performance of the business. Therefore, it should reflect the optimum level of revenue that the business can generate. Often, those who set the budget end up projecting less revenue than can be generated and projecting more expenses than needed. The difference is known as a slack. The budgetary team in an organisation has to negotiate and remove any such slack and improve the performance of the budget.

The budgetary team in an organisation has to negotiate and remove any such slack and improve the performance of the budget.

8.6.5 Review and Approval

The budget has to be approved by the topmost management, that is, the Board of Directors and the Chairman since it is the key document through which the business will be established in a financial year. Generally, the budget process is completed by the end of the calendar year, since by the beginning of the next calendar year, the new financial year is already approaching.

The budget has to be approved by the topmost management, that is, the Board of Directors and the Chairman since it is the key document through which the business will be established in a financial year.

8.6.6 Revision of the Budget

Budgets need to be revised to accommodate the changes and mitigate the discrepancies that may have occurred in the past year(s). Generally, budgets are revised in two ways, (a) systematic changes in the budget and (b) revision on special occasions.

In the first case, the budget provides for the flexibility to update and change on an 'as and when' basis. In order to achieve this, budget processes are approved for a short period, e.g., three or six months so that substantial changes can be made in the following period.

In the second case, when the controller of the budget feels that the budget is failing in its function as a controlling device, it is changed drastically with reference to the special needs, in consultation with the top management.

8.7 ADMINISTRATION OF A BUDGET

Once the budget is finalised, the budget department has to ensure that the budget is administered. Administration of the budget requires the support of the entire organisation. The steps to ensure administration of the budget in an organisation are given in the following sections.

8.7.1 Determination of Objectives

The first step in administering the budget is to percolate the objectives and spirit of the budget throughout the organisation. This ensures that the budget is accepted, and defines the purpose for which the budget was set up. The common objectives of the budget need to be identified with the help of all the employees and they should reflect the aspirations of the organisation as a whole.

8.7.2 Establishing the Objectives

Establishing the budget objectives means translating them into real terms of workable concepts. It has been found that an objective which cannot be translated into real monetary terms of the business does not serve the purpose of the budget. Establishment of the objectives also requires determining the budget centres for the establishment of the budget.

8.7.3 Making Available Accounting Records and Verifiable Records

A budget is based on past performance unless it is a scratch level budget (zero based budget). The reliable records of the past especially the accounting records are significant in establishing the budget and its codes.

8.7.4 Preparation of a Budget Organisational Chart and Fixing the Responsibility

In this step the line of authority and responsibility for the budget to work is set up. The clearer the lines of authority and responsibility, with regard to the budget, the better it can be implemented.

8.7.5 Establishment of the Budget Committee

It is important to include the right kind of personnel from all departments of the organisation, so that they represent all the interest groups of the business.

8.7.6 Preparation of the Budget Manual

The budget manual is the main part of all the budget activity. It contains the relevant budgets, the relationship between them and the logic by which they have been established. Further, it lays down the process of using the budget and the methods of implementing it.

8.7.7 Selecting the Budget Period

The budget period is selected keeping in mind the nature of the plan and the nature of the strategies that are going to be implemented in the business. Normally the period of a budget is one year. However, depending upon the intensity of the capital requirement (if large), it might be extended to 5 years.

8.7.8 Locating the Key Budget Factors that Influence the Budget

The key factors are those factors in which a change would drastically influence the budget. They are generally related to the environment. The external and the internal factors of the business decide which are the key factors, how they should be introduced into the budget and what steps should be taken to protect the business in case there is any change in them.

8.7.9 Determining the Cost Allocations of the Budget that a Budget Centre Expects to Implement

The responsibility centres have to calculate their individual budgets so that the overall budget is effectively implemented. This is done through negotiations between the top management and the functional heads that are responsible for the budget.

8.8 TYPES OF BUDGETS

Budgets are tools of action at the ground level of the organisation. They are established at the functional level in order to moderate the activity and help goal congruence.

Depending upon the requirements of the organisation and the purpose of the business budgets are classified into several types and groups some of which are as follows:

1. **Responsibility budget:** This is set for the operation departments and generally has an executive responsible for it.
2. **Program budget:** This is a separate budget for each plan or program of action of the organisation. This enables the management to assess the economics of any variation in programs.
3. **Operation budget:** This sets out the planned operations for the forthcoming period and includes the sales, production, production cost, and selling and distribution expenses.
4. **Functional budget:** This budget is set for each function of the business such as sales research, purchase and finance.
5. **Financial budget:** This includes the cash budget showing the anticipated sources and utilisation of cash, budgeted balance sheet and budgeted profit and loss account.
6. **Capital budget:** This relates to the capital expenditure of the business and it assesses the economics of capital expenditure and investment.

Some of the budgets and their implications are discussed in the following sections for a general understanding of their effect on the management control.

8.8.1 Master Budget

A master budget is the culmination of all the budgets of the business organisation. It is the relational budget of the organisation. It connects all the budgets and sets the common purpose of all the budgets. For example, the master budget links the cash budget with the expenses that are budgeted in the functional budgets such as the sales budget or the production budget. In fact, the master budget provides a link to understand the purpose for which the budgets are created according to the budget manual. The master budget also helps in understanding the overall variances in the business.

A proforma of a master budget is given for a conceptual understanding in Table 8.1.

Table 8.1: Proforma master budget

Master budget period:	**Normal capacity**		**Budgeted capacity**	
	Product I (Rs.)	*Product II (Rs.)*	*Product I (Rs.)*	*Product II (Rs)*
Sales				
Cost of sales				
(Add) opening stock				
(Less) closing stock				
Gross profit				
(Add) Administrative cost Selling and distribution cost				
Net profit				
Asset:				
Fixed				
Current				
Total Capital employed				
Ratios:				
Profit/capital employed				
Sales/capital employed				
Profit/turnover				
Current ratio				
Liquidity ratio				
Appropriations from profit				
Dividends				
Reserves				
Taxes				
Balance of profit and loss				

8.8.2 Sales Budget

A sales budget provides for the forecast of future sales and the costs required to support that particular level of sales in the budgeted period.

Several factors influence sales forecasts; the major ones are stated below.

1. **External factors** such as government policy, cycle of trade, purchasing capacity of the consumers etc.
2. **Internal factors** such as desired profit, sales trends, introduction of new products, to name a few.

A sales forecast may be prepared by one or more of the methods discussed below. Several methods are used since each method has some good points and generally act complementary to each other.

1. **Market research method:** Marketing research is a method of analysing the market by researching customers' and competitors' views on marketing strategies. The scope of this method is too large for this book to discuss. However, market research not only enables the organisation to decide about its future sales, it also strengthens its knowledge about the direction in which its sales and marketing efforts should move.
2. **Analysis of past sales reports:** In this method, the sales of the past years are analysed and an effort is made to fit the trend to the equation of a straight line, where the dependence on other factors which influence sales is determined.
3. **Salesman's assessment:** In this method the sales team is given a free hand to assess the market and give the sales forecast for the organisation. This method gives a ground reality about the sales and the market.
4. **Study of the competitors' sales pattern:** In this method, the competitors are the central focus of the sales budget. The idea is generally to replicate the best or the leader in the market. This method is generally used in collaboration with the market research method and study of the general trade practice.

A sales forecast indicates the quantity of anticipated sales of the various products at different estimated price levels. The total profits as well as the profit contribution of the individual products, which each of the forecast sales when materialised is likely to yield, are computed. Limiting factors such as shortage of raw material, skilled labour etc., if any, are taken into consideration and the profit contribution per unit of the limiting factor is projected. The accepted sales forecast is then converted into a sales budget. The sales forecast generally uses the objects of the business as assumptions to carry out the forecasts.

A product-wise classified sales budget is given in Table 8.2.

Table 8.2: Sales budget by products

SALES BUDGET
By Product and time of a calendar year
For the year ended 31st December 2005

Period	*Product A*		*Product B*		*Product C*		*Total*
	Unit Rs. 30 per unit	Amount per unit	Unit Rs. 40 per unit	Amount	Unit Rs. 20	Amount	Amount
January	4,000	1,20,000	5,000	2,00,000	10,000	2,00,000	5,20,000
February	4,500	1,35,000	6,000	2,40,000	8,000	1,60,000	5,35,000
March	5,000	1,50,000	5,000	2,00,000	7,000	1,40,000	4,90,000

cont...

Total 1st Quarter	13,500	4,05,000	16,000	6,40,000	25,000	5,00,000	15,45,000
2nd Quarter	12,000	3,60,000	18,000	7,20,000	30,000	6,00,000	16,80,000
3rd quarter	16,500	4,80,000	20,000	8,00,000	32,000	6,40,000	19,20,000
4th quarter	15,000	4,50,000	16,000	6,40,000	28,000	5,60,000	16,50,000
Total for the year	56,500	16,95,000	70,000	28,00,000	1,15,000	23,00,000	67,95,000

8.8.3 Materials Budget

The materials budget includes the quantities of raw materials. In this budget the quantities of each raw material needed for each finished product in the budget period are specified. The input data for this budget are obtained by applying standard material usage rates of each type of material to the volume of output budgeted.

The material budget serves the following purposes:

1. It gives a purchase plan for the material division.
2. It plans for the cash requirements for the purchase of raw materials.
3. It establishes cost of purchases.
4. It helps in fixing the levels of material holdings
5. It helps in control of raw material
6. It provides for calculation of the costs of raw materials for manufacturing each product.

In creation of the material budget, the cost of the material for each component of a product is taken into consideration. Thus this budget exercises control on the cost and quality of the product.

A proforma of a production cost budget is given below for conceptual understanding.

Table 8.3: Proforma production budget

PRODUCTION COST BUDGET
FOR THE PERIOD OF

Machine or department	Materials				Labour					Factory overhead		Total cost	Cost per unit
	Items of material	Qnty. Required for total production	Rate per unit	Cost	Operation	Trade and grade	Hours	Hourly rate	Cost	Department	Cost		
A	1 2 3 4				1 2					X Y			
B	1 2				1 2 3					Z			
C	1 2 3				1 2					X Y Z			

Administrative expenses budget

Administrative budgets are essentially administrative overhead budgets that classify the administrative costs and place them under the supervision of a particular manager who is responsible for the costs. Generally, the administrative costs are fixed in nature and hence it is not very difficult to establish such budgets. The method of control that is established is through standard variance analysis.

8.8.4 Promotion and Advertisement Budget

The purpose of promotion and advertisements is to increase and maintain sales. The advertisement and promotion budget is hence established in coordination with the sales budget. Since it is not possible to establish a direct link between advertisement and sales promotion with the actual sales it is not possible to make a budget by deciding the best method of advertisement or sales promotion. Hence one or many of the following methods are used to deal with the problems of discrepancies between the sales and advertisements when a budget is prepared.

1. **Percentage of sales budget:** In this method a percent of the current or previous year's sales is set aside for the purpose of creating the sales budget. It is set up on an incremental basis taking into consideration data from previous years.
2. **Funds available:** In this method, funds for advertisements and promotions are appropriated based on how much the company can afford to spend on these activities. This method is more or less arbitrary and controlled by the top management.
3. **What others spend:** Here the budget of a company is determined on the basis of the competitors' allocation for advertisement and promotion. This method often leads to 'one upmanship' and can cause problems, since the promotional budget of a competitor may be more than the company can really afford. It should be remembered that the size of companies in the same industry differs.
4. **Task method:** In this method each advertisement and promotion is taken as an independent task and generally funds are allocated according to the benefit that is expected to be received from each promotion.

8.8.5 Research and Development Budget

Since research and development generally has a long gestation period, the costs are also highly discretionary in nature. Research and development are really oriented towards perfecting a product and hence, the greater the perfection desired the greater are the costs and time required. In order to bring about a balance between cost effectiveness and optimisation in research, the following points need to be considered while setting up a research and development budget.

1. A clear definition of research and development should be developed based on which the funds are to be allocated.
2. The areas and sectors of responsibility should be clearly defined.
3. The budget defines the limits of each project or developmental work undertaken. The limits may be the percentage of sales, percentage of profit, ability of the concern to spend or experience of the past spending.

8.8.6 Overhead Budget

An overhead budget sets up a business' fixed and variable overheads. Since most of the overheads are activity driven, the overhead budget is influenced by the organisational activities, such as sales leading to sales commission, consignments leading to consignment commission etc. The operating expenses are disbursed on the basis of the operating costs and the overheads of each activity. Generally, about 50 per cent of the previous month's expenses are disbursed.

8.8.7 Financial Budget

A financial budget can be one of two kinds. The first is the cash budget and the second is the budgeted financial statement.

1. **Cash budgets:**

   Cash budgets are preceded by a cash forecast, which is an estimate of the cash requirements and availability in a future period of time. A cash forecast takes into account all sources of cash inflow and outflow in the business over a given period of time. The accrual items are not included in the cash forecast since they do not generally show the cash implications in a business. Cash forecasts and cash budgets are instruments for planning rather than control. A cash forecast is necessary as it:

   a. Indicates the level of cash requirements
   b. Preserves the liquidity
   c. Reveals the effect of sudden and seasonal requirements

d. Determines future fund requirements
e. Indicates whether funds are available for investment
f. Indicates availability of cash discount
g. Provides a basis of control

The length and period of a cash forecast depends on the requirements of the business and the nature of the business.

There are three methods of cash forecast, as follows:

a. Cash receipts and disbursement method: This method makes a short term forecast of all monetary requirements on the basis of the individual functional budgets including the capital budget. A forecast of the average collection is made through an analysis of the past collection periods. The figures for payments and receipts which are adjusted to the capital is obtained from the capital expenditure budget.

A typical cash forecast statement is shown below.

Table 8.4: Cash forecast statement

Cash forecast budget for the period				
A	First quarter	Second quarter	Third quarter	Fourth quarter
Opening balance				
Add: Receipts				
Less: Payments				
Closing balance				

Note: The closing balance of one period is the opening balance of the next period.

b. Balance sheet change or balance sheet forecast method: This method uses a change in the balance sheet item, which has a cash implication such as the debtors, creditors, work in progress etc., to forecast cash. This method does not take into consideration items in which expenses have a regular pattern of flow. It is a budget for the end of the period and does not reveal the periodic requirements of the cash.

c. Profit forecast method: This method assumes that the profit is the source of cash after making certain adjustments. Generally, before a forecast is made, the non-cash expenses such as depreciation and provisions are taken into account and the accruals such as advanced receipts are deducted. The adjusted profit denotes the cash requirement and availability.

2. Capital expenditure budget:

The costs of fixed assets are capitalised keeping in view the basic principles of classification of expenditure into revenue and capital. The conditions for capitalisation include one of the following:

a. It should benefit future periods
b. It should increase the serviceable life of the assets
c. It should contribute towards increased efficiency and productivity of the assets.

Capitalisation of the fixed assets serves the following objectives:

a. Accounting and control of cost
b. Charging of depreciation
c. Ensuring proper maintenance
d. Control over the proper working life of the asset.

A capital expenditure budget is the plan of outlay of the proposed outlay on fixed assets and is very closely associated with the cash forecast. Capital expenditure budgets are a continuous process and by nature a long term function.

An illustrative capital expenditure budget is given in Table 8.5.

Table 8.5: Capital expenditure budget

CAPITAL EXPENDITURE BUDGET FOR THE PERIOD OF							
	Original appropriation (1) (Rs.)	Expenditure to date (2) (Rs.)	Carry in from previous period (3) [(1)–(2)] (Rs.)	Fresh appropri-ation during the period (4) (Rs.)	Total (5) [(3)+(4)] (Rs.)	Budgeted previous period (6) (Rs.)	Carry over to next period (7) [(5)–(6)] (Rs.)
Machinery and equipment:							
Automatic production for shop 4	3,50,000	2,00,000	1,50,000	---	1,50,000	1,50,000	---
Milling machines	60,000	---	60,000	30,000	90,000	90,000	---
Cars and Vans	---	---	---	1,20,000	1,20,000	1,20,000	---
Building:							
Additional wing in hospital	80,000	20,000	60,000	---	60,000	60,000	---
Extension to Tool room	---	---	---	30,000	30,000	30,000	---
Building show room	---	---	---	1,30,000	1,30,000	70,000	60,000
Total	**4,90,000**	**2,20,000**	**2,70,000**	**3,10,000**	**5,80,000**	**5,20,000**	**60,000**

8.8.9 Cost Budget

A cost budget is based on the cost assumption depending on the output level of the organisation. This depends on the capacity utilisation and the plan outlay. On this basis, budgets can be divided into two kinds; the fixed budget and the flexible budget. However, in both these methods there is an assumption of a base year, i.e., they both depend on an actual amount of money which was spent in previous years. The other kinds of cost budgets include the 'scratch budget' and the 'Parta budget,' which are created on the assumption of no base year.

8.8.10 Fixed Budget

Fixed cost budgets are budgets in which no variable components are included and are generally established for a specific, planned output level. A fixed cost budget is not based on a variable output or any kind of change in the output. It is created independently by the top management, since fixed costs cannot be controlled by the functional heads. The idea is to divide the budgeting activity of the business into two discrete activities, one at the functional level and the other at the top management level. This segregation helps the business in controlling costs. In this method, budgets of the various departments are grouped under the fixed budgets of functional departments such as manufacturing, administrative and selling and distribution.

It should not be interpreted that a fixed budget is not subjected to change. Although it does not change to the level of activity, a fixed budget is liable to undergo change if there is a change in the business condition and the operational elements have changed drastically.

A fixed budget has very limited applications and is not a very good tool for control.

8.8.11 Flexible Budget

Flexible budgets are budgets that change according to fluctuations in the output level. Such a change allows for adjusting the business to the seasonal variances and length of the working period. Flexible budgets are more elastic, useful and practical since they take into account any changes that occur in the business.

In order to prepare a flexible budget, the anticipated expenses are classified into fixed, variable and semi-variable costs. The budget allowance for each activity of the business unit is then identified. These costs are then observed for their variation from actual performance. A fixed cost is established where there is no discretion available and variable and semi variable costs are established where there is discretion of management available to support the changed output level or changed business level.

The flexible budget is generally set at various levels of activities of output. An illustrative flexible budget is given below to clarify the above discussions.

Example:

The following data are available for a company that manufactures electric bulbs.

Information	*Rs (in lakhs)*
Wages and salaries	9.5
Rent, rates and taxes	6.6
Depreciation	7.4
Sundry administrative expenses	6.5
Semi variable expenses (At 50% of capacity)	
Maintenance and repairs	3.5
Indirect labour	7.9
Sales department salaries etc.	3.8
Sundry administrative expenses	2.8
Variable expenses (at 50% of capacity)	
Materials	21.7
Labour	20.4
Other expenses	7.9
Total	98.0

Whilst setting up the budget, it is assumed that the fixed expenses remain constant for all levels of production; semi variable expenses remain constant between 45% and 65% of the capacity, increasing by 10% for a capacity between 65% and 80% and by 20% for a capacity between 80% and 100%.

Sales at various levels are:

Capacity level	Rs. (in lakhs)
50% capacity	100
60% capacity	120
75% capacity	150
90% capacity	180
100% capacity	200

A flexible budget is set up as follows:

Flexible Budget

Period :

Particular	Capacity				
	50% Rs. *(in lakhs)*	60% Rs. *(in lakhs)*	75% Rs. *(in lakhs)*	90% Rs. *(in lakhs)*	100% Rs. *(in lakhs)*
Sales	100	120	150	180	200
Variable Expenses					
Material	21.70	26.04	32.55	39.06	43.40
Labour	20.40	24.48	30.60	36.72	40.80

Other expenses	7.90	9.48	11.85	14.22	15.8
Semi-variable expenses					
Maintenance and repairs	3.50	3.50	3.85	4.20	4.20
Indirect labour	7.90	7.90	8.69	9.48	9.48
Sales department salaries	3.80	3.80	4.18	4.56	4.56
Sundry administrative expenses	2.80	2.80	3.08	3.36	3.36
Fixed expenses	9.50	9.50	9.50	9.50	9.50
Wages and salaries	6.60	6.60	6.60	6.60	6.60
Rent, rate and taxes	7.40	7.40	7.40	7.40	7.40
Depreciation					
Sundry administrative expenses	6.50	6.50	6.50	6.50	6.50
Total	**98**	**108**	**124.8**	**141.6**	**151.6**

8.8.12 Zero Base Budget (ZBB)

Used and innovated by Peter Plyrr, in a company called Texas Instruments in 1969, this method does not advocate setting up a budget on a base year assumption. The idea in this budget is to start from scratch without any reference year or base amount that has been spent. Each unit of the budget is sanctioned on its own merit. The steps in a Zero Based Budget (ZBB) are as follows:

1. **Identifying decision units and developing decision packages:** This is akin to defining the responsibility centre and finding the requirements of both the capital and revenue expenditure in that decision unit.
2. **Evaluating and ranking the decision packages:** The decision packages are then ranked depending on the benefit that is derived from the decision unit. This helps in allocating the limited resources of the business to the decision points.
3. **Allocation of resources:** The resources are then allocated after several rounds of protracted negotiations between the functional heads of the decision centres and the top management, and funds are allocated on the basis of one unit of money earned to one unit of money allocated.

Merits of a ZBB

Since ZBB starts from scratch, some of its benefits are as follows:

1. Resources are allocated from lower priority items to higher priority items
2. It provides for better justification of resources
3. It makes the user of the budget more aware of the fund utilisation
4. It encourages better methods of fund utilisation
5. It reduces redundancy
6. It is highly flexible
7. It is a transparent system and allows sharing of information to run the business successfully

Limitations of a ZBB

1. It is a very cumbersome process, since it requires a lot of negotiation
2. It may not be effective for a business where there is forward integration of value
3. No fair methods of comparing innovative ideas accurately are available till date

8.8.13 Parta Budget

The Parta system refers to a daily budget based on the net cash flow from operations, post adjustment of tax and other financial charges. It generally benchmarks the efficiency factors of the business on a daily basis based on the actual inflow in the business. Tight credit and non-availability of funds is the main reason for this system.

The key factors that are considered in a parta system are the market position, targeted sales volume, pricing strategy, manufacturing efficiency and standard cost of raw materials. In the parta system there is generally an understanding between the topmost person in the organisation, such as the CEO, and the functional heads, as to how the cash will be regularly allocated.

Parta is a self regulatory system and motivates the personnel of the organisation to strive towards the best possible fund solution.

8.9 PROCESSES OF BUDGETING

The budgeting process requires the involvement of the personnel at all levels in the organisation. Generally, the strategic decisions are made by the top management and the functional inputs of the budget are collected from the lines and files of the business. However, there is no particular pattern available for the budget process. The two processes most frequently employed are discussed below.

8.9.1 Top Up Budget

Under the top up budget process the budget nuances are first finalised by the lowermost rung of the organisation who are in touch with the market and can feel the pulse of the customers. Their feedback is incorporated in the system and the process moves up until the organisational strategy is translated in terms of the budget.

8.9.2 Bottom Down Budget

In contrast to the top up budget, a bottom down budget is created by the top management, and the business units lower down only implement the budget. This method does not support the participative processes and hence is not favoured. But in a new business, this is perhaps the only solution, since the organisational learning is not sufficient to support a top up budget.

Many organisations use an intermediate approach. The direction of budget is given by the top management and information of the ground reality comes from the other units of the business.

8.9.3 Budget Report and Variance Analysis

Performance evaluation and budget reporting of variances are an integral part of the budgetary control system. Establishing a budget without comparing the actual results is of no practical use. A budget report shows the actual versus the budgeted amount on a regular basis so that necessary, corrective action can be taken. A typical budget report is shown in Table 8.6.

Table 8.6: Budget report

Department	Budget report for the period of				
Expenses	Budget (Rs.)	Actual (Rs.)	Difference		
			Increase (Rs.)	Decrease (Rs.)	Reasons
Controllable expenses					
Repairs to tools					
General shop labour					
Mechanical maintenance					
Lubricants					
Non controllable expenses					
Floor space					
Plant depreciation					
General prorated overhead					
Total					

As mentioned earlier in the chapter, a budget needs to be revised to accommodate change and to mitigate discrepancies in actual expenses with the budgeted expenses. Changes in the wage rate, prices, materials etc., lead to variance in the budget report. Amongst the other reasons are the errors in the budget that are detected after it is implemented and additional expenses needed to meet any contingencies that may arise.

A variance analysis is carried out in order to see the actual results of the business. Variance analysis is basically the difference between the budgeted and the actual expenditure.

A typical variance analysis sheet is depicted in Table 8.7.

Table 8.7: Variance analysis sheet

VARIANCE ANALYSIS Month: Jan 1999 Responsibility centre: Department 15		Standing order No. 02/0034/14 Expenses: Indirect Labour	
Reported by: Budget control			
Budget	Actual	Variance	Reasons identified
Rs. 4,850	Rs. 6,500	(–) 1,650	Excess labour strength
Corrective action report by department			
1. Cause of variance 2. Plan of corrective action 3. Effect on annual budget		1. 4 workers above the number allowed in the budget 2. Action in hand to transfer 3 workers to Dept: 14 and deploy one worker on direct job. 3. Will be met	
Sd/- Budget Controller		Sd/- Department Head	
Variance exceed 10% of the budget or Rs. 2000 (whichever is less) are only to be reported.			

8.10 CAPITAL BUDGETING

Capital budgeting refers to planning and accepting the projects with long term capital outlays (both outflow and inflows). These budgets require special attention since they involve greater risks and influence the business in the long run.

8.10.1 Process of Capital Budgeting

Capital budgeting is a long drawn out process and is outside the scope of discussion of this book. However, a broad outline is given in order for the reader to understand the process.

1. An economic analysis is carried out, which includes demand forecast, scale of operation and understanding the nature of the product etc.
2. A market analysis is carried out, which involves understanding the competitors' production and plan of action.
3. Projects are reviewed, this includes a review of the accounting and the discounted cash flow techniques to apprise the capital budgets.
4. Projects of a capital nature are accepted and implemented in the business.
5. The implementation process is reviewed.

8.10.2 Techniques of Capital Budgeting

1. **Non discounted techniques**

   Non discounted techniques, otherwise known as traditional techniques, fall back upon the earnings or cash inflows to evaluate a budget and do take the value of time into consideration.

They generally use the accounting information of the business. Two of the most commonly used non discounting techniques involved in capital budgeting are given below.

a. Pay back period method

This method is the most widely used method in India as it involves the least technical input. It works on the principle that the sooner the money is recovered the better, as the chances of losing are less. The payback period is defined as the time required to recover the original cash investment in a project. Mathematically it is expressed as:

Pay back period

$$= \frac{\text{Cash outlay of the project}}{\text{Annual instalments of cash inflow}}$$

The payback is received in a number of years and can be used as a criterion to accept or reject a project under capital budgeting consideration.

Merits of the method:

- It is simple to calculate
- It protects the interest of the investors
- It supports the efficient usage of cash and helps in building liquidity

Demerits

- It ignores the cash flows which are earned after the payback is completed
- It does not consider the time value of money
- The cost of borrowing is not considered

Example: Consider two projects 'A' and 'B', which require Rs. 10,00,000 capital outlay, with inflow is as follows:

No. of years	*Inflow in Rs.*	
	Project A	*Project B*
1	2,50,000	3,00,000
2	2,50,000	4,00,000
3	2,50,000	3,00,000
5	2,50,000	2,50,000
6	2,50,000	2,50,000

Then the pay back for project A is 4 years and that of project B is 3 years. Hence, project B is accepted as it requires less time to recover the initial outlay.

b. Accounting Rate of Return (ARR) method

This method uses the average income after tax and the average investment in a project to determine a rate of return, which is known as the accounting rate of return. The method uses the accounting information and hence is called the accounting rate of return. It can be expressed mathematically as:

Accounting rate of return

$$= \frac{\text{Average income}}{\text{Average investment}}$$

Merits of the method:

- It uses the entire stream of cash inflow for calculation of ARR
- It is simple to calculate
- It is based on available accounting data and therefore much more acceptable

Demerits:

- It ignores the time value of money
- It ignores the cash inflow and takes the profit instead
- The life of the project is not taken into consideration

Example: There are two projects, project 'A' and project 'B'. A business has to choose between them. Information regarding the projects is given below.

	Project A	*Project B*
Investment in Rs.	1,00,000	2,00,000
Life of the project	4 years	5 years
Cash income per year (After interest depreciation and taxes)		
1	5,000	7,000
2	15,000	15,000
3	20,000	18,000
4	16,000	20,000
5	—	15,000

Profit of project 'A'

= Rs. (5,000 + 15,000 + 20,000 + 16,000)

= Rs. 56,000

Profit of project 'B'
= Rs. (7,000 + 15,000 + 18,000 + 20,000 + 15,000)
= Rs. 75,000

Average profit of project 'A'
= Rs. 56,000/4 = Rs. 14,000

Average profit of project 'B'
= Rs. 75,000/5 = Rs. 15,000

Net investment in project 'A' = Rs. 1,00,000
Net investment in project 'B' = Rs. 2,00,000

A.R.R of project 'A'
= 14,000 × 100/1,00,000 = 14 %

A.R.R of project 'B'
= 15,000 × 100/2,00,000 = 7.5 %

Since the A.R.R of project 'A' is larger than that of project 'B', it should be accepted.

2. **Discounted techniques**

It can be seen that in both the above methods the time value of money and the cost of capital are ignored. This will lead to the problem of not being able to justify larger inflows during the later period of the projects and projects that have larger cash inflows during the earlier period will always be at an advantage. Hence, the discounted techniques take the time value of money and the cost of capital into consideration. These methods are more popular since they provide for a better comparison. The discounted techniques involved in the process of capital budgeting are stated below.

a. **Net present value**

The net present value method uses the concept that 'time is money'. According to this method, the net cash inflow, after being discounted for the capital costs, determines the acceptability of the project. The larger the net present value, the greater is the acceptability of the project. It may be noted here that the net present value is actually represented as an absolute value and indicates the value of the business in monetary terms. This method successfully recognises the fact that the large cash inlays, which occur during the latter period of the project, have more value than the ones that appear in the initial period and that the life of the project is an important consideration in determining the value of the project.

Mathematically, the Net Present Value (NPV) is defined as

$$\text{NPV} = \Sigma_{t-1}^{n} A_n/(1 + k)^n - C_o \qquad (8.1)$$

Where

A_n = Cash inflow of the project during the nth period of time

k = Cost of capital required for discounting the cash flows

C_o = Cash outlay or outflow in the project which happens in the '0th' year

t = The period for which the investment gives return of cash inflow

Merits of the method:

- It recognises the time value of money
- It gives weight to the cost of capital
- It is based on the entire cash flow of the project
- Ranking of the project is independent of the discounting rate.

Demerits of the method:

- It is a complex method and requires expertise to calculate the values
- It gives an absolute value and hence is difficult to compare
- It is based on the assumption of cost of capital

Example:

- A company has two projects, 'A' and 'B' to evaluate. The following information is available to them.

No. of years	*Value in Rs.*	
	Project A	*Project B*
1	40,000	1,20,000
2	1,20,000	1,60,000
3	1,60,000	2,00,000
4	2,40,000	1,20,000
5	1,60,000	80,000

If the cost of capital is 10% which project is more acceptable to the company?

(Given, the present value of Re. 1 for the next five years is .91, .83, .75, .68 and .62)

Present value of project A

(in Rs.)

Yr.	Discount factor	Cash inflow	Present value
1	0.91	40,000	36,400
2	0.83	1,20,000	99,000
3	0.75	1,60,000	1,20,000
4	0.68	2,40,000	1,63,000
5	0.62	1,60,000	99,200

Total present value = Rs. 5,18,400

NPV = Rs. (5,18,400 - 4,00,000)
= Rs. 1,18,400

Similarly,

Present value of project B = Rs. 5,23,200

NPV of project B
= Rs. (5,23,200 - 4,00,000)
= Rs. 1,23,200

Hence, project B should be accepted since it has a higher NPV.

b. Internal rate of return

The internal rate of return is the rate of return that equates the sum of the present value of cash inflows with the outflow. In other words, it is that rate at which the net present value is zero. This can be achieved by setting Equation (8.1) = 0.

Ideally if the cash inflow is equal to cash outflow than the IRR should be 1. If the present values of inflows are more than the outflow, then the IRR will be more than one and if the inflows are less than the outflow then the IRR will be less than one. Therefore, if a project has a higher IRR it is accepted. The IRR is always expressed in terms of percentage, which is an advantage as it is easier to compare the percentages. Besides it is free from the discounting rate at which the cash inflows are discounted.

Merits of the method:

- Provides an objective basis of evaluation
- It takes the time and magnitude of cash inflows into consideration

Demerits of the method:

- It is a very cumbersome process as often the rate has to be intrapolated
- Mutually exclusive projects with various discounting rates may give divergent results and cannot be used in this case.

Example: If machinery to be purchased requires a cash outlay of Rs. 18,000 and is expected to provide cash inflows of Rs. 5,610 at the end of each year for the next 5 years which is the life of the machinery, then the IRR of the machinery (the project) can be calculated as follows:

Cash outflow = Rs. 18,000

Cash inflow at the end of each year = Rs. 5,610

$18{,}000 = 5{,}600/(1 + r)^5$

By the trial and error method we see that the value of r is 18%

a. Profitability index method

The profitability index, also known as the benefit cost ratio, denotes the ratio of the present value of cash inflow to the present value of cash outflow. As in the case of the NPV, here a ratio of 1 means that the present value of cash inflow is equal to the present value of cash outflow or the IRR has been reached. If it is less than 1 it means the present value of cash inflow is less than the present value of cash outflow and if it is more than 1 than the present value of cash inflow is greater than the present value of cash inflow. This means we should accept the project that has a profitability index > 1 (more than the marginal project) and reject all projects whose profitability index < 1.

The mathematical equation for the profitability index is:

$$PI = \frac{\text{PV of cash inflows}}{\text{PV of cash outflows}}$$

Merits of the method:

- It provides for a sound system of comparison
- It accepts the logic of both the NPV and IRR methods

- It is index based and therefore free from the time taken to implement the project

Demerits of the method:

- It considers only the ratio and disregards the quantitative aspects of the value of the projects
- It involves cumbersome processes

Example: There are three projects which have the following information at a 10% rate of discounting, which one should be accepted?

	A	*B*	*C*
PV of cash inflow	1,20,000	80,000	30,000
PV of cash outflow	80,000	80,000	80,000
P.I	1.5	1	0.375

Here we see that A is the best project and should be accepted, B is a marginal project and therefore may or may not be accepted and C should not be accepted.

8.10.3 Concepts of Capital Rationing

Capital rationing refers to situation where there are constraints on the availability of the capital for investment in the business and the business has several projects to invest in with the limited capital available. Under such situation, taking a capital investment decision involves high risk. The factors that lead to capital rationing are as follows:

1. **External factors:** The external factors involved in the process are the non availability of funds in the market, a decision by the government to take drastic steps in curtailing investment in some areas of investment or any other trade cycle related problem.
2. **Internal factors:** The internal factors include the non availability of funds, more than one competing project for a given sum of investment and diverse business interests.
3. **Risk factors:** High risk in business also leads to capital reasoning since the higher risk tends to trade off the value of investment. This attracts a lesser number of investors to the business

8.10.4 Limitations of Capital Budgeting

The basic limitations of the capital budgeting are as follows:

1. All capital budgeting techniques assume that the projects are mutually exclusive and independent. This may not be true in many cases.
2. Estimation of future cash inflow is a serious impediment in all the techniques of capital budgeting, despite a number of probability models being used in practice.
3. Factors such as goodwill, relationships with others in the industry cannot be taken into consideration, as they cannot be quantified.
4. The time frame and urgency act as a limitation to the capital budgeting as often, urgency overruns logical business decisions.

SUMMARY

This chapter explored the requirements of a budget, the process of setting up a budget and the organisational support required to enable a budget process. The various kinds of budgets and their role in the control process were defined. The function budgets keep a tag on the process of the current business whereas the capital budget acts as a shield to any risk that might arise due to a wrong decision of capital investment. Setting up a budget with or without a base reference essentially draws our attention to the degree of strength required in the control process. In a flourishing business, a budget plays the role of a time keeper whilst in a business that is facing difficulties a budget acts as an instrument for effective allocation and control on the cash outlay. The limitations of the types of budgets have also been discussed.

Review Questions

1. What is a budgetary control? Discuss the various requirements that should be considered for adopting budgetary control?

2. Explain thé difference between a forecast and budget with examples.

3. What are the organisational requirements of a budget?
4. How does a budget help in the management control process? Explain with an example.
5. What are the key budgeting factors? What role do they play in the creation of a budget?
6. What is a functional budget? Explain one functional budget in detail.
7. What is a fixed budget and how does it differ from a flexi budget?
8. What is a zero based budget? How is it different from a general budget?
9. What is the parta system? Explain.
10. Explain the advantages and disadvantages of a budgeting system keeping in mind management control as a process.

Analytical Questions

1. You are the manager of production of a tea manufacturing unit in Assam. You have to set up a budget for the production department. State the key budgeting factors that you would take into account when you set up the budget. Explain why you intend to propose them as the key budgeting factors.
2. You have to provide a budget report that gives variance information as well as the action plan for a motor cycle manufacturing plant. What are the key issues that will be reflected in your report? Give a specimen of the report.

CHAPTER 9

Valuation as a Tool to Management Control

LEARNING OBJECTIVES OF THE CHAPTER

- Valuation of assets
- Valuation of liabilities
- EVA and MVA as a tool to value measurement

9.1 INTRODUCTION

The best methods of control are through assessing the financial performance of an organisation. However, this is not easy. To start with, the financial results show the overall well being of the corporation. A good performance in turn indicates that the business processes are in place and are working perfectly (we assume that there has been no severe window dressing of the business and it has been conducted under normal ethical terms acceptable to the industry and the business at large). Secondly, the financial performance gives a clue regarding the effectiveness of the business by providing information about critical decision areas in monetary terms. Needless to say, the first level of control in a business organisation starts with financial variance analysis (already discussed earlier in the book) and the ratio analysis, both of which are tools to observe the variations and to compare and contrast them with set figures or values. It is thus able to solve the problems, bring back normalcy and improve performance. Thus the financial performance is used for the purpose of management control.

The financial performance gives a clue regarding the effectiveness of the business by providing information about critical decision areas in monetary terms.

The financial performance is used for the purpose of management control.

It is appropriate to mention here that the financial performance of an organisation is related to the way the assets and liabilities are managed in a business. Subsequently, in this chapter, we will try to understand the relations that exist between the assets and liabilities of the business and how they can be used as a tool for control. The emphasis will be more on using the financial performance as a signalling tool to control.

9.2 UNDERSTANDING ASSETS AND LIABILITIES FOR THE PURPOSE OF CONTROL

The relationship between assets and liabilities and the expense and income in accounting terms are very well specified. Any income is treated as a liability since it is earned to be distributed to the ownership fund (equity capital). On the other hand, expenses are generated to carry out the basic functions of the business such as creating assets and resources and to earn a profit. Therefore they are related to the assets. In fact, as an accounting process all the fictitious expenses and losses are transferred to the asset side of the balance sheet (or are deducted from the liability side, which is equal to adding to the asset side of the balance sheet).

What does this have to do with management control? The essence of management control is to increase the efficiency of the business, which in turn will increase the value of the business and the assets of its stakeholders. Essentially this means that if the expenses and assets can be controlled and managed and the liabilities can be utilised in the right way, then the purpose of control is solved for the major part.

The essence of management control is to increase the efficiency of the business, which in turn will increase the value of the business and the assets of its stakeholders.

A good way to boost business is to increase the internal efficiency by creating an internal environment conducive to higher performance. This means pumping in huge funds to boost the production capacity and garnering large funds from the market to back it up. The argument often quoted for this is "money attracts money".

The window dressing corporate balance sheet is a fall out of this concept. Large fictitious assets boost up the performance of the business and makes the capital vulnerable to huge market risk. The risk arises, since there are no real assets to act as a fall out option for the business. This is actually a different kind of management control problem.

The corporate balance sheets window dressing is a fall out of this concept where, large fictitious assets boost up the performance of the business and makes the capital vulnerable to huge market risk.

Whatever the case, the managerial problem solving approach to maintain a balance between increasing value, decreasing costs (which includes the agency cost) is a difficult task. However the process generates a tremendous amount of support in implementing the basic business goal (profit maximisation) and in putting the management control in place.

9.3 MEASURING LIABILITY EMPLOYED: VALUATION OF SECURITIES FOR CONTROL

We start this exercise by first looking at the financial performance as a control from the liability angle. To understand this we will look at the valuation of liabilities first and then see how capital charges are used.

The valuation of liabilities gives us a basis to understand control from the investors' perspective. It is clear that goal congruence of the business is possible if the owner's fund is protected and increases in value.

9.3.1 Valuation Based on Earnings

The greatest problem in valuation of liability is that it tends to be concentrated on the book value, which is a problem in itself. Since, the book value is dependant on the face value it does not reflect the outstanding market value of the stock or debt. Hence, the only way out is to use a valuation which is based on the earnings (or at least the potential to earn) in the business. Valuing the debt capital is simple since there is a stated earning (or cost) in such instruments. The most common valuation method that is used for debt capital (with or without perpetual payouts) is known as Yield To Maturity (YTM).

The greatest problem in valuation of liability is that it tends to be concentrated on the book value, which is a problem in itself. Since, the book value is dependant on the face value it does not reflect the outstanding market value of the stock or debt.

The equation for the valuation model is

$$\text{YTM} = \frac{I}{(1+k_d)} + \frac{(P_1 - P_o)}{P_o} \qquad (9.1)$$

Where

P_o is the value of the single unit of a bond or debt capital (represented by the market price) in the 0th or initial year of investment.

P_1 is the terminal price of a single unit of a bond or debt.

I is the absolute value of interest or coupon received on the bond (one unit)

k_d is the rate of interest or cost of debt for that particular debt or bond instrument.

Example: A bond, which has a face value of Rs. 10, is sold in December 2004, at the face value. It carries 12% interest annually and was resold exactly at the end of one year of investment at Rs. 50 per bond. What is the yield to maturity value of the bond?

Given:

P_o = Rs. 10, P_1 = Rs. 50 and

$I = 12/100 \times 10$ = Rs. 1.20

Substituting the values in Equation 9.1 we obtain

YTM = Rs.[1.20/(1 + .12)+50 – 10/10]
= Rs. [1.08 + 4] = Rs. 5.08

The advantage of yield to maturity is that there is a capital gain in this valuation model and it can work for any kind of debt instrument.

For the equity capital the process of valuation becomes slightly more complicated. This is due to the fact that the cost of equity capital is implicit and is not readily available.

The most common valuation model available for the equity model is known as the dividend capitalisation model. This model suggests that the value of equity capital depends on the payout of the dividend and the retention of earning in the business. It establishes a relation between the equity cost, dividend and the growth of business to find the value of the equity. Mathematically it is stated as

$$k_e = \frac{D_1}{P_o} + g \qquad (9.2)$$

Rearranging Equation 9.2 we obtain

$$P_o = \frac{D}{k_e - g} \qquad (9.3)$$

Where,

P_o = The price (value) of one equity stock

D_1 = Dividend paid per stock

K_e = The cost of equity

g = The growth rate which is expressed as $b \times r$, where b is the retention ratio and r is the internal rate of return.

It may be noted here that if the payout is 100%, then retention is 0%. Therefore the payout ratio can be obtained as $(1 - b)$, where b is the retention ratio.

This method however has its limitations, since the cost of equity is difficult to estimate. Another model, which is popularly called the earning model overcomes this limitation. The earning model depends on the market price and the earnings of a business in a given period of time. The model is dynamic and accepts the market valuation of the stock price. The equation given below explains this model.

$$k_e - \frac{E_1}{P_o} \qquad (9.4)$$

The equation can be rearranged to get, P_o or the value of the stock, so that,

$$P_o = E_1/k_e \qquad (9.5)$$

This model is very convenient as it can be used on a regular basis.

Example:

If a company has quoted the price of a stock at Rs.100 and has paid a dividend of 40% in a certain year what would be the cost of equity of the company given that the profit earned that year was one crore and each stock gets about Rs. 60 dividend per stock? If the rate of return is 8% in the current year, what would be the price of the stock if the internal rate of return is about 10% per annum in the subsequent year of investment and the current rate of dividend and internal rate is retained?

Given: Dividend = Rs. 60, and P_o = Rs. 100 (assuming that the stock has been issued at par)

$g = b \times r$,

where r = 8% and the payout ratio is 40/100 therefore retention ratio $b = 1 - .40 = .60$

$g = .60 \times .08 = .048$ or 4.8%

$$k_e = \frac{60}{100} + .048$$

or k_e = .60 + .048

= .648 × 100 = 6.48%

If r = 10%, then g = .60 × .10

= .06 or 6%

$P_o = D_1/k_e - g$ = 60/.648 – .0 6 × 100 H

≈ 102

Example: If the profit before interest and tax is Rs. 15,00,000 for a company and that company has a debenture of Rs. 10,00,000 paying interest at 20% per annum, what would be the value of a stock if the market return in the same industry in equity is 24%? What would be the value of the stock of this company (per stock) if the company has 10,000 stock outstanding in the market?

Given, k_e = 24%, k_i = 20%

PBIT	=	Rs. 15,00,000
(less) interest	=	Rs. 2,00,000
PBT	=	Rs. 13,00,000
(less) tax (50%)	=	Rs. 6,50,000
PAT = EAC	=	Rs. 6,50,000

P_o = Earning/Cost of equity capital

Earning per stock = Rs. 6,50,000/10,000

= Rs. 65

P_o = 65/.24 = 15.6 × 100

= Rs. 1560 per stock.

Total value of equity is Rs. 1560 × 10,000

= Rs. 1,56,00,000

The price earning ratio of the company = 1560/65 = 24 which is equal to the market return of the industry.

9.3.2 Capital Charges

The other aspect of the liability is the capital charges that occur in a business. Some of the common capital charges on the liability side of the balance sheet are the profit carried over to the capital and reserves out of the current liability. In most cases, such charges occur in the revenue year and are therefore charged at the market price while being valued. The common valuation in the case of current liabilities is the market price or the book value whichever is higher. This is in accordance to the conservative prudence followed in the accrual system of accounting.

The common charges that are regularly transferred to the liability side of the balance sheet, do not pose any problem. In case, there is an unusual transfer, the valuation becomes a problem. For example, any deferred expenses, might be difficult to value since they arise in the current year but accrue in the subsequent year(s). In this case, the market value is the safest value since it will not lead to any under absorption of costs in the business.

9.4 MEASURING THE VALUE OF THE ASSET EMPLOYED

When a responsibility centre is evaluated, one of the prime considerations that is used is the utilization of assets employed in the business. There are two questions to be addressed: (i) Is the decision regarding the employment of asset correct? and (ii) Are the assets that have been deployed, used correctly?

When a responsibility centre is evaluated, one of the prime considerations that is used is the utilisation of assets employed in the business. There are two questions to be addressed: (i) Is the decision regarding the employment of asset correct? and (ii) Are the assets that have been deployed, used correctly?

Both the issues are related to the control of assets and their utilisation. The various assets and their effect on the management control system are discussed in the remaining part of this chapter.

9.4.1 Cash

Cash is a vital asset of the company. Generally, it is the difference between the actual receipts and actual payments (called float). Cash is usually controlled centrally and allocated to the various units. The normal practice to hold cash as a multiplier of the annual sales is quite

The reason for holding a larger amount of cash than the income from the annual sales is to be able to make a comparison with the outside companies.

common, often 3 to 4 times the annual sales are held by a company. The reason for holding a larger amount of cash than the income from the annual sales is to be able to make a comparison with the outside companies. Some companies hold cash at the actual level as they assume that cash approximates the current liability. The reason for showing higher cash holdings is also to allow a comparison with the earnings of the internal units. If higher cash holdings are not shown, the internal returns of the units might appear abnormally high, which could mislead the senior management. This might lead to tight cash control in the business. Cash is generally valued at its actual purchasing price (unless it is adjusted for inflation).

9.4.2 Receivables

The receivables in a business are directly influenced by the sales and the credit periods. The value of receivables is influenced by the collection pattern and the bad debts. The collection history can reveal the real value of the investment in the receivables. The debate as whether to value the inventory at the book value or market price has a number of arguments for both points of view. One side says the market value without any adjustment should be sufficient, but this argument does not hold if bad and doubtful debts are considered. The best policy is therefore to show receivables at the book value less the value of bad debts and allowances for doubtful debts. However, the valuation, as has already been discussed is directly influenced by the credit line and credit period, which need to be in accordance with industry practices.

The value of receivables is influenced by the collection pattern and the bad debts.

9.4.3 Inventories

Inventories are generally treated in the same way as receivables. However, their value depends on two factors. The first is the flow into and the outflow of goods out of the inventory. If the value of the outflow is lower than the value of inflow, the Last In First Out (LIFO) is used, in the reverse case First In First Out (FIFO) is used. The normal method is to calculate an average value on the basis of the usage and value of the inventory. The second factor is the value in the balance sheet, which should progressively influence the borrowing for working capital of the company; this uses the highest value between the market and book value. This facilitates two things: (1) the value of the inventory will not be under absorbed in the selling price and (2) the real amount needed to fund the inventory will be reflected.

If the value of the outflow is lower than the value of inflow, the Last In First Out (LIFO) is used, in the reverse case First In First Out (FIFO) is used.

Products which take a long time to process are generally funded by money given in advance at the time of booking. In such cases it is advisable that such advance amounts received be deducted from the value of the inventory or shown in the corresponding period as a liability.

9.4.4 Overall Working Capital

The overall working capital may be valued from a gross or net point of view. If only the current assets are taken into consideration for the working capital, then gross valuation is used. This method is useful, if the actual assets of the business are to be determined; however, it fails to answer a vital question, i.e., Is the back up of current liabilities more than the current assets? In other words: Is the company making a loss in terms of working capital? To answer these questions and help in generating a perfect control mechanics the second approach of using the net value is used, which shows the excess of the current assets over the current liabilities.

It fails to answer a vital question, i.e., Is the back up of current liabilities more than the current assets? In other words: Is the company making a loss in terms of working capital? To answer these questions and help in generating a perfect control mechanics the second approach of using the net value is used, which shows the excess of the current assets over the current liabilities.

9.4.5 Property, Plant and Equipment

The value of assets such as the plant and equipment, are generally written as the book value after deducting the value of the depreciation. However, there is a problem once the book value is down to zero. In this case, the accounting method would show a gain by acquisition of the assets but the Economic Value Added (EVA) will show a negative value addition.

Example: A company decides to replace some machinery, the following information is given:

The annual revenue generated by the replacement of the machine will be Rs. 10,000. The capital charges are 10% and the life of the plant will be five years. If the depreciation is charged at the rate of 20% what will be the economic implications of acquiring the asset?

The investment required for the machine is Rs. 10,000 (cash outlay)

The present value (annuity) of Re. 1 for 5 years is 3.791

Cash inflow discounted at 10% is Rs. 50,000 × 3.791 = Rs. 189,550

NPV = Rs. (189,550 – 10,000) = 179,550

Hence, the machinery should be bought.

Implications of EVA

	1st year	2nd year
Revenue	Rs. 10,000	Rs. 10,000
Less: Depreciation	9,000	8,930
Income before tax	1,000	1,070
Less: 10% capital charge on total income	500	600
EVA	**500**	**470**

(*Note*: The depreciation is calculated at an average value and 10% of the capital charges)

Hence, the investment in the machinery is not acceptable.

The problem occurs because there is a tendency to over value the book assets and also the question of inflation has to be addressed.

There is a tendency to over value the book assets and also the question of inflation has to be addressed.

In order to overcome this problem the terminal depreciation is generally calculated for the assets. The terminal depreciation is defined as the excess of the scrap value over the actual value. If the scrap value of the asset is less than the current value of the asset, the value is called the balancing charge and is treated as an income and added to the profit after tax for the purpose of accepting the project (that is the required investment).

9.5 BOOK VALUE: GROSS AND NET VALUE

The fluctuation in economic value added and the return on investment from year to year can be avoided by including depreciable assets in the investment base at the gross book value rather than the net book value. This will aggravate the problem of EVA as stated in the example given. However, it has been found that return on investment if calculated on the gross value of the assets tends to understate the actual return.

9.6 DISPOSITION OF ASSETS

If a new machine that has a low book value is being considered to replace an existing machine, then, as discussed earlier, the valuation will show terminal depreciation which will be deducted from the value of the investment outlay. This certainly decreases the chances of the investment being accepted. Hence, it is desirable that assets with a low book value be disposed of before the decision to replace the asset is made. If the investment is at its original price then the unit managers are motivated to get rid of these assets – even at the cost of their usefulness.

9.7 DEPRECIATION

Depreciation is vital in considering the value of assets and calculation of the Return On Investment (ROI) and Return on Net Asset (RONA). It is common knowledge that the straight line

It is often found that in diminishing balance method, the value of an asset does not become zero, leading to anomalies in the investment of assets as explained in the last section. It may therefore, de-motivate the unit managers to have an asset with a low book value and he/she may be keen to sell it rather than allow it to effect the overall performance by stating an under valued ROI as calculated on the gross value.

method and the diminishing balance method have various implications on the value of assets due to the residual value at the end of the depreciable period. It is often found that in diminishing balance method, the value of an asset does not become zero, leading to anomalies in the investment of assets as explained in the last section. It may therefore, de-motivate the unit managers to have an asset with a low book value and he/she may be keen to sell it rather than allow it to effect the overall performance by stating an under valued ROI as calculated on the gross value.

9.8 LEASED ASSETS

Many leases are actually financial arrangement akin to debt financing. They are reported in a similar way in the balance sheet (originally a lease was treated as an off balance sheet matter and was only treated in the income statement, however this is now not the case). This has serious implications on the cost of borrowing and therefore the value of the assets. Most leasing decisions are taken by the top management, and are not left to the unit managers. Leasing increases the EVA by decreasing the overall cost of capital. This appears as a slightly simplistic statement as tax consideration is not taken into account.

9.9 IDLE ASSETS

Idle assets lower the ROI of a unit and cause concern for the manager in charge.

Idle assets lower the ROI of a unit and cause concern for the manager in charge. Hence, a facility to share and transfer idle assets to other units will not only improve the ROI of the unit but will also lead to fruitful utilisation of assets in the business. Classifying assets as being available or not utilised will create awareness of the availability of assets and ensure that they are utilised.

However, if a fixed asset cannot be utilised by other units, the unit managers should be given the flexibility to remove it from the investment base so that the profitability of the unit increases.

9.10 INTANGIBLE ASSETS

Differed revenue expenditures are those expenditures which are capital in nature but revenue by implication. A large investment in R&D or advertisements in the current year cannot be recovered by the business in the same year, hence they need to be capitalised and recovered over a period of time. Unit managers should therefore have the flexibility to decide whether to recover the amount in the same year or recover it gradually by capitalising. This would improve the efficiency of the asset utilised by the unit manifold and increase the absorption capacity of the unit for such intangible (capitalised) assets in the future.

9.11 EVA Vs. ROI

Many companies consider ROI a better measurement for three reasons. The first is the familiarity of the concept, the second is the ease of calculation and the third is that ROI provides an easy and established comparison in the business. Often, in a business, situations arise where there is a specified ROI which is used to measure the efficiency of the business. For example, a 20% ROI is taken as a good indicator for the banking industry in India. It should be realized that the ROI is influenced by all items and any change in the financial statements.

The Economic Value Added (EVA) however, cannot be used in the same way as it is an absolute term, which provides for few comparisons and also it is difficult to calculate.

The EVA, which was proposed by G.B. Stewart III and Joel M. Stern in the early 1990s, can be calculated from the following equation:

$$\text{EVA} = \text{Net profit} - \text{Capital charges} \quad (9.6)$$

where;

Capital charges = Cost of capital × capital employed

Another way to derive the EVA is as follows:

$$\text{EVA} = \text{Capital employed} \; (\text{ROI} - \text{Cost of capital}) \quad (9.7)$$

The methods to increase the EVA are as follows:

1. Increase the ROI, without increasing the asset base. This can be done through better business processes or reengineering the activities of the business.

2. Divest and sell assets, products and sub business units where cost of capital is higher than the ROI.
3. Invest in assets, products or businesses where the ROI is higher than the cost of capital
4. Increase the profit margin and decrease the cost of capital wherever possible.

Merits of EVA

1. EVA has the same objectives as those of the business, especially when considering profit creation. It does not provide for a comparison and creates a rigid atmosphere for the business like ROI does.
2. EVA does not promote the profits of individual business sub units. Hence, it will never promote a system where there are water-tight compartments of improvement within the business. ROI on the other hand promotes the increase of divisional returns at the cost of the business.
3. EVA encourages a decrease in the cost of capital by negotiating different cost of capital for different assets. Thus, an inventory may have a different cost of capital from that of the long term assets. The idea is to reduce the overall cost of capital. This helps in management control by enforcing a common view and goal congruence.

EVA encourages a decrease in the cost of capital by negotiating different cost of capital for different assets.

4. It has been observed that companies that have a higher market value also have a higher EVA. This is a very strong point in favour of EVA as it reflects the desire of the investor and not that of the management.

9.11.1 Abstract of a Survey of EVA and MVA in India

A survey was conducted by the magazine *Business Today* in the year 2002 on wealth creation by Indian companies. The study surveyed 500 large Indian companies and came to the conclusion that most of the large companies failed to create wealth for the stakeholders. A status report of the best ten Market Value Added (MVA) showed that, there was a negative EVA despite the MVA being high. The other startling disclosure was that very few companies actually measure the 'addition to shareholders value' despite the fact that the word 'value addition' is most commonly used.

Table 9.1 shows the MVA and EVA of India's ten best companies.

Table 9.1: MVA and EVA: Top Ten Indian Companies (Source: India's Biggest Wealth Creators, February 17, 2002, Business Today)

Rank	*Name of company*	*MVA*	*EVA*
1	HLL	44,220	768
2	Wipro	36,322	128
3	Infosys Technologies	25,856	232
4	Reliance India Ltd	19,346	308
5	ITC	13,013	436
6	Satyam Computers Ltd	6,662	166
7	Ranbaxy Laboratories Ltd	6,511	-90
8	Dr. Reddy's Lab	6,411	-1
9	Cipla	6,021	49
10	HCL Technologies	5,599	-43

9.12 CONSIDERATIONS IN EVALUATING MANAGERS

As a process and a tool ROI has certain problems. It is used primarily as it is an easy process and partly to highlight the management's performance. Although the use of EVA is advocated, there are problems associated with it in India. The main problem is the calculation of cost of capital, other reasons are the non availability of reliable data for the several components of capital, non availability of proxy factors and volatile capital markets. In addition the large book value of assets held by companies also create problems. In the USA, for example many companies have eliminated a large amount of assets from their investment bases. This is endorsed by law in USA and helps in unnecessary tagging of assets to risk of obsolescence.

9.13 EVALUATION OF ECONOMIC PERFORMANCE

> *An economic analysis is a diagnostic instrument and helps in understanding the implementation of business strategies and the level of success they have achieved.*

Companies carry out an economic value analysis at irregular intervals. An economic analysis is a diagnostic instrument and helps in understanding the implementation of business strategies and the level of success they have achieved. Revealing the current plans is also a part of economic evaluation, however, this is not carried out on a regular basis. The relative attractiveness of the business is also determined by the economic analysis. The gap in current profitability and break-up value in a business is an indication that there is a need to change the business processes.

Since economic performances are futuristic, it helps the business focus on the future profitability rather than the current scenario only and causes the business to look for new challenges.

As discussed earlier in this chapter, since the value of the capital is arrived at by discounting the future cash flows, the economic value evaluation helps in estimating the most likely outcome of use of capital in the business.

SUMMARY

This chapter discussed the various methods of valuation of assets and liabilities, which are carried out to help the control process to be in accord with the desires of the investors. For this it is essential that the value of the business is increased. Conventional financial analysis of a business, by ROI, is limited because it is linked to the accounting processes. The EVA method proposed by Stern and Stewart, provides a broader framework of measurement, however non availability of data and complicated data calculations are difficulties in this method. It was noted that economic performance analyses are only carried out once in several years. However it is an accepted fact that economic evaluation provides a future picture and is a good way to control a business.

Review Questions

1. What are the methods of valuing the liabilities and assets? Why is valuation needed for designing a control system?
2. How does a company create hindrances in its business process by window dressing its balance sheet? Explain how such an act will affect the ROI and ultimately the control of the business.
3. What is Yield to Maturity (YTM)? How is it different from interest rate?
4. What are the various ways in which equity capital can be evaluated? Explain one of them in detail.
5. What is EVA? How is it helpful for the management to use EVA rather than ROI?
6. Which is a better control indicator, market value added or economic value added - why?
7. What are the advantages of economic evaluation of a firm over the traditional methods used?
8. State the reasons why EVA should be used to achieve better management control.

Analytical Question

In a recent report published by a company, which is trying to make a mark in the market by introducing a new product in the cosmetic and toiletries range, the finance manager finds to his dismay that, the company's MVA is lower than its own computed EVA. He is also concerned about the high ROI, which has prompted the company to take a decision to introduce new products and explore hitherto unexplored markets.

Try to identify, what could have caused such discrepancies and make a list of such items. Then comment on the changes that may be required to control each item.

CHAPTER 10

Transfer Pricing as a Tool to Management Control

LEARNING OBJECTIVES OF THE CHAPTER

- Concepts of transfer pricing
- Uses of transfer pricing
- Methods of transfer pricing
- Limitations of transfer pricing

10.1 INTRODUCTION

The delegation of significant amount of authority depends upon the ability to delegate responsibilities for profit generation, which further depends on two basic conditions as stated below.

1. The delegatee must have all the relevant information to make the optimum profit making decision.
2. The delegatee's performance is measured on how well he/she has made cost/ revenue trade offs.

In a corporate value chain, a transfer price system is required if these segments are to perform with profit and with responsibility.

Transfer pricing refers to the pricing of goods and services within a multi-divisional organisation, particularly with regards to cross-border transactions. For example, goods from the production division may be sold to the marketing division, or goods from a parent company may be sold to a foreign (outside) subsidiary, with the choice of the transfer price affecting the division of the total profit among the parts of the company. Such transactions have led to an increase in transfer pricing regulations as governments seek to stem the flow of taxation revenue overseas, making the issue one of great importance for multinational corporations.

10.1.1 Economic Theory

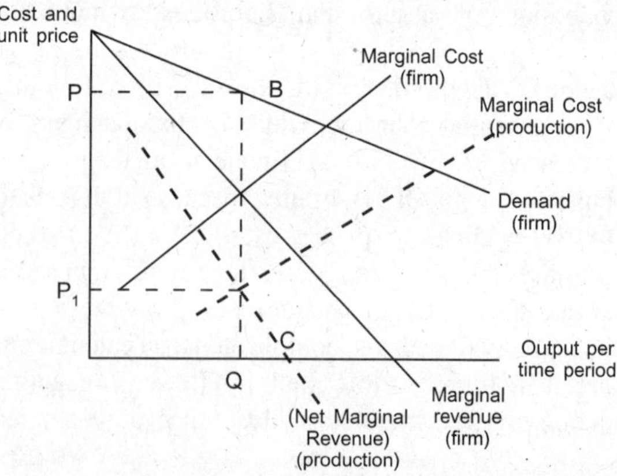

Fig. 10.1: Optimum level of output for a firm

Transfer pricing with no external market

The discussion below explains an economic theory, but in practice a great many factors influence the transfer prices that are used by multinationals, including performance measurement, capabilities of accounting systems, import quotas, customs duties, VAT, taxes on profits, and (in many cases) simple lack of attention to the pricing.

From marginal price determination theory, we know the optimum level of output is generally when marginal costs equal marginal revenue. That is to say, a firm should expand its output as long as the marginal revenue from additional sales is greater than its marginal costs. In Figure 10.1 this intersection is represented by point A, which will yield a price of *P**, given the demand at point B.

When a firm is selling some of its products to itself, and only to itself (i.e., there is no external market for those particular transfer goods), then the picture gets more complicated, but the outcome remains the same. The demand curve and the optimum price and quantity remain the same. Marginal cost of production can be separated from the firm's total marginal costs. Likewise, the marginal revenue associated with the production division can be separated from the marginal revenue for the total firm. This is referred to as the Net Marginal Revenue (NMR) in production, and is calculated as the marginal revenue from the firm minus the marginal costs of distribution.

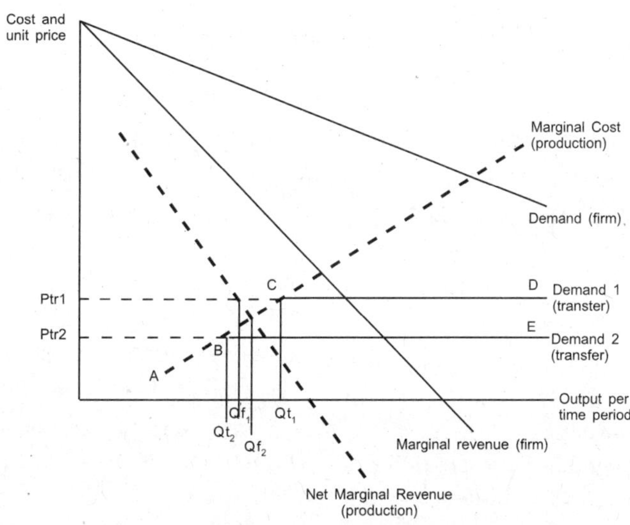

Fig. 10.2: Net marginal revenue

Transfer pricing with a competitive external market

It can be shown mathematically that the intersection of the firm's marginal cost curve and marginal revenue curve (point A) must occur at the same point as the intersection of the production division's marginal cost curve with the net marginal revenue from production (point C).

If the production division is able to sell the transfer goods in a competitive market (as well as internally), then both must operate where their marginal costs equal their marginal revenue, for profit maximization. Because the external market is competitive, the firm must accept the transfer price determined by market forces (their marginal revenue from transfer and demand for transfer products becomes the transfer price). If the market price is relatively high (as at the point Pt in Figure 10.3), then the firm will experience an internal surplus (excess internal supply) = $Qt_1 - Qf_1$. The actual marginal cost curve is defined by the points A, C and D.

If the firm is able to sell its transfer goods in an imperfect market, then it need accept the transfer price determined by market forces. There are two markets, each with its own price (Pf and Pt in Figure 10.3). The aggregate market is constructed from these two markets. This is represented by point C, which is a horizontal summation of points A and B (and likewise for all other points on the Net Marginal Revenue (NMRa) curve). The total optimum quantity (Q) is the sum of Qf plus Qt.

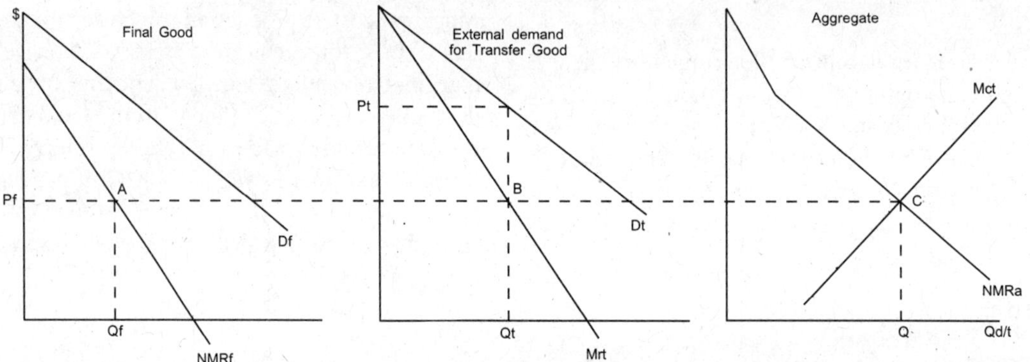

Fig. 10.3: Transfer pricing with an imperfect external market

10.2 OBJECTIVES OF TRANSFER PRICING

The transfer pricing system is generally established with the following objectives:

1. To provide relevant information to the value chain to determine the optimum trade off between cost and revenue
2. To induce goal congruence by providing a competent atmosphere, freedom to source out and negotiate
3. To measure the economic performance of the individual profit centre
4. To provide a single mechanism that is easy to administer.

10.3 THE FUNDAMENTAL ASSUMPTION IN TRANSFER PRICING

The transfer pricing is based on the basic assumption of two very important managerial decisions as given below.

1. The sourcing decision: Make or buy
2. The price at which it should be transferred if a 'make' decision is taken

Ideally, the transfer price should be approximately the same as the normal outside market price, with adjustments for costs not incurred in intra company transfer.

Even under a constrained sourcing decision, the market price is the best method of transfer.

If competitive prices are not available, transfer prices may be fixed on the basis of cost plus a profit.

Cost based transfer can be made at the standard cost plus profit margin, or by using a two step pricing system.

The example below explains the two way transfer pricing between two departments X and Y.

Business unit 'X' (manufacturer)
Product 'A'

Expected monthly sales to business unit 'Y'	5,000 units
Fixed cost assigned to the product	Rs. 20,000

Variable fixed cost assigned to product Rs. 5

Investment in working capital and facilities Rs. 1,20,000

Competitive return on investment per year 10%

Transfer price for product 'A' to business unit 'Y'.

Variable cost	Rs. 5
(+) Fixed cost	Rs. 4#
(+) Transfer price	Rs. 2*

Rs. 20,000/5000 = Rs. 4

* Profit per unit
= (Rs. 1,20,000/12) × .10/5,000 = Rs. 2

If the transfer price of the product A in a certain month is expected to amount to that of 5,000 units, then under the two step method, the calculations will be as follows:

1. Unit Y will pay the variable cost of Rs. 25,000 (5,000 × Rs. 5), plus Rs. 30,000 (Rs. 20,000 + 1,20,000/12 × .10) for fixed cost and profit equal to Rs. 55,000.

Under transfer pricing, the same amount will be paid, i.e., 5000 × Rs. 11 = Rs.55,000.

1. However, if the number of units are say 4,000, the unit Y would pay Rs. 50,000 [(4,000 × 5) + Rs.30,000] under the two step method, compared to Rs. 44,000 (4,000 × Rs. 11) under the transfer pricing method.
2. The difference of Rs. (50,000 – 44,000) is the penalty for not using the portion of unit X's capacity that it had reserved.

The method of negotiating transfer pricing should be in place, and there should be an arbitration mechanism for settling transfer price disputes. However, these arrangements should not be so complicated that an undue amount of the management's time is devoted to transfer pricing. It is very difficult to choose a perfect transfer pricing system and therefore in designing a control system, several less than perfect systems may be adopted.

10.4 THE IDEAL SITUATION FOR TRANSFER PRICING

Transfer pricing is a mechanism to cope with the cost of the business and its competitors in the business. The method of transfer pricing cannot be used unless certain conditions are fulfilled. The conditions that need to be fulfilled if transfer pricing is adopted in a business are as follows:

1. There has to be integration of business across the value line.
2. Business should not be diversified to unrelated businesses.
3. Transfer price best works in integrated horizontally integrated business.
4. There are common bases for calculation of variable and fixed costs.
5. The business has more than one location where the business is carried out and hence, seeking cost advantage is a must for the overall efficiency of the business.

10.5 LIMITATIONS

Transfer pricing is best adopted when an external market exists for the components of the value chain in an organisation. In most cases, this does not happen in practice since the big business houses have a lot of forward and backward integration in the business, giving them an internal cost advantage. The other reason why the system of transfer pricing does not work is if there is a lot of captive capacity building within the organisation. Such captive capacity works as profit centres and is highly cost competitive. As a result of this, even though there is an external market, it cannot compete with the internal business capacity. In addition, the decisions to invest in large facilities are sometimes strategic decision of a business and in such cases, the company cannot afford the luxury of negotiating with the external market even though there is a marginal difference in cost advantage for the external market.

10.6 METHODS OF TRANSFER PRICING

The transfer pricing has few accepted techniques that are used in practice. The fundamental assumptions of the pricing techniques are kept constant. The methods are different in terms of cost advantage.

10.6.1 Full Cost Based Transfer Pricing

The full cost method uses the total cost absorption techniques where the products to be transferred are transferred at the full cost minus the mark up. Under this method, the internal transfer has the advantage of charging the full cost but not a profit, thereby gaining the cost advantage. However, if such a technique is used in the value chain there is a lot of engineered cost.

10.6.2 Marginal Cost Based Transfer Pricing

Under the marginal cost technique the variable cost is used as the reference cost of transfer. The transferring unit takes the advantage of spread out fixed cost per unit of additional unit transferred. The idea is to generate contributory profit for the components of the value chain where the transfer takes place.

10.6.3 Negotiated Method of Transfer Pricing

Under this method the transferring units freely negotiate with each other. The negotiations are carried out on the basis of their performance and the prices are compared with the market price available for the business.

10.7 PROBLEMS WITH TRANSFER PRICING

The process of transfer pricing has a number of problems because transfer pricing works on the basic assumption that the business will work with cost and profit optimisation. This may be true conceptually, but often a business has to integrate across the value line or out of it in order to gain economies of scale or to simply beat the competition.

10.7.1 Problem of Integration of Fixed Costs in the Upstream Value Chain

One problem faced by integrated companies is that the profit centres higher up in the value line are not aware of the cost and profit which is flowing upstream. This makes most of the profit centres reluctant to reduce or negotiate their own profits to optimise the company's profit.

10.7.2 Profit Sharing

If the method of transfer pricing does not lead to goal congruence, a profit sharing method, which operates as follows, can be used. In this method:

1. The product is transferred to the marketing unit at standard variable cost
2. After the product is sold the business units share the contribution earned, which is the selling price minus the variable manufacturing and market costs.

The implementation of this system may lead to several problems, which include the calculation of the contribution of the two profit centres and the time in which this process will be implemented.

10.7.3 Two Sets of Transfer Pricing

Another problem that arises is the flat charge to profit centres up the value line for all the facilities used irrespective of time and usage reference in the organisation. This unnecessarily increases the cost and creates pressure on the profit optimisation of the product.

One way out of this is to use a two step or two charges for the transfer pricing. First, for each unit sold, a charge equal to the standard variable cost of production, is levied. Second, a periodic charge, equal to the fixed costs associated with the facilities reserved by the buying unit, is imposed. It is advisable to see that one or both of the components include a profit margin. The organisation should be careful about using this method because it involves the following issues:

- The monthly charges have to be negotiated periodically since the system works on this and an old price means under absorption of costs
- Accuracy of cost is always a question in this method. However, it can be overcome by taking an approximate accurate cost.
- The performance of manufacturing units is not affected by the sales volume under this method and hence sometimes acts as a de-link

between the business units across the value chain.

- The down stream units of the value chain can make a higher profit if the capacity is limited and they can outsource the products from the market

10.8 ADMINISTERING TRANSFER PRICES

Since, the transfer involves the operational profit of the responsibility centres, it requires long drawn out negotiations between the various profit and responsibility centres. Therefore, there is always scope for arbitration in the process.

10.8.1 Negotiations

Negotiations are generally carried out by the heads of the responsibility centres and do not require the intervention of the top management. This is done on purpose, since the functional heads understand, and have a role in increasing and optimising, the profit.

10.8.2 Arbitration and Conflict Resolution

Often the functional heads cannot come to a conclusion regarding the transfer price or are talking at cross purposes about the transfer price, leading to a dead end and no solution being reached. In such a case, the top management acts as an arbitrator to resolve the issues. In such cases, the business generally adopts an ad-hoc committee or a standing committee, depending upon the nature and frequency of the arbitration required. It has been found that both formal and informal arbitration are common practices in the case of transfer pricing. In the process of arbitration, goal congruence is the key issue.

10.8.3 Product Classification

The greater the non availability of a market reference price, the greater is the demand for transfer price mechanics. In case, the market prices are available, they act as a good benchmark for the top management to measure the efficiency and departments in the value line can take the transfer pricing decision more readily. In many cases the products are divided into two categories, the first category includes products on which the top management reserves the right to decide the transfer price and the second category includes those on which the functional heads or the heads of the responsibility centres have the right to negotiate the transfer pricing.

10.9 SOME THEORETICAL BASES OF CONCEPTUALISING TRANSFER PRICING

Although it may not be practical to use very complicated processes, a few theoretical frameworks of transfer pricing are discussed to help the reader gain a clear understanding of the business processes.

10.9.1 Economic Model

The economic model was first discussed by Jack Hirschleifier in 1956. He used several marginal revenues, marginal costs and demand curves for the transfer of intermediate products from one business unit to another, under various economic situations. His idea was to provide an optimization model of profit for the business as a whole. The problem with this model is that it does not provide any scope for negotiations and can only be used under a specific set of assumptions.

10.9.2 Linear Programming Model

Based on an opportunity cost approach, this model incorporates capacity constraints. It calculates a set of an optimum, company wide production patterns. Using these patterns it calculates a set of values that input the profit contribution of each of the scarce resources. This is called the 'shadow price' and one way of calculating it by what is called 'obtaining a dual solution'. The model would have been useful had there been scope of using the shadow price calculated under normal assumptions. However, this is not possible and hence, a lot of simplistic assumptions are made, such as a constant demand curve and linear cost function. This makes the model redundant in the real world.

10.9.3 Shapley Value

This was developed by L.S. Shapley in 1953, as a method of dividing the profits of a coalition of companies or individuals among its individual members in proportion to the contribution made by each of them. This is a game theory problem and the Shapley value provides an equitable solution to the problem.

10.9.4 Practical Application of Administrative Regulations and Guidelines

Although there is a sound economic theory behind the selection of a transfer pricing method, the fact remains that it can be advantageous to arbitrarily select prices such that, in terms of bookkeeping, most of the profit is made in a country with low taxes, thus shifting the profits to reduce overall taxes paid by a multinational group. However, most countries enforce tax laws based on the arm's length principle as defined in the Organisation for Economic Co-operation and Development (OECD) Transfer Pricing Guidelines for Multinational Enterprises and Tax Administrations. This limits how transfer prices can be set and ensures that a country taxes its 'fair' share. In the United States, the pricing of transactions between related parties that are reported for tax purposes, are governed by Section 482 of the Internal Revenue Code and the regulations there under. From the corporation's position, running foul of such regulations can prove to be a costly mistake, as illustrated by Glaxo Smith Kline's announcement on September 11, 2006 that they had settled a long-running transfer pricing dispute with the US tax authorities, agreeing to pay $3.1 billion in taxes related to an assessed income adjustment due to improper transfer pricing. However, proper use of the regulations also provides a method of protecting against double taxation provided that the transactions are carried out between divisions in countries bound by bilateral tax treaties. In the Glaxo Smith Kline case, however, the company had indicated that they would not pursue competent authority negotiations for the relief of U.S.-U.K. double taxation.

Application of the arm's length principle

There are discrepancies in the specifics of each country's laws concerning the application of the arm's length principle. However, the fact remains that they are primarily based on the OECD guidelines which means that although such a strategy carries a greater taxation risk than solutions tailored to each country global transfer pricing policies can be effectively used to determine an appropriate range representing the arm's length price for transactions carried out across a global enterprise.

However, different countries may accept different methods of calculating the transfer price (e.g., Japan requires that the three "traditional" methods, outlined above, be systematically discounted before allowing the use of alternative methods, while the United States accepts the most appropriate method). Therefore care must be taken in such circumstances. In addition, some countries may have immature transfer pricing regimes or apply the arm's length principle in different ways, Brazil, for example, does not apply the arm's length principle despite the existence of transfer pricing legislation.

SUMMARY

This chapter discussed the problems and importance of businesses, which are integrated across the value line and the equitable solution regarding optimization of the profits without disturbing the individual business or profits of the responsibility units. Transfer price is a mechanism that facilitates the continuous flow of value addition, gives the business a solution to provide a profit motive to the various responsibility units and provides a sense of competition to them. It was seen that there are several limitations in the process of setting a transfer price. The most common ways in which the transfer price are set include the negotiation, full cost and marginal cost methods. There is a need to implement an administrative process for the transfer price to work. This is due to the fact that there are several chances of conflict while the transfer price is being set up and a deadlock between the departments or the responsibility centres.

Theoretical models such as the economic model, the linear programming model and the

Shapley value model help us to understand the core discussion of the transfer price mechanism, even though, these models may not be used for practical reasons.

Review Questions

1. Why are transfer prices set up?
2. What are the methods of calculating the transfer pricing?
3. Which kind of transfer pricing is acceptable at what kind of responsibility centre in a value line?
4. Discuss the problems of the transfer pricing mechanism keeping in mind management control.
5. Identify three businesses that can use transfer pricing as a mechanism to optimise profits. Show how it can be used by taking imaginary data.

Analytical Question

1. Mohan Perambulator Ltd., has two operating divisions, each of which is a profit centre. Division 'A' makes the basic structure and Division 'B' makes the finished product. Division 'A' transfers part of its production to Division 'B' at the same price at which it sells it in the open market. This method has been adopted to facilitate divisional performance evaluation. However, accounts of Mohan Perambulator Ltd., are highly complicated because of the transfer price. A summary of the stock accounts of Division 'B' for three periods are given below.

	(in Rs. '000)		
	Transfer from Division 'A'	External purchases	**Total**
Period 1			
Opening stock	600	300	**900**
Purchases	500	100	**600**
	1100	400	**1500**
Consumption	750	150	**900**
Period 2			
Opening stock	350	250	**600**
Purchases	580	290	**870**
	930	540	**1470**
Consumption	400	500	**900**
Period 3			
Opening stock	530	40	**570**
Purchases	500	300	**800**
	1030	340	**1370**
Consumption	400	270	**670**
Closing stock	630	70	**700**

The transfer prices of Division 'A' include profit at the following rates.

Prior to period 1	Nil
In period 1	15%
In period 2	20%
In period 3	25%

Calculate the inter divisional profits to be eliminated from the stocks of Division 'B' at the end of period 1, 2 and 3.

CHAPTER 11

Management Control of Responsibility Centres through Audit

LEARNING OBJECTIVES OF THE CHAPTER

- Audit as a tool of management control for responsibility centres
- The techniques of audit
- Audit as a facilitator to strategic business planning and control

11.1 INTRODUCTION

Today the survival of a business does not depend on what is produced and how efficiently it is sold, but on the efficiency of the delivery system. Mistakes in business are becoming increasingly expensive. Millions of dollars are being spent internationally to run a mistake free system. Things like 'Six Sigma Corrections' are becoming the hall mark of quality control. Business processes are becoming proactive rather than reactive to problems in business processes to reduce errors.

Mistakes in business are becoming increasingly expensive. Millions of dollars are being spent internationally to run a mistake free system.

One way out is to establish an audit system (an internal audit is the most common method) which would monitor the business process and correct any erroneous processes. Quintessentially an accounting process, auditing has moved way ahead to become a management tool to control. Redefining parameters to fit the management perspective, there has been tremendous progress in the delivery and usage of the audit as a tool of management control system.

Quintessentially an accounting process, auditing has moved way ahead to become a management tool to control. Redefining parameters to fit the management perspective, there has been tremendous progress in the delivery and usage of the audit as a tool of management control system.

11.2 WHY AUDIT THE RESPONSIBILITY CENTRE?

In a financial audit, the idea is to compare the actual performance with standards and give an assessment of any deviations. In doing so, all items in the accounting are used, this is referred to as the census method. The assessment is carried out against the principles and postulates of accounting that have been laid down.

However, in practice, the audit covers a broader goal called the management audit that checks all the key items of the business against the standards so that pre established requirements can be gauged and necessary steps can be taken for corrective actions if there are deviations.

in practice, the audit covers a broader goal called the management audit that checks all the key items of the business against the standards so that pre established requirements can be gauged and necessary steps can be taken for corrective actions if there are deviations.

Another reason why a management audit is becoming increasingly popular is because it educates customers regarding the adequacy of the services and products of thc business.

A financial audit is external in nature and is carried out against standard, universally accepted principles. On the other hand a management audit is internal and is carried out against internal standards or the best practices of the business. Since it is much more flexible and can operate over a long period of time (usually 16 to 18 months) there is more scope to improvise a management audit for control in a business.

A financial audit is external in nature and is carried out against standard, universally accepted principles.

management audit is internal and is carried out against internal standards or the best practices of the business.

Management control focuses on a broad range of functions that contribute to the success or failure of a business in general, hence it can set the path for correct business practices.

The moot question is therefore, why audit the responsibility centres? The answer to this can be broadly given in three ways:

1. The responsibility centres are the key functions of the business. Their success or failure determines the overall success or failure of the business. Hence, monitoring these units is critical for the overall performance of the business.
2. The responsibilities centres are businesses prerogatives and hence have no precedence for comparison. A management audit will enable the business to set standards and propose compliance as required by the business itself. The business may consider internal parameters and measure them against a common benchmark in the industry for the purpose of compliance.
3. The responsibility centres are the units that create value in a business. Unless, a proper audit is carried out, the value chain may not be able to deliver and transmit the value to the end point, i.e., the customers. This is due to the fact that, each responsibility centre may become a watertight compartment and improve its own performance at the cost of the other units, leading to the loss of value in the organisation.

11.3 ROLE OF THE AUDIT

The role of an audit in an organisation is to facilitate an introspection of the business process and identify opportunities in order to improve the processes, which will finally benefit the business.

Since, an audit is a reality check it enlightens the management about the ground realities. Sometimes in a quest to prove a point and even to justify wrong behaviour (popularly known as entrapment[1]), managers move away from the reality of the business. The decisions of the management may then not really conform to the needs of the end users of the product of the business. This leads to loss of value in a business.

The role of an audit in an organization is to facilitate an introspection of the business process and identify opportunities in order to improve the processes, which will finally benefit the business.

Since, an audit is a reality check it enlightens the management about the ground realities.

[1] Entrapment is a situation where individuals try to justify their actions by logic and get trapped in the action. Such a situation starts by an individual carrying out what he/she knows to be a wrong act, and in their desire to justify the act, they become defensive.

Unrealistic assumptions and foreign concepts not tested in the actual environment may be used by the management to show their skills. An audit process acts as a check and balance in such a situation.

Due to the fact that an audit is a reality check and acts as a balancing method, it helps a business in identifying forthcoming strategies. In Chapter 7 we talked about the control of today becoming the strategies of tomorrow. An audit is perhaps one of the main tools of control that enables strategy building with ease and in addition helps in identifying outdated strategies.

Due to the fact that an audit is a reality check and acts as a balancing method, it helps a business in identifying forthcoming strategies.

Since an audit acts as a comparison between actual and ideal process, it improves the performance of the management. The concerns of the management in its current business are brought out by the audit. Hence, an audit provides the management a means to address the current concerns of the business.

An audit provides the management a means to address the current concerns of the business.

However, the role of an audit is sometimes confused with a fault finding mission, especially if things are not made clear by the heads of responsibility centres. It should be remembered that an audit is a process to see whether the desired path is actually being followed in the business and not a process to prioritise the management's opportunities and create a reward system.

Audit is a process to see whether the desired path is actually being followed in the business and not a process to prioritise the management's opportunities and create a reward system.

11.4 PROCESS OF AN AUDIT

An audit is a process and not an end in itself. This means that an audit is a continuous task to match the actual performance with a standard set of performances. If an audit is to be carried out in a meaningful way, there has to be a proper set up to facilitate it. Essentially, therefore an audit requires three things as given below.

1. **Establishing an audit team**

   A normal audit team consists of about four people. The qualifications and experience of the members of the audit team depend upon the nature of the audit. For example to carry out a cost audit, a cost and work accountant would be required. A combination of new and experienced auditors helps smoothen the process as new auditors will not be so fixed in their ideas.

   A typical management audit team consists of three to four persons who are conversant with the management processes of the business. The number of persons may be increased depending on the criticality of the audit and the volume of data and information to be handled.

   A typical management audit team consists of three to four persons who are conversant with the management processes of the business. The number of persons may be increased depending on the criticality of the audit and the volume of data and information to be handled.

   The eternal debate as to whether an external or internal audit is better, can be addressed, keeping in view a few essentialities of audit.

   An external audit is desirable when there is a legal need – say for example, the financial accounts audit by a qualified chartered accountant. That apart, an external auditor should be the last resort if there is a sufficient number of internal persons.

   The cost aspect is another vital component in deciding on an external or internal audit. For obvious reasons an internal audit will be less expensive than an external audit. However, if the services of the internal auditor compromise some vital functions and the cost of external auditor is only nominally higher, the business should resort to an external auditor. In such a case however, the experience and knowledge of the auditor in matters of the business should be of prime concern.

One reason why an outside auditor is preferred over an internal one is because the outside auditor gives a credibility which the internal auditor cannot give.

2. **Creating an audit plan**

   The second critical factor in establishing an audit process is to decide upon the audit plan. The audit is vital to the business. Therefore, while deciding the audit plan proper resources need to be allocated in the business. Right timing is essential for an effective audit plan to tap the right kind of information. The team members should have a clear picture of the audit process, as this brings about objectivity to the audit process.

Right timing is essential for an effective audit plan to tap the right kind of information.

3. **Executing the audit**

   Executing the audit requires a clear understanding of the task that lies ahead for the audit team. Unless, the team is clear as to how to go about the task, the audit may not be fruitfully executed. The audit process often uses the critical path method where the probabilistic time and the actual time for the business are taken into consideration. The slack time is eliminated by crashing the project and the critical path is obtained. This critical path primarily solves two issues, the issue of time and that of execution.

Unless, the team is clear as to how to go about the task, the audit may not be fruitfully executed.

11.5 SCHEDULING AN AUDIT

An audit, like any other management tool, works best when it is used at the right time in the right way. The best time for an the audit is that which suits the business. However, while deciding the time of the audit the following need to be kept in mind.

1. **Seasonal fluctuations of the business**

   An audit should follow the fluctuations and seasonal variations in a business. It is not correct to plan an audit when there is a slow-down in the seasonal fluctuation, as it will unnecessarily create an impression that the business is not doing well. An audit should be planned and scheduled in such a way that it shows a normal period of business.

2. **The time when most people in the organisation are available**

   An audit requires the coordination and support of the people in the organisation. Scheduling an audit at a time when the work force is busy, say the last quarter of the financial year will make the audit ineffective. However, this is not true for a statutory audit as it has to be completed before the end of the financial year.

3. **The period in which the overall performance is reflected**

   Since the period of the audit should reflect the best possible performance of the business, the best time would be in the first quarter of the business of the previous financial year.

11.6 AUDIT PLAN

A typical audit plan takes into consideration the proper utilisation of available resources and manpower. Inadequate resource planning will lead to a lopsided audit. Therefore, a proper audit plan should have a balance between the right number of people and the resources utilised in the business. In a typical management audit, personnel from the same department are also allocated to make the process smooth.

Planning also means providing a clear and time bound picture to the members of the audit team. Without this an audit will be impossible.

11.7 TOOLS AND TECHNIQUES FOR AUDITING

There are a number of tools required for an audit, which are discussed later in this section. The method and purpose of an audit decide how many and what kind of tools are necessary to obtain a comprehensive audit result. Some of the common tools of an audit are discussed below:

11.7.1 Surveys

1. **Types of surveys**

   A survey is a method of contacting individuals who can give desirable information about the audit requirements. Surveys are of two types. The first method is contacting individuals directly and the second method is through telephonic conversations. Surveys help in obtaining data and information on (1) demography, (2) beliefs and attitudes and (3) knowledge and behaviour. Surveys are conducted depending on the needs of the business. A mixed method of telephonic and direct survey may be used depending upon the intensity of the survey. If the survey requires quick responses and the individuals are spread over a large area and the time available is short, then a telephonic survey is desirable. Telephonic surveys are also desirable if the information required is to be kept secret or where an individual may feel uncomfortable about answering the questions face to face. However, if possible it is best to conduct a survey by the direct method.

2. **Advantages of surveys**

   A survey is advantageous when a large amount of data or information has to be accurately addressed. In such cases, a survey is a cheap technique.

   Another advantage of the survey method is the ability to address the problem from a quantitative point of view. Since, in a survey data or information is collected on an individual basis, the use of statistical methods to interpret the data becomes easy.

3. **Disadvantage of surveys**

   The disadvantage of a survey is that the surveyor has a substantial subjective influence on the data. This is because of lack of expertise in using the survey method. Since, a survey addresses a large population it is often superficial.

4. **Using a survey properly**

   For a proper survey, there are certain parameters that need to be taken care of. Foremost, is the timing of the survey. Audit surveys should be avoided just after the event has taken place, otherwise, the survey will be biased.

A survey should be carried out in such a way that respondents can answer the questions easily. Too many technical words may make a survey difficult.

A survey should not be carried out so that it forces respondents to give a particular kind of response. Leading questions should never be asked in a survey. A leading question is one which gives the respondent very little or no choice to answer differently.

A survey should not be carried out so that it forces respondents to give a particular kind of response. Leading questions should never be asked in a survey.

11.7.2 Questionnaires

Questionnaires can be used as an independent method as well as a tool in surveys and interviews. Questionnaires are designed so as to get a certain kind of response in the survey or interview method. Though questionnaires are created with the help of the audit group, they are not necessarily used by the people who carry out the audit.

1. **Closed and open ended questionnaires**

   Questionnaires are generally of two kinds: Open and closed ended. A closed ended questionnaire generally contains questions which have clear and defined responses for the respondent. An open ended questionnaire generally gives the respondent a choice in their answers.

Examples of closed ended questions:

What do you think are the causes for delay in delivery of goods to the customers?

i. Bad logistic system
ii. Poor distribution network
iii. Inefficiency in making the order
iv. Overworked staff
v. Demotivated work force.

Example of an open ended question

What in your opinion are the causes for the delay in goods reaching the customers?

(Give three opinions please)

i. ....

ii. ....

iii. ....

Mixed question

What do you think are the causes for delay in delivery of goods to the customers?

i. Bad logistic system
ii. Poor distribution network
iii. Inefficiency in making the order
iv. Overworked staff
v. Demotivated work force.
vi. Any other cause in your opinion

....

2. How to use questionnaires

In using a questionnaire it is best to judge the purpose of the data and information collection.

A questionnaire should be used judiciously according to the information required to be collected. Information collected through a questionnaire is mostly concrete and precise data. Therefore, in using a questionnaire it is best to judge the purpose of the data and information collection. If the purpose is to understand the environment of the business, it is better that an open or a mixed format is used. In case, the purpose is to understand a focused problem, the best method is to use a closed ended questionnaire.

The purpose of the questionnaire also determines how to use it. If the purpose is to guide an interview, then it should be an open ended questionnaire, but if the purpose is to reach a large audience, it is better to use a closed ended questionnaire.

3. Structure of a questionnaire

Structuring a questionnaire is a problem because one cannot determine the priorities of using such a questionnaire. In order to solve the problem the following five questions should be addressed.

i. Why do you want to prepare the questionnaire?
ii. What do you think you will learn from the questionnaire?
iii. Is the time for gathering the information correct according to you?
iv. Who do you think has the information you are seeking?
v. Do you think a person will be able to give the information through an open or a closed ended questionnaire.

While structuring a questionnaire the topics and contents of the questions should be clearly listed on paper. Then the order of the questions should be noted down. This will ensure that the problem is conceptually understood in terms of asking the questions and the answers will be clear and lucid.

4. Advantages of questionnaires

A few amongst the many advantages are given below.

i. It is easy for people to answer a questionnaire because it is mostly structured.
ii. It provides consistent information.
iii. It provides flexibility, which is not available in the other methods.
iv. It is easy to carry out over a large population and across geographical boundaries.

5. Disadvantage of questionnaires

Despite the fact that a questionnaire is the most common method of audit, it has several disadvantages, a few of which are given below.

i. It restricts flow of information because it is a guided form of information collection.
ii. It often contains the biases and subjectivity of the auditors.
iii. It creates an impression that the business is not much interested in the persons giving the information and therefore gives them a sense of alienation from the business.

11.7.3 Focus Group

1. **What is a focus group?**

A focus group is a technique wherein chosen participants from a homogeneous group are asked to participate in an interactive session with a moderator. The moderator helps to moderate and guide the group in the solution of a particular problem and additional information regarding the problem also emerges.

Originally started as a method of market research, the process is widely used today in various fields of study, including the audit processes.

The purpose of the focus group is to eliminate 'noise' in the information by being selective. An ideal homogeneous group is one where the participants are properly briefed about the focus group even before it is conducted. This avoids deviation in information dissemination.

The purpose of the focus group is to eliminate 'noise' in the information by being selective.

2. **Advantages of a focus group**

The focus group allows more data to be collected, in a shorter time, than is possible by interviews. In addition, the direct interaction in the process, leads to new insights into the problem under discussion.

3. **Disadvantages of a focus group**

The greatest disadvantage of this method is that the moderators are often not skilled enough to handle such a homogeneous group. As a result, the group may get fragmented and deviate from the focus discussion which is being carried out. Since the focus group discusses several issues, the results cannot be quantified. Besides, due to several reasons, it is very difficult for the group to maintain the focus.

11.7.4 Interviews

1. **What are interviews?**

An interview is a technique to gather information by talking to another person(s) face-to-face. The discussions are generally guided and the information flow is generally dynamic. It is one of the most flexible tools of an audit. Since, the interview is guided by the interviewer, it can lead to insights in the problem and may also lead to new information even about unaddressed problems.

An interview is a highly effective tool, since the respondent cannot evade the problem. Since an interview has a personal touch, the respondent feels comfortable answering the questions which could have been evaded in a questionnaire, say.

2. **Types of interviews**

Interviews are of three types as given below.

i. Structured interviews, where a set of formalised questions are put to the respondent without allowing any flexibility in the answers.

ii. Semi-structured interviews, which are like structured interviews but the questions and answers are flexible within the format of the interview.

iii. Unstructured interviews in which no protocol or formal structure is followed and hence the information flow is variable. The purpose of such an interview is to elicit as much information as possible and not to set boundaries for the information.

3. **Advantages of interviews**

The greatest advantage of an interview is that it allows the flow of information without intimidating the respondent. It is highly flexible if used properly and helps to understand the problem with ease.

The greatest advantage of an interview is that it allows the flow of information without intimidating the respondent.

4. **Disadvantages of interviews**

An interview is expensive to conduct and requires a lot of back up funds. Besides, the interviewer needs to have a certain maturity to be able to address the problem correctly, otherwise interviews can be very misleading.

11.7.5 Direct Observations

1. **What are direct observations?**

   Direct observations as the name indicates involve the process of observing the process directly from an outside point of view. There are several techniques of direct observation, which include the following:

   i. Participants' observations, where the researcher makes a mental note of the dynamics of the environment.

   ii. Field observations where the researcher observes the interaction between groups but does not get involved in the process.

   iii. Trace data, which takes two forms, accretion data and erosion data. Accretion data analysis examines the residue or evidence left by a certain process in order to estimate its use or popularity. Erosion method observes the usage factor of any item and determines the use to which it has been put.

   iv. Archival data are written records of past data, which are analysed for the performance of the business.

2. **Advantages of observations**

   The major advantage of observations is that the data or information collector does not get involved with the disseminator of the information, which allows freedom of expression, while being in continuous touch with the problem.

3. **Disadvantages of observations**

   One great disadvantage of the method is that it requires high expertise and does not help the auditor much.

11.7.6 Which Method Should Be Used?

While the audit team should be judicious in terms of using a technique, it is preferable to use a mixture of techniques, as a single tool cannot address all the problems of the business. The methods adopted depend on the availability of resources, time and requirements. It should be remembered here that, the purpose of the audit is to find deviations in the process, and no stone should be left unturned to achieve this.

11.8 CONTINUOUS IMPROVEMENT THROUGH AUDITING

The audit is used as a tool of continuous process improvement. Business processes are normally geared to a particular type of environment. However, the business environment changes very fast and therefore processes should be able to cope with these changes. The way to update a process is available through auditing.

An organisation which has the appropriate information regarding any change in its environment and the business process has a competitive advantage over the other firms. The audit process if properly equipped is generally capable of identifying the trigger points for the next level of changes necessary. A proper audit does not stop at finding deviations it also helps in developing a new action plan for the business.

It is often found that companies, which have reached a certain level of success, become complacent and do not take appropriate steps to remain abreast of a changing environment. This will lead to their failure. It is here that an audit comes to the help of the managers. Not only does audit provide quality data regarding the business and its change, but it also provides an action plan by a establishing a dialogue between the responsibility centres and the top management through audit reference notes and answers to audit compliance.

An audit report should not be underestimated, as it is carried out in consultation with the various heads of divisions. The audit may or may not be able to provide a complete picture of the problem but it will definitely provide a certain level of clarification and clarify any problems that may be imminent.

An audit should be used as a starting point for problem solving and analysis. The more coordination there is between the responsibility centres and the top management the better is the conditioning arrived at from the audit.

Apathy towards an audit starts with the top management using the audit as a fault finding mission. This will only make the audit a counter productive exercise.

11.9 GAINING STRATEGIC ADVANTAGE THROUGH AN AUDIT

Today, business is marked by fierce competition, demanding customers and a resource crunch, which are forcing modern firms to stream line their business processes and implement continuous improvements. The concept of continuous improvement comes from quality improvement theories, which state that the process should be continuously endorsed with quality. The idea of continuous improvement is based on the following beliefs.

1. No improvement can be carried out in one step, hence it needs to be implemented on a continuous basis.
2. The necessary improvements are continuously changing and hence require revaluation from time to time.
3. It should be realized that change is not always precise.
4. Priorities need to change, if improvement is to be a continuous process.
5. Proper feedback regarding the performance is necessary as it enables corrective action.

11.9.1 Acquiring a Competitive Advantage

A good audit has to incorporate the above points if it is to act as a tool of continuous improvement and enable a business to deal with its strategic issues. An audit will enable the management to understand the strengths, weaknesses, opportunities and threats properly. In addition it will enable the business to identify the capabilities of the business that can be converted into strengths. Bridging the gap between reality and the plan of action, an audit can enable the managers to set realistic goals and plans.

An audit should act as a sounding board for any forthcoming changes. This will enable the business to take the necessary steps before the changes actually take place.

An audit should act as a sounding board for any forthcoming changes. This will enable the business to take the necessary steps before the changes actually take place.

11.9.2 Improvement Through a Trigger Point

A trigger point is a point at which an organisation faces a significant challenge to its business. Events such as mergers and acquisitions, new entrants and new innovations trigger change and bring about an improvement in the business.

A trigger point may occur at any point be it the functional point, the entry point in a business unit, the maturity point or the point of saturation.

The trigger point should be treated as an opportunity rather than a threat. An audit program often helps to identify the correct trigger point of a business. Identification of a proper trigger point will result in a well organised program aimed at making the most of the trigger points.

11.9.3 Action Planning

Issues raised by an audit should be incorporated in the action plan of the business. In an action plan all issues regarding the audit should be raised and addressed. The action plan action should be a part of the audit report or a separate report and should incorporate the following vital issues.

1. The person responsible for preparation of the action plan
2. The time of the action plan
3. Content of the action plan
4. The person in charge of the action plan
5. The actions to be carried out by those who receive the action plan
6. The role of the auditor in the follow-up of the action plan

The action plan depends on the priorities of the business and the importance it attaches to the audit system. The need to change and improve continuously is a moot question in determining the action plan of a business. The greater the urge to change and improve, the greater is the need for an action plan of the audit system.

SUMMARY

Audit is a well established method in the financial world. The need for a more effective audit has been realised by businesses due to the changing needs of a business and the growing pressure to improve continuously.

Ideally, a business should be able to understand its internal strengths and weaknesses, build upon its opportunities and discard its weaknesses. This is possible through a continuous internal management audit.

The various methods of audit, from surveys and interviews to observation techniques all have their own merits and demerits. Judicious use of all these methods and processes improves the quality of an audit and helps in identifying the trigger points, which in turn help in creating the right choice of strategic mix in the business.

Review Questions

1. What is the rationale behind an audit?
2. Discuss the various ways in which an audit can help a business organisation.
3. Describe the audit process in detail.
4. Enumerate the various methods of audit. How do you think these methods should be used to obtain correct results for the business and implement a management control system?
5. What are the advantages of using a questionnaire?
6. How is the interview method a better method of audit than the questionnaire and survey methods?
7. How can a business achieve competitive advantage by using an audit?
8. How can an audit be used as a tool for management control?

Analytical Question

1. A manager of the Eastern Electronic Corporation which produces the mother board for computers finds that sales are increasingly falling. He realises that the market is saturated in the case of the current technology. Therefore, he asked the top management to incorporate necessary changes. However, the top management did not comply with his request. Subsequently the competitors rapidly gained a substantial share of the market. The top management realised its folly and quickly changed the technology, but the sales did not pick up. The management decided to set up an internal audit team including the manager of the mother board division to look into the problem.

   If you were the manager and a member of the internal audit team, what would you do in order to see that a good and meaningful audit is conducted which would address the problem.

CHAPTER 12

Management Control of Operational Processes

LEARNING OBJECTIVES OF THE CHAPTER

- Role of information in the operation process
- Total quality management as a tool to control operations
- Dealing with the decision support system to improve operations
- Target costing as a tool to management control
- Benchmarking as a tool to management control

12.1 INTRODUCTION

Operational processes are vital to the success of an organisation. In this light of the operational management plays a vital role in the overall functioning of the management. The right kind of processes supported by the right kind of manpower is what makes an organisation stand out from others.

How does an organisation put the right kind of operational practices into place? The key to success in most organisations is in fact, the right kind of manpower. This means that three processes should be in place, namely, induction of the right kind of manpower, training personnel to a higher level of competence and last, but not the least, being able to build and sustain the competency that already exists.

Another issue vital to the management is whether the operation has the right kind of information for the system to work both internally and externally. This is required to solve business problems quickly and to make the business environment effective and its work culture conducive to the employees.

In this context, information plays a vital role in the operations management.

12.2 THE ROLE OF INFORMATION IN OPERATION MANAGEMENT

When we talk about the process in a business, we should understand that it is the information exchanged by personnel that holds these processes together. It should be added that the information is a natural outcome of the business process. For example, let us look at the process of accounting which is in the fulcrum of business processes. The resultant outcome of accounting is a systematic recording of business transactions, but the most important fact of accounting is that it acts as a role model in the business information process.

The role of a business process is to support the system of an operation and in turn provide information that will support the business as a whole. The operational aspects of a business depend upon the efficiency with which information is disseminated within the business. The ideal use of information depends upon the source from which it is gathered.

12.2.1 Types of Information Available for an Operation

Managers procure various kinds of information from the system. Different types of information are required for different purposes, depending upon the sourcing of the information.

The use of the information helps in carrying out an operation in the business. Managers procure various kinds of information from the system. Different types of information are required for different purposes, depending upon the sourcing of the information. Some common types of information required in business are given below.

1. **Formal and informal information**

   Information can come from informal sources like observing and meeting people within an organisation. This style, which is called the 'management by walk around' has gained sufficient importance due to this reason. Gathering information by mingling with employees helps in getting to the root of any managerial problems that might have stemmed from any personal problems, even at a sub-conscious level.

   Formal information comes from the formal reports that are generated within a business. The reports are task compliance reports, budget reports or audit reports which generally give the managers specific information regarding the business.

   Formal information comes from the formal reports that are generated within a business. The reports are task compliance reports, budget reports or audit reports which generally give the managers specific information regarding the business.

2. **Budget information**

   Budget information is the information that comes out of making a budget comparison. As discussed in Chapter 8 in the book, this kind of information mostly comes in the form of variance in the budget as compared to the actual proposed budget.

   Budget information is extremely important, as setting up a business budget is a major intellectual exercise. A budget incorporates almost all the necessary information in a business.

3. **Task information**

   Task information is the information that is generated out of performance of the task at various points in the business. It is more or less like budgeted information except that it takes place at the grass roots level in a business. In fact, task information is a part of the budget information in a business.

4. **Audit information**

   Audit compilation reports are very important information for a business. They are different from the audit because they measure the processes in the operation against the requirements in the business rather than stating what the managers think should be done. Thus they provide an external view of the information and an outside perspective.

12.2.2 Some Approaches to Control of Operations

The process of controlling an operation is taken care of by the way operations are executed. Consider the following example: Suppose a business has a long drawn out production process, which requires continuous replacement of raw material. In addition, the raw material required by the business, is always in short supply and its price is very volatile. This makes it necessary for the business to procure large quantities of the raw materials. This leads to over absorption of costs and cost ineffectiveness, forcing the company cut costs on materials, which in turn leads to a marginal increase in sales but loss of quality. The business seems to be trapped in a dilemma of cost first or quality first. This has occurred because appropriate control is not taken to coordinate the control process. The problem can be solved through management practices, which have found great acceptance in practice and are based on certain realistic assumptions. The concepts of total quality and decision support system are worth mentioning in this regard. The Japanese method of Just-in-time inventory management has been a major step in this direction. Some of the systems are discussed in detail in the following sections.

12.2.3 Total Quality Control

The concept of total quality management was discussed by two pioneers, Juran and Deming, who showed why some corporations are more successful than the others. The analysis shows that there is a close relationship between 'cost – quality – times' (known as the Juran triangle). This fundamentally states that the coordination between the cost of process and manufacturing is directly affected by the quality and time of delivery of the product and the value thereof. For example, if you bring down the cost by compromising quality, the cost of rework will increase, decreasing the value added to the end user.

If you bring down the cost by compromising quality, the cost of rework will increase, decreasing the value added to the end user.

The consequence of poor quality may make it necessary to rework and change the product. In case of a service industry, poor quality may lead to loss of customers. Therefore, the first step to quality is to adhere to the specifications of the product and for a quality product the defects should be reduced to zero. It has been observed that the sooner a defect is detected in the process, the lower is the cost of replacement and its ultimate effect on the process is reduced costs and increased quality.

How to obtain total quality

1. **Documentation of the process:** The idea is to make the system thrive on a self supporting process. Total quality management stresses on documentation of the process to get the maximum out of the system. Documentation gives the details of the specified process and in addition, it gives a deep understanding into the past processes and the defects and the reasons thereof. A well documented organisation can detect the cause and reason of a problem faster than a non documented organisation.
2. **Responsibility of quality:** The age old practice was for the production department itself to set up a tight quality control process. This would often lead to a dispute between the production department and the quality department as they have divergent goals. The goal of a production department is to increase and optimise production whereas the goal of the quality department is to minimise defects. To avoid this, one has to understand the meaning of the word quality in the organisation and determine who are responsible for the quality. It should be remembered here that poor quality starts much before it reaches the production level. The design, the adaptation to commercialisation and delivery are essential parts of quality. However good the production system is and however defect free a product is, unless the above mentioned processes are in the right place, it will be difficult to assimilate quality in a business. It will be disastrous for a business if poor quality is passed down the value line. An ideal situation is one where a business is capable of identifying the defects at an early stage and allocate responsibility of removing the defects to various managers in the system.

   It should be remembered here that poor quality starts much before it reaches the production level. The design, the adaptation to commercialisation and delivery are essential parts of quality.
3. **Product design:** A good product design is half the battle won, therefore, it is essential that the product design is perfect. If the design has been adopted, then it should be adopted properly so that there are minimal problems at a later stage.

4. **Dealing with suppliers:** Poor quality starts with poor quality of the material. In the quest for quality it is essential that suppliers who are indispensable part of the business process also understand the quality process and become a part of the quality statement of the business.

12.2.4 Decision Support System (DSS)

The decision support system is essentially a support system for taking managerial decisions. It is based on a series of 'what if' situations and 'if then' answers given by experts in the relevant business in a natural language like English and converted into computer programs (called artificial language). These decisions are taken with the help of various knowledge bases such as neural networks, decision support systems and other artificial intelligence mechanisms. It is not mandatory for managers or experts to implement the decisions provided by a DSS. They may reject the whole proposal, modify it or take up a different course of action.

DSS helps the management control system in several ways. It streamlines the task delivery, as a result of which, the managers can focus their energies on more important tasks. The DSS also creates a second line of opinion for managers. It also helps them to understand the processes of the business and make the system more proactive. An example of a decision support system is given below for a general understanding of the process.

A DSS for the production line at one point of control is given below.

IF the order group for the order part = 270

AND the ordered part has been extended to the sequence 35

AND the order part has arrived in LESS than 2 minutes

AND the order part HAS ARRIVED and is passed on to the sequence 35

THEN display on the computer screen 'SEQUENCE OF RECEIPT OK'

IF the order group for the order part = 270

AND the order part has not been extended to the sequence 35

AND the order part has arrived in MORE than 2 minutes

AND the order part HAS NOT ARRIVED and is passed on to the sequence 35

THEN display on the computer screen 'SEQUENCE OF RECEIPT NOT OK'

'Call the sequence 34 for report at extension 111'.

The above example is an illustration of a two sequence DSS. In practice however, there may be several levels of a DSS module, which aims to give a direction to managers.

12.3 CONTINUOUS PROCESS IMPROVEMENT FOR OPERATIONS

The objective of the continuous process is to link the improvements to the activities in a business. Process modification is the key to continuous process improvement.

In order to improve an operation a firm has to enhance quality and set up a scheme of continuous process improvement. The idea is to strive for perfection. The objective of the continuous process is to link the improvements to the activities in a business. Process modification is the key to continuous process improvement. Modifying key and strategic business processes to achieve quality is the key to success in continuous process improvement.

Continuous process improvement however is not sustainable in the long run. A mix of technology improvement and continuous process improvement is needed.

Continuous process improvement however is not sustainable in the long run. A mix of technology improvement and continuous process improvement is needed. With improvement in technology a company could gain a cost advantage in the long run and through continuous process improvement a business can refine its process so that the quality of the product and the time of delivery is improved (see Section 12.2.3).

It is essential that managers are careful to integrate the various methods and their philosophies into the business. It has often been observed, that in the rush to accept 'management fads' (theories that are not really serious), the basic objectives of the business suffers.

Instead of taking on a number of continuous methods it is better to use one or two methods at a time. This gives the system time to react to the change rather than getting involved in too many things at a time and confusing the system and the employees.

Continuous process improvement requires that the personnel in the organisation believe in the methods. Hence, such improvements require people to go through a training and induction process so that they understand the philosophy of the process.

12.4 TOOLS IN CONTINUOUS PROCESS IMPROVEMENT

There are several tools in continuous process improvement. Foremost amongst them are quality certification, target costing, benchmarking (this has been discussed in some detail in Chapter 4 in a different context). We will discuss some of these factors for a general understanding of the management control process.

12.4.1 Target Costing

Target costing was developed and delivered by Sony of Japan. The idea of target costing is to feel the pulse of the customers first, and then design and price the new product. The method encourages the business design and R&D departments to develop less costly products, which can deliver the same function as the costlier ones.

Target costing goes through three phases as discussed below.

1. **Planning phase:** In a normal business the design department produces a product design that is passed on to the costing department which finalises the cost price. The product design goes back and forth between these departments, until they both arrive at a consensus on the price. The product is then sent to the manufacturing unit, which decides whether it is possible to produce it at the cost given by the design and the costing departments. Often, it is sent back to the design department for reconsideration. This process causes the business to lose precious time and money. As a result of this it becomes difficult for the business to reduce the cost of production and put the product on the market at the right price. Target costing shows a way out of this problem.

   In target costing, the consumers are taken into confidence, before the product is designed. Essential information is gathered from market research. First, it is determined whether the product is desired by the consumers or not. In this phase, the features of the product are also discussed with the consumers, sometimes through focus group. Second, the desired price of the product is taken into consideration.

   While, market research should cater to the above problems of the new design, it should also look at a niche market where it can be implemented with some competitive advantage.

2. **Development phase:** The development phase requires the design and the cost departments to integrate the information gathered through market research in the process, so that the best product in terms of the cost and acceptance of the product can be created. Advanced levels of costing methods are adopted to find the best possible cost in practice. In this, activity based costing is used to find the cost drivers so that the cost can be managed properly. At this stage the business should gear up all its resources to reduce costs and get the best possible product.

3. **Production phase:** In the production phase it is essential that the schedules are maintained so that the cost does not increase. Besides, Just-in-time is practised for the inventory and the float cost is reduced. The idea should be low cost with an even flow of goods.

Advantages of target costing

Target costing has several advantages some of which are given below:

1. Target costing enables an organisation to fix the cost of the design and the product in great detail.
2. Target costing allows the right product to be directed to the right group of customers.
3. The failure rate of a new product is negligible as the consumers have been taken into consideration before the product is manufactured.
4. It helps in setting realistic goals as it is based on realistic measurements.

12.4.2 Benchmarking

Benchmarking is a process in which an organisation continuously compares the standard and best practices in the industry. In the continuous comparison process, the standards, if available, are first looked into. In many businesses ready made standards are not available. Therefore, the standards achieved by the leader in the industry are used as best standards. The second important issue in benchmarking is choosing the best practice available. Best practices are generally defined by improved knowledge, better practices and high end processes. In benchmarking therefore, all the three issues of knowledge, practice and process need to be addressed.

Benchmarking is carried out in several phases as given below.

1. **Planning phase:** In the planning phase, the business tries to identify what they would like to benchmark, the process or the practice. Once that is determined, it is essential to identify whether it is to be done across the board for the business or for some specific parts of the business. The organisation should have a clear understanding as to what they are seeking through the benchmarking process.
2. **Analysis phase:** In the analysis phase, the issues of 'what is to be benchmarked,' are taken care of. This phase is marked by gap analysis where, the knowledge gap, process gap and the practice gap are measured.
3. **Bench trending:** Bench trending refers to the study of market variables, which affect the business and the product of an organisation in the long run. It includes a study of the various components in the market to get a fair view of the process. The performance gaps are monitored depending on the requirements needed to be fulfilled in the future. Bench trending is a method of gearing the business towards the future rather than the present. However, benchmarking uses all the components of bench trending to strengthen the business.

   The steps in bench trending are as follows:

   i. The market is determined by size, preference, competitors etc.
   ii. The direction of the industry, technology shift and geopolitical environment is studied.
   iii. The strengths of potential competitors are determined and evaluated.
   iv. Data regarding the performance of competitors are gathered and current and future performances are evaluated.
   v. The base line of performance in a business is established.
   vi. A set of activities that would improve the performance and maintain the strength of the business are identified and implemented.

   The process of bench trending is carried out through the following steps.

   i. The requirements of the process that is to be bench trended are understood.
   ii. The flow chart of the process is described.
   iii. The specific objectives of the bench trending process are identified and evaluated.
   iv. The bench trending methods adopted by competitors are identified.
   v. The best suited practice is chosen and adopted according to the need.
4. **Communication and integration:** The processes of benchmarking and bench trending are carried out through the organisation's formal and informal communication system.

While the formal system helps to disburse the information through a large forum of training and development, the informal information sustains it by making it a part of the value system of the business. Unless, a certain benchmark becomes a component of the goals of a business, it is very difficult to attain it.

5. **Implementation:** At the implementation stage, realistic goals are set up to realise the benchmarks. Teams are formed to accomplish the task. The processes are streamlined and linked to facilitate the implementation.

How the benchmarking process is carried out[1]

1. Two sets of information are scanned by the business organisation (a) from the environment and (b) from the internal information of the business.
2. From the two sets of information, the filtered information is identified and two further sets of information determined, (a) standards to be benchmarked, and (b) practices to be benchmarked.
3. In the case of standards to be benchmarked, the questions: How much? Where? and When are answered.
4. Regarding knowledge, the practice and process are verified.
5. If improvement in knowledge, practice and process are required to reduce the gap in performance, then they are carried out.
6. The organisation's commitment to the benchmarks is determined and delivered through communication in the organisation.

SUMMARY

In this chapter the various factors that affect the control process in a business were discussed. The role of appropriate information in setting the operation in place and keeping was seen to be one of the most important tools of control for a business. The idea of total quality management emerged from managing the time-cost and quality factors in a business. In doing so, two important concepts are used by the business, namely target costing and benchmarking. Target costing, which enables the costs to be reduced and benchmarking which helps in creating the appropriate knowledge base and reduces the gap between actual and best practices available.

Review Questions

1. Describe the role of the information system in controlling the operation of an organisation.
2. Describe the process of control of a business through the use of Total Quality Management (TQM).
3. Explain the process of developing a TQM process in a business.
4. What is target costing? How is it accomplished?
5. How does a business obtain continuous process improvement? Briefly describe the various tools used in continuous process improvement.
6. What is the meaning of benchmarking? How is it different from bench trending?
7. What are the steps in bench trending? Elaborate.
8. How is benchmarking implemented? Explain the steps involved.

Analytical Questions

1. In the shoe manufacturing industry how does one implement continuous process improvement? You may use sports wear, formal wear or fashion wear for your explanation.
2. The software industry is now involved in various CMM level certifications. What is the reason for this? Is it something to do with the control system?
3. Take up any hospital of your choice and explain how benchmarking can be carried out for it.

[1] For details on benchmarking and its economics refer to Chapter 4.

CHAPTER 13

Production Control

LEARNING OBJECTIVES OF THE CHAPTER

- Role of production in management
- Measurement of production performance
- Production control reports
- Supply chain management

13.1 INTRODUCTION

Production is the process in which inputs in the form of raw materials, consumables, spares and other material are converted into a finished product utilising land, human and other resources such as machinery, technology and information.

For example, for producing packaged food the basic ingredients to make the food, the technology, the machines and the information of the various tastes and recipes, are required.

The objective of controlling the production activities or operations is to ensure optimum utilisation of production capacities, minimal waste and reduction of the downtime of machines.

The objective of controlling the production activities or operations is to ensure optimum utilisation of production capacities, minimal waste and reduction of the downtime of machines.

Production management controls the production activities to achieve quick conversion cycles, optimal schedule of operations on the plant floor, efficient movement of materials on the plant floor and avoidance of spills and accidents. It also aims at identifying the various work points and measures the work point efficiencies to ensure high productivity levels.

Another important aspect of the production system is to achieve quality, for which quality checks are prescribed. This is a different dimension of control in the production system.

Production control is easier than controlling services, simply because most of the elements of production are measurable.

13.2 PRODUCTION CONTROLS

Production controls, which are established in a manufacturing organisation, depend on two broad variables: the nature of the production process and the degree of mechanisation involved in the production process, i.e., continuous production or discrete (assembly line) production.

In an assembly line production system, control is generally through a visual process rather than manual intervention. Random samples of the finished goods are checked in order to determine the quality of the goods being produced (the measurement is against set standards).

In a standard production system, a variety of components are combined to make the final product. This requires the production system to focus on the following points.

1. Production of the finished goods as per the specified design
2. Production of finished components as per the pre-determined time standards laid down
3. Synchronisation of the production processes of all the components so as to avoid excess production of one component *vis-á-vis* another component
4. Ensuring the right balance of production capacity of different production chains of the various components
5. Ensuring the right production capacity within a production process for a component
6. Ensuring that the work layout is appropriately designed and that there is a smooth flow of materials on the shop floor
7. Specifying the quantum of materials to be stacked on the production floor, for both the inputs and the outputs
8. Specifying the number of persons who can be present on the shop floor, the uniform or dress that the employees have to wear, etc.
9. Defining the wastage and spoilage norms and benchmarking the actual wastage and spoilage against these norms
10. Defining the quality norms that are to be met at each stage of the production process and strictly adhering to them, so that consistency of delivery can be met.

Another factor that directly influences the type of production control is the extent of mechanisation in the production process. If the production process is highly mechanised and uses advanced techniques like robotics and Computer Numeric Control (CNC) machines, where the degree of precision is very high and the chances of errors are very low, then the control element is in built in the mechanical system itself. In such a case the control element that the management should focus on is largely related to processes such as stock requirement etc.

If the production process is highly mechanised and uses advanced techniques like robotics and Computer Numeric Control (CNC) machines, where the degree of precision is very high and the chances of errors are very low, then the control element is in built in the mechanical system itself.

13.3 MEASURING PRODUCTION PERFORMANCE

In order to measure the performance of an organisation's production function, a tool that is commonly used is the organisation's productivity. Productivity is essentially a measure of an organisation's efficiency in terms of output to input ratio.

Productivity is essentially a measure of an organisation's efficiency in terms of output to input ratio.

1. The higher the numerical value of these ratios, the greater is the efficiency. It is an important tool, since it helps in tracking an inefficient production system and helps in judicious usage of resources of an organisation.

The higher the numerical value of these ratios, the greater is the efficiency.

13.3.1 Productivity Measurement

Productivity can be measured in relation to (a) a single (single factor productivity), (b) a combination of factors (multiple productivity) or (c) all the factors taken together (total productivity). Single factor productivity and multiple factor productivity can be termed as partial factor productivity.

Some of the measurements of productivity are given below:

1. **Labour productivity:** As labour is one of the major sources of production costs for an organisation, most productivity ratios are calculated considering labour as the specific input. This partial productivity ratio is called the productivity index or output per work hour ratio:

   Labour productivity ratio

$$= \frac{\text{Goods/services produced (units)}}{\text{Labour/man hours spent}}$$

2. Material productivity: Material costs also affects productivity as they may add up to 30% to 40% of the overall costs, or even more. Hence, operations managers also measure productivity in terms of materials used.

   Material productivity

   $$= \frac{\text{Goods and services produced}}{\text{Quantity of materials used}}$$

3. Multifactor productivity: Managers often develop specific ratios that gauge productivity in terms of change in combined inputs. These inputs can include raw material and labour hours used in the production of a particular output.

   Multifactor Productivity

   $$= \frac{\text{Goods/services produced}}{\text{Quantity of raw material} + \text{labour hours used}}$$

4. Total productivity: An organisation measures productivity in terms of partial productivity (single factor) as well as total productivity. However, it is difficult to understand the total productivity since the units of input need to be categorically identified for this purpose. Besides, total productivity fails to pin point the exact factor which has caused the productivity to fall.

   Total Productivity

   $$= \frac{\text{Goods and services produced (output)}}{[\text{Labour} + \text{Capital} + \text{Energy} + \text{Technology} + \text{Material}] \text{ (inputs)}}$$

13.4 PRODUCTION CONTROL REPORTS

For efficient production control, the management requires regular reports on various production-related parameters and activities. A few of these reports are discussed in this section to understand their role in the control system:

13.4.1 Production Efficiency Reports

A production efficiency report is prepared to determine the efficiency of the shop floor. Certain standards are set for the production departments based on machine capacity, required cycle time, manpower required to produce the yield etc., based on budgetary control and standard costing. The production efficiency reports give the details of the standard production within a given timeframe as against actual production, or the comparison of the standard time required to produce the given target as against the actual time utilized for the given target. Production efficiency reports are useful in taking corrective actions in case of irregularities.

13.4.2 Production Planning Report

The production planning report can be used to plan the production activity for a particular shift or day. Production planning is an important activity that takes care of crucial resources like manpower, machines and materials of the organisation. Lack of proper production planning will lead to wastage of the resources used in the production process.

13.4.3 Daily Production Report

The daily production report provides the production manager information about the activities carried out on the shop floor during the day. This report can be used to rectify any anomalies in the production process.

13.4.4 Downtime Analysis Reports

The downtime analysis reports are used to control the downtime. In order to ensure effective management of the shop floor, the production manager has to increase the efficiency of the production department by reducing the downtime of the machine. The downtime analysis report provides the production manager with the reasons for the length of the downtime.

13.4.5 Shift Handover Report

The shift handover report contains information about all the developments that have taken place during a particular shift. As the production process is carried out in two or three shifts, it is the responsibility of the persons in charge of a particular shift to give a report on the happenings in his/her shift to the person in charge of the next shift. The shift handover report typically contains details about the production achieved, the materials used, the utilities used, the problems that occurred during the shift, the actions taken to resolve or reduce the problems, etc.

SUMMARY

Production activities ensure optimal utilisation of production capacities and minimise wastage and downtime of the machines. In a manufacturing organisation, the production activity involves the conversion of inputs to outputs, and operations cover the dimension of the process involved in procuring the inputs to ensure optimal supply to the customers or consumers to satisfy their needs. The various activities executed during the production process are called production operations. Operations management and control cover production as well as non production operations.

The production controls, which are established in manufacturing organisations, depend on the nature of the production process and the degree of mechanisation involved in the process. The nature of a production process is defined in terms of whether it is continuous process production or discrete (assembly line) production. If the production process is highly mechanised then advanced tools like CNN machines and robotics are used.

Review Questions

1. Discuss the need for production control.
2. Discuss the major issues on which a production system should focus in order to enable control.
3. Explain the ways in which production performance can be measured.
4. Discuss the various measures of productivity with their shortcomings.
5. What are production control reports? Discuss some of them in detail.

Analytical Question

A tractor manufacturing unit engages about 90 labourers who work on ten different machines. There are three shifts in a day. On an average about 3 workers take leave in a month leading to at least one machine being down for lack of manpower in a month. Suggest ways of reporting, including what reports should be made. Also analyse how one measures productivity in this case.

CHAPTER 14

Marketing Control

LEARNING OBJECTIVES OF THE CHAPTER

- Types of marketing controls
- Marketing audit
- Sales control
- Distribution control
- Marketing communications control
- Marketing control in branding
- Information systems for marketing control

14.1 INTRODUCTION

Marketing is one of the most important functions of any business. Milan Kundera, the famous Czech novelist, playwright and poet, said, "Business has only two functions – marketing and innovation." In this chapter, we discuss some of the control techniques used in the marketing function and its sub-functions.

Marketing control deals with execution of marketing strategy and checking whether the organisation's objectives are being achieved or not.

Two aspects that are very important for any organisational function are: strategy and execution. Marketing control deals with execution of marketing strategy and checking whether the organisation's objectives are being achieved or not. In this chapter, we first discuss the different types of marketing controls, and marketing audit. We will then discuss the control related aspects of sales, distribution, marketing communication and brand management. Finally, we will discuss the use of information systems for marketing control.

14.2 TYPES OF MARKETING CONTROLS

Earlier, in Chapters 12 and 13, we have discussed the different types of controls used in operations management, such as production control, inventory control and quality control. We saw that control of R & D involves more personnel control than financial control. Thus, different types of functions use different types of controls. Marketing controls can be divided into four different types – strategic control, annual plan control, profitability control and efficiency and effectiveness control, which are described below.

14.2.1 Strategic Control

Schreyogg and Steinmann define strategic control as "the critical evaluation of plans, activities and results, thereby providing information for future action." This means that strategic control helps the organisation to evaluate its strategies by focusing on the outcomes of the activities undertaken. A major requirement for strategic control is

Strategic control helps the organisation to evaluate its strategies by focusing on the outcomes of the activities undertaken.

keeping a close watch on the internal and external environments and checking whether the strategies developed have been adapted to suit those changing environments. According to John F. Preble, strategic control has four components: premise control, implementation control, strategic surveillance and special alert control.

Premise Control

Premise control involves continuously monitoring certain specific environmental conditions, which form the basis of the strategy being devised. Continuous monitoring helps in adapting the strategy to fluctuations in the environment.

Implementation Control

Plans have to be implemented in the form of actions and these actions have an impact on the strategy already formulated. Implementation control is used to check the impact of the action on the strategy and to specify whether it is positive or negative. Implementation control is also used to check whether these actions are in line with the overall objectives of the organisation.

Strategic Surveillance

Strategic surveillance involves scanning the environment for any possible changes or developments that could affect the implementation process and the overall strategies associated with it. This component starts with the implementation phase and goes on continuously until the implementation is over. The very purpose of this component is to ensure that planned strategies are implemented fully and any changes detected in the environment that could possibly affect the implementation process are dealt with appropriately.

Special Alert Control

The most important component of strategic control is special alert control. This component ensures that the system is ready in the event of a crisis in the organisation or in the environment. As the name itself implies, this component is used only in an emergency.

14.2.2 Annual Plan Control

The targets set in the annual marketing plan are used as performance standards in annual plan control. Projected values of sales volume, market share, and profit are some of the typical performance standards under this type of control. Two important techniques used for tracking results and comparing them with the standards are variance analysis and marketing expenses-to-sales analysis.

Projected values of sales volume, market share, and profit are some of the typical performance standards under this type of control.

Variance analysis is used to ascertain the causes of any deviations and their impact on the business of the organisation. This technique has been discussed in detail in Chapter 5. Marketing expenses-to-sales analysis is used to analyse the impact on sales of the expenses incurred on promotional and other marketing activities. Managers often try to keep the ratio (or percentage) of marketing expenses to sales value as low as possible. A low value of this ratio implies that every unit of marketing expenditure has a high impact on sales.

Variance analysis is used to ascertain the causes of any deviations and their impact on the business of the organisation.

14.2.3 Profitability Control

A marketing manager is concerned with marketing profitability. Marketing profitability is the profitability achieved through marketing activities and is calculated based on the investment made in these activities. Profitability control ensures that profitability is maintained consistently in marketing activities.

The Strategic Profit Model (SPM) is a useful technique for profitability control. In marketing control, the model is used to identify the impact of the marketing

The Strategic Profit Model (SPM) is a useful technique for profitability control. In marketing control, the model is used to identify the impact of the marketing activities on the financials of the organisation, that is how they affect its financial performance in terms of profits and return on investment.

activities on the financials of the organisation, that is how they affect its financial performance in terms of profits and return on investment. As discussed earlier in Chapter 8, the SPM identifies three focus areas to improve an organisation's Return On Net Worth (RONW). The organisation can maximise its profitability in terms of RONW through profit margin management (net profit/net sales), asset management and debt management.

Two other important techniques used for profitability control are the segment margin report that generates a separate income statement for each customer segment or product line, and the Activity Based Costing (ABC) system that is used to analyse the whole marketing effort by analysing the marketing function based on different activities. The segment margin report was discussed in detail earlier as a part of Sales Budget. Both these methods can be used to analyse marketing activities based on customer segment, territories, product lines, channel structures, etc.

14.2.4 Efficiency and Effectiveness Control

Efficiency control is more of a quantitative control and deals with the efficiency with which the marketing activities are directed towards the achievement of the goals of the marketing function. Here, the controls mainly focus on the sales volume, the sales generated by each sales-person, number of accounts handled by each salesperson, etc. Thus, efficiency control is used to increase productivity in marketing activities.

Efficiency control is more of a quantitative control and deals with the efficiency with which the marketing activities are directed towards the achievement of the goals of the marketing function.

Effectiveness control, on the other hand, is qualitative in nature and aims at improving the effectiveness of the marketing activities. Customer satisfaction is one measure of effectiveness in selling. Con-ducting customer satisfaction surveys, tracking customer attitudes, and analysing customer feedback are some of the activities that help to assess the marketing effectiveness from the customer's perspective. For example, the retail outlets of Shopper's Stop have suggestion boxes and customer feedback forms to gather information about their products and services. These efforts help such retail outlets to improve their services and the product range they display.

Effectiveness control, on the other hand, is qualitative in nature and aims at improving the effectiveness of the marketing activities.

14.2.4.1 Marketing Effectiveness

The performance of an organisation in terms of sales growth, market share, profitability and customer satisfaction is considered to be a reflection of its marketing effectiveness. Marketing effectiveness is not easy to audit, measure or control. It depends on attributes like customer philosophy, marketing orientation, information about marketing, strategic orientation and operational efficiency of the organisation. These attributes are discussed below.

Customer philosophy: The basic requirement for marketing effectiveness is to be customer-oriented. This involves studying the market, identifying opportunities, selecting the best market segments and being prepared to provide superior value to the customers in order to meet their requirements. Customer philosophy differs from organisation to organisation. While product-oriented companies believe in offering good products to the customers, technology-oriented companies believe in offering products developed using cutting edge technology. However, an organisation that takes the requirements of the market place into consideration when designing its organisational structure and formulating its marketing plans may be more effective in its marketing efforts.

An organisation that takes the requirements of the market place into consideration when designing its organisational structure and formulating its marketing plans may be more effective in its marketing efforts.

Marketing orientation: For marketing to be effective, the organisational structure should have a marketing orientation. The major functions of marketing should be integrated and controlled by a top-level management executive and the marketing department should work in harmony with the other departments. The organisation should develop a structure that will help meet the requirements of the target market segments. This requires the organisation to have a well-defined structure of developing, evaluating, testing and introducing a new product in the market place. This structure has an effect on the long-term success of business.

Information about marketing: For marketing to be effective, adequate information is required for planning and implementing the marketing activities. The information should be up-to-date about the preferences of the customers and their buying behaviour. Marketing research helps organisations gather up-to-date information about the market.

Strategic orientation: Marketing effectiveness also depends on whether the management can formulate a marketing strategy based on the organisation's philosophy, organisation and information resources. To have a strategic orientation, the organisation should have a formal planning system that can operate on a long-term basis.

Operational efficiency: It is not enough to formulate marketing plans. The plans also have to be put into action carefully and the marketing activities should be implemented cost-effectively. This will determine the operational efficiency of the organisation. How efficiently the marketing plans are being implemented should be regularly monitored and corrective actions taken wherever necessary.

It is not enough to formulate marketing plans. The plans also have to be put into action carefully and the marketing activities should be implemented cost-effectively.

14.3 MARKETING AUDIT

A functional management audit is one type of management audit. The functional management audit of the marketing function is referred to as a marketing audit. It is a powerful tool for improving the marketing effectiveness of an organisation. It plays two important roles:

The functional management audit of the marketing function is referred to as a marketing audit.

1. It introduces or changes the market orientation and practices of the organisation, and hence acts as an intervention strategy.
2. It acts as framework for organisational analysis and control.

Such an audit helps the organisation to learn about the external business environment and industry, and make strategic choices regarding its positioning in the market. It can be used not only to assess past performance but also to enhance the future performance of the organisation's marketing function.

The marketing audit also serves as a vehicle for communication, an analytical framework to help take decisions and to frame policies. It is used as a vehicle by the management to communicate organisational policies and marketing ideas to the employees throughout the organisation. The audit can be used to structure the flow of marketing information in an organisation. It also enables the organisation to analyse the viability of its marketing activities against its marketing objectives. Finally, it helps a manager in decision making and in framing policies for each level of the organisational hierarchy.

14.4 EXTERNAL AND INTERNAL MARKETING AUDITS

Factors over which the organisation has total control like production capacity and budget allocations are called controllable factors. Factors like market demand, the business environment, customers and competitors, over which the organisation has no control, are called uncontrollable factors. The marketing audit can be either an external audit or internal audit, the first being concerned with uncontrollable factors and the second with controllable factors.

14.4.1 External Audit

An external audit involves an analysis of the organisation's external environment. The auditors conducting the external audit should have adequate knowledge of the organisation and the industry as well. The marketing requirements of the organisation and the problem areas as defined by both the top management and the middle-level management should be clearly communicated to the auditor. The external audit should be able to identify the opportunities and threats faced by the organisation in the marketing area, and help to formulate strategies to achieve the marketing objectives. It should also help in identifying the marketing resources, skills and assets, which the organisation should acquire.

The external audit should be able to identify the opportunities and threats faced by the organisation in the marketing area, and help to formulate strategies to achieve the marketing objectives.

14.4.2 Internal Audit

An internal audit is the analysis of the internal environment or the controllable factors of the organisation. It helps to analyse the direction in which the business is heading and where it stands at present. It is an ideal tool for introspection for an organisation. An internal audit involves an analysis of the strengths and weaknesses of the organisation and its product(s) in the market. It also involves identifying and analysing the changes in the market place and their negative effects on the business. The analysis of the positioning, pricing and targeting strategies of the organisation for a given product also comes under an internal audit. In addition an internal audit includes the analysis of the marketing activities of the organisation, and analysis of the marketing channels (such as e-marketing and direct selling) and the advertising media used. It also involves analysing the marketing budget of the organisation.

14.5 CHARACTERISTICS OF AN EFFECTIVE MARKETING AUDIT

A marketing audit is a detailed and systematic analysis. It helps the senior management to identify the strengths and weaknesses of the organisation, along with the opportunities and threats in the market place. An effective marketing audit is systematic, comprehensive, independent and periodic.

An effective marketing audit is systematic, comprehensive, independent and periodic.

14.5.1 Systematic

A marketing audit should follow a logical sequence of analytical steps. It should have a well-defined framework and should suggest improvements that will help accomplish the organisation's objectives. The audit should help the management in designing plans to meet the short- and long-term marketing objectives of the organisation.

14.5.2 Comprehensive

A marketing audit should take into consideration all the factors that have an impact on the organisation's marketing performance. This means that it should go beyond obvious factors like sales turnover and market share. At times, marketers are tempted to address the symptoms rather than the underlying problems. A comprehensive marketing audit helps them to identify and solve the underlying problems.

14.5.3 Independent

A marketing audit conducted internally by the managers may lead to biased results. Such audits do not meet the purpose for which they are conducted. Therefore, for an audit to be effective, it has to be conducted by people external to the organisation. Audits conducted by specialists of external consultants are more objective. Also, the external consultants have a broader knowledge about different industries.

14.5.4 Periodic

In practice, a marketing audit is usually carried out in a crisis, that is, when sales have fallen or when the morale of the personnel is very low. However, it would be very beneficial to conduct audits at regular intervals, without waiting for a crisis to arise. This is all the more important when the external market environment is dynamic and changing.

14.5.5 Conducting a Marketing Audit

The marketing audit is the starting point of marketing planning activities. This audit has three stages, which involve the following activities:

1. Extensive analysis of the present and past marketing activities of the organisation
2. Forecast of the organisation's growth relative to the changing market conditions.
3. Suggestions for improving the quality of plans and the marketing performance.

A marketing audit begins with collecting answers to a series of questions. The questions are framed in such a way as to guide the auditor in carrying out an extensive analysis of the organisation's present and past marketing activities and to forecast growth opportunities. These questions investigate the aspects related to the market and the marketing activities of the organisation. Exhibit 14.1 shows a marketing audit checklist.

Exhibit 14.1

Marketing Audit Checklist*

Agree/Disagree/Uncertain

Company has sometimes failed to meet production targets.
Suppliers are very reliable.
The majority of our sales are in one product.
We do not introduce new products as often as our competitors.
Our product range matches customer wants.
We monitor new product development in the industry.
We are aware of and comply with current legislation.
We are aware of how our customers perceive our products.
We do have system of quality control.
We monitor the quality of incoming supplies.
Level of sales returns is negligible.
Level of purchase returns is negligible.
Company collects feedback from after-sales complaints.
Company uses feedback from sales to influence new products.
Markets are sensitive to price changes.
Prices are in line with the competition.
Profit margins are wide enough to meet price competition.
Credit terms and discounts are in line with competitors.
An increase in credit sales with lead to cash-flow problems.
Company follows competitors in pricing the product/services.

***Adapted from *Marketing Audit Questionnaire*, Strathclyde European Partnership Project, Glasgow**

The process of conducting a marketing audit requires the deep involvement of both the management and the auditors. This ensures that the management learns to formulate policies based on the insights gained through its direct involvement in the work from the auditors. However, the marketing audit cannot be defined as a set of pre-determined activities, it is dynamic activity that differs from organisation to organisation.

In a marketing audit, initially there is a meeting between a person from the top management of the organisation and the auditor. Together, they identify the objectives of the audit, the format of reporting and other related issues. The auditor then reviews the business plans, the financial data of the organisation and the structure of the organisation; he/she conducts interviews with customers and competitors, analyses the marketing budgets, product costs and sales and presents the findings in the form of a marketing audit report.

14.6 SALES CONTROL

Sales control, which includes the control of the sales function and especially the sales force, is one of the most important components of marketing control. The sales function is primarily responsible for an organisation's revenue generation. It is also an important point of contact between the customer and the organisation. For example, in corporate banking, the salesperson (relationship officer or account executive) nurtures the relationship with the client and positions the bank as a long-term partner for the client.

Sales control, which includes the control of the sales function and especially the sales force, is one of the most important components of marketing control.

14.6.1 Sales Budgets

As discussed earlier in Chapter 8, the sales budget is a component of the operating budgets of the master budget of an organisation. A sales manager is responsible for developing budgets for the sales department. A sales manager prepares three types of sales budgets – sales revenue budgets, selling-expense budgets, and sales department administrative budgets. A sales revenue budget is a detailed plan showing the expected sales revenue for a future period. A selling-expense budget is a plan that estimates the expenses that the sales department will incur for achieving the planned sales. It includes the expenses incurred on salaries, travel allowances and training the sales force. The selling-expense budget is closely linked with the sales budget, as the selling expense budget is determined by the number of products that should be sold in a given period of time. The sales department administrative budget consists of budget allocation for administrative expenses like rent and electricity.

A selling-expense budget is a plan that estimates the expenses that the sales department will incur for achieving the planned sales.

As it is difficult to follow stringent budgets, managers make use of rolling budgets or flexible budgets. A rolling budget provides for an additional time period apart from the actual budget period. This allows managers to revise the performance in the budget period and carry forward pending activities/outcomes to the next budget period without inconvenience. Flexible budgets allow managers to revise and update the targets set at the beginning of the budget period. They are suitable for markets where the demand for products is uncertain. They are also suitable at times when there is uncertainty over the performance of the planned tasks due to internal or external factors.

14.6.2 Methods of Budgeting for Selling Expenses

Organisations use different methods for developing selling-expense budgets for the activities of the sales force. It is important for the organisation to let the managers participate in preparing the budgets. The different methods used for selling-expense budgeting are – the affordability method, percentage-of-sales method, competitive parity method, objective-and-task method and return-oriented method. Table 14.1 describes each of these methods.

Table 14.1: Selling-expense budgeting methods

Method	Description
Affordability method	The budget is developed depending on the organisation's ability to spend on the sales function. The allocation of funds will be arbitrary as the budgeted figure may fall short of or exceed the exact requirements of the sales department.
Percentage-of-sales method	The budget is prepared by multiplying sales revenues by a given percentage of sales. The sales revenues used may be a past or forecasted figure or a weighted average of both.
Competitive parity method	These budgets are based on the budgeted figures of the competitors of industry average. It is also based on the comparable (size or revenue) budget of a competitor so that the organisation does not its lose market share to competitors.

Objective-and-task method	Budgets are developed based on the objectives to be achieved.
Return-oriented method	Budgets are developed with the help of tools like Return-On-Investment (ROI), Return On Assets (ROA) and Return On Total Assets (ROTA).

14.6.3 Control through Budgets

Budgeting in itself is a control process. Control is a process of making a disciplined effort to follow an established plan of action and to identify any deviations that occur. As budgeting establishes the objectives and responsibilities of all departments and employees, it facilitates performance evaluation and control. Any deviation from the plan can be easily identified by conducting periodic reviews. This will help the management to take necessary steps to rectify the situation. It is also important for the management to impart sufficient training to employees about the best utilisation of budgeted resources.

In large organisations, budgets are used to achieve coordination between different business segments and to evaluate the performance of those segments. The annual budgets prepared as part of annual planning are used as controlling tools to ensure that the performance does not deviate significantly from the plan.

14.7 SALES QUOTAS

Sales quotas are the most common tools used to influence and improve the assignments of salespersons over a given time period; they can be specified in terms of sales volume or value, profit, expenses or activities. Sales quotas can be set not only for individual sales persons but also for a sales team or a territory. By setting a sales figure for certain product lines or for certain classes or customers, sales managers can direct the activities of the sales force toward reaching these targets.

By setting a sales figure for certain product lines or for certain classes or customers, sales managers can direct the activities of the sales force toward reaching these targets.

Quotas play a critical role in sales management because various selling activities are performed with quotas as the focal point. However, if failure to achieve the quotas is not followed by consequences such as warnings, extension of probation period, or dismissal, they may lose their effectiveness as a mechanism for sales force control.

Sales quotas should be fair, challenging, flexible and easy to understand. The management can set sales volume quotas based on market potential and/or sales forecasts, past experience, executive judgment, or sales force compensation or they can involve the sales force extensively in the process of setting the quotas to arrive at quotas that are mutually agreeable to both the management and the sales force.

Sales quotas should be fair, challenging, flexible and easy to understand.

14.8 IMPORTANCE OF SALES QUOTAS

The purpose of assigning sales quotas is to achieve organisational objectives and provide a direction to sales activities. Sales quotas have an effect on the entire organisation as they are closely linked to the productivity of the sales force and organisational growth. They serve as targets that help sales personnel orient their activities towards achieving these targets and also serve as a means for sales managers to direct the activities of the sales force. In other words, sales quotas motivate and control the sales force.

Sales quotas have an effect on the entire organisation as they are closely linked to the productivity of the sales force and organisational growth. They serve as targets that help sales personnel orient their activities towards achieving these targets and also serve as a means for sales managers to direct the activities of the sales force.

Setting sales quotas is important for a sales organisation due to a number of reasons, some of which are discussed below.

14.8.1 Performance Targets

Quotas provide sales personnel with fixed goals to be achieved within a certain time period. They help sales managers guide and direct the activities of sales personnel by setting goals for them. To attain these goals, sales personnel have to align their efforts with the organisation's overall objectives. Managers should communicate the importance of attaining quotas to the sales force. Assigning challenging goals prompts sales personnel to work harder and perform better. While higher quotas may motivate the sales force to perform better, unrealistic quotas will have a negative impact on sales force performance, thus managers have to be extremely careful while setting quotas.

Managers should communicate the importance of attaining quotas to the sales force. Assigning challenging goals prompts sales personnel to work harder and perform better.

14.8.2 Standards

Sales quotas are excellent tools to measure the performance of the sales personnel. They represent a standard for measuring actual sales results, and a uniform basis for comparing the performances of sales personnel throughout the organisation, irrespective of differences in territories, products sold, etc. Hence quotas are widely used as a basis for compensating the sales force.

14.8.3 Control

Quotas serve as a very good source of control as they facilitate evaluation of the performance of a sales force. Successful achievement of quotas indicates that sales activities are moving forward in the right direction. The failure of salespersons to achieve quotas set for them provides the sales manager with an easy index to spot any deviation in performance.

Quotas serve as a very good source of control as they facilitate evaluation of the performance of a sales force.

For example, setting expense quotas helps sales managers identify excess expenditure. Expense quotas are the amount of money allocated to each salesperson to increase sales in an assigned territory. If the expense reports filed by a salesperson consistently exceed the expense quota set for that person, the selling activities may have to be reoriented to enable achievement of the target within the expense quota.

14.8.4 Change of Direction

Sales quotas also aid sales managers to direct the efforts of sales personnel in the desired direction to achieve organisational goals. Sometimes, for certain strategic or operational reasons, sales managers set challenging quotas for specific products or product lines; attaining such challenging quotas brings significant rewards to the salesperson. This makes salespersons focus their efforts on selling these products. Thus sales managers can use quotas to direct sales efforts towards achieving an organisation's long-term goals.

14.8.5 Motivating the Sales Force

Quotas are a tool for motivating the sales force to enhance their efforts and performance. It has been observed in many studies that sales personnel will perform better if they have a specific target to achieve rather than when they have no such target. Sales quotas also motivate salespersons to compete among themselves, leading to improved performance and sales volumes.

14.9 SALES AND COST ANALYSIS

Sales analysis involves gathering, classifying and studying the sales data of an organisation. It is one means by which an organisation can analyse its performance and it helps sales managers to plan and direct the sales efforts. A sales analysis classifies and presents the sales data that the organisation has gathered in an organised manner and thereby reveals market and competitive changes to the management. It produces a wide variety of information that sales managers can use to improve the efficiency of sales functions.

A sales analysis classifies and presents the sales data that the organisation has gathered in an organised manner and thereby reveals market and competitive changes to the management.

In addition to directing and controlling the selling efforts of the sales force, sales analysis helps the management in many other ways. It helps to identify the strengths and weaknesses of the organisation, thereby allowing the management to formulate suitable marketing strategies. Sales analysis also helps the management in production planning, cash management, inventory management and other non-marketing functions. Most important of all, it helps in the overall management of the organisation by providing the management with an orientation and direction in which to focus its competitive efforts.

Marketing cost analysis involves the collection, classification, comparison and study of marketing cost data. Conducting a marketing cost analysis helps an organisation to identify opportunities to increase the effectiveness of its marketing expenditure. In addition to tracking profitability, cost analysis helps generate accurate cost information that is required for planning pricing strategies, promotional campaigns, etc.

The next sections discuss sales variance analysis, market share analysis and marketing expense-to-sales variance analysis.

14.10 SALES VARIANCE ANALYSIS

Sales variance analysis is used to identify the reasons for discrepancies between the expected and actual outcomes. A thorough analysis of the variance will help in better control of sales activities. Sales variance analysis can be of two types: the value method where the variances are calculated in terms of sales value and the profit method (also called margin variances) where variances are calculated in terms of their impact on profit. Sales value analysis can be further divided into sales price variance and sales volume variance. Sales volume variance is again sub-divided into sales quantity variance and sales mix variance. Variance analysis has been discussed earlier in Chapter 8 and later in Chapter 15.

14.11 MARKET SHARE ANALYSIS

The aim of a market share analysis is to determine the market share of an organisation by comparing its sales with the total sales in the industry. Since the market share is not a static figure and changes from time to time, the marketer has to conduct the analysis on a regular basis. Market share acts as standard for developing action plans and forecasting demand, with a higher market share indicating that the organisation is doing well in the market.

Market share analysis also helps an organisation that operates in international markets. Regular analysis of market shares helps an exporter to know the organisation's relative position in the world market. Based on this analysis, exporters can formulate strategies for the foreign market to counter competition from domestic players of the importing country and other exporters.

14.11.1 Marketing Expense-to-Sales Variance Analysis

Marketing expenses are a function of sales value. They are made up of two components - fixed and variable. The fixed component does not vary with the sales. The variable component is calculated as a percentage of sales. Sales budgets and marketing expense budgets are prepared considering both the fixed and variable components. The actual sales and expenses are compared with the budgeted sales and expenses. If the actual sales are higher than the budgeted sales and the actual expenses are lower than the budgeted expenses, the variance is favourable. If the actual sales are lower than those budgeted and the actual expenses are higher than the budgeted expenses, then the variance is unfavourable.

Example: Fashion Textiles Ltd. is a cloth manufacturing company. The company also markets its own products. The marketing manager of the company has set the budget for marketing expenses at Rs. 100 million for the year 2007. This budget has been allocated to different functions as mentioned in Table 14.2(a).

Table 14.2(a): Budgeted marketing expenses

(Rs. Million)

	Fixed	Variable	Total
Direct selling	15	20	35
Distribution	10	20	30
Promotion	10	15	25
Other marketing	10	-	10
Total	**45**	**55**	**100**

The sales for the year were budgeted at Rs. 500 million. The quarterly sales that were budgeted for each quarter are given in Table 14.2(b).

Table 14.2(b): Budgeted quarterly sales

Quarter I	Rs. 150 million
Quarter II	Rs. 100 million
Quarter III	Rs. 130 million
Quarter IV	Rs. 120 million

At the end of two quarters, the actual sales and the actual expenses for the first two quarters were compared with the budgeted sales and budgeted expenses respectively. The actual sales for Quarter II stood at Rs. 175 million and Rs. 80 million respectively; the actual marketing expenses for Quarter I and Quarter II stood at Rs. 22.5 million and Rs. 19 million respectively. Based on this data, we shall prepare a fixed budget and flexible budget for the company for Quarters I and II.

Using fixed budgets: If fixed budgets are used, the total marketing expense budget of Rs. 100 million will be uniformly spread over the year with the quarterly marketing expense budget being Rs. 25 million per quarter. In Quarter I, the actual sales (Rs. 175 million) are more than the budgeted sales (Rs.150 million) for the quarter. Therefore, it is a favourable situation for the company. The marketing expenses were budgeted at Rs. 25 million for Quarter I while the actual expenditure incurred was Rs. 22.5 million. This is again a favourable situation for the company as the company has spent less than the budgeted expenses. On the other hand, in Quarter II the actual sales (Rs. 80 million) were less than the budgeted sales (Rs. 100 million) and this resulted in an unfavourable variance. The actual marketing expenses (Rs. 19 million) were less than the budgeted marketing expenses (Rs. 25 million) and hence the situation was favourable for the company in Quarter II. In this case, the sales and marketing expenses report will be as shown in Table 14.2(c).

Table 14.2(c): Using a fixed budget – Sales and marketing expense report

(Rs. Million)

	Quarter I			Quarter II		
	Budgeted	Actual	Variance	Budgeted	Actual	Variance
Sales	150	175	25(F)	100	80	20(U)
Marketing expense	25	22.50	2.50(F)	25	19	6(F)

(F) – Favourable
(U) – Unfavourable

Using flexible budgets: In flexible budgeting, both the fixed and variable components of the budgeted marketing expenses are taken into consideration. It may be assumed that the fixed marketing expenses of Rs. 45 million will be incurred uniformly over the year. The variable marketing expenses will vary with the sales value in each quarter. The variable expenses of Rs. 55 million are 11 percent of the budgeted sales (55/500 × 100).

The break-up for the budgeted marketing expenses is shown in Table 14.2(d).

Table 14.2(d): Budgeted marketing expenses

(Rs. Million)

	Total	Qtr I	Qtr II	Qtr III	Qtr IV
Fixed expenses	45.00	11.25	11.25	11.25	11.25
Variable expenses	55.00	16.50	11.00	14.30	13.20
Budgeted marketing expenses	**100.00**	**27.75**	**22.25**	**25.55**	**24.45**

In flexible budgeting, the actual expenses should be compared with the budget in order to arrive at the variances. For this purpose, the budgeted variable expenses will have to be modified to suit the actual sales value, as mentioned in Table 14.2(e).

Table 14.2(e): Marketing expenses allowed for sales achieved

(Rs. Million)

	Quarter I	Quarter II
Fixed expenses	11.25	11.25
Variable expenses (11% of actual sales)	19.25	8.80
Marketing expenses allowed for sales achieved	**30.50**	**20.05**

In this case the sales and marketing expense report will be as shown in Table 14.2(f).

Table 14.2(f): Using flexible budget – Sales and marketing expense report

(Rs. Million)

	Quarter I			Quarter II		
	Budgeted	Actual	Variance	Budgeted*	Actual	Variance
Sales	150	175	25(F)	100	80	20(U)
Marketing expenses	30.50	22.50	8(F)	20.05	19	1.05(F)

* " Sales is 'budgeted sales': Marketing expenses are 'allowed marketing expenses for actual sales'
(F) – Favourable
(U) – Unfavourable

In Quarter I, the actual sales (Rs. 175 million) are more than the budgeted sales (Rs. 150 million) for the quarter. Therefore, it is a favourable situation for the company. The marketing expenses were budgeted at Rs. 30.5 million for Quarter I while the actual expenditure incurred was Rs. 22.5 million. This is again a favourable situation for the company as it has spent less than the budgeted expenses.

On the other hand, in Quarter II, the actual sales (Rs. 80 million) were less than the budgeted sales (Rs. 100 million) and this resulted in an unfavourable variance. However, the actual marketing expenses (Rs. 19 million) were less than the allowed marketing expenses (Rs. 20.05 million) for the actual sales, and hence the situation was favourable for the company on this front.

In Quarter II, if the actual marketing expenses had been Rs. 21 million, which is more than the allowed marketing expenses (Rs. 20.50 million) for the actual sales, then the situation would have been unfavourable for the company on both the sales and expense fronts.

14.12 SALES REPORTING

Sales' reporting is used as a method of tracking and monitoring the performance of the sales force. Information on sales, expenses, etc., is collected from the sales personnel through a formal reporting system.

The activities undertaken by the sales force can be controlled in two ways: one, by giving incentives to the salespeople to motivate them to perform and to align individual objectives with organisational objectives; two, by closely monitoring the sales force to check that the activities they undertake are performed well. Sales' reporting is used as a method of tracking and monitoring the performance of the sales force. Information on sales, expenses, etc., is collected from the sales personnel through a formal reporting system. Information used to evaluate the performance of the sales personnel can also be gathered from a manager or supervisor who keeps the sales force under observation.

Richard R. Still, Edward W. Cundiff, and Norman A.P. Govoni describe two primary types of sales-related reports—sales and expense reports, and other reports. The sales and expense reports are used by the sales management to evaluate actual performances. The other reports include reports from the sales personnel and other employees lower in the hierarchy of the sales function. For example, they may include sales forecasts which are very important for the planning of sales management as well as for the strategic planning of the organisation.

Sales managers are expected to evaluate the sales representatives and give their appraisals of them on quarterly or monthly basis. The reports generated help in this evaluation process. Reports can be obtained from the sales force and also from the sales management team.

14.12.1 Reports from the Sales Force

The field staff or sales force submit different types of reports at different times depending on the requirements of the management. The different types of reports are described below.

1. **Call reports:** Call reports cover details about the sales calls made daily or weekly. These reports consist of information regarding the different customers, their preferences, competitors and their products, etc. For example, in a pharmaceutical company, a sales representative may be expected to call on around 12 to 15 doctors and five to six retail chemists a day, to promote the company's products. The relevant details of these calls have to be reported to the management in the daily call report, as per the company's prescribed format. While some organisations require a handwritten submission, others have online reporting systems in place.
2. **Expense reports:** The sales personnel are reimbursed for the official expenses they incur, such as travel expenses and promotional activity expenses. Expense reports also help the management in monitoring and controlling the type of expenses that the sales force incurs.
3. **Sales work plan**: The sales force has to plan their calls ahead of time and submit the report to the management. This helps the management track the sales representative's calls when he/she is in the field.
4. **Potential new-business report:** This report generates information on the possible new areas where business can be developed or new prospects can contribute to the business. It helps the management in gauging the level and effectiveness of business development initiatives a sales representative undertakes.
5. **Lost sales report**: This report helps the management check the capabilities of the sales force in retaining customers and fighting competition. It helps in gauging the requirements for sales training and improvements in customer service and products.

14.12.2 Reports from Sales Management

The regional and divisional managers submit periodic reports to the senior management regarding the expected sales and actual sales in a specific month, quarter or year. They also have to report on the sales that are expected from each of the sales representatives in their region or division. The reports generated by the sales management also include information regarding the promotional activities to be undertaken by the sales team in a specified time period and the forecast or result of the activity in terms of sales.

14.13 CREDIT CONTROL

Organisations offer credits to customers and channel members to increase sales. There should be a proper credit policy in place to control the credits. The organisations should ensure that the credits given do not end up becoming bad debts. Employees of the organisations may offer unwarranted credits to customers and channel members if a credit control system is not in place. A proper credit control mechanism involves two steps. The first step is to analyze the accounts

A proper credit control mechanism involves two steps. The first step is to analyse the accounts receivables and bad debts. This helps in determining why some of the debts have gone bad, and also the amount and type of receivables. The second step is the credit rating of customers and channel members.

receivables and bad debts. This helps in determining why some of the debts have gone bad, and also the amount and type of receivables. The second step is the credit rating of customers and channel members.

14.14 RECEIVABLES MANAGEMENT

As discussed in the above section, analysing accounts receivables or receivables management is an important step in devising the credit control policy. Having a proper receivables management methodology in place is the most crucial step in maximising the profitability and cash flows from the increasing revenue. The three important ways in which this profitability from receivable management can be increased are:

1. **Devising and implementing an appropriate portfolio strategy:** It is necessary to have different collection methods in place for different customers. As positioning of a product is different for different segments, collection methods differ depending on the customer. These methods differ based on whether the customers are from the government or private sector, whether they are domestic customers or international customers, etc. There should be a portfolio strategy in place for the customers, and this should be implemented using the correct methods, resources and organisational structure. This will help in maintaining the cash flows and reducing bad debts.
2. **Precise fulfilment of orders and invoicing:** The extent of receivables depends a lot on the quality of service offered to the customers. Any mistakes in the process from order taking to order fulfilment will increase the chances of delayed payments. Precise order fulfilment and invoicing and quick conflict resolution will help in maximising the cash flows and also improve the organisation's image. It will also help in enhancing the productivity of the employees in terms of order processing, customer service and collections.
3. **Having an efficient conflict resolution procedure in place:** Conflicts may arise when the price or quantity stated in the invoice is incorrect, or quality of the products or services are not up to standard. Most instances of outstanding receivables are due to such conflicts. Finding a solution to the conflict by direct discussions with the customer will help in reducing the delayed receivables. It will also help in maximising cash flow through clearance of pending payments.

14.15 CREDIT RATING

Depending on the credit rating, customers are graded as no-risk through high-risk customers.

Credit rating helps in calculating the amount of credit that can be given to customers or channel members with minimum risk. Depending on the credit rating, customers are graded as no-risk through high-risk customers. This helps the organisation in deciding to whom it can give credit and to whom it cannot. If there is no credit rating policy in place, the organisation would have to either deny credit to all customers or have a standard credit that is extended to all customers. Both these alternatives are risky.

14.16 PERFORMANCE EVALUATION AND PERFORMANCE-BASED COMPENSATION

Performance evaluation is a formal and planned system for measuring and evaluating the performance of salespersons. It is used by sales managers to monitor and measure the performance of the sales force. Though the basic objective of performance evaluation is to assess the performance of a salesperson, it can be used as a tool by the management to motivate him/her. Further, performance evaluation acts as a tool in developing a sales plan, which will help to improve the performance of the person in the future. Performance evaluation also helps the salesperson to adjust his/her work to suit the expectations of the management, on the basis of the feedback received. Thus, it is helpful in discovering those areas that can be improved in the performance of each and every salesperson. If the performance of a salesperson is found to be unsatisfactory, he/she can be counselled and motivated, which will help him/her in improving his/her performance. If all these measures fail to yield the required results, the salesperson may be discharged from service.

The output or sales volume generated by a salesperson usually depends on his/her individual effectiveness. In this case, the performance of the salespersons is usually measured on the basis of the sales volume that they generate. The incentives provided to them are also related to the sales volume. In this situation, the organisation has to ensure that all the salespersons are treated equally, and that there are no factors that will unduly influence the output of any salesperson. For example, while allocating territories for sales, it has to be ensured that everyone gets territories that have equal potential for generating sales.

The output or sales volume generated by a salesperson usually depends on his/her individual effectiveness.

In addition to the ability of a person, there are many other external factors like new products launched by competitors in the market and the economy of the country, which affect the sales volume generated. Organisations have to therefore, be sensitive to such external factors while developing a performance measurement system, if generation of sales volume is not directly related to the efforts like number of sales calls made, the frequency of these sales calls and so on.

Organisations have to therefore, be sensitive to such external factors while developing a performance measurement system.

14.17 COMPENSATION AND INCENTIVE SYSTEMS FOR THE SALES FORCE

Sales force compensation is generally made up of two components: salary and incentives. There are various factors and situations to be considered while deciding when incentives should be more or when salary should be the higher component.

To give incentives, the measure used should be objective. Hence, in a situation where the output is not attributable to the performance of a single salesperson, the salary component of compensation should be higher than the incentives components. If the salesperson has to put in higher efforts in selling the products and services, incentives play an important role in motivating the sales force. On the other hand, if the sales are due to the position of the organisation in the market or sales promotion, then salary plays an important role. The higher the number of people in the sales force, the higher is the emphasis on salary as compared to incentives. For sales people working in an uncertain and risky environment, salary plays a crucial role.

14.18 SALES FORCE MANAGEMENT AUDIT

A sales force management audit is a cross-function exercise that evaluates the entire selling operation in an organisation. It covers the environment, planning system, organisational evaluation and functions of sales management. Figure 14.1 presents a diagrammatic representation of a sales force management audit.

Evaluation of the organisation's sales force management process helps the sales manager improve the performance of the sales and effectively allocate resources for achieving the sales objectives. If conducted effectively, a sales force management audit will help the management to identify problems with the present system and prevent them from recurring.

14.19 DISTRIBUTION CONTROL

The distribution function ensures that the products of the organisation reach the markets. The distribution channel consists of the manufacturers, the intermediaries, and the end user. Performance standards can be set for the sales volume generated by the distributors, the number of accounts maintained by each distributor and their contribution to the total sales as a percentage and costs incurred by the organisation. To maintain a relationship with the distributors (in terms of trade discounts, promotion activities, etc.,) for logistics partners like warehousing companies and transportation companies, performance standards may be set for the ratio of cost of transportation to the sales revenue, costs incurred in warehousing and inventory management, etc.

The distribution channel can be controlled in different ways. One method is through channel integration and another is through channel management. Evaluating the channel performance is another control mechanism in the distribution function. As conflicts often arise between channel members, channel conflict management also becomes important in distribution control.

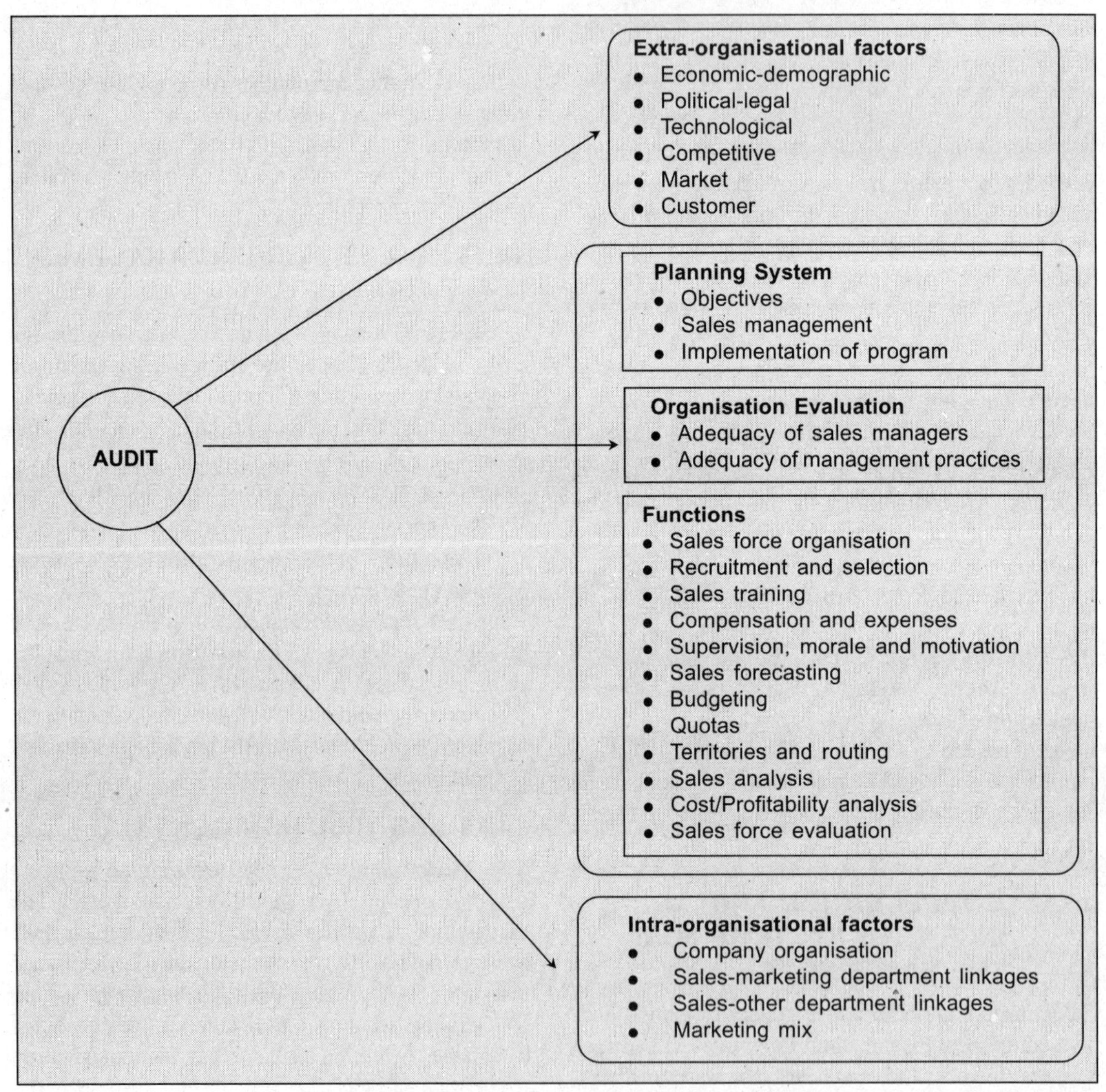

Fig. 14.1: Representation of a sales force management audit (Adopted from Dubinsky, Alan J. and Richard W. Hansen, 'The Sales Force Management Audit', California Management Review, Vol. 24, No. 2, Winter 1981, p86-95.

14.19.1 Channel Integration

Channel integration requires cooperation between the various channel members. Ownership of the channel integration is of great significance not only to manufacturers but also to other channel members like retailers. It serves a host of functions in the present day competitive environment. These include maintaining minimum inventory levels; improving mutual relationships among channel members; reducing transaction costs; helping and enabling organisations to manage their skills and resources better; and enabling organisations to develop a competitive advantage over their rivals in different markets.

There are two ways in which channel integration can be achieved: Vertical Marketing Systems (VMS) and Horizontal Marketing Systems (HMS).

Vertical Marketing Systems (VMS)

A Vertical Marketing System (VMS) is a common model of channel integration in which one of the channel members owns the channel or exerts a substantial influence or control over the activities of the members along the channel. This 'channel leader' oversees the functions of the channel members and ensures that everyone performs only those functions which they are good at. A VMS usually consists of manufacturer(s), distributor(s), and retailer(s) pooling their individual strengths together to achieve operating economies or a competitive advantage.

In a VMS, channel plans and policies are clearly laid out so that each channel member performs a specific that benefits the whole channel. This helps in reducing channel conflicts and achieving better channel cooperation and coordination.

Vertical marketing systems are most prevalent and successfully used in the food service industry. Companies like Kentucky Fried Chicken (KFC) have successfully streamlined production, distribution, and retailing into a single efficient system to succeed in the global market.

In a VMS, the channel leader owns other channel members, franchises them or influences other channel members to cooperate through the channel power vested with the leader. Based on these aspects, VMSs can be divided into:

1. Corporate VMS: Many petroleum refining companies, which have company-owned, company-operated retail outlets, have this type of VMS.
2. Administered VMS: Retailers like Marks and Spencer, which have a strong hold on small suppliers, use this kind of VMS.
3. Contractual VMS: An example of this type of VMS is seen in McDonald's, which is the channel leader for its franchisees.

Horizontal Marketing Systems (HMS)

A horizontal marketing system is an arrangement within a distribution channel, in which two or more organisations at the same channel level work towards a common goal. In this system, the two organisations are unrelated to each other and come together with the objective of cashing in on a market opportunity. Most organisations operate through a strategic alliance or a joint venture. This type of an arrangement is arrived at because the organisations on their own do not have the resources, experience, or the know-how to exploit the marketing opportunity. Horizontal systems have become popular due to the fact that cooperating organisations pool their skills and resources. Organisations have started making use of horizontal integration to gain advantages that are not possible in the vertical system.

The success of a horizontally integrated system depends on: operational integration – the standardisation of the production and distribution processes between the cooperating organisations; intellectual integration – sharing information about the requirements among the cooperating organisations; and social integration – the ability of personnel in the cooperating organisations to discuss and analyse issues with their counterparts, and implement joint programs.

Horizontal arrangements have been successful in distribution of hospital supplies and the pharmaceutical and retailing segments. This type of arrangement is generally formed at the R&D level for new product development or at the wholesaler or retailer level for products, like electrical appliances and hardware. Such arrangements are mostly seen in US market.

14.19.2 Channel Management

Factors such as convenience and service are not under the direct control of manufacturers as intermediaries play a key role in providing them to customers. Efficient channel management helps organisations reduce costs, reach potential customers and make profits. A number of steps are involved in managing channels efficiently.

First, the organisation has to recruit and select the right channel members. The selection criteria may include: a member's ability to sell the organisation's products in the market; the channel member's expertise and knowledge of the products to be handled; the type of customers handled in the past and their satisfaction levels; the amount of work the channel member is handling; the distributor's pricing patterns and risk factors; evaluation of the potential channel member's past performance; the channel member's commitment to the organisation's progress; the cost incurred in selecting a member and subsequent dealings with all stakeholders of the organisation.

Second, it has to focus on motivating channel members and increasing profitability. Relationship management, personal contact with distributors, and formal mechanisms such as distributor advisory council are useful in determining the needs and problems of channel members. The role of the distributor advisory council is to encourage channel members to contribute significantly to the planning process and improve channel performance. Thus, these councils give channel members a sense of belonging, which motivates them to put in their best performance. The organisation should offer appropriate benefits and incentives to distributors to help them improve the supply chain, reduce the capital employed, lower the operating costs, lower the risks involved, enhance customer finance schemes and engage in sales promotion.

Third, the organisation has to periodically evaluate the performance of channel members to ensure that they remain competitive in the market.

Fourth, based on market changes, it should suitably modify the existing channel arrangements.

14.20 EVALUATION OF CHANNEL PERFORMANCE

The performance of a marketing channel can be evaluated from various perspectives. The evaluation assesses the channel's financial performance and looks into societal contributions made by individual members of the channel. The channel performance is evaluated at both the macro- and the micro-level.

14.20.1 Evaluation of Macro-level Performance

Performance at the macro-level is evaluated in terms of the contribution made by the intermediaries to society. Major elements that will determine the contribution of an intermediary are channel efficiency, productivity, effectiveness and equity.

Channel efficiency judges the ability of intermediaries to undertake necessary channel functions by incurring minimal costs. Productivity deals with the extent to which the total channel investment in the form of inputs has been optimised to yield maximum outputs. Productivity and efficiency deal with maximising outputs for a given level of inputs while keeping costs down irrespective of the problems encountered during the distribution process.

Channel effectiveness measures channel performance and considers its ability to satisfy customer needs. It focuses on issues like lot size, delivery time, location convenience and assortment breadth.

Channel equity refers to the distribution of opportunities available to all customers in accessing the market channels of a region.

14.20.2 Evaluation of Micro-level Performance

Channel performance at the micro-level involves a closer look at the performance of individual intermediaries associated with a marketing channel. The five objectives to be considered for evaluating performance are: probability, goal attainment, pattern maintenance, integration and adaptation.

Channel probability considers the financial performance of channel members in terms of Return On Investment (ROI), liquidity of the channel member, financial leverage, growth patterns and potential for sales and profits. Of all the financial dimensions, it is probability or ROI that is accepted as an indicator of good performance in both the wholesale and retail trades. Probability forms an important element in ascertaining the financial well-being of a business. The Strategic Profit Model (SPM), (which was discussed earlier in this chapter) in the context of probability control of the marketing function, can also be used to evaluate the profitability of channel members.

Goal attainment refers to the organisation achieving its goals by interacting with the task environment and maximising of costs and company-specific obstacles. Pattern maintenance involves coordination of processes and functions among organisational units to help the system function smoothly. Integration refers to the coordination among the components of a channel or an organisation to meet common objectives and maintain the entity as one single unit. Adaptation is the modification of resources required to meet system objectives.

14.20.3 Management of Channel Conflicts

Faulty channel design is probably the most important cause of channel conflicts.

Channel conflicts can arise from either structural causes or attitudinal causes. Faulty channel design is probably the most important cause of channel conflicts. Goal divergence or goal incompatibility among channel members is another important cause. Conflicts can also arise from clashes over domains. Domain clashes may be in terms of range of products handled, coverage of territory or customer segments, and responsibilities for performing different channel functions. The differences in attitudes and perceptions among channel members are another key source of channel conflicts. Unexpected changes in the competitive environment, consumers and markets, differences in economic and ideological objectives among channel members, etc., also lead to conflicts. Exhibit 14.2 discusses ways in which channel conflicts can be prevented through e-commerce.

Exhibit 14.2 : E-Commerce in Preventing Channel Conflicts

Using multiple distribution channels has become a common phenomenon in the business environment today. Multiple distribution channels help organisations to increase their reach in the marketplace and also to capture the right target market. However, utilising multiple distribution channels may lead to undesirable channel conflicts especially due to domain clashes.

Linking e-commerce channels with the conventional distribution channels helps in preventing the conventional conflicts. The most important reason for incorporating the internet in the channel is to identify customer preferences and to check whether these preferences are being catered to. Multiple channel distribution allows the marketers to cater to a varied customer base and the manufacturing organisations to improve the product presence in the market. Some ways in which channel conflicts can be prevented are:

1. When using a website for marketing, the products should not be priced lower than the selling price of the other channel members.
2. The channel members should be asked to fulfil the Internet orders.
3. The website should be used only for promoting the product and not for selling.
4. The website should be used to advertise the channel members' activities as well as to promote the channel members.
5. The entire product range should not be offered on the website; or a different brand name should be used for products on the website.
6. The website should be used for promoting relatively new products.

14.20.4 Conflict Resolution Strategies

Efficient cooperation and coordination among channel members can help prevent channel conflicts, and resolve them when they arise. The commonly used conflict resolution strategies are – negotiation and bargaining, problem-solving strategies, persuasion, political strategies and co-operation. Table14.3 shows these conflict resolution strategies.

Table 14.3: Conflict resolution strategies

Strategy	Description
Negotiation and bargaining	• Used to resolve conflicts arising due to issues related to price, cash credits, discounts, delivery, etc. • Used to reach a consensus; no attempt is made to change the objectives of the members involved • Generally takes place between the marketer and the channel member and not between two channel members
Problem-solving strategies	• Used when both the marketer and the channel member have common objectives but are not able to reach a common decision • Information is transferred openly, and solutions sought through cooperation
Persuasion	• Marketers try to influence decisions by changing the objectives and perspectives of the channel members.
Political strategies	• A third party is appointed for conflict resolution • Used when the marketer and the channel member are not able to reach a consensus
Co-optation	• An information-intensive mechanism that involves free transfer of information between members. Coordination and cooperation are prerequisites for co-optation • A new member from outside the organisation is selected and involved in the top management decisions and policies • Involves responsibility sharing; members from different levels can become prominent in the entire channel system and committed to the programs and policies of one another

Source: Compiled from various sources

14.21 MARKETING COMMUNICATION CONTROL

To market a product successfully, it is not enough to ensure that it is the right product, available at the right place at the right time; information about its availability, utility and price must also be effectively communicated to prospective buyers. For the communication process to be effective, the marketer must be able to create the right message and deliver it to the right prospective customers at the right time, using the right medium. Although this may sound simple, in a competitive environment with increasingly similar products and services, proliferation of media options, and complexity in segmenting audiences, it is very difficult to get all the elements of the communications process right.

For the communication process to be effective, the marketer must be able to create the right message and deliver it to the right prospective customers at the right time, using the right medium. Although this may sound simple, in a competitive environment with increasingly similar products and services, proliferation of media options, and complexity in segmenting audiences, it is very difficult to get all the elements of the communications process right.

In section 14.6, we

discussed sales control, which included the control of the sales force, which is responsible for the personal selling component of the marketing communications mix. In this section, we will focus on the control aspects of advertising, sales promotion, direct marketing and public relations. Marketing control in branding will be dealt with in detail in the next section.

14.21.1 Advertising

Advertising can be defined as a paid form of communication in various media (indoor or outdoor) used to convey information about products or services in a way that can persuade people to make a purchase.

Advertising can be defined as a paid form of communication in various media (indoor or outdoor) used to convey information about products or services in a way that can persuade people to make a purchase. The common forms of advertisements are in newspapers, magazines, on television and radio, hoardings and online.

Measuring advertising effectiveness

The effectiveness of an advertisement can be measured either before the advertising campaign takes off (pre-testing) or after the advertisement is run in select media (post-testing).

A commonly used method for measuring the effectiveness of an advertisement is copy testing or message testing. This helps in evaluating the appeal of the advertisement to the target customer, and whether the message is being communicated properly. The effectiveness of an advertisement can be measured either before the advertising campaign takes off (pre-testing) or after the advertisement is run in select media (post-testing). While pre-testing helps advertisers avoid the risk of releasing ineffective advertisements, post-tests provide useful information about the performance of the advertisement campaigns already released, the latter can be used for planning future advertisement campaigns.

The effectiveness of an advertisement can also be measured by monitoring the following parameters: recognition, recall, persuasion (attitude change) and purchase behaviour.

Measuring the effectiveness of Internet advertising

The Internet has become an effective medium for advertising. Many organisations spend a substantial amount of their advertising budgets on online advertising. The various ways in which organisations advertise on the Internet are through banner advertisements and sponsorships, or through their own websites.

While launching a website or advertising online, the first and the foremost aspect is to decide the purpose of doing so, that is, whether the website was launched to directly sell a product, create more leads, generate donations, etc. Secondly the effect that the advertisement has on the customer, that is, whether the customer buys the product, reads the page for information, donates money, etc., should be gauged.

Once the purpose is decided, the next aspect to be decided is the value of the intended outcome. This value could be profit gained per sale, or value generated from a consumer reading an article, etc. For instance, if the percentage of leads converted are 15% and the average value of each conversion is Rs. 500, then the value of the lead is 0.15×500 = Rs. 75.

The third aspect is to monitor the number of times the purpose of the advertisement is fulfilled. This can be done through installing software that tracks the number of landings on the page, conversions, and from where the conversions resulted – through banner advertisements, keyword search, email, newsletters, etc.

The fourth aspect to be tracked is the costs incurred for gaining the revenue. This can be done by tracking the amount of money being spent on the clicks against the revenue being generated and by checking – on a conversion-to-conversion basis – which advertisement creates value. If it is found that a specific advertisement is not contributing to the revenue, that advertisement could be discontinued.

Through these measurements, organisations can monitor which campaigns are beneficial and which are not and, in turn, track the effectiveness of the advertising campaign. These measurements will help organisations bring out better Internet advertisements and use the information generated to improve the effectiveness of their online advertisements.

14.21.2 Sales Promotion

The decreased effectiveness of advertising and a desire for short-term gains are the two main reasons why sales promotions have become so much in demand in recent times. There are two types of sales promotions: trade promotions and consumer promotions. Trade promotions are targeted at channel members (usually retailers) to motivate them to stock the organisation's products and promote them more effectively. Thus, trade promotions aid in the implementation of an organisation's 'push' marketing strategy. On the other hand, consumer promotions are aimed at end consumers so as to create a consumer pull for the product. Thus, consumer promotions help an organisation implement its 'pull' marketing strategy.

Measuring the effectiveness of sales promotion

Different criteria are used for measuring the effectiveness of different types of sales promotions (coupons, price-offs, bonus packs, etc.) This is because the objectives of each type of sales promotion are different. The effectiveness of sales promotions can be measured in two ways: direct evaluation and indirect evaluation. In direct evaluation, sales volume is used as the parameter for measurement, whereas in indirect evaluation, indicators of sales are used as the parameters for measurement. Some indicators of sales that can be used are given below:

1. The number of promoted units sold and profits from the sales
2. The number of un-promoted units sold whose sales can be attributed to the promotion, and profits from the sales
3. The increase in the number of units in distribution and display
4. The increase in impulse buying

The effectiveness of sales promotions can also be measured in terms of the number of inquiries generated regarding the product being promoted. For coupons-related sales promotions, a simple form of measuring effectiveness is the number of coupons redeemed. The effectiveness of sweepstakes can be measured by the total number of entries.

14.21.3 Direct Marketing

According to the Direct Marketing Association of Washington, direct marketing is an interactive system of marketing which uses one or more advertising media to effect a measurable response and/or transaction at any location. Direct marketing involves direct communication with customers to obtain an immediate and measurable response. The changes in the demographic profile of customers, advent of newer advertising media, improvements in technologies and increased focus on relationship marketing have increased the importance of direct marketing. The different ways in which organisations undertake direct marketing are – direct mailing, telemarketing, mass media advertising, and internet advertising.

While developing a direct marketing campaign, the organisation decides the objectives of the campaign undertaken, chooses the profile of the target audience and the different media that it wants to use for the campaign, and creates the content of the campaign. Then the specific set of customers to be targeted is decided. The implementation process involves launching the campaign, receiving orders, processing the orders, managing the inventory, and managing customer queries and complaints. The main advantages of direct marketing are measurability and flexibility. The evaluation of direct marketing campaigns is discussed below.

Evaluation of direct marketing campaigns

The organisation evaluates the campaign in terms of the response to it and its profitability. Response needs to be evaluated both quantitatively and qualitatively. The quantitative measurement of response is conducted in terms of the number of responses received per 1000 mailings or number of responses received per call centre. The quality of the response is measured in terms of the number of sales inquiries and the number of information requests that are generated. A high quality response is one that generates more sales inquiries than information requests.

Profitability analysis is another way of measuring the effectiveness of the direct marketing campaign. This is done by assessing the costs incurred by and the profits generated for the organisation. Costs can be measured in terms of cost per 1000 mailings, cost per order or cost per response. Profits can be measured in terms of the sales obtained from the campaign, profit margin and the actual profit obtained. The evaluation should be carried out on a continuous basis so that the organisation can identify the issues that arise during the campaign and take corrective action to achieve the set objectives.

14.21.4 Public Relations (PR)

The institute of Public Relations defines Public Relations (PR) as "*the deliberate, planned, and sustained effort to establish and maintain mutual understanding between an organisation and its public*." According to The Chartered Institute of Public Relations, "*Public relations are the discipline which looks after reputation, with the aim of earning understanding and support and influencing opinion and behaviour. It is the planned and sustained effort to establish and maintain goodwill and mutual understanding between an organisation and its public.*" PR efforts are aimed at identifying and closing the gaps that exist between the image that the public holds about the organisation and the one that the organisation wants to project.

Measurement and evaluation of PR is a process which involves assessment of the success or failure of PR strategies, activities and tactics in producing the desired output, outtakes and outcomes. Measurements and evaluations of PR aim at monitoring the success of PR efforts in establishing the required relationships between the organisation and the public and improving them over a period of time. PR output is the short-term result achieved by a PR effort and includes the amount of press coverage received or exposure gained by a specific message. PR outtakes relate to the information that the public gathers or obtains from a particular PR effort. PR outcomes are usually long term in nature and refer to the behavioural and business impact of the PR efforts. They are measured in terms of awareness and attitude levels, change in behaviour patterns, change in sales, etc. Measurements of PR aim at quantifying the results of various PR efforts and comparing them with a predetermined target, usually expressed in numerical terms.

Measurement of PR output

Every result that a PR program, activity or tactic generates in the short term is considered as PR output. Usually, the output is the most tangible response shown by the target audience immediately after being exposed to a PR program. Some of the aspects of media output measurement that an organisation can consider are described in Table 14.4.

Some tools used for measuring PR outputs are: media content analysis, cyber space analysis, trade show and event measurement, and public opinion polls.

Measurement of PR outtake

While PR output is concerned with immediate results, measurement of PR outtakes concentrates on finding out whether the target public received the message in the form intended by the organisation and whether they understood and retained the message so that it could be recalled when required. Measurement of PR outtakes is important, as it is necessary for the organisation to know what the target audience has gathered from a particular PR effort. One popular measurement is the favourable or positive attitude shown by an audience toward a PR effort or the various components of that effort.

Outtakes can be measured by parameters such as understanding, recall and interest. Some of the tools for measuring outtake are: awareness and comprehension measurements, recall and retention measurements, surveys, ethnographic studies and experimental research.

Table 14.4: Aspects of media output measurement

Aspect of output Measurement	*Description*
Impressions	Readership (as opposed to circulation) of clips, that is, the number of persons in the target audience who may have been exposed to a news article or story
Ad value of PR	The equivalent advertising value of media coverage resulting from a PR effort
Cost	The cost per media impression or the cost per thousand of campaign
Frequency	Number of times exposure was gained
Reach	The degree of coverage across target audiences
Prominence	How and where the coverage occurred within specific media
Message delivery	Whether the story delivered specific pre-determined messages
Tone	Whether the story was positive, neutral or negative
Share of ink	Total amount of coverage devoted to a topic, that is, quantitative measurement of volume of coverage against competitors in areas, such as media type, article type, and prominence
Share of voice	Percentage of coverage devoted to a client or product compared to competitors

Adopted from "Measuring PR: Output – The First Essential Step," ***PR Influences Newsletter,*** **July 2003**

Measurement of PR outcome

Outcomes are the end responses that a PR effort aims to achieve from its target audience. These responses can be changes in opinions, attitudes and behaviour. Outcomes of a PR program are not immediate. They are responses from the target audience that occur in the long run, as a result of consistent exposure to various PR efforts. It is difficult to measure PR outcomes since they are not immediate or visible just after a PR effort. Since PR outtakes and outcomes are qualitative in nature, in-depth surveys, reviews and analyses of the responses are required for measuring them. The measurement process involves the use of various statistical tools and survey techniques like correlation and regression analysis, multivariate studies, focus groups and qualitative attitude surveys. Some of the PR outcome measures include: attitude and preference measurement and behaviour measurement.

14.22 MARKETING CONTROL IN BRANDING

Customers have the freedom of choice to evaluate the product based on various criteria, such as search attributes, which allow them to assess the value of the brand before purchase; experience (use) attributes which allow assessment only after use; and credence attributes which cannot be completely assessed. Organisations respond to such pressures from the marketplace by nurturing strong brands. A brand is the proprietary, visual, emotional, rational and cultural image that one associates with an organisation or a product. It is always associated with a communication message, which it communicates to the consumers. It is this communication that binds the consumers in some psychological aspects to a brand, thus enhancing the brand image, brand personality and customer loyalty.

Brand equity denotes the value of a brand to the customer and the organisation. Organisations try to leverage the equity of an established brand to enter other categories of products. Brand equity not only creates a positive brand image, but also drives demand because customers are attracted towards a brand with better brand equity. In this section, we will discuss the concepts of brand equity and brand measurement. We will also discuss the technique of brand portfolio management.

14.22.1 Brand Equity

Apart from its role in adding value to customer, brand equity also adds value to the organisation by generating marginal cash flow. It helps organisations attract new prospects and retain old customers. High brand equity facilitates premium pricing and cost savings, because an organisation spends less on promotion. It also paves the way for brand extensions. Strong brand equity, when extended, will draw people to buy a product depending on their perceptions about the parent brand. Brand equity can also provide an advantage in the distribution channel, as more dealers and retailers will be willing to store more units of the product. It also acts as a deterrent to competitors by providing a competitive edge to the organisation.

Brand equity can be understood in terms of three underlying concepts: brand assets, brand strength, and brand value. Table 14.5 describes the three concepts.

Table 14.5: Brand equity – Underlying concepts

Concepts	*Definition*	*Remarks*
Brand assets	Attributes of the brand that affect the consumers' decisions	These attributes include brand awareness – whether the brand is well-known among customers, brand personality – the set of human characteristics associated with the brand, brand reputation, patents and right, etc.
Brand strength	The power that the brand exerts due to the presence of the brand assets at any given point and in any of the markets	Brand strength depends on market share, growth rate, loyalty rate, price premium, etc.
Brand value	Capability of the brand to generate profits for the organisation	It is estimated based on net discounted cash flows

Adopted from Kapferer, Jean-Noe, The New Strategic Brand Management, Creating and Sustaining Brand Equity Long Term, First South Asian ed. Kogan Page India Private Limited, 2004, p. 14.

14.22.2 Brand Measurement

Brand measurement is used to evaluate the brand equity of a brand. It helps in integrating the brand with an organisation's performance. Brand measurement can be conducted through different types of measurements: perception measurement, performance measurement, and financial measurement. Perception measurement includes attributes such as brand awareness and customer perceptions of quality, credibility, etc. Performance measurement includes attributes like customer preference and repeat purchase. Financial measurement includes market share analysis and market capitalisation.

A balanced scorecard for the brand helps the organisation to measure important behavioural dynamics and compare the position of the brand vis-à-vis its competitors.

A balanced scorecard for the brand helps the organisation to measure important behavioural dynamics and compare the position of the brand *vis-à-vis* its competitors. This helps in checking the strengths and weaknesses of the brand and in turn helps the organisation in strategic planning and marketing. The different perspectives of the balanced scorecards (as discussed in the earlier chapters) can be utilised to link brands to organisational performance.

The framework of the scorecard will vary from business to business depending on the business environment, the maturity of the business and the industry in which it operates. Some attributes like market share and goodwill will be common to all businesses.

The framework of the scorecard will vary from business to business depending on the business environment, the maturity of the business and the industry in which it operates. Some attributes like market share and goodwill will be common to all businesses.

14.22.3 Brand Portfolio Management

A brand portfolio includes all the brands that are managed by an organisation. Generally, it is seen that less than 20% of the brands in the brand portfolio contribute to the organisation's profits. For example, as of 1996, Nestle Ltd., had a portfolio of 8,000 brands of which only 200 that is, 2.5% of the brand portfolio, contributed to the overall profits of the organisation. Organisations may need to rationalise the number of brands in their portfolio. One of the ways of doing this is by conducting a brand audit.

Brand Audit

In order to carry out a brand audit, all the brands in the portfolio should be reviewed in terms of their respective market shares, their percentage contribution to the yearly sales and profits, and their positioning in the market. The figures showing the market and the percentages of sales and profits will help in understanding whether investing in any specific brand is feasible or not. Brands that are ranked low are the ones that have to be removed from the portfolio.

In order to carry out a brand audit, all the brands in the portfolio should be reviewed in terms of their respective market shares, their percentage contribution to the yearly sales and profits, and their positioning in the market.

Once the brands to be removed are short-listed, the organisation has to review the choices and decide which of the four strategies – merging (two brands are made into one), selling, milking (continue to use), or killing (stop producing) – it will adopt. The brands are merged when the products serve a specific segment in the market that has the potential to grow in future. Organisations adopt the selling strategy when a particular brand does not fit the corporate strategy of the organisations. When a product cannot be removed due to some strategic reasons or due to the emotional bonding that the customers have with the product, organisations minimise the expenditure on advertising these brands and market them only to gain profits. This is called milking. Organisation can decide to kill brands that do not appeal to the customers and the retailers.

There are brand management consultancies and market research companies that help organisations in managing their brand portfolio. For example Interbrand is one such company which offers services in brand research, integrated marketing and brand valuation. Another example is ACNielsen. Exhibit 14.3 outlines the brand management consulting service of ACNielsen.

Exhibit 14.3

Brand Cubed from ACNielsen

Brand Cubed from ACNielsen is a leading company in providing marketing information. It is a division of The Nielsen Company, which has its headquarters in New York, USA. Brand Cubed from ACNielsen offers measurements and analysis of market fluctuations and consumer preferences and behaviour.

The company launched a new brand management consulting service called Brand3 (Brand Cubed) in May 2007. Brand3 linked the measurement information from the retail market with household panel data and personalised survey results to get a comprehensive perspective of the brand equity in terms of consumer beliefs regarding the brand, style of shopping, buying behaviour, etc. This helped the organisations to assess their sales and positioning strategies, identify problems, recognise newer opportunities, and modify their marketing activities in such a way that to maximise the results. Brand3 could be customised to suit different users' needs through discussions with experts in the organisation.

Alastair Gordon, Managing Director for Customised Research Asia Pacific, The Nielsen Company, said, "*Brand3 breaks the boundaries of conventional analytics and unscrambles complex networks of data to offer an entirely new approach to brand-management consulting. This is the first service that delivers a truly three-dimensional understanding of their brands to clients – the attitudes that consumers hold in their minds about a brand, their actual purchasing behavior, and the place the brand holds within a product category. We are blending our advanced, proprietary customised research capabilities, our continuous market measurement and analytical research and our consultative expertise to help out clients develop unique and optimal marketing strategies for each of their brands.*"

Adapted from *"Nielsen Launches 'Brand Cubed', A Revolutionary, Integrated Brand-Management Consulting Service,"* ***ACNielsen News,*** *May 28, 2007, <http://www.acnielsen.co.in/news/20070528.shtml>*

14.23 INFORMATION SYSTEMS FOR MARKETING CONTROL

With the ever-changing nature of business operations, the information requirements of marketers are also changing rapidly. Another important feature of today's business operations is the speed with which decisions are taken. To be able to make such speedy decisions in a dynamic environment, a decision-maker should have the necessary data and information at his/her disposal, and the relevant tools to analyse these inputs and take effective decisions.

There are many ways in which information systems can be used in marketing control. In this section, we will discuss the marketing decision support system and marketing intelligence.

14.23.1 Marketing Decision Support System

The Marketing Decision Support System (MDSS) is a set of decision models with supporting hardware and software made available to marketing managers to assist them in analysing relevant business data and making better marketing decisions. Today more and more organisations are moving toward the use of MDSS in their decision-making. MDSS is mainly used in situations where semi-structured or unstructured data are available, that is, in situations where a lot of uncertainly exists and in which managers are forced to take decisions. These situations can be either internal or external to the organisation. Estimating market potential for a new product before its launch is one such situation.

MDSS can be used in the controlling function due to its ability to provide features such as system integration, aggregation and dis-aggregation of organisation data, and analytical efficiency.

MDSS can be used in the controlling function due to its ability to provide features such as system integration, aggregation and dis-aggregation of organisation data, and analytical efficiency. System integration refers to pooling of data into a large database that is shared by all the decision-makers whose decisions have an impact on the marketing function. These decision-makers are marketing managers, production managers, finance managers, etc. The aggregation and dis-aggregation features mean that data can be combined or broken down by the MDSS depending on the needs of the managers. This process saves a lot of time for the decision-makers thus allowing them to focus on the decision-making process rather than on data processing. Analytical efficiency is another feature of MDSS that detects the performance of the marketing function and its various sub-functions and tracks down any deviations in performance. This feature provides the decision-maker with a complete picture of the performance, deviations, if any, and their possible causes, and the extent to which these deviations may affect the whole organisation. This information enables the marketing managers and other managers to take the steps necessary to control the deviations and avoid them in future.

Benefits of MDSS

MDSS has many advanced features that help the decision-makers in the process of decision-making. It acts as a supportive tool, provides information about various activities, and helps in information analysis. Some of the benefits an organisation can avail of from MDSS are given below.

1. It increases the effectiveness of marketing decisions by providing quality information.
2. MDSS can break down complex chunks of information into simple parts, thereby allowing the decision-maker to analyse each part thoroughly.
3. It can be used to integrate information with other departments in the organisation. This enhances coordination between departments and leads to effective functioning of all the departments.
4. MDSS also analyses the decision situations and presents the analysis reports to the decision-makers. This reduces the time consumed in analysis, which can be used to select the best course of action from the choice set.
5. It helps the marketing managers in the controlling function by identifying the deviations at an early stage. This gives the managers sufficient time to control the deviations and prevent their recurrence.
6. MDDS is flexible enough to allow the decision-makers to tackle unforeseen marketing situations efficiently and effectively.

14.23.2 Marketing Intelligence

Business intelligence involves collecting information through human, electronic or other means and analysing it with respect to both the internal and external environments in which the organisation functions. Business intelligence offers managers updated and precise information that helps them devise and execute policies that can assist the organisation in catering to or sustaining its competitive advantage. The business intelligence system used in marketing is called the marketing intelligence system.

The systems for customer relationship management and database marketing are the systems that utilise the most sophisticated business intelligence functions. These systems help to measure the correlation between marketing activities and their business outcomes. Marketing intelligence systems also help managers monitor the performance of their sales force and assess the contribution of the marketing function to the organisation's profits.

Two companies that offer marketing intelligence systems are Oracle Corporation and SAP AG. Exhibit 14.4 describes the Oracle® Daily Business Intelligence (DBI) for marketing applications.

Exhibit 14.4

Oracle® Daily Business Intelligence (DBI) for Marketing

Oracle Corporation (Oracle), based in California, USA, was established in 1977. It is one of the leading developers of Database Management Systems (DBMS) and Enterprise Resource Planning (ERP) software.

The Oracle® Daily Business Intelligence (DBI), developed for marketing applications, helps managers track and control the most important activities in the marketing function. It was one of the components of the Oracle E-Business Suite of applications. These applications helped in converting the collected data into information, which helps the organisation enhance its competitive edge. Some of the salient features of DBI are given below.

Analysing the marketing expense: Organisations could use DBI to set a threshold Return on Investment (ROI) for the activities undertaken. By comparing the market budget utilisation and the ROI for an activity, the marketer could decide whether to continue with the activity or abort it.

Evaluating the effectiveness of the market segment: DBI offers a detailed segment analysis intelligence, which helps organisations to determine whether a given segment is viable and profitable.

Monitoring the impact of marketing activities on revenue trends: DBI helps managers to calculate the contribution of their activities to the profits of the organisation.

*Adapted from **Oracle Daily Business Intelligence for Marketing.** <http://www.oracle.com/applications/cpm/dbi_marketing_ds.pdf>.*

14.24 SALES FORCE AUTOMATION AS A CONTROL TOOL

Managers find that sales force automation gives them more control over the activities of their sales force. Sales force automation can be used in the following ways:

Surveillance and control: Surveillance is used for closely supervising and monitoring the behaviour of the sales force. This function of sales force automation should be used carefully as employees should not feel that their privacy has been encroached upon. Also, enough information should be available to facilitate productivity improvement of the sales force.

Sales force automation brings about standardisation in the way business is conducted. Sales force automation may help in preventing the sales force giving unwarranted and unacceptable discounts to customers.

Accountability: Sales force automation helps in increasing the interaction between managers and the sales force. This increase in interaction encourages the sales force to take responsibility for their actions. It also helps the sales force by allowing them to voice their questions and concerns easily and to get answers faster.

14.25 MOBILE CRM

Advancements in technology of mobile communications have provided organisations with new ways of conducting business and reaching out to their customers. One of the most widely known solutions in this aspect is Mobile Customer Relationship Management (mobile CRM), which can be defined as an extension of the traditional CRM, wherein a mobile, remote access or wireless component application is incorporated into the standard CRM system. Mobile CRM makes it more convenient and efficient for mobile field forces such as sales, service and technicians to interact with customers. Typical examples in this regard are Mobile Sales Force Automation (Mobile SFA) and mobile field services.

Mobile Sales Force Automation (SFA): Mobile SFA is an extension of corporate CRM/SFA systems to mobile devices. This solution enables personnel to access product information, pricing, and inventory status and customer information on their mobile devices and enables them to perform contact management, calendar entries, opportunity analysis and order management functions while away from their office.

Mobile Field Service Management (FSM): Mobile FSM involves extending the relevant components of FSM to mobile devices used by the service technician to deliver services to customers in the field. This facilitates bi-directional interaction with customer support, scheduling and dispatch, service order and contracts management, service parts management, and possibly other components of the FSM application such as knowledge management.

14.26 ENTERPRISE-WIDE APPLICATIONS

Enterprise-wide applications are used by many organisations to improve their overall control over business operations, such as customer relationship management and enterprise resource planning. Sales force automation is a part of enterprise-wide applications. Exhibit 14.5 explains how enterprise-wide applications can be utilised to improve the business operations in the marketing function.

Exhibit 14.5
Use of Enterprise-Wide Applications in Marketing Control

Many organisations invest in information technology in the form of Enterprise-Wide Applications (EWA). EWA comprises Enterprise Resource Planning (ERP), Customer Relationship Management (CRM), Sales Force Automation (SFA), etc. According to a survey conducted in India by *Network* magazine, 45% of the organisations surveyed had invested in EWA (as of June 2006). The highest number of users used the ERP systems which formed the first step toward implementing CRM. ERP is implemented to integrate data with their programs.

CRM offers a comprehensive list of customers to the organisations and SAF helps the organisation to have fairly good control over the supply chain and improved communications with the sales force. These attributes triggered investments in these applications by Fast Moving Consumer Goods (FMCG) and pharmaceutical companies, which have a diverse and large presence in all types of markets.

The investments in data warehousing and business intelligence was the highest in the FMGC sector, which involves longer supply chains and larger retail networks. Data warehousing and business intelligence help organisations to improve their decision-making capabilities.

Patni computer used ERP systems for their finance and HR functions, and Siebel CRM module for their customer relationship function. They also implemented SEA to track the sales form the acquisition of the customer to closing of the deal. Rallis India invested in SAP for their applications like sales and distribution and quality management.

SUMMARY

Marketing controls are used to implement marketing strategies and to check whether the objectives of the marketing function are achieved or not. Marketing controls are of four types - strategic controls; annual plan control, profitability control, and efficiency and effectiveness controls.

Strategic control helps the organisation to evaluate its strategies by focusing on the outcomes control, implementation control, strategic surveillance and special alert control.

Annual plan control involves the use of annual marketing targets as performance standards. Projected values of sales volume, market share, and profits are some of the typical performance standards under this type of control. Two important techniques used for marketing are expenses and sales analyses.

Marketing profitability is the profitability achieved through performance of marketing activities and is calculated based on the investment made in these activities. Some of the techniques used for profitability control are strategic profit model, segment margin report and activity based costing.

Efficiency control is more of a quantitative control and deals with the efficiency with which the marketing activities are directed towards achievement of goals of the marketing function. Here, the controls mainly focus on the sales volume, the sales generated by each salesperson, the number of accounts handled by each salesperson, etc. Effectiveness control, on the hand, is qualitative in nature and aims at improving the effectiveness of marketing activities. The marketing effectiveness of any organisation is reflected through its market share, profitability, customer satisfaction, etc. It is not easy to audit, measure or control and depends on attributes like customer philosophy, marketing orientation, information about marketing, strategic orientation, and operational efficiency of the organisation.

A functional management audit of marketing is referred to as a marketing audit. It is used as a communication tool, an analytical framework to help take decisions and to frame policies. A marketing audit can be of two types: external in which the factors audited are external to the organisation and cannot be controlled: and internal where the factors audited are internal to the organisation and can be controlled.

A marketing audit is a detailed and systematic analysis. It helps the senior management to identify the strengths and weakness of the organisation, along with opportunities and threats in the market. An effective marketing audit is systematic, comprehensive, independent and periodic.

The audit is conducted in three stages: extensive analysis of the present and past marketing activities of the organisation, forecast of the organisation's growth relative to the changing market conditions, and suggestions for improving the quality of plans and the marketing performance.

Sales control is a major component of marketing control and involves the control of the sales function as a whole and the sales force in particular. Sales control includes sales budgets, sales quotas, reporting, credit control, performances evaluation and performance based compensation and sales force automation.

There are different types of sales budgets: sales revenue budget, selling-expenses budgets and sales department administration budget. A rolling budget provides for an additional time period apart from the actual budget period. Flexible budgets allow managers to revise and update the targets set at the beginning of the budget period.

A selling-expenses budget can be developed using different methods, such as the affordability method, the percentage-of-sales method, the competitive parity method, the objective-and-task method and the returns-oriented method. Budgeting establishes the objective and responsibilities of all departments and employees and in turn facilitates performance evaluation and control. Budgets are used to achieve coordination between different business segments, and for seeing that the performance does not deviate significantly from the plan.

Quotas are quantitative sales goals assigned to sales people for a given time period: the quotas can be specified in terms of sales volume or value, profit, expenses or activities. Sales quotas can be set, not only for individual salespersons, but also for a sales team or a territory. Sales quotas are used to specify performance targets and standards, communicate change of direction, and motivate the sales force.

Sales analysis involves gathering, classifying, and studying the sales data of an organisation. It is one of the means by which an organisation can analyse its performance and it helps sales managers to plan and direct the sales efforts. It helps the organisation in the overall management of its operations.

Marketing cost analysis helps an organisation to identify opportunities to increase the effectiveness of its marketing expenditure. The different types of analysis used are: sales variance analysis, market share analysis and marketing expenses-to-sales variance analysis.

Sales reports are used as a method of tracking and monitoring the performance of the sales force. Information on sales, expenses, sales personnel performance, etc., is collected through a formal reporting system. The two primary types of sales reports are: sales and expense reports and other reports. The sales and expense reports are used by the sales management as a tool to evaluate actual performance and the other reports include sales forecasts and other inputs for planning.

The credit control mechanism involves two steps: analysing the accounts receivables, which helps in finding out why some of the debts have gone bad and also the amount and type of receivables; and credit rating of customers and channel members. Not having a proper credit policy in place will affect the profitability of the organisation.

Performance evaluation is a formal and planned system for measuring and evaluating the performance of salespersons. Performance evaluation is generally used to assess the performance of a salesperson; it can also be used as a tool by the management to motivate him/her.

Sales force compensation is used as a way of controlling the sales force and is often dependent on the sales volume generated. Sales force compensation is generally made up of two components: salary and incentives. There are various factors and situations to be considered in deciding when the incentives component should be higher and when the salary component should be higher.

Sales force management audit is a cross-functional exercise that evaluates the entire selling operation of an organisation. A sales force management audit involves evaluation of the sales management environment (both extra-organisational and intra-organisational), sales management planning system, sales management organisation and sales management functions.

Distribution control involves channel integration, channel management, evaluating channel performance and managing channel conflicts.

Channel integration can be achieved in two ways: through vertical marketing systems and horizontal marketing systems. Channel management helps organisations reduce costs, reach potential customers, and make profits. It involves four steps: selection and recruitment of channel members, motivating channel members, evaluating the performance of channel members and modifying the existing channel arrangements to suit the market changes.

Evaluation is carried out at both the macro-level and the micro-level. At the macro-level, the societal contributions made by the intermediaries are assessed in terms of channel efficiency, productivity, effectiveness and equity. The objectives of performance management at the micro-level are profitability, goal attainment, pattern maintenance, integration and adaptation.

Channel conflicts can arise from either structural causes or attitudinal causes. The commonly used conflict resolution strategies are negotiation and bargaining, problem-solving strategies, persuasion, political strategies and co-operation.

Apart from sales control, marketing communications control includes control of advertising, sales promotion, direct marketing, public relations and brand management. Advertising effectiveness can be measured through copy testing or message testing and by monitoring recognition, recall, persuasion (attitude change) and purchase behaviour. The effectiveness of internet advertising can be measured by considering four aspects: the purpose of the advertisement, the value of the intended outcome, the number of times the purpose was fulfilled and the cost incurred on advertising.

The effectiveness of sales promotions can be measured in two ways: direct evaluation and indirect evaluation. In indirect evaluation, volume is used as the parameter for measurement, whereas in indirect evaluation, indicators of sales are used as the parameters.

Direct marketing involves direct communication with customers to obtain an immediate and measurable response. The steps in direct marketing are developing a framework for the direct marketing campaign; developing the direct marketing campaign; implementing the campaign and evaluating the campaign. Evaluation of the campaign is carried out through evaluation of response and profitability. The response needs to be evaluated both qualitatively and quantitatively. Profitability analysis is carried out by assessing the costs incurred by and the profits generated for the organisation.

Public Relations (PR) are defined as any effort or measure undertaken to promote a strong image of an organisation or its products in the mind of the public. PR measurement and evaluation involves assessment of the success or failure of PR strategies, activities and tactics in producing the desired outputs, outtakes and outcomes.

Brand equity can be understood in terms of three underlying concepts: brand assets, brand strength and brand value. Brand measurement, which is used to evaluate the brand equity of a brand, includes perception measurement, performance measurement and financial measurement. A balanced scorecard for the brand helps the organisation to measure important behavioural dynamics and compare the position of its brands with those of its competitors. This helps in checking the strengths and weaknesses of the brand and, in turn, helps the organisation in strategic marketing and investment planning.

Brand portfolio management is an important activity for organisations. It can be carried out through a brand audit, which helps organisations to rationalise the number of brands in their brand portfolio to achieve better profitability.

The Marketing Decision Support System (MDSS) is a set of decision models with supporting hardware and software available to marketing managers to assist them in analysing relevant business data and making better marketing decisions.

Marketing intelligence offers managers updated and precise information which helps them to devise and execute strategies that can help the organisation increase its competitive advantage. It helps organisations assess the contribution of marketing activities to the profits of the organisation and also monitor the performance of the sales force.

Sales force automation helps in improving relationships with customers, and monitoring the activities of the sales force. It helps in standardisation of processes and procedures that are used in business. Sales force automation can be used for surveillance and control and also to increase the accountability of the sales people. Some of the ways in which automation is achieved are through mobile CRM and enterprise-wide applications.

Review Questions

1. What are the various types of control in marketing?
2. Explain the concept of marketing effectiveness.
3. What is a marketing audit? Explain the concepts of internal and external marketing.
4. How does one achieve sales control? Explain with an example.
5. Enumerate the role of sales and marketing budgets in controlling an organisation's revenue generation.
6. Explain sales reporting with an example.
7. How does credit control help in sales control?
8. What is marketing communication control? How does one achieve it?
9. How can the sales force automation help in control?

Analytical Question

The sales team of Raj Furniture is facing severe competition from local manufacturers. Earlier, loyal buyers were shifting to local manufacturers in the gray market because of lower prices and the facilities of easy instalments available for credit purchase.

Raj Furniture is known for good quality material and artistic finishing, which made their products costlier. In addition they use a distribution channel which includes stockists and their commission. Recent inclusion of new technology has made the cost of the furniture even higher. Raj Furniture knows that it would not be able to do without these interventions if it has to target the up market customers, but it is leading to a loss of lower end customers.

Explain how Raj Furniture should deal with this situation and its strategies in marketing control.

CHAPTER 15

Performance Report and Reward System as a Tool of Control

LEARNING OBJECTIVES OF THE CHAPTER

- The concepts of variance analysis
- The use of variance analysis
- The concepts of a reward system in the organisation
- The concepts of designing a reward system for the business

15.1 INTRODUCTION

The variances can be positive or negative depending on the trend of the business, the well being of the business and the direction in which the economy is moving.

Budgets are made to accomplish business goals with appropriate financial control. The actual performance of a business may vary from the budgeted value of an activity. The difference is called the variance. The variances can be positive or negative depending on the trend of the business, the well being of the business and the direction in which the economy is moving.

It should be remembered that variances are always determined on the basis of a reference and the correctness of that reference is very important in calculating that variance.

The idea of calculating the variance is to find the deviation, the cause of deviation and the corrective measures that need to be taken to bring the values to those in the budget. The control system should be designed in and around the deviations where larger variances are observed.

15.2 ANALYSIS OF VARIANCE

The financial aspect of a business organisation is divided into two categories: expenses and the income (revenue). Therefore, variance analysis is also of two kinds, variances in revenue and variances in income. Both of these are divided into two further categories: volume variance and price variance. The classification is based on the practical assumption that the factors that determine all expenses and revenues are dependant on volume and price. Expenses are further divided into manufacturing and non-manufacturing costs. The manufacturing costs can be of three types: variable, semi-variable and fixed costs. A diagrammatic representation of the cost allocations is given in Figure 15.1.

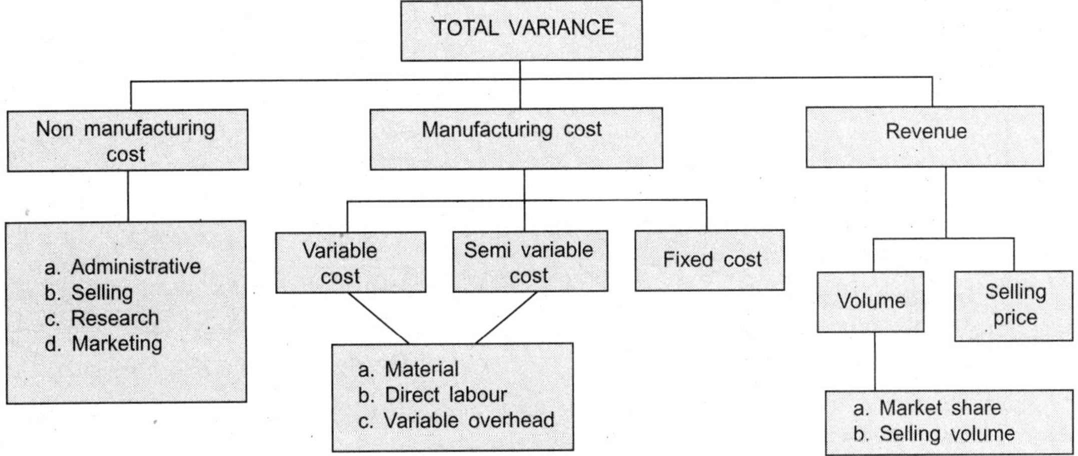

Fig. 15.1: Cost allocations for the purpose of variance analysis

Information on costs is collected to determine the extent and the dimension to which the revenue are affected by the business operations. The costs are measured against the standard cost set up by the management.

Eric L. Kohler defines standard cost as "*a forecast or pre determination of what actual cost should be under projected condition, serving as a cost control and as a measure of production efficiency or standard of comparison when ultimately aligned against actual cost. It furnishes a medium by which the effectiveness of the current results can be measured and the responsibility for the deviations can be placed.*"

Variance analysis helps the management to identify each variance and identify the manager responsible for it. The reasons for conducting a variance analysis are as follows:

1. To identify the key factor likely to affect operational profit
2. To focus on the key variables, if the variance of the profit is negative
3. To segregate the causal factor by keeping another independent factor constant
4. To identify the sequence of impact on the variables and their impact on the operational profit

15.3 TYPES OF STANDARDS IN STANDARD COSTING

There are three types of standards as given below.

1. **Current standards:** Standards related to current conditions, which are established for use over a short period of time.
2. **Ideal standards:** Standards which can be attained under the most favourable conditions in a business.
3. **Expected or attainable standards:** Standards which are expected to be attained during a future specified budget period. These standards are taken to be more realistic rather than those under the most ideal conditions. These type of standards are best suited from a control point of view since they reveal the real variance from the attainable performance.

15.4 SETTING STANDARDS

Setting standards involves the following steps:

1. Setting up a standard committee, which involves persons from all levels of management and includes the key functions of the business.
2. Identifying costs for which standards are set. These include:
   a. Labour costs where the standard quantity and standard price is determined.

b. Direct labour costs, which involve standard time and standard rate of wage.
c. Overhead costs where the standard variables overhead and standard fixed overhead rate are considered.

15.4.1 Analysis of Variance

Analysis of variance is helpful in controlling the performance and achieving the planned profits.

The deviations of the actual cost or profit or sales from the standard cost or profit or sales are known as "variance(s)".

When the actual cost is less than the standard cost or the actual profit is better than the standard profit the variance is 'favourable'. If the reverse occurs it is called 'un-favourable'.

Variances of different items of cost provides the key to cost control because they show whether and to what extent the set standards have been achieved. This in turn helps to set up a reward system so that managers who minimise variance are rewarded.

Variances of different items of cost provides the key to cost control because they show whether and to what extent the set standards have been achieved. This in turn helps to set up a reward system so that managers who minimise variance are rewarded.

Another common method of classifying variance is as controllable and non controllable. Controllable and non controllable variables depend on a set of exogenous and endogenous factors.

Analysis of variance may be carried out with respect to each of the element of cost i.e., materials, labour and overheads.

Material cost variances

The material cost variance deals with the variances in the materials used. Material cost variance is calculated under the following five heads.

1. Material cost variance
2. Material price variance
3. Material usage variance
4. Material mix variance
5. Material yield variance

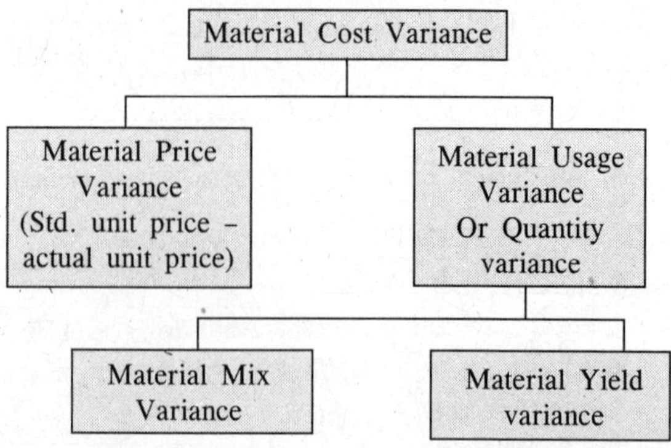

Fig. 15.2: Material cost variance

We will try to understand these variables one by one.

1. **Material cost variance**

Standard cost of material for actual output – Actual cost of material used

or = Material price variance + Material usage or quantity variance

or = Material price variance + Material mix variance + Material yield variance

2. **Material price variance**

This is the part of the material cost variance that is due to the difference between the standard cost of materials used for the output achieved and the actual cost of materials used. In other words, it can be expressed as:

Material price variance = Actual usage (Standard unit price – Actual unit price)

Here, Actual usage = Actual quantity of material (in units) used and

Standard unit price = Standard price of material per unit

Actual unit price = Actual price of material per unit

3. **Material usage (or quantity) variance**

It is that portion of the material cost variance, which is due to the difference between the standard quantity of materials specified for the actual output and the actual quantity of materials used. It may be expressed as:

Material usage variance = Standard price per unit (Standard quantity – Actual quantity)

Example 15.1 explains the variables.

Example 15.1

The standard materials required to manufacture one unit of product of 'X' = 10 kgs and the global price per kg of material is Rs. 25. The cost accounts records, however, reveal that 11,500 kgs of material costing Rs. 2,76,000 were used for manufacturing 1,000 units of product 'X'. What are the relevant material variances observed?

Solution :

Standard price of material per kg = Rs.25

Standard Usage unit of products 'X' = 10 kgs

Therefore, standard usage for an actual output of 1,000 units of product 'X' = 1,000 × 10 kgs = 10,000 kgs

Actual usage of material = 11,500 kgs

Actual cost of material = Rs. 2,76,000

Actual price of material per kg $= \frac{\text{Rs. } 2{,}76{,}000}{11{,}500} = \text{Rs. } 24$

(a) Material cost variance
Standard cost of material – Actual cost of material
or Standard usage × Standard rate – Actual usage × Actual rate
= 10,000 kgs × Rs. 25 – 11,500 kgs. × Rs. 24
= Rs. (2,50,000 – 2,76,000) = Rs. 26,000 (Adverse)

(b) Material price variance
Actual usage (Standard unit price – Actual unit price)
11,500 kgs (Rs.25 – Rs.24) = Rs.11,500 (Favourable)

(c) Material usage variance Standard unit price (Standard usage – Actual usage)
Rs.25 (10,000 kgs – 11,500 kgs) = Rs. 37,500 (Adverse)

4. Labour variance

The value of wages paid and use of labour often do not match in terms of the budget. As a result there is always a problem in assessing the efficiency of the labour and deciding on the rewards to be given. The labour variance is a measure to find out the cost and time variance in use of labour as against the set standards.

The labour variance can be classified as follows:

a. Labour Cost Variance (LCV)
b. Labour Rate Variance (LRV)
c. Total Labour Efficiency Variance (TLEV)
d. Labour Efficiency Variance (LEV)

The variances are explained below:

a. Labour cost variance: This is the difference between the standard cost and labour allowed (as per standards laid down) for the actual output achieved and the actual cost of labour employed. It is also known as wages variance.

This variance is expressed as:

Labour cost variance = Standard cost of labour – Actual cost of labour

b. Labour rate (of pay) variance: It is that portion of the labour cost variance that arises due to the difference between the standard rate specified and the actual rate paid. It is calculated as follows:

Rate of pay variance = Actual time taken (Standard rate – Actual rate)

c. Total labour efficiency variance: It is that part of the labour cost variance that arises due to the difference between standard labour cost of standard time for actual output and standard cost of actual time paid for it. It is calculated as follows:

Total labour efficiency variance = Standard rate (Standard time for actual output – Actual time paid for)

d. **Labour efficiency variance:** It is that portion of labour cost variance that arises due to the difference between the standard labour hours specified for the output achieved and the actual labour hours spent. It is expressed as:

Labour efficiency variance = Standard rate (Standard time for actual output – Actual time worked).

Here standard time for actual output means the actual time allowed for the actual output achieved. Actual time worked means actual labour hours spent minus idle hours.

Example 15.2

Malavya DTP centre which processes the daily data for a local paper in India is largely a labour oriented company. Given below are the data of the company in terms of the labour (workers) used. It is required to find the labour variances from the information given below.

	Standard	Actual
Number of men employed	100	90
Output in units	5,000	4,800
Number of working days in a month	20	18
Average wages per man month	Rs. 200	Rs. 198

Solution:

To calculate the standard rate, actual rate, standard time and actual time which are not directly given in the example.

Standard wages per man per month = Rs.200
Standard working days in a month = 20
Standard rate per day = Rs. 200/20 = Rs.10

Actual wages per month = Rs.198
Actual working days in a month = Rs. 18
Actual rate per day = Rs. 198/18 = Rs. 11
Standard man days for an output of 5000 units = 100 × 20 = 2000 man days
Standard man days for the actual output of 4,800 units = 2000/5000 × 4,800
= 1,920 man days
Actual man days = Men × working days = 90 × 18 = 1620

a. **Labour cost variance**

Labour cost variance = Standard cost of labour – Actual cost of labour

For, 5,000 units standard cost of labour = 100 workers @ Rs. 200 = Rs. 20,000.

Therefore, for the actual output of 4,800 units, standard cost of labour = Rs. 19,200 – Rs.17,820 = Rs. 1,320 (Favourable).

b. **Rate of pay variance**

Actual time × (standard rate – actual rate)
1,620 man days × (Rs. 10 – Rs. 11) = Rs. 1,620 (Unfavourable)

c. **Labour efficiency variable**

Standard rate (Standard time – Actual time)
Rs. 10 (1,920 man days – 1,620 man days) = Rs. 3000 (Favourable)

5. Overhead variance

The overhead cost variance can be defined as the difference between the standard overhead allowed for the actual output achieved and the actual overhead cost incurred. In other words, overhead cost variance is under or over absorption of overheads. The formula for the calculation is:

Actual output × Standard overhead rate per unit – Actual overhead cost

or

Standard hours for actual output x Standard overhead rate per hour – Actual overhead cost

Overhead cost variance can be classified as:

a. Variable overhead variance
b. Fixed overhead variance

a. Variable overhead variance: It is the difference between the standard variable overhead cost allowed for the actual output achieved and the actual variable overhead cost. This variable is represented by expenditure variance only because variable overhead cost will vary in proportion to production so that only a change in expenditure can cause such a variance. It is expressed as:

Actual output × Standard variable overhead rate – Actual variable overhead

or

Standard hours for actual output x Standard variable overhead rate per hour – Actual variable overheads

Some accountants also determine the variable overhead efficiency variance in the same way as labour efficiency variance. Variable overhead efficiency variance can be calculated if there is information relating to the actual time taken and the time allowed. In such a case variable overhead variance can be divided into two parts as given below:

a. Variable overhead expenditure variance or Variable overhead budget variance

= Actual hours worked × Standard variable overhead rate per hour – Actual variable overhead

or

Actual hours (Standard variable overhead rate per hour – Actual variable overhead rate per hour)

b. Variable overhead expenditure variance or Variable overhead budget variance

= Standard time for actual production × Standard variable overhead rate per hour – Actual variable overhead – Actual hours worked × Standard variable overhead rate per hour

or

Standard variable overhead rate per hour (Standard hours for actual production – Actual hours)

Variable overhead efficiency is similar to the labour efficiency variable and is calculated in the same way.

Example 15.3

Malavya DTP centre has furnished the following information regarding their overheads. From the data, calculate the variable overhead variance.

	Budgeted	Actual
Variable overhead	Rs.2,50,000	Rs. 2,60,000
Output in units	25,000	20,000
Working hours	1,25,000	1,10,000

Solution:

Standard variable overhead per unit = Rs. 2,50,000/ 25,000 = Rs. 10

Standard variable overhead per hour = Rs. 2,50,000/1,25,000 = Rs. 2

Time allowed per unit of output = 1,25,000/25,000 = 5 hours

Variable overhead expenditure variable

Actual hours worked × Standard rate per hour – Actual overhead

1,10,000 × Rs. 2 – Rs. 2,60,000 = Rs. 40,000 (adverse)

Variable overhead efficiency varianceStandard time for actual performance × standard variable overhead rate per hour – Actual hours worked × Standard variable overhead rate per hour

= 1,00,000 × Rs. 2 – 1,10,000 × Rs.2 = Rs. 20,000 (adverse)

Now, standard time for actual production = time allowed for 20,000 units of actual output @ 5 hours per unit i.e., 1,00,000 hours

Total variable overhead variance

20,000 × Rs.10 – Rs.2,60,000 = Rs.60,000 (adverse)

b. Fixed overhead variance

It is the difference between the Standard Fixed Overhead Cost and the Actual Fixed Cost Overhead. In normal circumstances, this may be nil, however, when overhead of machinery and other fixed assets are done, this variance is observed.

6. Some other variances used in the control of a business organisation

Some other common variances that are used in a management control system are given below.

a. **Selling price variance:** The selling price variance is calculated by multiplying the difference between the actual price and the standard price by the actual sales volume. This is clearly explained in Table 15.1.

Table 15.1: Selling price variance

Particular	*Product X*	*Product Y*	*Product Z*
Actual volume	100	200	150
Actual price	9.00	20.50	25.00
Budget price permitted	10.00	20.00	30.00
Actual overhead (under price per unit)	(1.00)	(0.50)	(5.00)
Price variance	(100)	100	(750)

b. **Market penetration variance and industry volume variance:** One extension of revenue analysis is to separate the mix and volume variance into the amount caused by the difference in market share and the amount caused by difference in industry volume. The idea is that the business unit managers are responsible for the market share, but the state of the economy decides the industry volume. For this purpose, the industry sales data are also needed to exactly represent the performance of a business unit. The calculations due to the market share and due to industry volume variance are shown in Table 15.2.

Market share variance = [(Actual sales) – (Industry volume) × Budgeted market penetration × Budgeted unit contribution)]

Industry volume variance = [(Actual industry volume – Budgeted industry volume) × Budgeted market penetration × Budgeted contribution per unit]

The variance is found for each product separately and the sum of the variance of all the products gives the total variance. Table 15.2 shows that Rs. 1,040 is the variance due to market penetration and the remaining Rs. 460 results from industry volume variance.

Table 15.2: Variance in market share and industry volume

A Budgeted Sales Volume				
Particulars	*Product X*	*Product Y*	*Product Z*	***Total***
Estimated industry volume (units)	833	500	1,667	**3,000**
Budgeted market share	12%	20%	6%	**10%**
Budgeted volume (units)	100	100	100	**300**
B. Actual Market Share				
Industry volume, units	1,000	1,000	1,000	**3,000**
Actual sales	100	200	150	**450**
Market share	10%	20%	15%	**15%**
C. Variance due to Market Share				
1. Actual sales (units)	100	200	150	**450**
2. Budgeted share at industry value	120	200	60	**380**
3. Difference (1 – 2)	(20)	-	90	**70**
4. Unit contribution (budgeted)	2.00	9.00	12.00	-
5. Variance due to market share	(40)	-	1080	**1,040**
D. Variance due to Industry Volume				
1. Actual industry volume	1000	1,000	1,000	**3,000**
2. Budgeted	833	500	1,667	**3,000**
3. Difference (1 – 3)	167	500	(667)	-
4. Budgeted market share	12%	20%	67	-
5. (3) × (4)	20	100	(40)	-
6. Unit Contribution (budgeted)	2.00	9.00	12.00	-
7. Total (5 × 6)	**40**	**900**	**(480)**	**460**

b. Expense variance: Expenses are divided into fixed and variable costs. The variance between the actual and budgeted fixed costs is obtained simply by subtracting one from the other, as these costs are not influenced by the market sales or volume. The budgeted variable manufacturing costs must be adjusted to the actual volume of production. Table 15.3 explains how the amount has been spent at the actual level of production.

Table 15.3: Variable manufacturing expenses variance

	X	*Y*	*Z*	*Total*	*Actual*	*Variance*
Material	75	84	300	459	470	(11)
Labour	15	18	20	53	65	(12)
Overhead (variable)	30	30	40	100	90	10
Total	120	132	360	612	625	(13)

It is assumed that all the products that are manufactured are sold in the same period. In reality however, the production volume differs from the sales volume, and so the cost difference would definitely change.

15.5 VARIANCE IN PRACTICE

The different ways to calculate the variance are: time period comparison, focus on gross margin, evaluation standards, full cost systems and amount of detail information. These approaches are described below:

1. **Time period comparison**

   Year to date information is used by some companies for the basis of comparison. They use data up to the end of June as a comparison for a six month period. Other companies use the budget for the whole year and compare it against data of the whole year. The actual figures are taken for the first six months and the estimates of revenues and expenses for the next six months.

   A comparison of the annual budget with the current expectation of actual performance for the whole year shows how closely the business unit managers are expected to meet the annual profit target. If the performance for the year to date is worse than the budgeted for the year to date, the deficit is likely to be overdue in the remaining month. However, the reason why the actual performance is below that budgeted for the year to date may be expected to continue for the remainder of this year, which is likely to make the final figure significantly different from the budgeted amounts.

2. **Focus on margin**

   In preparation of a budget, selling prices are assumed to remain constant throughout the year, however, in practice this is often not feasible. Moreover, the task of the marketing manager is to obtain a budgeted gross margin – that is, a constant spread between costs and selling prices. So, it is necessary to consider the 'gross margin variance' rather than actual performance of profit.

3. **Evaluation standards**

   The formal standards used in the evaluation of reports on actual activities are of three types: (a) predetermined standards, (b) historical standards and (c) external standards.

   a. *Predetermined standards*: These are also called budgets and are carefully planned and coordinated, so they are considered to be excellent standards. Most companies take these as a basis against which actual performance is compared. But, environmental uncertainties affecting the performance of a responsibility centre are often large in number, and so these become unreliable.

   b. *Historical standards*: These are records of past actual performance. Results for the present month are compared with the results of the last month or with results for the same month a year ago. However, there are two serious weaknesses in this: (i) the environmental conditions might be different in the two periods, (ii) the performance in the prior period may not have been acceptable. Despite these inherent weaknesses, these standards are used in many companies where valid predetermined standards are not available.

   c. *External standards*: These standards are derived from the performance of other responsibility centres or other companies. The performance of the sales office of one branch may be compared with the performance of the sales offices of other branches. Such a comparison may provide an acceptable basis when the conditions in the responsibility centres are similar.

4. **Full cost system**

   In a full cost system, the manufacturing cost of a product includes both its variable costs and an allocation of fixed costs. Companies that operate under a full cost system may not be able to separate the volume of production for absorption of variable cost and even if they do so, they have to identify the variance in manufacturing costs that result from the difference between actual and standard production volumes. A 'production volume variance' occurs when the actual volume is different from the standard volume.

15.6 LIMITATIONS OF VARIANCE ANALYSIS

Variance analysis tells us that there is a variance but does not explain why the variance occurred. Another problem with variance analysis is to decide whether a variance is significant or not. Yet another limitation of variance analysis is that, as the performance reports become more aggregated, offsetting variances might mislead the interpreter. For example, a manager might notice that the business unit manufacturing cost performance was as per the budget, which may have been the result of a good performance of one plant offsetting the bad performance of another plant.

Some variances occur due to exogenous factors such as inflation. There is no point in investigating them and this should be understood by managers using such variances. Besides, we should understand that variance analysis is regressive in nature and thus does not give a future vision. It only tells what has happened and not what might happen. Variance analysis is limited to those events, which are recorded in the accounts and not beyond it.

15.7 TIGHT VS LOOSE CONTROL

The concept of tight control emanates from the idea that subordinates work most efficiently and effectively, if they are monitored closely, when they are forced to meet specific goals. Under 'tight control' the profit goal of business unit managers is considered to be a firm commitment against which he or she will be measured. Thus, a manager's performance is evaluated primarily on his or her ability to attain the budgetary objectives of the organisation. The idea of such a control closely endorses the variance analysis and helps in generating a control mechanism, which is based on deviation measurement. Loose control on the other hand is based on the philosophy that people work best if they are not forced by the management to do the work. The idea here is that the best people were chosen for the job and they will perform as per expectations. They consider that the cause for failure is not the employees' fault. The management overviews the entire project, but it does not study each and every report in detail. Here the concept of variance analysis is used only as a guideline, rather than a measurement of performance.

15.8 REWARD FOR GOOD PERFORMANCE

Variance analysis shows whether the performances of the managers are up to mark or not. Good or better variances are indicative of good performance and are accordingly used for revising the standards. Good performances are generally associated with rewards. A reward system is directed towards inducing a high performance by an individual, group or organisation. Care is also taken to see if the reward system is integrated with the overall goal realisation of the business. Generally, in India, the rewards system is skill based since it relies heavily on parameters which are drawn from the skill sets. Rewards are also used to motivate employees. Hence, rewards are looked upon as important source of communication and feedback. The rewards act as a positive communication about the good performance of the individuals in an organisation.

15.9 PURPOSE OF A REWARD SYSTEM

There are three purposes of a reward system: First, rewards act as a recognition of the good work done by an individual in a company, and creates a sense of belongingness for the individual in the company. Since, most of the employees are considered as internal customers, a reward system is taken as a method of recognising their status in the company.

Second, a reward system acts as a good communication line in a business. Rewards help in matching the needs of customers and managers, since they are the outcome of a performance measurement system. It may be noted here that, good performance can be expected through a proper performance system only when the aspirations of the employees are reflected in the appraisal system and such aspirations are a part of the greater good of all the stakeholders in the business.

Third, it acts as a morale booster for the employees, in either a monetary or non monetary form. It also helps employees upgrade their skills as the rewards are directly related to the skill sets.

15.10 REWARD THROUGH COMPENSATION

Apart from performance rewards, certain monetary and pecuniary benefits come to the employees through regular payments such as salary, benefits and incentives. Salaries are contractual payments, which are given at the end of the month depending upon the number of days worked and certain other conditions fulfilled. Benefits depend on the nature of the business and the kind of contract that is entered into between the employees and the company and of course the kind of benefits the employees of other competing firms receive. Incentives on the other hand are completely performance based and depend on the kind of targets laid down and that were actually accomplished.

1. **Salary:** Salaries are contract payment given to the employees by the employer at the end of each month. Calculated on the basis of the number of working days, it is either expressed as a part of the yearly payment or monthly payment, depending upon the nature of the contract. Salaries generally depend upon the nature of the business, the payments made by competitors, the inflation rate, the negotiation forums such as workers' unions and last but not least, the legislation passed by the government in the state. Salary generally comprises the basic payment, the dearness allowance and the housing rent allowance (based on the cost of living index of a city). Salaries are a very critical area of management and are directed towards providing the right kind of motivation to the right group of employees, retaining employees and acknowledging the efforts made by individuals towards the organisation.
2. **Benefits:** Benefits are provided to employees to meet contingencies and social obligations. They help in meeting the social and psychological needs of the employees. Safety measures, health insurance and pension are some of the common benefits that are given to employees across the board, the world over. The objective of providing benefits is to boost the morale of the employees, improve their work life and help them to develop loyalty to the company.
3. **Incentives:** Incentives are the third component in the compensation package. The first two components are more or less fixed in nature, but the third one is a variable component and varies with the performance of the individual. In the spirit of it, it is one of the most important tools in the hand of the management.

Incentives are designed to give benefits to employees. Incentives are mainly used to motivate employees. Hence, it is the duty of the senior managers to see that the incentives planned, are the best the industry can offer. The second reason for incentives is to control non performing managers. However, incentive plans should be designed on a positive note and not as a tool to punish employees, although in most cases the concept of the carrot and stick works. Corporate incentives are designed keeping in mind the best practices in the industry and the laws, which allow corporates to have the incentive plans approved by their stakeholders.

Incentives are given based on either long term or short term performance. Short term incentives are usually based on the performance of employees in the year for which they are given the incentives. Long term incentives are given as a part of the long term accomplishments in the business.

15.11 PERFORMANCE VARIABLES

Performance variables are established to coordinate the interests of stakeholders with those of managers. These variables ensure that the reward system is able to match the pay to individual performance, taking into consideration individual competencies, skills and team input. The different types of performance variables are:

1. **Controllable:** Managers should be rewarded on the basis of variables that are under their control and influence. Such a reward system will be fair. On the other hand, when the rewards are based on variables that are outside the control of the managers, the reward system is more arbitrary.
2. **Non controllable:** Some unfairness does creep into the reward system when the managers hold their subordinates responsible for things beyond their control. In such a case, the attention of the subordinates leans towards the uncontrollable variable. The compensation that the corporate has to pay for these undesirable factors is quite heavy and sometimes unethical.
3. **Financial:** Performance variables are of two kinds, financial and non financial. Financial variables are widely used and understood and are drawn from accounting information.
4. **Non financial:** There are a number of variables that are non financial like motivation, appreciation etc. which are important in a business. Such variables are the key to the reward system.
5. **Feedback:** A reward system based on behaviour and performance sends signals to the employees as to what the organisation expects from them. The most powerful positive communication about performance is the reward given by the company to its employees.

15.12 DESIGNING A REWARD SYSTEM

The largest problem in designing a reward system is to understand what is considered as a reward to the management or a manager for that purpose. Whereas monetary rewards act as the best motivator in some case they may work against the system at a later time.

In most cases, integrating a reward system with that of a management control system, gives autonomy to a manager. The sense of authority that comes along with it is considered to be the best reward, which complements the management control system.

The values and culture of an organisation strongly influence the reward system of an organisation. Communication and integration of structures are strong motivators. The involvement of the employees in the decision making process and the problem solving process are a powerful incentive.

In designing a reward system it should be kept in mind that targets for the employees should be attainable. Targets that are easily achieved are poor motivators as they do not give individuals the scope to extend themselves and grow.

Both formal and informal rewards should be given. Whereas performance should be directly related to a formal reward system, such as monetary incentives, improvement of self respect and morale should be linked to an informal reward such as awards, trophies and promotions.

SUMMARY

This chapter laid down the concepts of variance analysis and how rewards can be used to reduce variance and induce good control in an organisation. The cost of production, which has essentially two forms, i.e., direct and overhead, varies from the budgeted targets due to several reasons including abnormality of performance, and unreachable and improperly designed targets. Often the management focuses on performance only through cost measurement, which may be undesirable. Disconnections between the purpose of the business and the achievements, as seen by the variance, are often not taken into consideration when designing a reward system. This makes the process more difficult. In order to promote connectivity, it is necessary that both short and long term goals are set by the management in a more achievable and measurable way. The attainment of these goals should be linked to formal rewards, such as monetary incentives and non monetary and informal rewards such as esteem and autonomy.

Review Questions

1. Why is it necessary to carry out a variance analysis for a business?
2. What are the major considerations in carrying out a variance analysis for a business?
3. How is variance analysis used in setting a target for the employees?
4. What is the role of a reward system and how can it be linked to the variance analysis of a business?
5. What are the major considerations in designing a reward system for management control?

Analytical Questions

1. If you were to design a control system for a computer production business, which operates offshore as well as onshore, what factors will you consider while measuring the variance?
2. In the same context as above, what factors should you keep in mind while designing a reward system?

PART—D

MANAGEMENT CONTROL OF SPECIAL ORGANISATIONS

CHAPTER 16

Management Control in Multinational Companies

LEARNING OBJECTIVES OF THE CHAPTER

- Issues in transfer pricing
- Issues in exchange rates
- Issues in designing a control system for an MNC
- Issues in translation effects
- Issues in economic exposure
- Issues in transaction effects
- Consideration in management for control systems

16.1 INTRODUCTION

As a business grows in size it is difficult to limit the operations to one geographical location.

The search for new markets leads most of the big companies in the world to establish their business across the globe. Due to this expansion and changes in the business scenario a number of problems have arisen.

To start with, there are the cross cultural issues leading to varied business issues, which can only be addressed if all the differences in the cultural issues can be addressed completely, which is not possible.

Then there are long and short term legal issues that a business with global and/or offshore operations will have to address.

Challenges also arise pertaining to the revenue reorganisation and consolidation in the business. The nature of the problem is compounded due to the various accounting practices and different exchange rates that prevail in the business and market.

Generally, inter-national business houses which have an international business (normally called a multinational company) operate the responsibility management way, i.e., creating revenue, investment profit and cost centres. However, this does not change the complexity that was discussed earlier. This means that problems have to be approached in a way that will allow for the issues discussed above.

Generally, inter-national business houses which have an international business (normally called a multinational company) operate the responsibility management way, i.e., creating revenue, investment profit and cost centres.

16.2 CONSIDERATIONS OF MANAGEMENT CONTROL IN MNCS

The main issue that is faced by such businesses is the problem of price fixation, especially, when the product is transferred between the holding and the subsidiary company. In this case equity becomes a key issue.

The domestic laws which bind the parent company are different from the laws faced by the subsidiary. Hence, the prices and tariffs these companies charge are different, leading to a major challenge for the management in designing a control system.

The various business issues that arise out of international joint ventures encompass legal and socio-economical dimensions, which have to be addressed by managers when they are designing a control system for the business.

A multinational business faces a large number of issues that are related to foreign exchange and the risks associated with it. Consolidation of revenue in the business is affected by the various issues associated with foreign exchange.

16.2.1 Transfer Pricing

Transfer pricing is a method, which tries to measure the value of the services and products between two responsibility centres within the same company.

The need for transfer pricing arises due to a number of factors. Some of these factors are purely aimed at the measurement of profit whereas others are a result of managing the costs (refer to earlier Chapter 10 for the details). In addition, multinational companies have to address the various tariffs and rates, taxation laws and the different kinds of exchange that the business functions with.

Transfer pricing is a method, which tries to measure the value of the services and products between two responsibility centres within the same company.

16.2.2 Tariffs and Rates

Tariffs and rates are levied on imported goods, and generally increase their price. This has a huge impact on transfer pricing since the value of the transfer price and consequently the resultant profit will be affected by the rate of such tariffs. A multinational company has to be careful about the value of transfer and match the same with the value of the export to the host country.

16.2.3 Foreign Exchange

The problem of foreign exchange, for a multinational company, from the transfer pricing angle is two-fold. In the first place, if the host country's exchange is stronger than that of the domestic country, the resultant transfer of goods would result in an increase in the price of the goods in the domestic country. In such a case, the resultant profit will fall due to decreased demand if the prices cease to be competitive.

The second dimension of the problem starts with the fact that many domestic countries may restrict the availability of foreign exchange for transferring goods. In this case, a lower transfer price allows the firm to transfer a larger amount of goods.

16.2.4 Funds Accumulation

Transfer pricing serves as a method for a firm to siphon funds from one country to another. There may be several reasons behind this, and the motive may vary from one firm to another or from one country to another, but there will definitely be legal implications of some kind.

16.2.5 Joint Ventures

Joint ventures may lead to further complication as there is a tendency to price the components higher, depending upon the economic position of the party and its share in the venture. The higher transfer may be resisted by the country where the transfer is taking place, because this will result in a higher price of the product.

16.2.6 Legal Aspects

From a legal point of view, transfer pricing has to be addressed on two issues, the first being tax laws and the second being the pricing.

Since, the taxation laws prevalent in various countries are different, multinational companies have a tendency to evade tax by using these loopholes. For example assigning profit to a low tax country may decrease the total tax burden of the company. However, this may have serious implications on the pricing, since assignment of profit will lead to higher investment in the domestic country, higher cash flow and resultant higher idle assets.

Transfer pricing in itself is highly regulated in many countries because of the ulterior motives of the multinational companies. The Organisation for Economic Cooperation and Development (OECD) and the World Trade Organisation (WTO), have acknowledged three methods of transfer pricing which are given below in order of descending priority.

Transfer pricing in itself is highly regulated in many countries because of the ulterior motives of the multinational companies. The Organisation for Economic Cooperation and Development (OECD) and the World Trade Organization (WTO), have acknowledged three methods of transfer pricing which are given below in order of descending priority.

1. **Comparable uncontrolled price method**

   Transfer price = Price paid in comparable uncontrolled sales +/– Adjustments

   In this case one of the members of the group involved in transfer pricing is not in the control group.

2. **Resale price method**

   Transfer price = Applicable resale price – Appropriate mark ups +/– Adjustments

   Applicable resale price denotes the price at which property purchased in a controlled sale is resold by the buyer in an uncontrolled sale.

   Appropriate mark up = Applicable resale price × Appropriate mark up percentage

   Appropriate mark up percentage = Percentage of gross profit (expressed as a percentage of sales) earned by the buyer (reseller) or by another party in an uncontrolled purchase and resale similar to controlled resale.

3. **Cost-plus method**

   Transfer price = Cost + Appropriate mark ups +/– Adjustments

   Appropriate mark up = Cost × Appropriate gross profit percentage

   Appropriate gross profit percentage = Gross profit percentage (expressed as a percentage of cost) earned by the seller or another party on uncontrolled sales similar to controlled sales.

16.2.7 Environmental Aspects

Multinational corporations are affected by two kinds of environmental issues. In the first place, they have to deal with the natural environment and the consequences that their business has on it. Each country has a different set of laws that guides such issues besides the international standards that are faced by the country. This apart, there are the pressure groups, which act to achieve several issues ranging from political to social causes, which have to be addressed by multinational corporations.

they have to deal with the natural environment and the consequences that their business has on it. Each country has a different set of laws that guides such issues besides the international standards that are faced by the country. This apart, there are the pressure groups, which act to achieve several issues ranging from political to social causes, which have to be addressed by multinational corporations.

The governments of the various countries where these MNCs operate also act as legal and regulatory boundaries for these companies. One example here would be the tobacco and cigarette manufacturing companies, which face several levels of regulatory prohibitions in different countries. Yet, they are perhaps one of the most successful multinational businesses.

Internationally, transfer prices are decided in such a manner that the transfer of tangibles and intangibles are carried out at the

Internationally, transfer prices are decided in such a manner that the transfer of tangibles and intangibles are carried out at the same price for the related parties across the globe. By the same price it is meant that the price is the same as that which would have been charged to an unrelated party. This is otherwise known as an ***'Arms Length Transfer Pricing'****.*

same price for the related parties across the globe. By the same price it is meant that the price is the same as that which would have been charged to an unrelated party. This is otherwise known as an **'Arms Length Transfer Pricing'**.

Multinational companies interact with the related parties in such a way as to transfer income from a higher tax jurisdiction to a lower tax jurisdiction. Therefore, it is essential that countries that have a high tax enact laws to see that multinational companies do not withdraw the profit they earn in these countries[1].

16.3 ISSUES OF EXCHANGE RATE

Multinational corporations carry out transactions in various currencies. This means the domestic country faces a number of disparities in terms of foreign exchange, which result into differential cash flow and various kinds of profit. The problem is compounded when the MNCs try to consolidate their account in terms of the currency of one country. The MNCs face three kinds of currency exposure, namely, translation, transaction and economic.

16.3.1 Exchange Rate Exposures and MNCs

The exchange rate denotes the price of one currency in terms of another currency. It can be expressed either as the number of units of the home currency required to buy one unit of foreign currency (referred to as the 'direct quote') or the number of units of foreign currency that are required to buy one unit of the home currency (referred to as the 'indirect quote'). For example, if the Indian rupee is the home currency and the US dollar is the foreign currency, then to express the exchange rate as $ 0.03/Re is the direct quote, and to express it as Rs. 47.75/$ is the indirect quote. Both types of quotes are used in the market for foreign exchange. However, traders usually use one type or the other for a particular currency.

The exchange rates that are usually quoted (such as those given in Table 16.1) are termed as normal exchange rates. The normal exchange rate that prevails on a given day is called the 'spot' exchange rate. The spot exchange rate, after adjusting for inflation differentials between the two countries in question, is the real exchange rate. Forward exchange rates are the exchange rates at the present time at which a transaction can be entered into for completion at some future date.

Table 16.1: Exchange rates for various foreign currencies (as on November 2006)

Country	Monetary unit	Rupees per unit foreign currency (direct quote)	Foreign Currency units per Rupee (indirect quote)
United States of America	US Dollar	44.86	0.022
United Kingdom	Pound Sterling	85.24	0.011
European Community	Euro	56.99	0.017
Germany	Deutsche Mark	54.19	0.018
France	French Franc	35.36	0.028
Japan	Yen	37.98	0.026

Source: **The Economic Times of India**

In using the direct quote if there is a rise in the number of rupees required to buy a unit of dollar, then the rupee is said to have undergone depreciation in relation to the foreign currency and vice versa.

With the advent of a floating exchange rate system in the early 1970s, there have been substantial swings in real exchange rates, even for the most traded currencies. If the currency of one country becomes stronger in terms of another currency by a certain percentage, then the companies in the country, whose currency has become stronger, become competitively stronger by the same percentage against the country whose currency has lost value.

---

[1] It is a matter of concern that India as a country is one of the highest tax jurisdictions in the world. We may therefore say that if laws relating to transfer pricings are not set in India, there may be a shift of income by multinational companies.

1. **Translation exposure**

Fluctuations in the exchange rate affect the income and balance sheets of companies either positively or negatively. The depreciation or appreciation of the value of earnings, assets and liabilities is referred to as translation exposure. This exposure arises out of the MNCs' maintenance of accounts in a single currency in the parent country. However, an MNC conducts its business in several currencies. For example ITC maintain its account in rupees in India. As the value of the rupee fluctuates in various countries where it has its operations, the income in the profit and loss account and balance sheet is affected.

The depreciation or appreciation of the value of earnings, assets and liabilities is referred to as translation exposure.

2. **Transaction exposure**

Transaction exposure indicates the exchange rate exposure that the firm has in its cross border transactions, when such transactions are entered into at a particular time, but payments to settle the transaction are made at some future date. If nominal exchange rates change during the interim period, and the payment or receipt commitments are outstanding, the value of the transaction is put to risk. Examples of such transaction costs include receivables and payables, and debts or interest payments outstanding in foreign currencies.

Transaction exposure indicates the exchange rate exposure that the firm has in its cross border transactions, when such transactions are entered into at a particular time, but payments to settle the transaction are made at some future date.

3. **Economic exposure**

Economic exposure, also referred to as the operating exposure or competitive exposure, occurs when the firms' cash flows change in the real exchange rate. Such exposure may occur due to several reasons including currency rate adjustment by the parent country where the MNC operates.

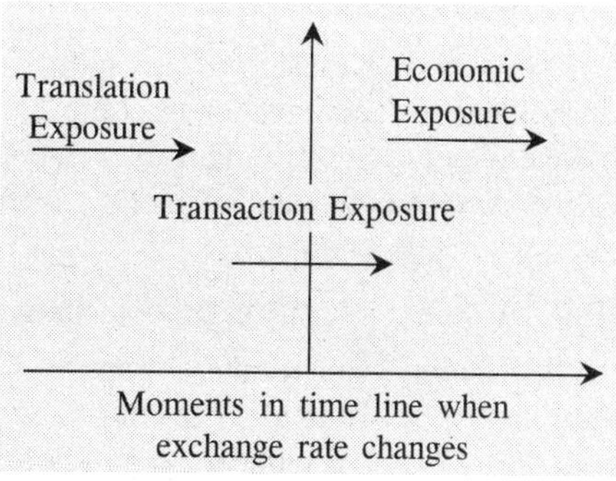

Fig. 16.1: Different types of exchange rate exposure on various moments on a time line.
Source: D. Eitman and A. Stonehill, *Multinational Business Finance*, Reading Mass: Addison Wesley, 1989

16.4 ISSUES IN DESIGNING A CONTROL SYSTEM FOR AN MNC

In designing a control system, the questions that need to be answered are mostly for performance evaluation. Some of them are listed below.

- Should the responsibility for the impact of exchange rate fluctuation on the bottom line be that of a subsidiary manager?
- Should the home currency or local currency be used by the parent company to carry out performance evaluation? Further, should it make use of the initial exchange rate, the project exchange rate or the ending exchange rate in setting and tracking budgets?
- Should a distinction be made by the parent company between the effects of various types of exchange rate exposure while evaluating the performance of the subsidiary managers? If yes, how is this to be done?
- How should various types of exchange rate exposure affect the evaluation of the economic performance of the subsidiary, as distinct from the evaluation of the subsidiary managers?

16.5 ISSUES OF MANAGEMENT CONTROL IN MULTINATIONAL COMPANIES

There are many issues that a multinational corporation has to face in order to control foreign operations, chief amongst them is the issue of strategy in determining the design for the control system for foreign companies.

1. Role of control in foreign operations

To determine the control for a foreign company by a multinational corporation it is essential that the strategy that is to be adopted for it is determined. The next step is to determine the key success factors under the strategy for the business. This enables the company to decide the appropriate degree of autonomy for its foreign operations as well as the appropriate management control system that needs to be in place.

The most commonly followed strategies in such a case are:

(*a*) To penetrate a host country market with new and innovative products that are appropriate for the host markets.

(*b*) To fully utilise the production capacity in the home country by producing additional products for the host market

The first strategy requires paying closer attention to the host market characteristics. More innovations in product development are required under this strategy.

If the first strategy is followed a significant amount of autonomy and decentralisation has to be in place for business in the foreign companies. The management control system has to therefore give a substantial amount of thought to the autonomy in this case.

Depending on the nature and volume of the business, the parent company may allow a production facility at the host location and give it a substantial amount of cost and quality responsibility. In this case a profit centre establishment in the foreign country will be in place.

In the second strategy, since it is based on economy of scale, the production should be carried out at a place where it can be done best and most probably in the parent country and not the host country.

In this case establishment of a revenue centre in the foreign market will be in place since the market is to host the revenue for the parent company.

Since all the profits are recorded by the parent company, transfer from the domestic to the foreign market would probably take place at the standard cost. There would be very limited autonomy for the foreign operations, which would be reflected in the design of the management system.

Apart from these two strategies there are many other strategies for entering the foreign markets. Some of them are discussed in detail hereafter along with the additional issues involved in them.

2. Analysis of foreign projects

In the analysis of foreign projects, there are a lot of surprises in store for the unwary analyser having only a domestic orientation. A number of refinements to the net present value model are necessary in order to evaluate foreign investments properly. The principle differences between domestic and foreign investments that should be considered during an analysis of a foreign project include political and economic risks, which are dealt with later in this book.

3. Evaluation of foreign projects

According to Persen and Lessig (1979), '*Almost without exception, the procedures used in measuring domestic profitability were expanded and modified to apply to foreign units when the firm expands overseas.*'

'Firms' attempt to 'export' their control systems to their overseas operations by making appropriate adjustments for the new demands that arise as an outcome of foreign operation.

'Firms' attempt to 'export' their control systems to their overseas operations by making appropriate adjustments for the new demands that arise as an outcome of foreign operation.

4. Transfer pricing for affiliates

Except for one very important difference, the transfer pricing problem for a multinational firm is similar to that of a domestic firm. In the case of a domestic firm, transfer pricing mainly affects the allocation of the firm's total profit amongst the various profit centres. It does not have a direct impact on taxes paid by the corporation. In a domestic firm, the transfer price does create strong motivations, and may have an impact on the total profit of the firm, but will not affect the total tax burden for a given level of income before taxes. For a multinational corporation on the other hand, transfer prices affect the level of taxes paid for a given level of income before taxes, and thus their importance, not only to the firm but also to the government of the present company as well as to the government of the host company.

5. Budgeting for foreign affiliates

Comparison of actual versus planned financial performance in the context of the operating budget is the most common method of evaluating the performance of foreign affiliates. The complexities that may be encountered in budgeting for overseas operations revolve around exchange rate considerations. The issues faced in this context are use of the correct exchange for consolidation of accounts and performance reports. The responsibilities of the manager regarding the management of the various kinds of risks arising out of the foreign exchange, which is going to affect the business in the long run, need to be determined.

6. Taxation issues for foreign affiliates

Ordinarily taxes are levied by the host country on the income of an MNC earned in that country. These rates, which differ from country to country, are sometimes offset by the concessions granted to the MNC in return for some desired services (such as generation of employment, transfer of technology etc.) provided by the MNC to the host country.

Further, an additional tax is levied by many countries on the portion of the profits repatriated to the home country in the form of dividends. In addition, profits repatriated from the foreign operation are taxed by many home countries.

Major variations occur from country to country in the taxation of MNCs. The complications that arise due to taxation in evaluating foreign projects of MNCs may be directly incorporated into the NPV models when project evaluations are done.

7. Political and social considerations

The businesses are subject to expropriation by the government of the host country due to economic reasons. Such expropriation may result in the nationalisation of corporate property with or without full compensation. There are several cases where the government of countries such as Bolivia, Chile, India had expropriated the property of MNCs.

There may also be other political and social interference, which although not as dramatic as expropriation, is also a risk to MNCs in certain foreign countries where they operate.

To counter political risk, it is possible to insure an investment at book value against expropriation and include the insurance premium as a charge against the project.

In dealing with political risk, many MNCs adopt a 'go or no go' approach and refuse to consider investment in nations deemed to have an unfavourable investment climate, unstable political conditions or where the courts cannot be relied upon to uphold contractual relationships.

In politically unstable nations, the minimum discounted payback period is a practical guide to investment decision making. This criterion, coupled with the purchase of political risk insurance, enables MNCs to reach satisfactory results in foreign countries.

8. Economic and exchange rate risks

Economic risks are much easier to manage than political risks. Exchange rate changes and inflation are the two principle economic risks that can influence the success of a project. In many respects, these two risks are opposite sides of the same coin because, if allowed to seek their own level, exchange rates will move in the opposite direction to the relative rates of inflation.

The exchange rate influences the dollar cash flow from foreign investments and also influences the revenue of a project denominated by local currency. Prices for output will fall relative to the price charged by the competitors in the event of devaluation.

Changes in exchange rate not only affect the local revenues, but also the costs. There will be an increase in the prices of raw materials imported from countries against which the local currency has been devalued. Moreover, since domestic inflation often accompanies devaluation, the prices of raw materials purchased locally will rise. As costs and prices rise, so will wages. Therefore, if there are risks of exchange rate changes, these risks should be reflected in estimates of project cost and benefits.

Changes in exchange rate not only affect the local revenues, but also the costs. There will be an increase in the prices of raw materials imported from countries against which the local currency has been devalued.

9. Goal congruence issues

The primary concern of the parent company is that its earnings and return on investment capital are translated into the parent country's currency. If the parent company is in the United States, consolidated statements prepared by it shall be in terms of dollars. Payments of dividends and statements of its objectives and goals for the foreign operations shall be in terms of United States dollars.

Hence, from the perspective of goal congruence, the parent company would like to budget using projected exchange rates at the end of the period since this is most reflective of the parent company's interests. Furthermore, using the same criterion, the parent company would like results reported in terms of actual exchanges rates, which reflect the actual translated sums that the parent company receives.

SUMMARY

In this chapter we focused on the issues that a multinational corporation faces while transacting its business. The fact that the business needs to be integrated across the globe exposes them to various risks, which include political, social and economic risks. Integration and consolidation of the earnings by the parent company in the parent country from the host countries face several challenges, including the challenges of appropriate transfer pricing system. The value at which the transfer takes place is affected by the cost as well as the exchange risk exposure by the company. Currency risk exposure is of several kinds, so the business needs to respond to each risk with a different strategy. Each strategy therefore uses different kinds of control mechanics. An internally and externally focussed strategy combined with a centralised control mechanism with decentralised function is often sought. Depending on the strengths of the parent country's economy and the economy of scale that the MNC needs to achieve, the control response changes.

Review Questions

1. Why is it that multinational corporations try to consolidate the accounts in terms of the currency of the parent country? Is there any exception to this?
2. What are the issues in transfer pricing that a multinational corporation faces?
3. Enumerate the various risks that are associated with currency exchange in business.
4. While designing a management control system for a multinational corporation what are the major factors to be considered? Does culture play any role in the issue?
5. What do you think an MNC based in India should do to minimise its exchange risk in the business? (Answer from a control view point).
6. Why should a country like India insist that multinational companies operating in India, be incorporated in India?

7. Do you think there are any issues where there is a goal conflict in deciding the transfer pricing?

Analytical Question

A company is based in India and wants to expand its business in terms of operation and production in two countries where it is currently having good sales figures. It has found that production in these countries will bring down the inventory and freight costs drastically, besides leading to a reduction in certain other costs like insurance and currency risk coverage cost. The options open to them are the United States of America and Uganda. If the goods are produced in Uganda, they can be exported to the USA. However, the laws in Uganda require a subsidiary with a host partner, whereas the laws of the United States of America are liberal on such issues.

As a student of control, what will be your suggestions to the company so that control of the company will not be jeopardised and the business will benefit from the decision? Defend your answer from as many angles as possible. (Note: Advice not to opt for the business expansion will lead to substantial losses).

CHAPTER 17

Management Control for Service Organisations

LEARNING OBJECTIVES OF THE CHAPTER

- The characteristics of a service organisation.
- The key issues of designing the control system for a service organisation.
- The issues relating to the management control of some specific service organisations, like financial organisations, insurance companies, non profit making organisations and government organisations.

17.1 INTRODUCTION

Service organisations are a major contributor to the economy all over the world. In India alone 52 percent of the GDP accounted for service organisations in both the organised and unorganised sector.

Service organisations refer to organisations that produce and market intangible products. They range from hotels and personalised services on one hand to health care, banking, insurance and research and development on the other. In between there are organisations which provide necessary services and social services.

Service organisations refer to organisations that produce and market intangible products. They range from hotels and personalised services on one hand to health care, banking, insurance and research and development on the other. In between there are organisations which provide necessary services and social services.

In this chapter we will examine the nature and problems associated with the service organisations and management control in particular. We will also deal with the specific problems of service organisations in general and industries such as banking, insurance and NGOs in particular to address the issues of management control.

17.2 THE SERVICE SECTOR

All over the world there has been a shift in the way human beings are looking at work. A brief review shows that mankind has moved from agriculture to manufacturing and is slowly shifting towards services. Although all forms of organisations coexist in the world, the number of persons employed in service industries has drastically increased. In India, the maximum number of people in service organisations are employed in the banking and financial sector.

17.3 CHARACTERISTICS

Exercising management control in a service organisation is different from that in other organisations discussed in earlier chapters. This is mainly due to the fact that service organisations are very different from other organisations.

17.3.1 No Inventory Buffer

Unlike manufacturing organisations, services organisations do not have an inventory buffer.

Unlike manufacturing organisations, services organisations do not have an inventory buffer. Thus unlike manufacturing organisations, they cannot use the inventory to manage the cost of production. Also in the short run in a manufacturing organisation, there are little or no variable costs as they are essentially fixed. It is not possible for an accounting firm to reduce its cost by laying off staff for a short period or for a hotel to gain a cost advantage by closing the booking in one of its wings.

It is not possible for an accounting firm to reduce its cost by laying off staff for a short period or for a hotel to gain a cost advantage by closing the booking in one of its wings.

In service organisations, the current capacity and matching demand serve as a key success variable to design a control mechanism.

In service organisations, the current capacity and matching demand serve as a key success variable to design a control mechanism.

In service organisations there is often a peak season and an off-season. Service organisations manage these key variables by way of lower prices and higher marketing efforts during the off season and vice versa. Some examples of key factors in these industries are the load factor for an electricity company, student enrolment in management schools, occupancy rates in hotels, hospital enrolment to bed availability in a hospital, and programming hours to available manpower in the software industry. These factors are used extensively by these industries to sensitise their control systems.

17.3.2 Problems in Quality Control

It is extremely difficulty to ensure quality control in a service organisation. This is because there is no physical product on which the quality parameters can be judged. The quality of a service organisation cannot be set like that of a manufacturing organisation where the defects per number of product manufactured can be gauged. The method used today to ensure quality in service organisation is by standardising the processes involved to attain the end result. However, this is not a fool proof system as a good educational system does not essentially ensure the best manager or the best judiciary does not always give the correct judgment.

17.3.3 Labour Intensive

Since service organisations are highly labour intensive, it is unlikely that costs can be reduced through reducing labour costs. Besides, most of the service industries depend heavily on the knowledge of the workers. The higher the knowledge requirement of the industry, the greater is the cost associated with it.

Since service organisations are highly labour intensive, it is unlikely that costs can be reduced through reducing labour costs. Besides, most of the service industries depend heavily on the knowledge of the workers. The higher the knowledge requirement of the industry, the greater is the cost associated with it.

17.3.4 Multi Unit Organisations

Service units operate through several small and medium size operating units. These units provide similar services to customers. Analysing their performance is difficult, since they operate through a profit centre mechanism. It is essential that organisations that have several units choose a statistical technique to determine the good, average and bad performers and this forms the basis of the control system.

17.3.5 No Quantity to be Measured

Service organisations face the problem of identifying which factors constitute the quantity of the service provided by them. This often makes it difficult for the organisation to keep a track of their output. Though there are quite a number of complex units that can measure the units of service, it is almost impossible to make a correct estimation of the number of units the service organisations can have in terms of output.

17.3.6 Difficulty in Using Costing Techniques

Cost management techniques are based on historical data assimilated from the manufacturing units which have enriched management control systems in their own way. The services sector and industries do not have such data, hence cost management becomes a difficult proposition.

17.4 PROFESSIONAL ORGANISATIONS AND THEIR CHARACTERISTICS

Professional organisations are those that provide specialised services rendered by an individual or a group of professionals. Organisations such as chartered accounting firms, law firms or engineering firms are examples of such professional firms. They are largely impacted by the design of management control and are therefore different from organisations that are into manufacturing.

17.5 ISSUES IN PROFESSIONAL ORGANISATIONS

Due to their nature, the issues of control in professional organisations are different from those in other organisations. For example, the goals are based on the clients they are dealing with and therefore change accordingly.

1. **Organisational goals**

   Unlike a manufacturing unit, the goal of a professional organisation is not just to maximise its earnings. The goals of a professional organisation depend on the skill set of the professionals and the direction in which they would like to grow in their profession. For example, a goal of a law firm may be "not to deal with clients whom they believe to be on the wrong side of the law." However, such a goal could be a deterrent to the profession, because it is not professional to deem a person guilty without proof. Thus organisational goals of a professional firm are highly subjective depending on the needs of its clients.

Unlike a manufacturing unit, the goal of a professional organisation is not just to maximise its earnings. The goals of a professional organisation depend on the skill set of the professionals and the direction in which they would like to grow in their profession.

2. **Professionals**

   Professional organisations are created and sustained by the knowledge of a group of professionals. The assets of the organisation are therefore knowledge and human capital which is very difficult to price and articulate (in fact there are hardly any organisations which are completely involved in it).

3. **Output-input measurement**

   It is very difficult to measure the output and input of work in a professional organisation. Therefore it is not possible to measure the productivity of the organisation or the individuals accurately. As a result, designing a control system around such issues as productivity is not possible for a professional organisation.

   The work carried out by professionals is non repetitive and hence no correct measurement is possible. Several task level controls have been designed by various accounting firms, but they are only applicable to clerical work.

The work carried out by professionals is non repetitive and hence no correct measurement is possible. Several task level controls have been designed by various accounting firms, but they are only applicable to clerical work.

   Keeping track of the time spent on work by a professional is not possible since there is hardly any line of divide between personal and professional work in the case of many professionals.

4. **Size of an organisation**

   Most professional organisations are small in size and operate at a single location where seniors in the business monitor and motivate the juniors in the profession. Therefore, there is not much need of developing sophisticated control mechanics.

5. **Marketing**

   The concept of marketing cannot be clearly defined in a professional organisation. Clients are approached through word of mouth, professional contacts and sometimes by means of informal meetings, which arise out of the current business. Therefore, designing a control system around marketing inputs as in a manufacturing company is not possible.

17.6 ISSUES IN MANAGEMENT CONTROL SYSTEMS

The considerations for a management control system are directed more towards issues concerned with pricing, profit centres, transfer pricing, budgeting, operational control and performance reporting. These issues are very different from those faced by other organisations.

17.6.1 Pricing

Pricing is an important consideration in designing a management control system. The difference in a service organisation is that it cannot work out a typical unit cost of its services as in a manufacturing company. The most common method of pricing in a services organisation is by taking the unit of time of the service rendered. Another common method is the 'service fee,' which is the total charges for the services rendered. This is a common practice in stock broking and merchant banking firms. Software services also add the cost of training and development while valuing a service. However, all factors of pricing in the services industry are directed towards finding a 'profit' in the service fee.

17.6.2 Profit Centres and Transfer Pricing

The use of profit centres in manufacturing companies is common. In the case of service organisations a profit centre pertains to support centres and the actual service providing centres. It is customary to set a profit centre for all support centres that can be run on a standalone basis of business.

17.6.3 Budgeting

In a service organisation the principle asset is the quality of human resources in the firm. The budgeting (which is the essence of control in a business) generally revolves around the manpower budget which takes care of both short and long term requirements.

17.6.4 Control of Operations

Estimating the idle time and the actual hours of work as against the total hours available (called the billed time) is an important issue in designing the control of such an organisation. One of the greatest problems of a service organisation is not being able to set a task level control, since the level of a task is mutually decided between the members of the professional team.

17.6.5 Reporting Progress

Reporting progress in a service organisation is difficult because it is not possible to measure the end product. Also, trivial matters may be reported by the professionals being evaluated and may not yield the results. Besides level of participation in formal reporting is generally low in case of services organisations, since the services tend to spill from one point of time to another, making it difficult both to report and control.

17.6.6 Performance Measurement and Appraisal

The absence of objective criteria for measurement in the case of service organisations makes performance measurement difficult. The performance measurement of the top level management is relatively easy since it can be assessed against the goals reached. The lowest level is even easier to assess, since it is a measurement of a task set and completed. It is the middle level management, which is the most difficult to measure.

17.7 SOME SPECIAL SERVICE ORGANISATIONS

The design of a control system for service organisations has several characteristics that are specific to them. There are some service organisations that have their own specific processes which need special consideration while determining the control system. Some of these specific services organisations, which are unique and need special consideration, are discussed below.

The design of a control system for service organisations has several characteristics that are specific to them. There are some service organisations that have their own specific processes which need special consideration while determining the control system.

17.7.1 Financial Service Organisations

The assets and liabilities of financial organisations are denoted in terms of money. The assets for a financial organisation are the loans given out and the liabilities are the deposits it has taken in. Financial organisations earn a profit by the difference in interest between that received by it and that paid out by it. This is bound by the time factor associated with the lending and borrowing. Hence, the control factors revolve around safe investment and safe lending criteria. At the same time, financial organisations have to ensure high returns to its investors. Hence, a balance between the expectations and matching the returns requires a specific control mechanism and effort on the part of financial organisations. Since the processes of investment are becoming more complicated, there is a need for rapid information dissemination and transfer of information to investors. While designing the control of a financial organisation the following issues need to be addressed.

Since the processes of investment are becoming more complicated, there is a need for rapid information dissemination and transfer of information to investors. While designing the control of a financial organisation the following issues need to be addressed.

1. Establish a customer relationship management program, which will take care of timely information dissemination of investments, keep a tab on prospective investments, enable the current borrower to pay in time and current investors to receive their dues in time.
2. Establish "star performer" criterion for the frontline managers in the business to motivate them, as there is a lot of monotony associated with the financial business.
3. Ensure rapid flow of information to the various parties in the business and ensure faith in the investment.
4. Focus on short term performance as the funds involved in the business need to turn in short run.
5. Measure the financial performance in terms of funding association and time spent on dealing with customers rather than cost (since cost involved is much less in a financial organisation as compared to a physical organisation).

17.7.2 Insurance Organisations

Insurance is of two kinds, life and non life. Life insurance is taken as an investment as persons pay an insurance premium for a given period of time and are covered for the risk of life or accident and are paid the whole amount invested at the end of the stipulated investment period along with a bonus.

On the other hand, the non life insurance companies collect a premium from individuals who want a particular kind of casualty or peril to be covered over a year's time. This means that at the end of the period if the peril or casualty does not occur, then the insurance policy lapses. In other words, non life insurance cannot be taken as an investment.

Insurance policies are generally sold by insurance agents, who earn a specific percentage on the premium of the policy.

Implications of management control

The profit from a product of insurance cannot be determined immediately and usually takes a long time. Despite the fact that fund inflow and outflow considerations are taken care of while designing the product of insurance, it has been found that the gap is far more and skewed towards the expenses in the long run in practice. It is seen that insurance companies are far more expense conscious then their counterparts in the financial industry.

The facts that should be kept in mind when designing a control system for an insurance company are given below.

1. **Product pricing:** Insurance companies provide various prices for the same product to different groups of people. For example, the policy premium for the same kind of life annuity policy will be different for a person of 21 years of age and 35 years of age. Some of the considerations taken in pricing an insurance product (known as actuarial science) are as follows:
   a. Acquisition cost like sales agents' commission
   b. Servicing cost such as collecting the premium of the policy
   c. Desired profit from the policy
   d. Probability of lapse
   e. Earnings from investment of money in the fund collected from the policy
   f. Probability of payment, arising out of death, peril or any other event
   g. Consideration of income tax regulations, which are substantially different for insurance companies as compared to other companies
   h. The discounting rate to discount the current inflow of income from the fund invested for the insurance product
2. **Sales performance:** Since profitability of the insurance product is a difficult issue, the insurance companies manage the performance control by focusing on the volume. An agent's commission is fixed on the basis of the yearly or early year premium, or on the face amount of the policies written. Such appraisal methods are used to appraise the branches.

   Since profitability of the insurance product is a difficult issue, the insurance companies manage the performance control by focusing on the volume.
3. **Expense control:** Control of expenses is a fundamental activity of insurance companies as the profits fluctuate for the various products of the insurance industry. Expenses are generally controlled through close monitoring of the budget set for each insurance product.

17.7.3 Non Profit Organisations

Non profit organisations like trusts and societies are basically philanthropic in nature but are a business by organisational structure. In practice, non profit organisations do not make a profit but have revenue surpluses. The key issues in designing a management control system stem from the fact that such organisations do not have a single time frame for performance like that of a business or profit making organisation.

The key issues addressed while designing a control system for such organisations are: the goals of the organisation, the period through which they are supposed to achieve the desired goals and the costs associated with them. It has often been seen that such organisations design their control system in and around the cost factors, which are associated with fulfilling the organisations goals. Such organisations have been dealt with in detail in Chapter 19 under the head of control for Non Governmental Organisations (NGOs), which are mostly non profit making bodies set up with a social cause.

17.7.4 Government Organisations

Government organisations are service organisations and tend to be non profit organisations with business-like activities. The characteristics of government organisations are given below.

Characteristics of a governmental organisation

1. Political influences in a democratic country like India are a major characteristic of government organisations. The ruling political party has its predetermined political manifesto, which it has to fulfil as a part of the electoral promise. Government organisations are used as an instrument to deliver government

programs, which are a part of the electoral promises made by political parties during general elections.

2. Another problem and feature of a government organisation is over exposure to public information. The disbursement and interpretation of information regarding their performance and activities sometime gets misinterpreted due to wrong connotations or politically motivated reasons.
3. Since government organisations in India do not usually make a profit, they are not driven by customer satisfaction. There are quite a number of misnomers in the mind of people working in these organisations, namely that they are not responsible for good customer service and only have to perform their duty. Besides, their job security often leads them to feel that even if they do not perform they are not going to lose their jobs. This makes them even more liable to non performance of duty at the cost of the customers.
4. Since the work requirements are often not matched by the compensation, the motive to work is less.

Issues of a management control system

The key issues, which should be taken care of while designing a control system for government organisations, are as follows.

1. **The designs of programs and budgeting:** All government organisations have to fulfil the programs laid down by the legislature. For this purpose, the state lays down the annual budget, which is strictly followed in order to maintain control on the activities of the business.
2. **Performance measurements:** These are carried out through both process control and measurement of end results, especially in the activities associated with welfare activities. Social indicators are broad measurements of a government organisation's performance. At the micro level however, the government may decide to design appropriate measurements of performance depending upon the need of the organisation.

SUMMARY

This chapter dealt with management control in service organisations. Service organisations differ from organisations that have physical products to sell. The key issues on which the control of such organisations is based depend on the nature of the services and the way they are delivered. Financial service organisations design their control system around the information disbursed, whereas insurance organisations design their control around the cost per product. Government organisations and non profit making organisations are controlled on the basis of budgets laid down for the programs they have to comply with and the level of compliances. Different service organisations are affected by different issues, which are specific to a particular industry and therefore need to be addressed while designing the control system.

Review Questions

1. Explain, with a relevant example, how service organisations differ from other organisations.
2. What are the difficulties one might face in control of a service organisation?
3. What factors should be kept in mind in designing a control system for a service organisation? Can a control system of a physical product industry be replicated in a service organisation? If yes, how?
4. What issues are faced while designing a control system for a financial organisation?
5. Why does the insurance industry use cost to design a control system? What are the other issues that can be used by an insurance company to design a control system?
6. Government organisations are victims of the political system. Can this statement be referred to while designing a control system of a government organisation?

Analytical Questions

1. What issues should you address to design the control system for a nursing home?
2. Can regulatory authorities play any role in the design of a control system for a financial or insurance company? If yes, how?

CHAPTER 18 Management Control of Projects

LEARNING OBJECTIVES OF THE CHAPTER

- The project control system
- The tools used in project planning, execution and control
- The various reporting needs for the project control to operate

18.1 INTRODUCTION

Projects are a set of activities, which are carried out with a desired end result. They are commissioned by the management of a company or a business organisation to benefit the business.

Projects may either be a new part of the existing business or be associated with a new venture of the business. Generally, projects are a set of activities, which are carried out with a desired end result. They are commissioned by the management of a company or a business organisation to benefit the business. A project goes through phases of planning, implementation and evaluation. Projects are of various size and dimensions. Many projects are very large and require large resources to complete them, whereas others may require very little resources and manpower. Since projects have a stipulated end result that is to be achieved within a given time frame, it is necessary to keep control over it, as an uncontrolled project would result in loss of resources both in terms of time and money. This chapter examines the essential components of a project in view of the control process in the projects.

18.2 KEY ISSUES IN THE CONTROL OF A PROJECT

The key issues in the control of projects are time, cost and quality of the work carried out.

The key issues in the control of projects are time, cost and quality of the work carried out. It is evident that the quality of the project depends on the time-cost overrun. This is especially true in the case of long term projects such as those pertaining to infrastructure. In fact, while designing the management control system, the schedule of the time available for the project should be calculated as meticulously as possible.

The elements of cost and time are deciding factors in the overall quality of the project and the quality of the work. The time calculated for a project to be completed should be the optimum time, i.e., it should ensure that the best possible work is carried out in the specified time, otherwise the quality of work may suffer. For example if a project in the normal course should have taken three years, but is completed in one and a half year, the quality of the work in the project may suffer. Such issues in terms of the quality of the project should be taken into account, while designing a control system.

18.3 ROLE OF CONTROL IN PROJECTS

A project is a set of critical activities, which are co-ordinated with the help of the persons who work towards its completion. It follows a set of budgeted activities, which are schematically scheduled. The closer the congruence of the actual activity with the budgeted activity, the better is the quality of the project management. The managers who monitor, implement and deliver projects have to set controls that encourage behaviour and effects that will deliver the required results. The way control is exercised should generate positive participation and goal seeking. If for some reason these processes do not work for some individuals in the project, passive participation by the individual(s) should be taken up in order to avoid loss.

The managers who monitor, implement and deliver projects have to set controls that encourage behaviour and effects that will deliver the required results.

An individual's re-action to various controls depends on several vari-ables, such as the specific control mechanism used, the nature of goals being sought, the individual's self image, assessment of the value of the goal, expect-ations of being able to achieve the goal, and basic tolerance enduring control. The common controls and their resultant behaviour are explained below. The three types of control which are used in a project are (a) cybernetic control (b) go/no go control and (c) post performance controls.

An individual's reaction to various controls depends on several variables, such as the specific control mechanism used, the nature of goals being sought, the individual's self image, assessment of the value of the goal, expectations of being able to achieve the goal, and basic tolerance enduring control.

1. **Cybernetic control:** Cybernetic control is a close loop control where the performance is measured against a set standard through an assessor and detector tool. Depending on the intensity of the variance between the actual values and the standard values, control is exercised. Cybernetic control systems are of three kinds, the first order sets a highly rigid system that does not allow for any alteration in the set standards. The second order allows a few changes in the set standards and in the third order, standards are changed from time to time depending upon requirements and hence there are no pre-programmed instructions, allowing the project managers to act independently.

Cybernetic control is a close loop control where the performance is measured against a set standard through an accessor and detector tool.

2. **Go/no go controls:** Cost and time overruns are common in projects. Go/no go controls are used to ensure that the project is completed within the specified time and budget. These control systems are flexible and are used in most projects. Go/no go controls are used at periodic and regular intervals, but they can also be exercised at the discretion of the controller. When the controls are used periodically at pre set intervals, the intervals are determined on the basis of a clock, calendar or the operating cycle of the machines.
3. **Post performance controls:** Post performance controls are reviews that are carried out after the project has been completed to see whether the objectives of the project have been met in terms of cost, quality and time. In order to organise the controls effectively, management should provide a congenial environment and incentives for the project managers to study the reports and to determine corrective procedures for the problems that come to light in the reports.

A prerequisite for control system is that it should have a well balanced approach. Costs increase exponentially with a linear increase in the degree of the control. The optimum level of control can be set considering the size of the project. Controls must be directed towards the correction of errors rather than towards reprimand and retribution. A balanced control system is one that is geared towards the end results.

18.4 PROCESS CONTROL IN PROJECTS

When dealing with the control of a project the two most important objectives are: (a) the regulation of results through the alteration of activities in the project and (b) the appropriate control and usage of the assets of the project.

Therefore, it is necessary that while designing a control system both regulation of results and conservation of the assets is achieved. The three most important resources (and therefore the processes involved in them) that need to be controlled are the physical assets, the human resources and the financial resources. All of them are critical and should be handled with care to deliver the desired results of a project.

18.4.1 Control of Physical Assets

Control of physical assets involves the scheduling, maintenance, repair and replacement of physical assets. Physical asset management requires both preventive and corrective control.

Physical assets are always a constraint on the project since they may be redundant once the project is over, hence they are procured with caution.

Control of physical assets involves the scheduling, maintenance, repair and replacement of physical assets. Physical asset management requires both preventive and corrective control. Preventive control means ensuring that the physical assets are used appropriately and that they are replaced in due course. Corrective control means that, the physical assets are controlled once there is a problem or deviation of the assets.

18.4.2 Control of Human Resources

Controlling of human resources requires controlling and maintaining the growth and development of people in the organisation (project). Projects provide an effective platform for gathering people, but they have to be utilised carefully. Devices such as employee appraisals, personnel performance indices and screening methods for the appointment, promotion and retention are not satisfactory devices for ensuring that the conservation function is properly handled. This can be accomplished through the familiar audit procedures. 'Human resources accounting' is one of the devices that can produce effective results.

18.4.3 Control of Financial Resources

Different tools are available for the conservation, regulation and utilisation of financial resources. Financial control techniques involve working capital management (managing the current asset and liability gap), budgeting and capital investment decisions and controls (these have been dealt with in Chapters 8, 9 & 10).

18.5 VARIOUS PHASES OF A PROJECT AND CONTROL

A project consists of three phases namely, (a) project planning, (b) project execution and (c) project evaluation. The desired results of a project can only be achieved if sufficient care is taken to reduce the deviation between the budgeted requirements and the actual requirements.

18.5.1 Project Planning

Project planning is defined as 'the process of developing the basis for managing the project, including the planning objectives, procedure, organisation, routines, finance and other activities'.

Project planning is defined as 'the process of developing the basis for managing the project, including the planning objectives, procedure, organisation, routines, finance and other activities'. A project plan describes how all the major activities of each project management function are accomplished, including overall project control. The project plan evolves through successive stages of the project cycle.

Project planning takes place on two levels, technical and operational. At the technical level, decisions are taken regarding the implementation of these activities. The development of the project plan is not a single stage exercise. It goes through several stages, before the final proposal is prepared. The project plan requires induction of several control devices into the project. The concepts of time, cost and quality are taken into consideration.

The final plan of a project should consist of three important parts: scope, schedule and cost.

1. The scope states the specification of each work package and the name of the persons or the organisation responsible for taking the project to completion. If the project specifications are vague, as in consultation and research and development projects, the scope of the project is necessarily brief and general.
2. The schedule estimates the time required to complete each work package and the interrelationship among the work packages. The sequence of the activities should be properly planned so that the entire project is not changed or delayed even if a particular activity is delayed. Network techniques are popularly used to estimate the schedules.
3. Total project cost is defined as all the costs that are specific to a project and are incurred through the start up of a facility, prior to the operation of the facility. Thus, Total Project Cost (TPC) includes Total Estimated Cost (TEC) and Other Project Costs (OPC).

$$TEC + OPC = TPC$$

Project costs should be properly planned taking into account all the necessary components of the project. Long drawn out projects often have a time-cost over run. In such a case the management has to be reactive to the situation and create appropriate changes to accommodate the cost. Therefore, the original plan should be changed according to the demands of the time and situations that may arise.

The CPM deals with the time-cost estimates for each activity and provides a standard method for communicating project plans, schedules, time and cost performance.

The project uses network techniques such as Project Review and Evaluation Techniques (PERT) and Critical Path Method (CPM). The CPM deals with the time-cost estimates for each activity and provides a standard method for communicating project plans, schedules, time and cost performance. CPM identifies the most critical elements where attention has to be paid to the cost element. This allows the best possible method, among the alternatives available, to be used, by calculating the total duration of the project. Through crashing of the critical activities, CPM reduces the project's duration at an increase of the cost.

PERT on the other hand deals with the problem of uncertain activity times by application of statistical analysis for determining the estimated time for each activity. This tool coordinates the activities that must be carried out to successfully accomplish the objectives of a project on time.[1]

The activities that are performed in the planning phase include ordering of material[2], obtaining necessary permission and selecting personnel to name a few.

18.5.2 Project Execution

The execution of the project starts after identifying the specification of the work packages, schedule, budget and the managers responsible for each activity. The schedule gives the estimated time for each activity and the budget shows the estimated cost of each principal part of the project. In the control process, data of actual cost, actual time and actual accomplishments are compared with the estimates.

The management requires three different types of reports, namely, trouble reports, progress reports and financial reports.

***Trouble reports** emphasise the problems that have already occurred or are anticipated to occur. Critical problems are identified and highlighted.*

1. **Trouble reports** emphasise the problems that have already occurred or are anticipated to occur. Critical problems are identified and highlighted. It is essential that these reports be sent to the appropriate managers in time so that corrective actions can be taken as early as possible.

---

[1] PERT and CPM are in the realm of project management and can be studied in detail from any good book on project management. Ideally, students should get an idea of optimistic time, pessimistic time and the most likely time while studying these techniques. A good understanding into probability will also help in this case.

[2] EOQ and levels of inventory are critical to project completion.

Trouble reports can take the form of oral report in case of an emergency.

2. **Progress reports** compare the actual schedules and costs with the planned schedules and costs for the work carried out. They also contain similar comparisons for the overhead activities that are not directly related to the work. Variances associated with costs, schedule delays and similar factors are identified and measured quantitatively.

***Progress reports** compare the actual schedules and costs with the planned schedules and costs for the work carried out. They also contain similar comparisons for the overhead activities that are not directly related to the work.*

3. **Financial reports** project costs accurately where cost reimbursements are to be made. These are not necessary if the project is based on a fixed cost contract. However, maintenance of the reports gives a clear picture of the manner in which the financial resources are being spent.

Use of reports

Reports show the actual time as compared to the scheduled time and actual costs as compared to the budgeted costs. While interpreting the time report, questions are raised if more than the estimated time was spent. Analysis of the cost report is somewhat different. Actual costs are compared with the budgeted costs, if the processed quality is maintained. If the actual costs are less than the budgeted costs, quality might have suffered. So, all the reports must be studied individually and jointly.

SUMMARY

A project is a set of activities that are to be accomplished with a specific end result of sufficient importance for the business. The essence of control of the project depends on the control of the time, costs and quality of the project. Since the time factor is very important in the control of the project, the project manager should use control that encourages the managers. Cybernetic control, go or no go controls and post controls are some of the most common tools of control in the management control system. It is essential that the project managers both regulate and conserve assets while dealing with a project. PERT and CPM are used to analyse the scope, schedule and the cost of the project. Various kinds of reports such as a progress report, trouble report and financial report are generally used to monitor the projects. The reports are evaluated to determine the outcome, and corrective steps are taken to overcome the errors.

Review Questions

1. Describe the various ways in which a project can be controlled. Explain one of the methods in detail.
2. What is post performance control? Explain the key issues in post performance control.
3. Write a short note on project execution.
4. What are the various ways of reporting involved in a project control system? Give a detailed explanation of the various reports that are resorted to in project control.
5. What are the key elements in carrying out a project? How should the key factors be used in terms of designing a control for the project?

Analytical Question

1. A bridge is to be built across a river near the mouth of the river. The time estimated for the project was 10 years and the project was supposed to cost about Rs. 100 crore. Over time, due to several faults in the design, and labour problems, the project was delayed by 15 years over its schedule. The time cost overrun was about 103% of the total cost estimated. This apart, the construction company had to pay a penalty of 30% of the original cost for the time cost overrun to the government.

   In view of the above information provided to you, answer the following questions:

   a. What are the major issues that should have been addressed while designing a control for this project?
   b. What do you think is the major cause of the delay and how could the control design possibly have helped in avoiding it?

CHAPTER 19

Management Control in Non-Governmental Organisations and Development Programs

LEARNING OBJECTIVES OF THE CHAPTER

- The nature and kinds of NGOs and development programs
- The ways NGOs and development programs can be monitored
- The various research methods used in collecting and enumerating data regarding these organisations, and the need to use them

19.1 INTRODUCTION

Despite the will of the government, it is always not possible for it to carry out all the development activities and peripheral issues in development issues. In this context, the Non Governmental Organisations (NGOs) play a major role. The government also floats a number of development programs, which are directed towards delivering its agenda of development programs, especially the ones in the social sector.

The non governmental organisations are set up to supplement the government's development works or address the problems at the grass root level in the management. These organisations aim to maximise the benefit of the target group, which can range from weaker sections of society to the women and unemployed youth of rural India.

Both NGOs' and governments' development projects require coordination between the government, the public at large and the political will of the state. Therefore, there has to be a flow in the process of the activities that are carried out by these organisations.

As we know the non governmental organisations are set up to supplement the government's development works or address the problems at the grass root level in the management. These organisations aim to maximise the benefit of the target group, which can range from weaker sections of society to the women and unemployed youth of rural India. Since, these programs are self motivated and are non profit making by nature, their implementation sometimes takes a backseat.

NGOs and development programs are divided into two categories: self regulated programs and administered programs.

Broadly, NGOs and development programs are divided into two categories: self regulated programs and administered programs. Self regulatory projects are voluntary in nature and are undertaken by people who decide to form an association or organisation of their own through a collective effort so that they will benefit from the program.

The administered development programs are those that are initiated and implemented by the government or by any other agency. In India the '*Sarva Shiksha Avijan*' or education for all children and illiterate adults is directed by the government and executed through the NGOs and the development agencies.

19.2 THE KEY ISSUES IN THE MANAGEMENT CONTROL OF NGOS AND DEVELOPMENT ORGANISATIONS

The key issues, in the control mechanism of NGOs and development organisations, revolve around two issues, the core objectives of such organisations and the process through which they are implemented.

In both cases the perspective of the project and degree of self regulation involved are critical to the success of the project. The control should change according to the nature of the program. Members of the organisations that undertake self regulated programs are more interested in these programs as they are aimed at benefiting the members themselves. An example would be the members of a "Self Help Group of Women" from economically backward parts of society. In the case of administered programs, officials who are away from the scene of action of the projects have to implement the entire program. Moreover, they are not the actual beneficiaries of the groups, and hence they may be negligent in carrying out the program. Such programs have to be evaluated to ensure that the target group is gaining the benefits of the programs. Control is more explicit in an administered program.

The key issues, in the control mechanism of NGOs and development organisations, revolve around two issues, the core objectives of such organisations and the process through which they are implemented.

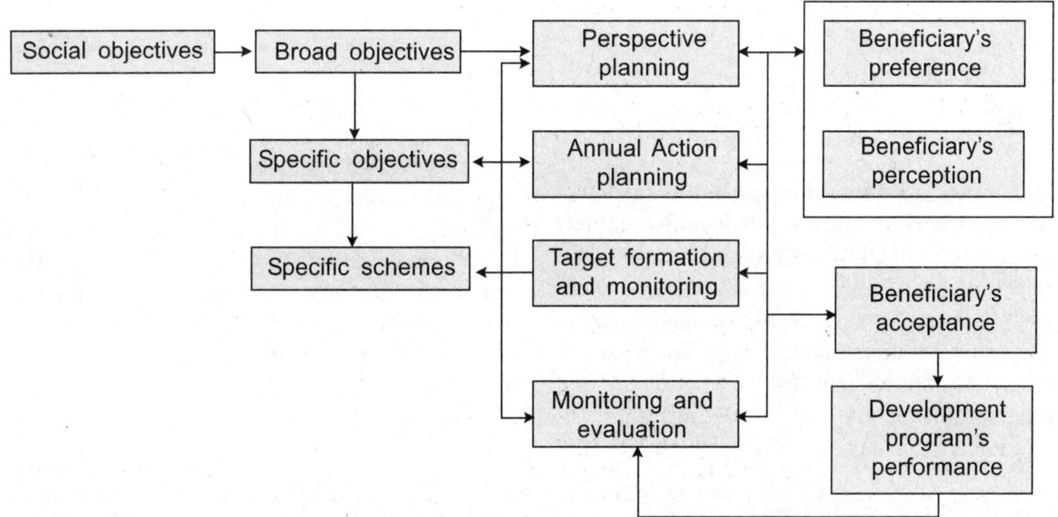

Fig. 19.1: Monitoring and control of projects (Source: Subhash Sharma, Management Control System, Text and Cases, Tata McGraw Hill Publishing Company Limited, India, Seventh Edition)

19.3 EVALUATION SYSTEM FOR DEVELOPMENT PROGRAMS AND NGOS

The NGOs and the development programs carried out by development organisations have to be continuously monitored. There has to be a balance between the work carried out and the expenses incurred. All good work needs to be rewarded and all unworthy work needs to be eliminated through a feedback and review system. It is also important that the expenses are controlled.

The deviations from the actual plan are recorded, the cause/s for the deviation analysed, and follow up action taken if necessary. This requires reviewing the organisation periodically, depending upon the changes that are noted in the plan of action from time to time.

Objectives of the organisation need to rechecked, since the environment and the assumptions under which the original objectives were set might have undergone a sea change. There might be a drastic change in the environment, which would force the organisation to reorient its line of actions. Even in a constant environment, there are chances that the objectives require refocusing and sharpening.

There are several ways to monitor a NGO and its development program. Some of them are given below.

1. **Indicator based monitoring:** In this method, the appropriate management information system highlights the key parameters of performance. These key parameters are used as indicators. The deviations for each indicator are recorded and suitable follow up action is taken as per the deviations. There may be conceptual problems in deciding such parameters since it is difficult to isolate the effect of an individual casual variation on the success/failure of the entire program.
2. **Monitoring through the beneficiaries' method:** This is a method of monitoring, where the beneficiaries are directly questioned about the usefulness of the program. Suggestions from the beneficiaries about how to make the program more effective are welcomed.
3. **Monitoring through field visits:** This is carried out either through periodic monitoring or by surprise checks. Observations are made during the field visits and reported to the higher officers. In the case of a public interest program, the visits are made by a public representative.
4. **Monitoring by legislators:** In this case the field visit and the checks are carried out by state legislators. This is aimed at reducing discrepancies in the reporting and safe-guarding the public interest.
5. **Monitoring by the media:** The media is a very powerful monitoring device, especially with today's electronic media reporting. One advantage of media reporting is that it acts as a third party monitoring system.

The process of evaluation can be carried out by an internal or external team or by an independent agency. Since the internal team is usually emotionally attached to the development program or NGO, an independent agency should really carry out such a process. Donor agencies, which fund the program, accept external evaluation as being more authentic. While internal evaluation could be a useful tool for the managers of the development organisations for improving overall effectiveness, external evaluation is helpful in assessing the socio-economic impact of the program.

The process of evaluation can be carried out by an internal or external team or by an independent agency. Since the internal team is usually emotionally attached to the development program or NGO, an independent agency should really carry out such a process.

To determine the impact of the program on the target group, ex post evaluation is conducted for some development programs. An assessment of the impact of the program in terms of meeting its objectives is made once the program is completed.

To determine the impact of the program on the target group, ex post evaluation is conducted for some development programs.

The **'before and after approach'** can also be used to determine the impact of the program in some cases. This is done by collecting information on the important socio-economic development parameters of the beneficiaries for whom the program is intended. Comparison between the beneficiaries who were covered under the program and the group that were not covered determines the variance. Besides, survey research, known as 'with' and 'without' approach can also be considered for comparison. The evaluation of a development program is shown in Figure 19.2.

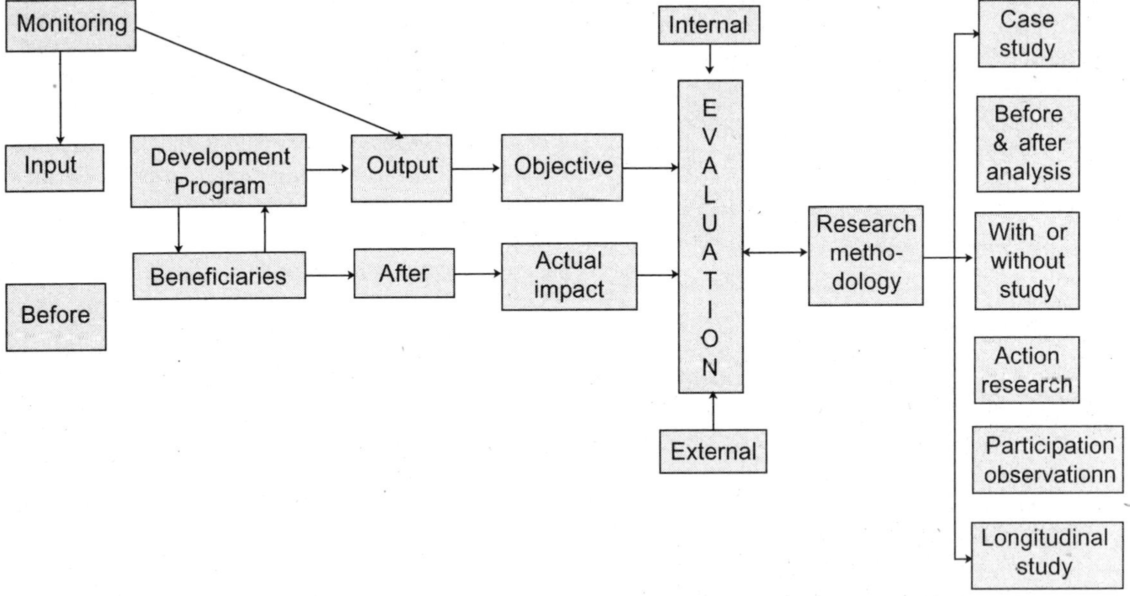

Fig. 19.2: Monitoring and evaluation of NGOs and development programs, (Source: Subhas Sharma, Management Control System, Text and Cases, Tata McGraw Hill Publishing Company Limited, Seventh edition, 1997)

19.4 RESEARCH METHODOLOGY

The NGOs and the development program need to be monitored, and data on an empirical basis need to be collected. Data collected are to be judiciously used as feedback so that necessary action can be taken if there are any problems. There are several ways to carry out such research. Some of the common methods are given below:

1. **Participation observation method:** In this method, the researcher participates as a member of the group and notes down his or her findings and observations. This is a very good method as it helps the researcher to determine the causal relationships. The problems associated with the implementation are reviewed in this method.
2. **Longitudinal research method:** In this method a long period is taken into consideration for data collection as against a single reference time period. The idea is to observe the trends and overall changes.
3. **Action research method:** In this method, the researcher actively takes part in the implementation of the program and tries to measure the impact of the program on the beneficiaries. The researcher records and evaluates the effect of various combinations of the program variables, their timings, levels of acceptance and the responses of the beneficiaries.

SUMMARY

Non Governmental Organisations (NGOs) and developmental programs have similar issues of control since the purpose of both organisations is similar. The organisations generally depend on a third party view of the development. The idea in this case is to provide continuous monitoring of the program. The monitoring can be carried out through an indicator base or by monitoring the beneficiaries. Common methods of monitoring are through field visits and use of legislators. The research methods play a very important role in data collection and the process of taking corrective action. For example participation, observation and action research are finding a meaningful place in monitoring NGOs and development programs.

Review Questions

1. How are development organisations and NGOs different from other organisations? In light of their differences, what factors should be kept in mind for developing a control system for them?
2. What is the role of research in the control of NGOs and development organisations?
3. Enumerate the ways through which NGOs and development organisations can be monitored.
4. Can a development program be monitored with reference to a single point of time? If not why?

Analytical Question

During the cyclone that hit the coast of Orissa in 1999, thousands of human establishments were annihilated. It took several years to deal with the problem of rehabilitation. Million of rupees were spent and not less than 60 NGOs and 30 corporates took part in the rehabilitation process. The area covered was more than 1200 square kilometres. The government, the WHO and the WFP were largely involved in the process. The main problem was access to information pre and post rehabilitation.

(i) Design a control system for the development program if you were to monitor it.

(ii) State, the methods of data collection you would have used and the reasons behind them.

PART—E

SPECIAL ISSUES IN MANAGEMENT CONTROL SYSTEM

CHAPTER 20

Use of a Management Information System in a Management Control System

LEARNING OBJECTIVES OF THE CHAPTER

- The need and use of an MIS
- Dosigning an MIS
- The various kinds of MIS in practice
- The use of MIS in the various functional areas including control
- The evaluation process of an MIS

20.1 INTRODUCTION

Modern businesses are complex in terms of their global spread and diverse activities. This has made the task of controlling a business difficult. The crux of any control is the availability of correct information and using such information at the right time for the right purpose. Thus in a modern business, storage and retrieval of data are crucial.

The crux of any control is the availability of correct information and using such information at the right time for the right purpose. Thus in a modern business, storage and retrieval of data are crucial.

Management Information Systems are information management systems that use computerised data, and they are of vital importance. A Management Information System (MIS) provides a process to coordinate, assimilate and disburse managerial and business information in a meaningful way. It also helps to keep real time accounting in place and provide an information based decision system.

A Management Information System (MIS) provides a process to coordinate, assimilate and disburse managerial and business information in a meaningful way.

20.2 WHAT IS MIS?

A Management Information System refers to an automated computerised system, which helps in assimilation, storage and disbursement of business information to the appropriate managers, when they need to take a decision.

A Management Information System refers to an automated computerised system, which helps in assimilation, storage and disbursement of business information to the appropriate managers, when they need to take a decision.

An MIS is able to discriminate between the different information required by managers at different levels. It gives support to managers, as to the data and information they need to retrieve and use, to make a decision.

The information that is used and disbursed by a MIS at the different levels of management includes:

1. At the top level it disburses strategic information. The information, which is important at this level includes, informa-tion on the industry and competitors and information that is needed to formulate policies and strategic planning.
2. At the middle level the information required is tactical in nature. This information endorses the top level strategic information and helps in creating a path for the execution of the strategic decision.
3. At the lowest level, the information required is oriented towards operations and tasks. It helps in creating a base for carrying out the actual business.

An MIS system should be designed in such a way that it provides all levels of the business with the appropriate inform-ation in an effective, timely and relevant manner. In addition, it should provide the requisite information to all functions of the organisation. The MIS should ensure that erroneous and un-wanted information is not generated.

An MIS system should be designed in such a way that it provides all levels of the business with the appropriate information in an effective, timely and relevant manner. In addition, it should provide the requisite information to all functions of the organisation. The MIS should ensure that erroneous and unwanted information is not generated.

20.3 DESIGNING A GOOD MIS

To design a good MIS system the following should be kept in mind:

1. Information from all areas of the business should flow freely and reach all relevant points in the management.
2. Both a top to bottom and a reverse flow of information should be ensured. This includes reports, summaries and feedback information.
3. There should be a horizontal flow of information, i.e., from a manager in one function to other managers at the same level in other functions.
4. The cost of data processing, data collection and data access has to be taken into account. All the managers would like to use as much information as possible, but cost may act as a constraint.
5. The trade off between the use of information and its cost of collection and storage has to be worked out and economised. Data or information should be collected in such a manner that it can be used by as many managers as possible.
6. The value of information is always cumulative, thus collection of information is never redundant, just because it cannot give enough decision support immediately. It may so happen that over a period of time, data and infor-mation systematically collected will help in taking a meaningful decision. The expected value of perfect inform-ation should be calculated in order to get information in its correct perspective, otherwise there is a chance that redundant inform-ation is collected.

The value of information is always cumulative, thus collection of information is never redundant, just because it cannot give enough decision support immediately. It may so happen that over a period of time, data and information systematically collected will help in taking a meaningful decision.

20.4 THE FEATURES OF AN EFFECTIVE MIS

The features of an effective MIS are as follows:

1. An effective MIS system is linked to all the responsibility centres, whether vertical or horizontal, to provide linkages to all decisions taken by the managers.
2. The MIS should provide for both financial and non financial information. If possible it should be able to provide for linkages in these data.

3. An effective MIS system takes into consideration the key functions of the business and collects information on these areas. It should also sensitise the business regarding any changes in these key indicators.
4. The MIS should take into account the frequency of reporting required, which decides the level of use of the system.
5. The database should be upgraded regularly, so that there is no gap between the real time data and the time of decision of a manager at any level of the business.
6. The MIS should be able to provide two kinds of reports, information reports and control reports. While the information reports provide a factual base, the control reports provide a comparison between the budgeted and actual achievements in the business.

   The MIS should be able to provide two kinds of reports, information reports and control reports. While the information reports provide a factual base, the control reports provide a comparison between the budgeted and actual achievements in the business.

7. The MIS should take the entire organisation as one system and work out a "system-subsystem linkage" throughout the business.
8. The MIS should provide relevant information and a reasonable degree of precision.

20.5 TYPES OF INFORMATION SYSTEMS

There are different types of information systems that are currently in use. They cater to various kinds of need. Some of the commonly used MIS systems are the external information system, continuous information system, systematic information system and social information system. These are explained below.

20.5.1 External Information System

External information is vital to a business. Such information consists of the competitors' advantages and strengths, the customers' preferences and changes in the economic legislation. Such information is required at all the three levels of a business. However, the need is more at the strategic level. Often, collection and assimilation of such information is outsourced to an external organisation with the necessary expertise.

20.5.2 Continuous Information System

Many business decisions affect the business in the long run. In order to derive a meaningful conclusion from such decisions, it is essential that information is collected over a sufficiently long period of time so that a meaningful trend emerges. Such trend analysis is specially needed in the case of marketing information. Continuous information systems are used to evaluate a long time-bound program.

20.5.3 Systematic Information System

Systematic information systems are used to appraise the decisions made by the managers. The views of the managers are evaluated considering the assumptions under which the managers have made such decisions. This system helps in safeguarding against improper assumptions. It takes a **dialectical approach,** which proposes a thesis, or the original idea and an antithesis or an alternative idea. A structured data base decreases conflicts and leads to the emergence of a synthesis.

This system helps in safeguarding against improper assumptions. It takes a ***dialectical approach,*** *which proposes a thesis, or the original idea and an antithesis or an alternative idea.*

20.5.4 Social Information System

Such information systems capture the changes in social indicators, which occur due to any development program taken up. They are similar to continuous information systems as they collect data over a very long period. However, in this case, the system should enable cross checks and cross reference to verify data.

20.6 ROLE OF MIS IN THE FUNCTIONAL AREAS OF MANAGEMENT

20.6.1 Role of MIS in Marketing

A management information system in marketing is vital. It helps in planning and controlling the total effort of marketing. Besides, MIS provides a very sound basis for the purpose of forecasting demand and sales in a future period.

A well designed management information system helps in identifying the drop in sales as well as identifying strong points in the current market scenario. Information such as which segment or product is doing well, in which territory sales are increasing and how to compute the market share appropriately takes priority in designing such a management information system.

20.6.2 Role of MIS in Finance

Finance is greatly dependent on the MIS. The MIS system helps three-fold in finance. In the first place it helps in appropriately collecting financial data through a computerised accounting system. In the second place it helps in coordinating the working capital needs both through data analysis and computerised enterprise-wide resource planning. In the third place it helps by providing a computerised decision support system and business intelligence.

20.6.3 Role of MIS in Human Resource Management

Human resource depends on human resource allocation, knowing the availability of the resources and mapping the competency of the individuals in the organisation. A good centralised data base helps the HR manager in all these respects.

20.6.4 Role of MIS in Control

The role of MIS is the greatest in the control field. It helps in setting the performance standards by laying down appropriate benchmarks, measuring the required data against standards and suggesting corrective actions to the managers. An MIS supports both the open and close loop management control systems. In a close loop control system, the MIS is a part of the corrective action, whereas in an open loop system the corrective action lies outside the purview of the control system.

MIS helps in feedback and feed forward mechanism. The feedback mechanisms are post operative, whereas the feed forward mechanism helps in passing the required information to the future so that it acts as a good reference point.

MIS helps in feedback and feed forward mechanism. The feedback mechanisms are post operative, whereas the feed forward mechanism helps in passing the required information to the future so that it acts as a good reference point.

20.7 HOW TO IMPLEMENT AN MIS

Implementation of an MIS includes selection of a hardware platform, scheduling project planning activity, resource allocation, develop-ment, and testing. Implementation is carried out by the 'freeze-unfreeze' technique. This technique provides for controlling the changes in the environment in a stipulated period.

The freeze-unfreeze technique helps in three stages. In the first stage or unfreeze stage, all the required modifications and changes to the existing procedures and practices are identified. In the second phase or the change stage, the modifications are carried out along with an awareness campaign for the employees. In the third phase or the freeze stage the changes are implemented.

The freeze-unfreeze technique helps in three stages. In the first stage or unfreeze stage, all the required modifications and changes to the existing procedures and practices are identified. In the second phase or the change stage, the modifications are carried out along with an awareness campaign for the employees. In the third phase or the freeze stage the changes are implemented.

20.8 HOW TO EVALUATE AN MIS

The evaluation of an MIS is carried out in three stages as discussed below :

1. The technical review, which includes the issue relating to the IT tools that have been used in the implementation of the MIS. It covers areas like hardware, software tools, designs, structures, Operating Systems feature, security and built in checks and control.
2. The utility review, which reviews the activities are aimed at the improvement of the information collected by the MIS.

3. The economic review is aimed at identifying the actual costs and benefits by comparing them with the budgeted ones. The review also addresses issues of delays in implementation and overrun in terms of time and cost.

SUMMARY

An MIS is a system of collecting, processing and presenting information to help a business take appropriate decisions at all levels of the management.

Various forms of MIS are in vogue, such as: external, continuing, systematic and social MIS.

MIS reduces the amount of information through standardising the procedures, categorising information and putting a proper feedback system in place. Implementation of an MIS system employs a 'freeze-unfreeze' technique. Evaluation of an MIS is through three types of reviews, namely: technical, utility and economical.

Review Questions

1. Enumerate the needs of a good MIS. What role does it play in the management control system?
2. What are the characteristics of a good management control system?
3. What are the various MIS systems in use in the modern business world?
4. What are the features of an efficient MIS?
5. What is meant by a dialectical approach to a systematic information system? Give an example from an actual business.
6. How does one evaluate an MIS?

Analytical Question

1. Design a management information system for a general hospital. Keep in mind the following key factors while doing so.
   a. The hospital has a chain of hospitals to cater to its out patients, besides its own OPD.
   b. There are some doctors, who are not on the rolls of the hospital, but work at the hospital as and when required for a fee.
   c. The hospital is linked to some hospitals in the USA and the UK for specialised diagnostic services carried out on-line.
   d. The hospital has a free ward where poor patients are treated free of cost. The cost of treatment for patients in the free ward is recovered from fees charged to well to do patients.

CHAPTER 21

Ethical Issues and Moral Issues in Management Control

LEARNING OBJECTIVES OF THE CHAPTER

- Role of ethics in control
- Why do ethical problems occur in an organisation?
- Designing a control system that supports ethical behaviour
- Ethical principles in designing a control system

21.1 INTRODUCTION

The learning process in human beings takes place in three steps: opinions, beliefs and values. Opinions arise out of casual discussions and may change. After being put to the test of arguments and logic, the opinions become beliefs. Beliefs are often difficult to change as by then substantial learning has occurred. Beliefs will become values when a person is absolutely certain that the ideas are totally acceptable to them. Values therefore, will be the most difficult to change. The collective values of individuals are reflected as the ethical choice of society as a whole. Values impact on a business in several ways, as a business operates in a social environment.

The word ethics is derived from the Greek word 'ethicus', which means the moral character of an individual. Ethics in the context of business means conducting the business in a way that is conducive to society as a whole and does not create any moral, legal or social problems for people and the society at large.

The word ethics is derived from the Greek word '*ethicus*', which means the moral character of an individual. Ethics in the context of business means conducting the business in a way that is conducive to society as a whole and does not create any moral, legal or social problems for people and the society at large.

The ethical approach to business has been studied from various angles. Milton Friedman, believed that a business has to generate profit and there is no connection between morality and business. It was Talcot Parson, who gave the connection between ethics and business. In his view there is a consequential effect of ethics on business, i.e., if the business is carried out ethically, the results shall be positive. Talcot's opinion has been largely accepted in the business community.

The role of ethics in business needs to be understood by managers for several reasons. Some of the major reasons are as follows:

1. Business is a social activity and society is guided by moral and social ethics.

2. The law of the land derives its essence from the law of natural justice, which is a major area of ethical consequence.
3. Business is conducted by and for human beings and therefore, an ethical approach brings about goodwill which otherwise is not possible.

It is essential to be fair when taking decisions in business, especially at the time of executing control.

4. It is essential to be fair when taking decisions in business, especially at the time of executing control. Hence, ethics is a natural part of business.

21.2 ROLE OF ETHICS IN CONTROL

It is essential for managers, while designing the control system, to keep the ethical issues in mind. The ethical parameters set by the organisation decide the behaviour and the interaction of the employees of the organisation. They also help in setting a minimum standard of organisational behaviour. For example, the ways to deal with a fraud or to tackle a case of bribery in an organisation are essentially governed by the ethical code of the business, which is an integral part of the design of the control system.

The ethical parameters set by the organisation decide the behaviour and the interaction of the employees of the organisation.

When designing a control system basic rationality, creativity, mastery, morality and human association need to be considered. All these values are linked to ethical and moral issues in business. Hence while designing a formal or informal ethical system; ethical behaviour amongst the employees should be encouraged by the system.

Hence while designing a formal or informal ethical system; ethical behaviour amongst the employees should be encouraged by the system.

21.2.1 Why there are Ethical Misgivings in Organisations

In today's business world, ethical misgivings happen because of several reasons, which are related to the way the business operates. Some of them are enumerated below.

1. There is tremendous pressure to perform and achieve goals and targets in modern day businesses. This may lead to unethical practices, which have to be controlled by addressing the Do's and Don'ts in the control system itself.
2. Exogenous factors like practices of the competitors in the business.
3. Corporates failing to take care of the financial needs of their employees leads to bribery and stealing, within an organisation.
4. Employing incompetent personnel in the organisation may lead to them using unfair means to cope with the pressures in the organisation. Hence, the employment of personnel should be commensurate with the quality that the organisation requires.
5. Improper human resource practices might put the employees under stress and make them resort to unfair practices.

21.3 DESIGNING A CONTROL SYSTEM THAT SUPPORTS ETHICAL BEHAVIOUR

Designing a control system with an ethical perspective requires it to be designed in a way that takes care of the goals of the organisation, the perception of the employees and the needs of the business. One way of doing this could be by using a cybernetic approach. As discussed earlier in Chapters 1 and 18, the cybernetic approach gives a feedback to the system via the preceptor and deals with a corrective action by comparison. Figure 21.1 gives a representation as to how the system works.

Designing a control system with an ethical perspective requires it to be designed in a way that takes care of the goals of the organisation, the perception of the employees and the needs of the business.

Organisations usually adopt a cybernetic approach to develop an ethical program. Such an approach consists of six steps.

Step I: Develop a control system which complies with all laws, ethical codes and policies of the organisation

Step II: Sensitise all managers and employees as to what kind of behaviour is improper.

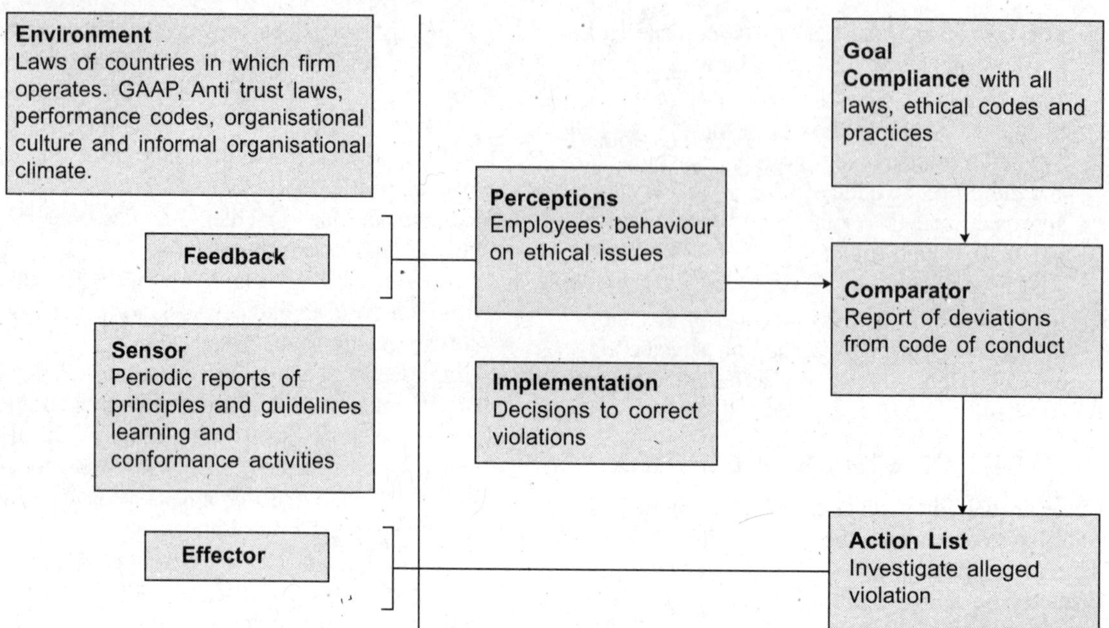

Fig. 21.1: Cybernetic processes for control with an ethical premise, (Source: Joshep, A. Maciariello and Calvin, J. Kirbey, Management Control System: Prentice Hall of India, Second edition)

Step III. Audit the behaviour of employees regarding their interaction with all stakeholders

Step IV: Report significant deviations from the desired ethical conduct

Step V: Investigate the violation in the prescribed ethical code

Step VI: Implement regulations to ensure the prescribed ethical behaviour

The style and culture of the organisation greatly influences the attitude of employees. A good work culture nourishes the ethical conduct of the employees.

The style and culture of the organisation greatly influences the attitude of employees. A good work culture nourishes the ethical conduct of the employees. Since there are two kinds of management styles, external and internal, the ethical approach depends on the style of management adopted.

The external formal process tends to measure and reward all the good work of employees. This may lead to employees indulging in corrupt and unethical practices to gain rewards. On the other hand, an internal formal process, while recognising the work of employees, does not measure and judge it. In this case, the employees are under less pressure and may not indulge in unethical practices. It is important for a firm to respect individuals and their thoughts, and treat employees and customers well.

It should be remembered that ethical programs do not apply only to employees, but should be extended to the highest level of the organisation. There should be a staff member in charge of the ethical standards. He/she will be responsible for issuing an ethical code to all personnel. The legal and the human resources department should conduct trainings to sensitise the employees in an organisation regarding the consequence of ethical problems and the stand the organisation will take on ethical issues. This training should be carried out at the time of induction and promotion of the employees.

Control systems for ethics are designed to establish formal communication channels that help in reporting ethical violations (whistle blowing).

The channels ensure that employees who report these violations are protected from their fellow employees and their superiors. This is known as "whistle blowing protection." Ethical behaviour can be used by the top management as a yard-stick when deciding on promotions.

Control systems for ethics are designed to establish formal communication channels that help in reporting ethical violations (whistle blowing). The channels ensure that employees who report these violations are protected from their fellow employees and their superiors. This is known as "whistle blowing protection."

21.4 ETHICAL PRINCIPLES IN DESIGNING A CONTROL SYSTEM

The objective of control systems is to assist managers in achieving the goals and objectives of the organisation. A control system, in which all the subsystems are designed to achieve these goals and objectives, is a goal congruent subsystem. For a control system to be ethical, it requires an environment conducive to the ethical conduct. This requires an environment that is conducive to ethical behaviour, the business objectives and stakeholders' objectives. Thus, the concept of fairness is stressed to achieve an environment, which is conducive to ethical behaviour.

An unfair control system increases mistrust amongst employees and distorts information, which in turn results in poor control. The ethical administrator in an organisation should keep a disciplinary record so that the ethical program is perceived to be fair. This is one of the key ways to increase trust and trust is the key factor in improving performance.

In order to increase the effectiveness of ethical control it should be extended to all personnel in the organisation as well as stakeholders. In the case of customers, truthful and fair advertising is a way to gain their trust and lead the business forward. The suppliers form a vital link in a business. They should be taken into confidence on all counts, especially when major decisions are taken for the business. This will ensure relationship based on trust.

In order to increase the effectiveness of ethical control it should be extended to all personnel in the organisation as well as stakeholders.

SUMMARY

Ethics are very important to a business in today's world. Conducting a business for the social and collective good is not just desirable, but essential. While designing a control system it is essential to see that it complies with the law of the land and the ethical code of the business and becomes goal congruent. Sensitising the employees and the stakeholders regarding the ethical code of the organisation is necessary. Training and development programs regarding the ethical concepts and goals of the organisation should be conducted. A person, who will be in charge of the ethical and moral values, should be employed. An organisation should disseminate information about its ethics and should ensure that its employees behave ethically and morally with its customers and the suppliers who repose their trust in the business. The ethical aspects of the business should take a cybernetic approach of assessment and feedback leading to corrective results. In designing the control system the concept of fairness should be kept in mind. Flexible, informal control helps employees to deal correctly with ethical issues.

Review Questions

1. What are the issues that cause concern for a control system when ethical issues are not taken into consideration?
2. How does one ensure that ethical issues are taken care of in the management control system?
3. What is the role of cybernetic control in designing a control system with an ethical code?
4. What steps should an organisation take to increase its ethical standards?

Analytical Questions

1. If a bank has to design a control system what points should it keep in mind to make the control ethical?
2. List the ethical issues that should be taken into consideration while designing a cybernetic control for a hospital.

PART—F

CASES FOR MANAGEMENT CONTROL SYSTEM

Long Cases

CASE 1—Action Learning as a Form of Management Control—Dutch Elevator Company

What is management control? According to Emmanuel, Otley and Merchant (1990), management control may be defined as: "... the processes by which managers attempt to ensure that their organisation adapts successfully to its changing environment."

Through management control, goal and behaviour congruence between organisational members may be established (Emmanuel, Otley and Merchant *ibid.*). Thus, situations of opportunistic behaviour may be overcome. Management control information can also help to reduce the uncertainty that surrounds specific activities, processes or projects.

Why are management control measures useful in an action learning situation?

An argument against their use is that they introduce the idea of 'accountability' in action learning. However, we feel that learning is not the prime incentive of an action learning program. We presume that organisational members are always intrinsically and highly motivated to participate in an action learning program, solve a problem, and learn from it. This would be the case if participants in an action learning program take part in it voluntarily, however, this seems to be occurring less and less in practice. This raises a question as to the motivations of the participants. Another reason why we have assumed that action learning participants are intrinsically motivated is the fact that literature concerning the action learning almost exclusively discusses success stories in which such motivation is (allegedly) present.

However, it is not their *involvement* in action learning as such that will motivate participants to tackle a problem, but rather whether they are really facing the problem under discussion. If participants are not allowed to bring in their own problem(s) in an action learning program, management control measures might help to increase participants' motivation to tackle a problem seriously and thoroughly.

In an action learning program, personal learning can occur, but whether or not organisational learning takes place depends on a number of factors. The first is that what the individuals have learnt should fit in with the organisation's current institutional framework and secondly the organisation must be willing to accept and work with what has been learned by participants, outside of the program, even if this runs contrary to its present institutional setting.

How can management control measures be used to facilitate personal and organisational learning in an action learning situation? There are two ways in which this can be achieved. Firstly, management control measures may be specifically tailored to an action learning program and secondly, action learning may be used as a form of management control itself.

Let us start by looking into the first way to use management control in an action learning situation.

When setting up concrete management control measures for the activities taking place in an action learning program, Hofstede (1981) asserted that one must look at four characteristics of the activities that are to be controlled in order to find a 'suitable' form of management control. These characteristics are:

- The goals of an activity (are they unambiguous or not?)
- The output of an activity (is it measurable or not?)
- Advance knowledge about the effects of management interventions (does it exist or not?)
- The repetitiveness of an activity (will it happen again or not?)

Only trial and error control remains as a possible control type in the case of action learning. This conclusion is endorsed by Hofstede's (1981) reflection that: "... as soon as people are part of the process ... our routine control tends to become trial and error control because learning about human behaviour usually takes place through trial and error."

When using trial and error control, it may be hypothesised that since action learning needs to be a repetitive activity if its effects are to appear in an organisation in the long run, the learning process of organisational members must be encouraged. It is here that the alleged relevance of controlled experimentation in action learning comes in, as it states that experimentation is the basis of learning. Often however, an organisation, albeit unwittingly, hinders experimentation by participants in action learning programs, when it installs performance measures that reward routine behaviour that was already present before the program began. Standard performance measures are hardly ever attuned to organisational learning and tend to be based on backward-looking, diagnostic reward schemes that refer to previously set budget targets among others. In such a case, management control measures will not help to foster an action learning program.

Alternatively, action learning can be used as a form of management control *itself*. Experimentation in an action learning program can be targeted (by an organisation) towards specific problems in specific contexts. This effectively comprises a control structure. Increasing the number of repetitions of an action learning program, in which one can have different roles, may strengthen the retention of behaviour associated with the program. When an organisation finds action learning relevant or even crucial for organisational conduct, it can subsequently lead to the institutionalisation of such behaviour at the organisational level.

In a recent case the latter view on management control came to the fore. This case will be examined below, as it may shed some new light on the conduct of action learning programs that aim to achieve both personal and organisational learning. Besides, it highlights a different (and less rigid) approach to management control, in which control is used interactively and proactively.

The more that control systems are used interactively, and the more that top managers are involved in giving out signals that an organisation needs to adapt to changing environmental circumstances the greater is the positive effect of employees' activities on organisational performance. Thus, a (interactively used) control system can help to translate employees' activities into increased organisational performance.

Company 'M' is an elevator company located in the Netherlands that installs and maintains elevators in (mostly) residential buildings. The company operated as a separate entity between 1996 and 2004, when it was sold to one of the larger players on the market. In the heyday of the company, which occurred between 2001 and 2003, problems pointed out by organisational members could be tackled via an action learning program (called an 'initiative') upon approval by M's top management.

Many company documents were available upon request from the company director (denoted as 'F' hereafter). Apart from the company director, interviews of the sales manager, finance manager, and head of operations were conducted. These managers were all involved, at some point of time, in M's initiatives. F claims that many processes in his company were shaped by initiatives and asserts that their implementation was always safeguarded (provided that their outcome had been accepted by both the so-called 'resonance group,' which is explained below, and M's management team).

F strongly believed in employee empowerment, *kaizen* and operating as a coach in stimulating organisational success, stressing the need for open communications and mutual trust between employees. This was acknowledged by all the stakeholders, who were interviewed. In a SME like M, which F had started (partly with the help of one of his brothers), and for which he personally hired and fired all personnel (amounting to 60 employees in M's halcyon days), this approach turned out to be a fruitful one, despite some very turbulent times. F had decided to draw on a focus strategy, with the aim of becoming one of the main players on the market in terms of customer satisfaction. Although M's price for elevators generally was 20% over the price of the market leader, F was able to realise this goal about halfway through the company's existence. In order to put M's focus strategy into operation, F employed repetitive, rolling budgets as an explicit management control mechanism. These budgets, after having been pinned down at the beginning of the year, were open for structured discussions halfway through the year and thus functioned as a communication device in the company. Throughout the year, employees could apply for an 'initiative' if they felt that the mode of business should be changed in order to fulfil M's strategic targets contained in the aforementioned budgets. In an initiative, which basically started as a form that had to be filled in and sent to a special e-mail address, one had to signal a problem and ask to be allowed to work on it. Provided that a problem could not be solved easily or routinely, and that attention was indeed considered essential by M's management, an initiative could generally be undertaken, although at most five of them were allowed to run in M at a single point of time (so that the regular work process would not be impaired). In 2001 and 2002, M's management team received a total of 109 initiatives. Every initiative had the same basic set-up. It firstly included a project leader who was appointed by the management team (and who often differed from the person who had handed in the initiative, for the latter would mostly have strong strategic ties). Project leaders coordinated initiatives, which were subsequently carried out by a project team. A project team was selected by the project leader and could in principle comprise *all* of M's employees, and even people from outside the company (customers, suppliers, co-producers, etc,). A project team usually contained 5-8 members. The project leader was not part of the team. Both a so-called 'resonance group' and a (principally external) facilitator accompanied a project team, although resonance groups were only installed when an initiative was clearly tied to customer demands. Resonance groups consisted of members of external parties relevant to M (like its suppliers). When asked by the project leader, they would get involved in an initiative to provide feedback on the solutions proposed by a team. They had to discuss whether these met the quality standards prevailing on the market and were realisable, so that their implementation could follow. However, M's management ultimately decided whether implementation could take place. The facilitator functioned exactly like in an action learning program, attempting to safeguard a team's process and progress, whilst highlighting the need for controlled experimentation through processes of trial and error. The general set-up of an initiative is shown in Figure 1 below.

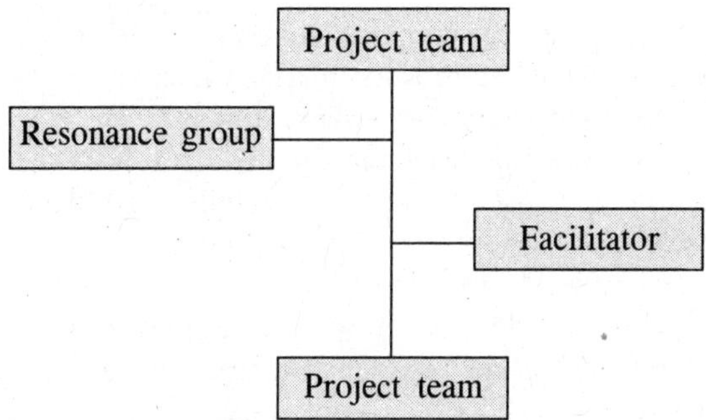

Fig. 1: General set-up of an initiative

An initiative typically lasted between two to nine months. Organisational members could be involved in different roles in different initiatives at the same time, but also had their regular tasks to accomplish. Most of the stakeholders interviewed claim that working with initiatives helped to enhance organisational performance and learning, the more since their outcome was almost always implemented, which was a strong incentive to work through an issue constructively and thoroughly.

When the outcome of an initiative was implemented, it led to changes in M's so-called 'Handboek Algemeen' ('General Handbook'), in which all processes and procedures in the company had been codified (by its employees). This information was gathered through interview techniques. Several new versions of the handbook were issued up until its final version dated December 2002. Working with initiatives was however not a success that happened overnight in M. Employees, in particular those who had previously worked for other (elevator) companies, often had difficulties to come to terms with the concept. F asserts that when being involved in an initiative for the first time, these employees tended to take shortcuts instead of thoroughly working out a problem and openly discussing it from all angles. F literally had to teach them, through repeated group and personal discussions, that their behaviour was likely to lead to unproductive solutions. At times however, employees had to be laid off, for they could or would not work with the initiative concept and/or for M's management team made strategic decisions that led to this.

Shaping the initiative concept as described above was also a process of trial and error. Only after various discussions and experiments, involving several external consultants, did it finally take the shape previously set out (in the fall of 2001). F feels that one of his biggest problems was to differentiate between complex problems 'worthy' of an initiative and problems that could more easily be tackled through *kaizen* approaches. There obviously existed a grey area between these types of problems, which he found to be (at least partly) indecipherable. Explanations as to why an initiative had been accepted or not were thus not always easy to give, and this sometimes led to conflicts with employees (when an initiative had been rejected).

What does the foregoing example tell us in terms of management control? In the first place, it illustrates that in M, management control was used in a much 'looser' fashion than one normally finds in organisations. For instance, M's (rolling) budget did not form the foundations of a reward system (which M never had) and did not contain strict financial targets. It was debatable once a year and functioned as a beacon to see whether organisational performance was still on track. Therefore, budgets were used interactively in M. When organisational performance was not on track, initiatives could be handed in to correct possible deviations. These generally led to new routines and procedures in the organisation, which were subsequently codified in the 'Handboek Algemeen'. M's budgets thus *indirectly* spurred on organisational learning (and perhaps also organisational performance) as well. Secondly, although M's control framework was laid down in a top-down fashion (by F), the input thereof was primarily a bottom-up process in which action learning principles played a considerable part (most notably through the initiatives). Thereby, these principles comprised a form of management control *themselves*.

M's initiative concept thus was an interactive control system that aimed to develop the focus strategy the company had adopted, at least during its heyday. Action learning and management control can thus readily be tied together. That the company was finally sold had probably nothing to do with the success or failure of the initiatives but with external conditions that a SME like M could not influence. All interviewees deem working with initiatives a valuable experience, which they have almost all tried to ingrain in their new work setting.

However, they acknowledge that initiatives will probably not work in all organisations (listing political organisations and multinationals as possible exceptions), and indicate that top management support and involvement is a crucial success factor for the concept to take hold in an organisation over an extended period of time.

Final remarks

What happened in company 'M' should not be considered the final word in action learning. The case was only intended to highlight one of the ways in which management control can be used in an action learning situation, which is an issue that is often neglected in the action learning literature. This neglect may be due to an apparent negative connotation associated with the term 'control', that is, with the (supposed) hindrance of personal creativity. There may be added value in considering management control issues in action learning, as this can help to increase both organisational learning and performance. This issue has to be treated more extensively in the action learning literature.

CASE 2—Strategic Planning and Programming – ITC Limited

Strategic planning is the process of deciding on the programs that the organisation will undertake and the amount of resources that will be allocated to each program in the next few years. For strategic planning to be effective it should be accompanied by an appropriate organisational structure, an effective management information system, a budgeting system and a reward system. The programming process is a long-term organisational process for making resource allocation decisions.

There are four elements of strategy: domain sought, differential advantage, strategic thrusts and targeted results. The domain sought relates to analysing the business environment in which the organisation is functioning. It addresses issues related to the changing needs of the business activity, the changes in the business environment, changes in the customer's perception regarding the company's product and best practices to deal with competition. Differential advantage relates to identifying the strengths and weaknesses of different businesses, improving upon the strengths and overcoming the weaknesses. After an organisation analyses the domain sought and differential advantage, the next step is to plan the strategies required to achieve the goals. This involves issues related to costs, marketing new products and services, planning the training and development strategies required for the staff to work in congruence with the organisational goals. The last stage involves analysing performance. To know whether an organisation is moving in the right direction, it is important to measure the actual results against expected results at regular intervals.

The strategic planning process involves the following steps:

- Reviewing and updating the previous year's strategic plan
- Deciding on assumptions and guidelines for the plan
- First iteration of the new strategic plan
- Analysis
- Second iteration of the new strategy
- Review and approval

ITC is one of India's foremost private sector companies with a market capitalisation of around US$ 13 billion and a turnover of US$ 3 billion. Rated among the world's best big companies by Forbes magazine, ITC ranks third in pre-tax profit among India's private sector corporations. ITC has a diversified presence in cigarettes, hotels, paperboards & specialty papers, packaging, agri-business, packaged foods & confectionery, branded apparel, greeting cards and other FMCG products. While ITC is an outstanding market leader in its traditional businesses of cigarettes, hotels, paper-boards, packaging and agri-exports, it is rapidly gaining a market share even in its nascent businesses of packaged foods & confectionery, branded apparel and greeting cards. As one of India's most valuable and respected corporations, ITC is widely perceived to be dedicatedly nation-oriented. Chairman Y.C. Deveshwar calls this source of inspiration "*a commitment beyond the market*". In his own words: "*ITC believes that its aspiration to create enduring value for the nation provides the motive force to sustain growing shareholder value. ITC practices this philosophy by not only driving each of its businesses towards international competitiveness but by also consciously contributing to enhancing the competitiveness of the larger value chain of which it is a part.*" ITC's diversified status originates from its corporate strategy aimed at creating multiple drivers of growth anchored on its time-tested core competencies: unmatched reach of distribution, superior brand-building capabilities, effective supply chain management and acknowledged service skills in hotels. Over time, the strategic forays into new businesses are expected to garner a significant share of these emerging high-growth markets in India. ITC's agri-business is one of India's largest exporters of agricultural products. ITC has been one of the country's biggest foreign exchange earners (US$ 2 billion in the last decade). The company's 'e-Choupal' initiative is enabling Indian agriculture to significantly enhance its competitiveness by empowering Indian farmers through the power of the Internet. This transformational strategy, which has already become the subject matter of a case study at Harvard Business School, is expected to progressively create for ITC a huge rural distribution infrastructure, significantly enhancing the company's marketing reach. ITC's wholly owned information technology subsidiary, ITC Infotech India Limited, is aggressively pursuing emerging opportunities in providing end-to-end IT solutions, including e-enabled services and business process outsourcing. ITC's production facilities and hotels have won numerous national and international awards for quality, productivity, safety and environment management systems. ITC was the first company in India to be rated for Corporate Governance by ICRA, an associate of Moody's Investors Service, which accorded it the second highest rating, signifying "a high level of assurance on the quality of corporate governance." ITC employs over 20,000 people at more than 60 locations across India. Ranked among India's most valuable companies by 'Business Today' magazine, ITC continuously endeavours to enhance its wealth generating capabilities in a global environment to consistently reward more than 3,58,862 shareholders, fulfil the aspirations of its stakeholders and meet societal expectations. This over-arching vision of the company is expressively captured in its corporate positioning statement: "*Enduring Value. For the nation. For the Shareholder.*"

Organisational structure to support the strategic planning of a diverse portfolio:

Formal 3-tiered governance structure:

1. Board of directors, comprising
   - executive (4) and non-executive directors (8)
   - strategic supervision
2. Corporate management committee, comprising
   - executive directors and senior managers
   - strategic management
3. CEO and divisional management committee
   - executive management

Strategic thrusts

1. Sustain multiple drivers of growth, matching internal capabilities with emerging market opportunities
2. Pursue world class competitiveness in all businesses and across the entire value chain
3. Best-in-class in terms of:
   - Internal vitality
   - Market standing
   - Profitability
4. Strategy of organisation and governance processes geared to manage multiple businesses
5. Blend core competencies and leverage ITC umbrella strengths to create new avenues of growth

Strategic planning among the various business divisions

FMCG - Cigarettes

In the face of the extremely challenging environment, ITC continues its strategic focus on product quality, technology upgradation, productivity improvement and enhanced value addition to brands. Investments of nearly Rs.1100 crores over the last eight years in state-of-the-art technology enables ITC to offer products to Indian consumers that represent the finest global quality standards. Product innovation, spurred by deep consumer insights nurtured over time, reinforced ITC's leadership position in the industry. An array of packaging formats were launched in key value segments, enlarging the portfolio of world-class products. 'Insignia', launched in the unique shoulder box packaging style, redefined the premium segment and strengthened the association of ITC's brands with superlative quality. 'India Kings' became the first Indian brand to be offered to consumers in a state-of-the-art international contour pack, significantly reinforcing its premium imagery. The ultra premium bevelled edge packaging of 'Classic Milds,' established this brand's superiority amongst its competitors, which include international and contraband offers. Buoyed by this experience, consumers of 'Classic Menthol' were also offered their product in this packaging format. A new wave pack was introduced in the 70-75 mm filter category and is rapidly gaining consumer acceptance.

In addition to investments in brands to provide world-class standards to the Indian consumer, ITC is committed to continuously improving in-house standards of environment, occupational health and safety. This commitment continues to earn international recognition. The trade marketing and distribution capabilities of ITC, widely acknowledged as industry benchmarks, have been further expanded to cater to ITC's growing portfolio of FMCG products. Concurrently, ITC's R&D competencies were enhanced, creating the Integrated Group Research and Development Centre with capabilities to lead a wider gamut of R&D initiatives in the FMCG sector.

FMCG - Others

ITC, with diverse competencies residing in its various businesses, is ideally positioned to leverage the significant growth opportunity inherent in these broader trends. It is the strategic intent of ITC to secure long term growth by synergising and blending this pool of competencies to create new engines of growth. Investments in product development and design complement the deep consumer insights gained by ITC over time to create a range of value added FMCG products across categories and segments. ITC's Integrated Group Research and Development Centre at Bangalore and the state-of-the art Master Design Facility at Gurgaon provide cutting edge capability in product development and innovation thereby creating a franchise in the minds of consumers as providers of world-class value added products. Each category within this business segment of ITC also serves to widen and deepen the FMCG trade marketing and distribution capability, which already services about 1.5 million convenience outlets. Further, ITC's pioneering e-Choupal model is engaged in addressing the issues of the last mile in rural India, thereby providing the foundation for unmatched delivery capability that can encompass not only FMCG but also a host of other products and services. As one of the largest users of consumer research in the country, ITC is constantly engaged in creating products in anticipation of consumer needs, creating in the process competitively superior offerings straddling a wide range of segments from staples to lifestyle products. Towards this end, ITC continues to invest in people systems and proprietary processes and protocols. ITC is also engaged in creating low cost demand fulfilment capacity by upgrading capabilities across value chains. This business model envisages retaining critical elements of each value chain in-house while manufacture is outsourced largely to Small and Medium Enterprises (SMEs). Such a model enables ITC to draw upon key internal competencies including agri sourcing skills, cuisine knowledge and services expertise, paperboard and packaging domain knowledge, state-of-the-art IT services capability and the well known trade marketing and distribution strength to enhance the competitiveness of the entire value chain.

Lifestyle retailing

In line with evolving consumer preferences ITC's lifestyle retailing business continued to enhance the portfolio of offerings in three distinct usage segments, namely formal wear, relaxed wear and evening wear, to provide discerning consumers with unmatched variety and vitality. The expanded 'Wills Classic' range, which caters to the high potential formal wear segment, reinforced its exclusive, world-class brand proposition, accounting for nearly 40% of turnover of the 30 select 'Wills Lifestyle' stores offering this range. The launch of the 'Wills Clublife' premium evening wear range in select stores enabled fuller representation in the fashion portfolio. In the highly competitive arena of branded apparel, Wills Lifestyle is gradually gaining acceptance as a preferred fashion destination. In order to enhance accessibility to the consumer, brand availability was extended to a chosen few high profile large format retailers and multi-brand outlets in the country. Apart from consolidating its presence in the premium, western ready-to-wear segment, ITC also registered progress in the high growth branded mid-price segment. The size of this segment is estimated to be about Rs. 2400 crores with annual growth rates in the region of 10%.

ITC, which made a national entry into this segment in 2003 with a range of high quality, attractively priced men's wear under the brand 'John Players', consolidated its presence in over 3000 outlets up to March 2004. The business geared up the supply chain to address the challenge of the significantly higher scale of operations, in terms of both product range and outlets serviced. The state-of-the art master facility in Gurgaon continues to engage in R&D activities to offer superior products to the consumer, besides facilitating prototyping of designs. The business' internationally benchmarked quality continues to earn industry recognition, with 'Wills Lifestyle' winning the 'Most Admired Exclusive Brand Retail Chain of the Year' at the Images Fashion Awards 2003.

Greetings, gifting and stationery

Focused improvement in product quality and supply chain processes enabled the Greeting, Gifting and Stationery Business (GGSB) to capture 20% market share in the greeting cards segment in 2003-04, with value added products available in 12,000 outlets across 700 markets. The strengthened design capability was corroborated by increasing retailer confidence, with 395 stores opting to partner the business as 'expressions' valued customers. The business also established new value chain partnerships encompassing design, and manufacturing to enhance efficiency through streamlined back-end operations. The range of cards supporting social causes introduced in partnership with the SOS Children's Villages of India is established amongst the top social cause greeting card brands in the country. The year 2003-04 also witnessed the launch of the 'Paperkrafts' and 'Classmates' range of notebooks across major markets, leveraging ITC's capability in high quality paper manufacture to offer superior products at competitive prices. Market response has been encouraging; with the range exhibiting potential to garner a sizeable share of the Rs.500 crore, fast growing stationery market. The expanding range of world-class products, aggressive penetration in the domestic market and progressive entry into export markets provide a platform for addressing the growth challenge over the medium term.

Safety matches and incense sticks

ITC possesses a number of strengths that can be leveraged to enhance the competitiveness of the small scale and cottage sectors and thereby give expression to ITC's philosophy of creating shareholder value through serving society. Safety matches and incense sticks represent two such endeavours. The product development capability of the Integrated Group Research and Development Centre, blended with ITC's paperboard and packaging domain expertise and the FMCG trade marketing and distribution capability, provide the wherewithal to service evolving consumer needs for value added products in fragmented markets estimated at over Rs.2,000 crores. ITC commenced marketing high quality safety matches sourced from the small scale sector in August 2002 under ITC's brands, 'i Kno', 'Mangaldeep', 'Vaxlit', 'Delite' and 'Aim'. The 'Mangaldeep' brand of incense sticks was launched in December 2003 in varied fragrances at different price points and pack combinations in unique in-house developed 'fragrance locked' packaging. Visibly superior product quality coupled with rapid market rollout enabled the capture of a growing market share, with 'Aim' achieving the distinction of becoming by far the single largest match brand in India. Encouraged by the consumer response in the domestic market, ITC commenced its forays into international markets through export of safety matches to the USA and West Africa. ITC continues to support the competitiveness of the small scale and cottage sectors through induction of appropriate technology and best practices. Mid 1990s, 44 such upgraded small scale units supplied high quality safety matches to ITC. In pursuance of its abiding social commitment, ITC forged partnerships with select NGOs to train economically disadvantaged women in rolling agarbattis and thereby provide vocational opportunities.

Hotels

Successful execution of the ambitious investment program over the last seven years enabled ITC's Welcomgroup to regain its position as the fastest growing premium hotel chain in the country. The service edge of the ITC Welcomgroup chain and the land bank in future growth markets like Bangalore and Chennai represent formidable assets that strengthen the ability of ITC's hotels business to address future growth challenges. ITC is therefore well positioned to sustain leadership in this infrastructure industry, the growth of which is perhaps one of the best indicators of the nation's economic progress.

Paperboards and specialty papers

The business seeks to address growth challenges in a fast globalising market through a number of interventions aimed at improving competitiveness through internal efficiencies. Such interventions include: (a) implementation of total productive maintenance for production loss minimisation, and enhancement of quality and productivity, (b) installing e-procurement systems for improving buying efficiency of key inputs and (c) leveraging synergies across businesses within ITC through integrated logistics management for lowering transportation and warehousing costs. The growing sophistication of the Indian consumer is expected to accelerate the demand for high quality packaging, and in turn for world-class paperboards. With expectations of robust growth in the Indian economy, the per capita consumption of paper in India can increase beyond the current 5 kg per annum to progressively approximate the world average of 54 kg per annum. ITC, on the strength of its growing competitive capability is best poised to tap this potential.

CASE 3—Tracing the Transfer Pricing in Philips India Ltd.

***"It's a critical application because the transfer pricing determines who gets what revenue from the ultimate sale,"* says Philips Semiconductors' Bostock.**

Royal Philips Electronics of the Netherlands (NYSE: PHG, AEX: PHI) is one of the world's biggest electronics companies and Europe's largest, with sales of US$ 33 billion. Having activities in the three interlocking domains of healthcare, lifestyle and technology, the company has 165,600 employees in more than 60 countries. Philips has products in categories like medical diagnostic imaging and patient monitoring, colour television sets, electric shavers, lighting and silicon system solutions. In December 2003, Philips reached the impressive milestone of 100,000 patents. Some 20,000 inventions underlie the 100,000 patents. Philips is also the owner of 22,000 brands, 11,000 model rights and 2,000 domain names. Some examples of important patented Philips inventions are the audiocassette, CD, DVD, JPEG, MPEG (digital video), Xenon car lights, UHP lights for projectors and GSM speech codification.

Philips in India started operations in 1930, with 75 employees as "Philips Electrical Co. (India) Private Ltd". Philips India grew over 4,500 employees by 2003 with a turnover of over US$ 333 million. Philips India is a leader in lighting, semiconductors, consumer electronics, medical systems, domestic appliances and personal care, with a wide range of internationally current products backed by superior design and technology. Philips has seven manufacturing sites at various locations in India and a world class innovation campus and research and development centre in Bangalore contributing to over 20% of Philips' global resources for high-tech R&D and software development. Philips has made an investment of over US$ 150 million in the Indian operations over the past few years.

Philips India is a market leader in almost all its product categories. It has a 45.8% share (revenue) of the audio market, which includes radios, hi-fi stereos, monos, CD players, DVD products and home theatre systems. Fifty per cent of cardiac examinations in India are done on Philips equipment. Philips has a leading market share in lighting systems, particularly in lamps, lighting electronics and automotive lighting. Philips has maintained a leading position in the semiconductor industry in India. Three out of five TVs in the country have Philips chips. Philip chips are present in the world's thinnest watch made in India. Philips India has a leading market share in the juicer-mixer-grinder category and dry iron category.

Philips India has several recognitions to its credit:

- Recognised as one of the best Indian employers by the Business Today (BT)-Hewitt Survey
- Rated No. 16 in the Economic Times Brand Equity - India's Most Trusted Brands 2003 survey.
- Recognised by Business World magazine as "The Most Respected Company in India in the Consumer Durables Sector" in 2002.
- Philips India's Philips Software Centre (PSC) was placed in the top five in the Business World-Grow Talent "Great Places to Work" survey.

Transfer pricing: Emerging issues

Corporates, the world over are expanding in an effort to gain a share of the global pie. There is talk of the world fast turning into a global village with economies increasingly becoming inter-connected. But with cross-border trade there comes a whole new set of problems. Transfer pricing* (Refer to Exhibit 1) is one of them.

When a company opens a branch in another country, manufactures its products there and then imports them, there is a question as to what price the parent company should pay for buying the product from the subsidiary. This price, until now, has been subject to the parent company's discretion and has been used by many corporates the world over to control tax outgoings to their governments. The price at which goods are transferred from one arm of the company to another is known as transfer pricing.

IT initiatives in transfer pricing

Philips Semiconductors, a US$ 4.3 billion division of Philips Electronics NV, implemented Baan financials. However, reports from the new Baan system could not be used to achieve a key corporate goal in the United States: rationalising a costing system that involved transfer pricing among development, manufacturing, testing, and sales units worldwide. The existing costing application suffered from outdated Cobol programming. It was difficult to update, required centralised data entry from faxes and other media, and created confusion because of multiple cost listings for the same item. So Philips Semiconductors turned to the consulting firm KPMG.

"*It's a critical application because the transfer pricing determines who gets what revenue from the ultimate sale*," says Philips Semiconductors' Bostock. "*Our vision was to create a simplified costing system that would provide much greater access and the ability to quickly change pricing methodologies and other calculations*." The system would also give an executive-level view of how revenue and costs are distributed along Philips' internal value chain.

With these marching orders, Philips and KPMG developed a Java-based application that accurately calculates internal transfer pricing information as items move internationally from one business unit to another – for example, from production facilities in Asia to sales offices in Germany. The application not only standardises business rules so all units operate consistently, but also allows data input and report access via the Web. The application is being tested in the United States before a worldwide rollout in the first quarter of 1999. It is also being integrated with existing mainframe order processing, shipping, and invoicing systems.

As companies become increasingly global in their operations inter-company transactions are becoming more commonplace. With the increase in transactions tax authorities have been attempting to ensure that they are optimising the tax revenues in their respective jurisdictions with the applications of new transfer pricing laws, new documentation requirements, and the installation of stricter penalties.

Companies are facing an increasing documentation burden with respect to their inter-company transactions in order to show that the transactions have been conducted on an "arm's-length" basis. Therefore, there is an increased need for companies to have a consistent approach to identifying, collecting, and documenting the data needed for a reasonable defence of their transfer pricing policies.

PriceWaterhouseCoopers has developed *e*MAXIMIN, a first of its kind web-based product that has been specifically designed to handle repetitive, routine, time-consuming aspects of transfer pricing work, while providing companies with a consistent transfer pricing collection and documentation methodology.

*e*MAXIMIN enables a company to better deal with transfer pricing issues by:

- Automating the time-intensive data collection task
- Identifying, collecting and evaluating relevant data for transfer pricing methodology
- Assessing issues and evaluating risk areas
- Creating and editing documentation to substantiate transfer prices and policies and defend against penalties

Operational difficulties

- Some intra-group transactions are so unique that they cannot be compared with others
- TP reports of two AE's would have conflicting conclusions
- No recommended Profit Level Indicator (PLI) – wide fluctuations may result depending upon each PLI
- Corporates are hesitant to disclose information.

Database difficulties

- Time gap in search of databases
- Non availability of recognised databases
- Lack of comparables

EXHIBIT 1

Transfer Pricing Regulations in India

Introduction

The Finance Act of 2001 introduced detailed Transfer Pricing Regulations (TPR) in India, with effect from 1stApril 2001 corresponding to the assessment year 2002-2003. The rules for transfer pricing were notified on August 21, 2001.

Need and rationale for introducing TPR

A need was felt for detailed and separate regulations for administering transfer pricing with globalisation of the Indian economy. Absence of such regulations not only results in litigation but loss of revenue to the exchequer. In absence of transfer pricing regulations, India was losing its legitimate share of revenue.

New provisions

The sections and rules under the income tax act, which deal with transfer pricing regulations are sections 92 to 92F and rules 10A to 10E and sections 271(1) (c) , 271AA, 271BA and 271G.

Section 92

- Any income arising from an international transaction shall be computed having regard to arm's length price. [Section 92(1)]
- The allowance for any expense or interest shall be determined having regard to the arm's length price while determining income under sub-section (1) above. [Section 92(2)]
- The cost or expense allocated or apportioned between two or more associated enterprises shall be at arm's length price. [Section 92(3)]

This is a case of cost contribution arrangement or cost sharing arrangement between intra group entities.

Associated Enterprise (AE) [Section 92A]

Basic criteria

The basic criterion to determine associated enterprises is the participation in management, control or capital (ownership) of one enterprise by another enterprise.

The participation may be direct or indirect or through one or more intermediaries. It appears that one may go to any layer of management, control or ownership in order to find out association.

1. Direct control
2. Through intermediary

If enterprise B is managed, controlled or owned, either directly or through an intermediary, then Enterprise B is said to be an AE of enterprise A.

If Mr. A and Mr. B control both Enterprise A and Enterprise B then both Enterprise A and Enterprise B are associated enterprises.

Additional criteria

Additional criteria to determine associated enterprises are based on:

- Holding 26% of the voting power
- If Enterprise A controls 26% of the shares that carry voting rights of Enterprise B, directly or indirectly, then Enterprise A and Enterprise B are associated enterprises.
- Advance of loan not less than 51% of the total assets of borrowing company

Enterprise A has given a loan of Rs. 51 to Enterprise B.

Book value of assets of Enterprise B is Rs.100.

Loan by Enterprise A to Enterprise B is 51% of the book value of the assets of B.

Therefore Enterprise A and Enterprise B are associated enterprises.

The term "book value of assets" has not been defined, hence there will be questions such as inclusion or otherwise of intangible assets, accumulated losses, deferred revenue expenditure, etc.

- Guarantees not less than 10% on behalf of borrower
- Total borrowing of Enterprise B is Rs.100. Guarantee by Enterprise A is Rs.10. Therefore, Enterprise A and Enterprise B are associated enterprises.
- Appointment of more than 50% of the Board of Directors or members of the governing board; Total number of the Board of Directors of B is ten. Enterprise A appoints six of them.
- Therefore, Enterprise A and Enterprise B are associated enterprises.

  If however, Enterprise A has the power to appoint six directors of Enterprise B, but in fact does not do so, Enterprise A and Enterprise B will not be associated enterprises.

  If Enterprise A or Mr. A appoints more than 50% of the directors/governing board members or one or more executive directors or governing board members of both the enterprises, then all such enterprises will be associated enterprises.

- Dependence (wholly) on the enterprise possessing exclusive rights, for manufacturing or pricing of goods or articles by using know-how, patents, etc.
- This refers only to technology transfer and not financial participation.

  If Enterprise A manufactures product 'X' under a brand owned by Enterprise B, then Enterprise A and Enterprise B are associated enterprises.

  Large MNE's supplying technology to users worldwide will thus become associated enterprises, perhaps without knowing that they are associated enterprises!

  Technology could be by way of transfer for use of:

  i) Know-how; ii) patents; iii) copyrights; iv) trademarks; v) licences; vi) franchises; or vii) any other business or commercial right of similar nature.

  It is pertinent to note that technology for services e.g., software is not included in this definition.

- Dependence for up to 90% or more of raw materials and consumables on another enterprise, coupled with influence over price and other terms of supply.

If Enterprise A procures 90% of raw materials from Enterprise B on prices and terms determined by Enterprise B, both Enterprise A and Enterprise B will be associated enterprises.

Influence of prices for goods or articles manufactured or processed; If price is influenced by Enterprise B then Enterprise A and Enterprise B are associated enterprises.

One individual (or his relative jointly or separately) controlling two different enterprises;

E.g., Mr. P and Mr. Q may or may not jointly control Enterprise A and/or Enterprise B. Even if the brothers have separate economic activities, this condition will still continue to apply.

***Note** : The term "Relative" under section 2(41) of the Income tax Act 1961 means the husband, wife, brother, sister and any lineal ascendant or descendent enterprise.*

One Hindu Undivided Family (HUF) (or relative of a member of HUF - either jointly or separately) controlling two different enterprises.

Firm/AOP/BOI holding not less than 10% interest in another firm/AOP/BOI.

E.g., Firm A holds 10% interest in firm B. The two are associated enterprises.

- Relationship of mutual interest to be prescribed

AE comes into existence if any of the above criteria are met *at any time* during the previous year. However, transactions entered into by an enterprise before becoming an AE and after ceasing to be an AE would not be covered. In other words, the relationship of an AE must subsist at the time of entering into an international transaction.

International Transaction [Section 92B]

An international transaction is defined as a transaction between two or more associated enterprises of which either both or any one is a non-resident, in the nature of:

- Purchase, sale or lease of tangible property or intangible property; or
- Provision of services: or
- Landing or borrowing of money: or
- Any transaction having a bearing on the profits, income, losses or assets
- Mutual agreement or arrangement between two or more associated enterprises for the allocation or apportionment of any contribution cost or expense

The requirement of one of the parties to be non-resident would remove transactions between the Indian company and its overseas branch from the purview of the transfer pricing regulations as both entities will be residents. However, transactions between the foreign entity and its permanent establishment (Indian branch) would be covered. Similarly, any transaction between two permanent establishments in India would be covered as both will be non-residents of India. These regulations cover transactions of borrowing and lending.

CASE 4—Reward System in Centurion Bank of Punjab Ltd

Centurion Bank of Punjab was amongst the earliest banks to offer a technology enabled customer interface that provides easy access and superior customer services. The bank offers a wide spectrum of retail and corporate banking products and services and is a leader in the field.

Centurion Bank of Punjab is a new generation private sector bank offering a wide spectrum of retail, SME and corporate banking products and services. Centurion Bank of Punjab has a nationwide reach through its network of 240 branches and extension counters and 388 ATMS. The bank aims to serve all the banking and financial needs of its customers through multiple delivery channels, each of which is supported by state-of-the-art technology architecture.

Centurion Bank of Punjab was formed by the merger of "Centurion Bank" and "Bank of Punjab" both of which had strong retail franchises in their respective markets. Centurion Bank of Punjab has a well-managed and growing retail assets business, including leadership position in two-wheeler loans and commercial vehicle loans and a strong capital base.

As on March 31, 2004, Centurion Bank of Punjab had a network of 61 fully networked branches covering 45 cities, 148 ATMs, 20 extension counters and 23 marketing offices. Centurion Bank of Punjab provides various other facilities such as the ability to operate accounts from any of their branches on a 'real-time' basis, make e-payments and transfer funds instantly. Centurion Bank of Punjab's key focus remains a successful retail banking strategy.

Centurion Bank of Punjab (CBOP) was incorporated on June 30, 1994, under an overall economic reform program initiated by the Government of India in 1991, when the RBI granted nine new licenses for the establishment of commercial banks in the private sector. It obtained a Certificate of Incorporation on July 20, 1994 and subsequently received the banking license (BOM: 57) from RBI vide their letter no. DBOD/4577/16.01.104/95 dated January 13, 1995; it was founded by the erstwhile TCFC (The Centurion Finance Company) in the financial year 1999, TCFC was merged with Centurion Bank of Punjab Ltd vide a scheme of arrangement under the Act. The merger increased its branch network by adding 40 marketing offices of TCFC to its existing 30 branches at that time. The merger also marked its entry into retail asset financing, ahead of our peer banks, and strengthened its presence in southern India. It undertook a rebranding exercise and introduced new products like global debit cards, cash management services and depository services. It was among the first banks to enter the profitable 2-wheeler, commercial vehicles and construction equipment financing businesses.

Reward system

A reward system is a major motivational tool to secure participation of individuals to achieve organisational goals. It is usually felt that only the employees of an organisation are entitled to rewards. However, organisations also reward their stakeholders.

Reward systems are an important source of communication and feedback. Rewards create a sense of belonging, which makes an individual feel more committed towards his work.

Why reward systems?

The only way employees will fulfil their dreams is to share in the dream. Reward systems make this happen. "*However, reward systems are much more than just bonus plans and stock options. While they often include both of these incentives, they can also include awards and other recognition, promotions, reassignment, non-monetary bonuses (e.g., vacations), or a simple thank-you. The journey is the reward,*" says Steve Jobs.

The greatest management principle is that the things that are rewarded get done. "*You get more of the behaviour you reward. You don't get what you hope for, wish for or beg for. You get what you reward.*"

When employees do reach the target and meet a stretch standard set for them, they should be rewarded immediately. By doing so, employees will directly connect the reward with behaviour and higher performance they have attained. "*Fail to reward the right behaviour and you will most likely get the wrong results.*"

Designing & implementing reward systems in Centurion Bank of Punjab

Effective reward and motivation management is so challenging because a reward system that delivers positive results in one organisation may have the totally opposite effect in another. Equally baffling is the fact that good reward systems require constant updating to remain effective and relevant.

As a global leader in reward management consulting, Centurion Bank of Punjab helps organisations in every aspect of reward strategy, design and implementation and to delve deeper into the specific areas of reward strategy, design and implementation.

Reward strategy and design

How organisations reward their employees makes a statement about what they value. How employees are engaged and motivated deserves strategic attention. Hay Group helps put rewards into context, by understanding how different pay practices affect an organisation's and an individual's performance.

What is actually meant by reward strategy?

- To outline the organisation's objectives of reward
- Deliver clarity/shared understanding of how reward will be managed
- Identify how values will be expressed through reward management
- Provide boundaries within which reward policies operate.

Building on this, the approach focuses on:

- What performance matters most to the organisation?
- What rewards are valued most by the employees and management teams?
- How are performance and rewards aligned to advance the organisation's strategy?

There is increasing realisation that rewards comprise more than just the tangible elements of pay and benefits. Research has demonstrated that a wide range of factors, collectively, have a major impact on employee motivation and performance – factors that address the important question: 'Why should I work here?' – which include the working environment – career opportunities – personal/professional development – organisational reputation – leadership and management style – recognition etc.

This is the total reward approach to reward management and it is essential that all these elements of working life are underpinned by a consistent set of appropriate values and principles.

What is actually involved?

1. Information gathering: review of employee attitudes to rewards
2. Analysis: how these findings can be integrated with other HR strategies
3. Development: agreement on proposed reward strategy principles by HR and senior management and winning consensus
4. Documentation: concisely/formally documenting the reward policy
5. Communication: the reward strategy needs to be internally communicated to all employees

Organisational benefits

In short, an effective reward strategy will:

- Support the delivery and communication of an organisation's values
- Enable the development of consistent reward policies
- Provide clarity to all employees regarding the various elements of rewards being offered
- Lead to optimal levels of employee engagement and performance
- Maximise the return on reward investment

Taking a long-term view of reward is essential in today's competitive market if organisations are to recruit and retain the talented staff they need.

Total remuneration

Today's business realities - sharper competition, globalisation, rising costs, the need for improved performance with fewer resources to continuously satisfy ever more discerning customers and shareholders - means that more and more organisations will need to ensure that their total investment in human resources directly supports their business objectives. Remuneration strategies need to be closely aligned with their business strategies. This is driving a change to managing total remuneration.

In Centurion Bank of Punjab Ltd., total remuneration comprises base pay, short and long-term incentives and benefits. Increasingly, organisations are taking this broad view when they develop compensation and benefits policies.

- Employers need to ensure that the total package is competitive and appreciated
- Organisations need to manage compensation and benefit programmes to provide the maximum value to employees. The total remuneration approach provides a framework for doing that
- This approach will have a direct impact on organisational performance, profits and shareholder return by exerting more control over employee costs.

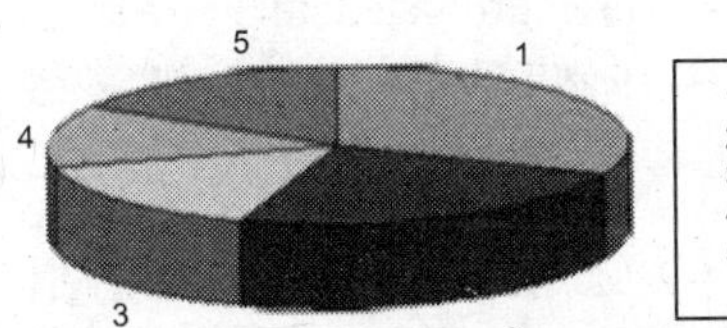

Centurion Bank of Punjab Ltd., has an intimate understanding of local job markets, employment practices and industry conditions. It builds its database with a globally consistent methodology, through which employees can compare jobs across a variety of functions, industries and countries with a high degree of confidence.

Innovative tools

Centurion Bank of Punjab Ltd. offers quick and easy access to information through internet-based reporting and analysis tool. Its total remuneration practice will allow employees to quickly and accurately address the following concerns with greater clarity:

- Does the total remuneration package reflect the current and long term reward philosophy, business strategy and is it cost effective?
- Does it attract, retain and motivate the right employee talent?
- Is it competitive within the industry and other relevant markets?
- Are benefit practices out of step with current employee needs?
- Can 'return on employee spend' be improved by making adjustments to package components?

Total Remuneration (TR) statements

Organisations can maximise their returns on reward investment by ensuring that their employees clearly understand the true value of their remuneration package.

A TR statement in Centurion Bank of Punjab Ltd. is a personalised statement of the tangible remuneration and benefits offered by the employer.

Why produce TR statements?

- Ensure employees understand the full value of their package
- Improve internal communications
- Improve the perception of external market competitiveness
- Highlight the existence and appreciation of little known or understood benefits
- Raise awareness of benefit issues as a precursor to making revisions of the package or introducing flexible benefits
- Make before and after comparisons after such revisions.

Pay and grade frameworks

Building on appropriate job measurement can work with an organisation to develop a tailored pay and grading framework to meet business objectives and the reward and recognition needs of employees.

Pay structures exist to help organisations in a number of ways, e.g., managing payroll costs effectively, providing clarity about what is expected and working as a basis for career progression.

A flexible approach to flexible benefits

There is a growing appreciation that it takes more than a good base salary to attract and retain top talent.

Flexibility of tangible and intangible benefits can play a key role in a reward strategy and in response Centurion Bank of Punjab Ltd. has developed a unique and independent proposition around flexible benefits.

Flexible benefits such as pensions, cars, childcare, incentives etc., can have a marked affect on motivation, retention and recruitment.

It is believed that implementation is a must for progressive organisations. Employees with a fully flexible 'cafeteria' scheme typically have a clearer understanding and appreciation of its value.

A flexible approach to design

Centurion Bank of Punjab Ltd. believes "the best scheme may not necessarily be the one that offers the maximum choices to employees. It is important that the plan design reflects the business reasons for introducing flexibility and the on-the-ground realities of the organisation as well as employee demand.

Incentives and performance pay

One of the enduring trends in reward management over the last decade has been the continuing development of variable pay schemes.

Variable pay now accounts for nearly 10% of the typical pay package and significantly more for certain roles.

Centurion Bank of Punjab Ltd., mobilises these assets to deliver support relating to incentives such as:

- Performance management
- Management incentives
- Sales commission
- Staff bonus schemes
- Team-based incentives
- Performance-based pay progression

Working with organisation, Centurion Bank of Punjab Ltd., ensures that the incentive strategy supports the business. This ensures that the organisation's motives for introducing them are clear, that the incentives are easy to understand, motivational and that they are communicated properly.

Pensions

The issues that surround pension schemes can be complex and difficult to discern. While it is clear to most companies that it is important to implement the right scheme, the constantly changing market can make this hard to do without expert and independent advice.

Centurion Bank's benefits consultants and actuaries are well informed about pensions. They can steer customers through the issues, suggest alternative approaches and talk with scheme actuaries about changes. The approach is in the context of total remuneration value. Pension schemes are considered as a part of the whole reward package and are grounded in knowledge and understanding of employee behaviour and attitudes.

It is a given that all people in an organisation should work for the same goal; to competitively manufacture a quality product on time. This could be measured in overall production efficiency or production reliability or prime tons/cost. If this overall measurement is applied to all departments and coupled with each department's measurement and reward systems, an organisation stands a better chance to work in collaboration towards the same goal.

CASE 5—On Capex Assurance in Telecom Industry

A capital expenditure decision may be defined as the company's decision to invest its current funds most efficiently in long-term assets in anticipation of an expected flow of benefits over a number of years. Capital expenditure decisions occupy a very important place in corporate finance for the following reasons:

Once the decision is taken, it has far-reaching consequences, which extend over a considerably long period, and influence the risk complexion of the firm. These decisions involve huge amounts of money and are irreversible once taken. They are among the most difficult to make if the company is faced with various potentially viable investment opportunities.

While capital expenditure decisions are extremely important, the management may find it extremely difficult to analyse the pros and cons and arrive at a decision because measuring costs and benefits of an investment proposal is difficult, since all costs and benefits cannot be expressed in tangible terms. The benefits of capital expenditure are expected to occur for a number of years in the future, which is highly uncertain. Because the costs and benefits occur at different points of time, investment proposals, for a proper analysis of the viability of all these have to be brought to a common time-frame. Hence, the time value of money becomes very relevant here.

The capital expenditure decision starts with the identification of investment opportunities and potential business prospects. It is followed by a preliminary screening of the investment opportunities, implementation of the project and performance review.

Identification of the investment opportunities and potential business prospects

Identification means identifying the potential sources for project ideas, market characteristics of different industries, product profiles of various industries, imports and exports, emerging technologies etc.

Preliminary screening of the investment opportunities

The criteria that are typically applied for the preliminary evaluation are:

1. Compatibility with the promoter
2. Compatibility with government priorities
3. Availability of raw materials and utilities
4. Size of the potential market
5. Reasonableness of cost
6. Risk inherent in the project

Implementation of the project

The various stages of implementation are:

1. Construction of buildings and other civil works, erection and installation of machinery, preparation of blueprints and designs for project and plant engineering, selection of machineries and equipment
2. Negotiating for project finance with various financial institutions, entering into technical know-how agreements if necessary, entering into contracts for construction of machinery, marketing of the company's products etc.
3. Actual construction and installation of equipment
4. Training of engineers, technicians, workers, etc.
5. Commissioning of the plant and a trial run
6. Commercial production (radiation of sites in case of telecom industry)

Performance review

Once the project has been implemented, the trial run has been successful and commercial production is started, a review of the actual performance with the performance projected in the feasibility study is required.

A performance review throws light on how realistic the assumptions underlying the project were. It is a valuable tool for decision-making in the future.

The major infrastructure hurdles common to operators wishing to build networks in emerging markets include transmission and power.

Transmission

Backbone transmission networks usually do not exist in the rural areas of emerging markets. When networks do exist, the price for a leased line tends to be high. Satellite access exists virtually everywhere, but is even more expensive than leased lines. However, in remote areas, satellite transmission is sometimes the only solution available.

Power

Telecom infrastructure in rural areas depends on a reliable supply of electricity. Because rural areas are often outside the power grid, the default solution is to install diesel-driven electric generators.

Alternative power sources are, however, being developed. Renewable energy solutions such as hydropower, solar, wind, biogas and biodiesel are well known and the increase in oil prices, is putting these solutions more in the limelight.

Solutions based on solar power are today limited to small radio base stations, as they cannot generate enough energy to power a base station for large area coverage. Biodiesel on the other hand, is an especially interesting option for standalone radio base stations because it can directly substitute fossil-fuel diesel.

Solution for telecom and other industries

Companies in all industries, including telecom operators and telecom service providers, have three main areas of concern: customers, products and resources. Customers can be consumers and/ or enterprises, as well as other operators. Products include deliverables, prices and terms of payment, distribution channels and even public relations. Resources include staff, capital, equipment and infrastructure.

A successful company in any industry has a working business strategy to manage the three areas: its customers, products and resources.

The relationship and fit between the areas are implemented with end-to-end business processes and supported with a business management solution.

Each industry, regardless of its business area, has similar business management requirements for dealing with customers and products. This includes sales automation, order management, customer care, customer service level agreement management, invoicing, accounts receivable, accounts payable, general ledger and payment collection.

From a resource perspective, each type of industry has unique business management characteristics and behaviours. Resources specific to the communications industry are services, nodes in the access, core and service networks. Some examples of specific resource characteristics in the communications industry are real-time mechanisms and session supervision, large numbers of events, "telecom grade" performance, and complex network dependencies.

Consequently, the overall needs for business management can be divided into:

- Customer and product management to support cross-industry generic needs for products and customers
- Resource management to support industry-specific needs for resource management

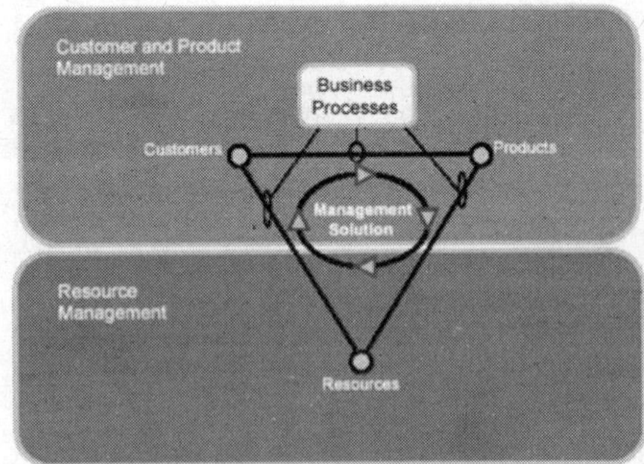

Source: www.ericsson.com

Using cross-industry business support systems

Telecom operators have two primary perspectives to manage their business. One is their commercial offerings, customers and partners. The other is their infrastructure investments.

These perspectives provide the following separation of concerns:

- Customer and product business perspective
- Resource business perspective

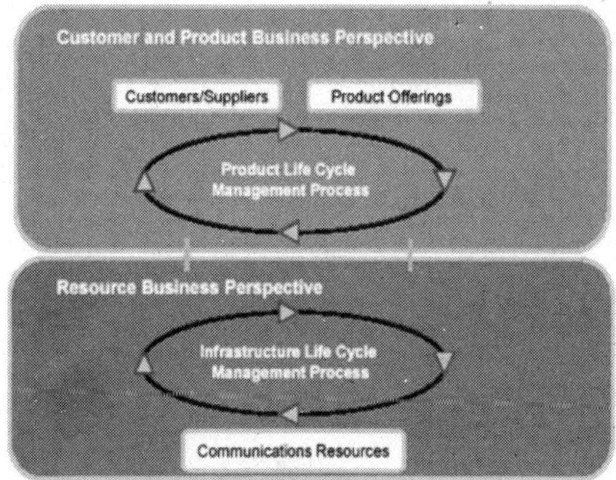

Source: www.ericsson.com

The customer and product business perspective concentrates on revenue creation, offering attractive and profitable products to focused market segments in order to attract new customers and maintain existing profitable ones. This also makes the operator attractive to third parties that can help build the end-user value chain. Cross industry business support solutions support the customer and product business perspective. Many telecom operators have not yet explored the full potential of such solutions. Instead, the telecom industry often relies on vertical solutions that are specific to telecom. However, vertical solutions[1] are one of the main factors behind the problems many operators face today.

The resource business perspective is driven by efficiency: optimising deployed investment in infrastructure resources (capex) and operational resources (opex), optimising service and traffic volumes delivered with controlled quality levels (customer satisfaction), and charging usage of services in the network (revenue).

Telecom industry-specific support solutions support the resource business perspective.

By closely integrating standard cross-industry business support systems with standard telecom-industry specific systems, Ericsson believes operators can efficiently support their end-to-end business processes with improved cost-of ownership.

Target telecom management solutions

End-to-end business processes applied to well-defined management domains are central to telecom management. As further elaborated below, Ericsson, based on its experience with operators throughout the world, recommends telecom management architecture be built on:

1. End-to-end business processes that increase automation and simplification
2. Dual-layered implementation based on standard cross industry business support solutions that are closely integrated with standard communication industry management solutions
3. Simplified architecture based on management domains that have clear roles, responsibilities and inter-dependencies, with a network domain manager as an integral part of each network domain.

Effective end-to-end business processes

Telecom management focuses on cross-domain, end-to-end business processes. This includes all processes, ranging from customer requests for service, to service activated, service disruptions to problems fixed, and customer consumptions to payments and revenue shared. Effective telecom management systems and processes allow operators to manage and operate all the phases involved in managing customers, products and resources.

To improve competitiveness, operators need to simplify and automate these processes as much as possible.

Telecom management supports end-to-end business processes such as operation and readiness, fulfilment, assurance and revenue management.

[1]Vertical Solutions for telecom industry refers to use of voice and related services and VAS (value added services).

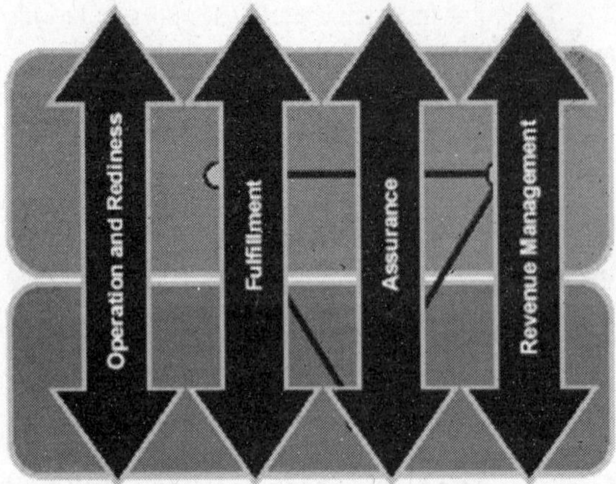

Source: www.ericsson.com

What simplified architecture does

The simplified architecture model contains four management domains. Each one possesses well-defined functionality and responsibilities, and clearly described interfaces for cost-efficient integration.

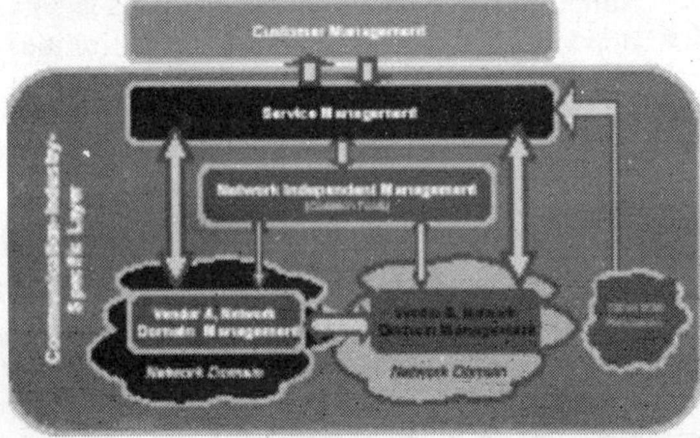

Fig. 2: Telecom management domains

Source: www.ericsson.com

To simplify telecom management, operators should:

- Manage cross-dependencies, and minimize overlapping information and redundant data between management domains. This will increase the interoperability capabilities in the telecom management solution.
- Use network domain managers to strengthen management support as part of each network domain. This hides the network domain complexity from other management domains, and reduces the integration tax.
- Consolidate the current telecom management environment by reducing the number of vertical management solutions.

The evolution

Step-by-step evolution should start with an end-to-end gap analysis. The objective is to identify and analyse heavy cost-consuming operational and business processes, as well as requirements from network infrastructures and services.

The gap analysis identifies what steps need to be taken and in what order. This is based on the suggested improvement areas and the business cases for each of them, which are also identified by the gap analysis.

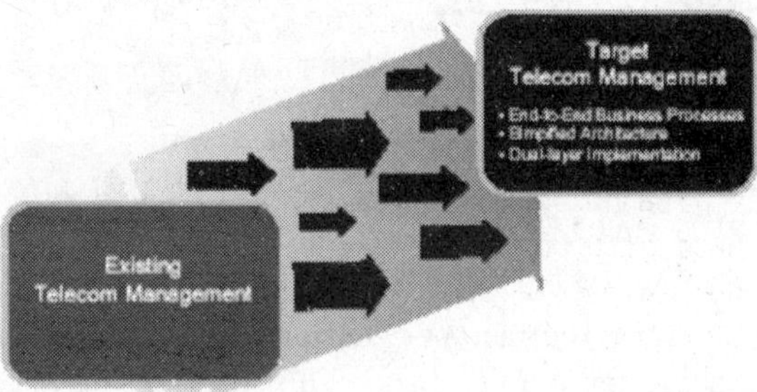

Fig. 3: Step-by-step evolution of telecom management systems and processes

Source: www.ericsson.com

Concluding remarks

Operators can turn telecom management into an efficient business tool for competitive differentiation and lean operations. Effective telecom management systems and processes enable operators to attract and retain customers, increase operational readiness for short time-to-market for new services and technologies, as well as reduce operational expenditures by, for example:

- Tracking and tuning the performance of services to ensure customers experience quality and perceive the value of the services offered.
- Automating and simplifying end-to-end processes.

- Simplifying telecom management by incorporating management capabilities within each network domain. Utilizing a network domain manager to make the capabilities and features of each network domain available to all other management domains.
- Reducing their dependency on stand-alone vertical systems.
- Moving to cost-efficient, integrated telecom management based on a dual layered architecture with clear roles, responsibilities and interfaces between management domains that can handle cross-dependencies and minimize redundant data.

Finally, operators should maximize their chance for success by taking a step-by-step approach to evolving their telecom management systems and processes, and working closely with a business partner that has a thorough knowledge of end-to-end communication solutions.

Questions

1. What is the right approach for Capital expenditure?
2. Design an appropriate control structure for Capex
3. What should be the ideal steps for Capex, keeping in view the customer satisfaction?

CASE 6—Management Control in an MNC: Standard Chartered Bank

Standard Chartered Bank has a history of over 150 years in banking and has a presence in many of the world's fastest growing markets. It has an extensive global network of over 1,200 branches (including subsidiaries, associates and joint ventures) in 56 countries in the Asia Pacific Region, South Asia, the Middle East, Africa, the United Kingdom and the Americas. As one of the world's most international banks, Standard Chartered employs almost 44,000 people, representing 89 nationalities, worldwide.

Standard Chartered uniquely derives 95% of its profits from Asia, Africa and the Middle East. Serving both consumer and wholesale banking customers, the bank combines deep local knowledge with global capability to offer a wide range of innovative products and services as well as award winning solutions.

Some of the major awards won in 2005 by the bank include:

1. IFR Asia's Domestic Bond House of the Year
2. Finance Asia's Best Local Currency Bond House & Best Securitisation House
3. Asia Risk's Interest Rates Derivatives House of the Year
4. Trade Finance's Best Trade Finance Bank in Sub Saharan Africa
5. Global Custodian's Best Agent Bank in Asia
6. The Asset's Best Cash Management Bank for South Asia
7. Retail Banker International's Best Retail Bank in Asia Pacific.

Standard Chartered meets all relevant international legal obligations and all relevant local legal obligations in the countries in which it operates. It is also committed to the principles of the global compact.

Background

The Standard Chartered Group was formed in 1969 through a merger of two banks: The Standard Bank of British South Africa founded in 1863, and the Chartered Bank of India, Australia and China, founded in 1853. Both companies were keen to capitalise on the huge expansion of trade and to earn the handsome profits to be made from financing the movement of goods from Europe to the East and to Africa.

In 1969, the decision was made by Chartered and by Standard to undergo a friendly merger. All was going well until 1986, when a hostile takeover bid was made for the group by Lloyds Bank of the United Kingdom. When the bid was defeated, Standard Chartered entered a period of change. Provisions had to be made against third world debt exposure and loans to corporations and entrepreneurs who could not meet their commitments. Standard Chartered began a series of divestments notably in the United States and South Africa, and also entered into a number of asset sales.

From the early 1990s, Standard Chartered has focused on developing its strong franchises in Asia, the Middle East and Africa using its operations in the United Kingdom and North America to provide customers with a bridge between these markets. Secondly, it focused on consumer, corporate and institutional banking, and on the provision of treasury services - areas in which the group had particular strength and expertise.

In the new millennium the bank acquired Grindlays Bank from the ANZ Group and the Chase Consumer Banking operations in Hong Kong in 2000.

Leading the way in Asia, Africa and the Middle East

In its unique position as an international bank with strong franchise, Standard Chartered combines an in-depth knowledge of local markets with global product expertise to offer effective financial solutions. The bank capitalises on its onshore presence across Asia, Africa and the Middle East to offer customers convenient and reliable access to the widest range of currency markets to date, local market information, country-specific global risk management strategies, raising customised capital and liquidity management solutions.

- With 150 years of emerging market experience, its in-depth understanding of the local market is unrivalled by most other financial institutions, especially in the currencies of Asia, the Middle East and Africa. The bank has been able to meet the needs of local corporates, multinational companies, development organisations, investment and financial institutions, and central banks around the world.
- Understanding that each customer's needs are unique, Standard Chartered customizes *client solutions* for risk management, yield enhancement, liquidity management and debt financing.
- Its structured yield enhancement products match risk appetites and investment requirements.
- It provides solutions for currency and interest rate exposures.
- It has access to more than 100 onshore and offshore illiquid and restricted currencies.
- It has a US dollar liquidity fund for effective cash management.
- It offers local currency and G3 currency fixed income and loan syndications
- It offers asset securitisation
- Structured trade and export financing for importers and exporters
- Project financing services
- Corporate advisory services

To meet the diverse needs of its customers, Standard Chartered also offers a broad range of **Foreign exchange products and services,** as given below.

- Money market products
- Interest rate and cross currency derivatives
- Foreign exchange, forwards and swaps
- Non-deliverable forwards and exotic options
- Money market funds
- Online electronic trading services
- Global FX and economic research

Management control through reward and recognition in Standard Chartered

- **Differentiating high performance**

The bank is committed to providing compensation and benefits competitively positioned to attract, retain and motivate talented individuals. As a high performing organisation, rewards are linked to individual performance and the extent to which the employee has demonstrated a commitment to the bank's values.

Consistent with the bank's values, base salaries bonus and share awards are benchmarked against key competitors, focusing on high performing employees.

Share ownership is encouraged across the bank to engage individuals in the performance of the overall business. Over 40% of the employees participate in an all-employee share save scheme.

Core benefits such as annual leave, retirement benefits, sickness and medical benefits are provided across the businesses and geographies in accordance with local customs and practices.

- **Harnessing diversity through inclusion**

Standard Chartered employs over 33,000 people across 56 countries and territories. The workforce comprises over 80 nationalities (including 45 at senior management level) and close to half is female. The bank wants to lead by example in building a multi-talented, diverse and representative workforce and leadership. The simple logic behind the commitment to diversity and inclusion is to attract and retain the best talent and harness the differences individuals bring, enabling them to realise their full potential. Individual differences are seen as strengths, allowing the bank to deliver higher performance and true competitive advantage. The bank's diversity council provides a strategic, global focus to diversity and inclusion in the bank.

- **Identifying future leaders**

The bank's on-line, global, graduate recruitment site provides an effective method of attracting and recruiting talented graduates. Successful applicants join a two-year international graduate program, which stretches them through on-the-job learning and rotations, in-depth business training, performance coaching and three international, residential workshops. Following the completion of the programme, the graduates receive continued support in building their careers.

- **Creating winning teams through engagement**

The bank believes that providing employees with the right working environment encourages the application of their individual talents and discretionary effort. Investing in the measurement of employee engagement is a key element of building the high performance culture to drive the business forward.

In 2000, the bank introduced Q12, an annual survey to measure employee engagement. It is not an employee satisfaction survey. Instead, it measures improvement in the engagement of teams. Teams use the results to discuss and develop action plans, whilst continually monitoring the follow-through. In 2004, the survey covered all 56 countries with 97% of employees participating voluntarily. This is a significant achievement and a clear indication that employees are committed to improving individual and team performance.

- **Developing people's strengths**

This strengths-based approach lies at the core of the bank's development philosophy. Managers are encouraged to help employees identify and develop individuals' strengths to help themselves and their teams to deliver sustainable performance. A large percentage of employees have benefited from formally identifying their strengths using an on-line self-assessment system. This is supported by trained in-house experts, or strengths coaches, who facilitate the development of action plans to help individuals and teams improve their effectiveness.

- **Effective service delivery**

Effective service delivery is a priority of the human resource function, for value-added service across the bank.

The Human Resources Shared Service Centre (HR SCC), based in Chennai, India, became operational in 2002. It maintains a central employee database and administers a range of services including payroll, retirement benefits, organisation learning administration, and share schemes across the bank.

The HR SSC serves over 27,000 employees in 29 countries. Year-on-year, the HR SSC delivers higher value services, freeing local HR to provide greater strategic support to the business. The HR SSC is now considered an industry benchmark and is continually improving and growing.

- **Creating a healthy and safe place to work**

The bank is determined to provide employees with a healthy and safe place to work, wherever they are in the world. Although local legislation varies between countries, the bank is increasingly applying efforts to ensuring consistently high principles of health and safety across all operations. The bank aims to provide its community with the structures, systems and support to ensure the health and safety of all employees, customers, visitors and contractors. To achieve this, the bank aims to facilitate, guide and encourage management and employees to create a work environment where hazards are kept to a minimum and safety is seen as a core value. The different local health and safety legislation in the many countries make this a challenging task. Health and safety for the bank is not just about legislative compliance, it is about creating the right culture.

The bank is therefore in the process of creating a health and safety management system using the British Standard 8800 as the framework to improve its safety culture and performance. Health and safety coordinators have been appointed and trained in each of the countries the bank operates in. In addition, health and safety training will also be extended through all members of staff using an online training programme.

- **Environmental policy**

The bank is committed to minimising the environmental effects of operations and aims to achieve continual improvement in the management of environmental issues. The bank's operations span a wide range of countries with differing cultures, climates, infrastructures and legal requirements. Consequently, a number of environ-mental commitments have been developed, which can be applied universally across the organisation. These are as follows:

Legal compliance: The bank aims to comply fully with all government legislation applicable in each country in which it operates. Where no regulations apply, the bank adopts its own international environmental standards.

Energy & resource use: The bank will seek to reduce its per capita consumption of resources, specifically: energy, water, transportation services and paper, wherever practicable opportunities exist.

Hazardous substances: The bank is endeavouring to eradicate the use of ozone depleting substances and to use only refrigerants with a low global warming potential in Standard Chartered controlled premises. Hazardous substance use is managed to ensure that releases are minimized both during operation and at the end of life.

Procurement: The major operational centre procurement processes consider environmental issues surrounding the production, consumption and disposal of products and services. Wherever practicable, products are procured, that are derived from sustainable resources. Wherever appropriate, the use of suppliers who can demonstrate environmentally sound business practices is preferred.

Banking services: Due consideration is given to the presence of environmental and social risks in banking transactions. The bank expects its banking customers to comply with the prevailing environmental and social regulations applicable to their sphere of operation.

Air emissions & waste management: Greenhouse gas emissions arising from the bank's activities, are identified, recorded and monitored, wherever the bank's global environmental management system is implemented and reliable means to do so exist. When possible, targets for reducing greenhouse gas emissions will be set and progress towards them will be reported annually.

Wherever practical, the production of wastes are minimised and staff are encouraged to participate in reuse and recycling initiatives. The bank ensures that wastes that are not reused or recycled are disposed of in a safe and responsible manner.

Supply chain management in Standard Chartered

Implementing a global system for sourcing is a tough task. Standard Chartered introduced the Know Your Supplier (KYS) scheme in phases. This allowed us to focus on one region at a time, learn lessons and make improvements as the programme proceeded.

	Phase 1	*Phase 2*	*Phase 3*
EAST:	Hong Kong, Singapore	India	Malaysia
WEST:	UK	US	UAE

Rollout of the above schedule will be according to the following schedule:

Phase 1 – Complete
Phase 2 – Completed on June 30th 2005
Phase 3 – Completed on December 31st 2005

The bank considers suppliers typically, in each country, the number of suppliers engaged on a business as usual basis is high. It was not practical to proactively monitor all suppliers for compliance with the bank's standards. Initially all suppliers entering into a business relationship with the bank in the above countries, were monitored. Typically suppliers are appointed on anything between a one and three-year contract so as anticipated, after a period of three years, the supply base was fully assessed. On assessment suppliers were categorised into one of two types - high Social, Ethical or Environmental (SEE) risk and low SEE risk. If the supplier's product or services involves two or more of the risk elements identified in the table below then they are deemed "high risk". If they only exhibit one or less factors then they are deemed "low risk".

The bank focused its resources on suppliers that posed the greatest potential risk to the bank, to the environment and to the communities they operate in. The relative scale of social and environmental impact of the supplier was also taken into account in the assessment of whether a supplier is deemed high risk or low risk.

[A] On human rights

	Checklist items	*Method*	*Things to look at*
A1	Use of child labour	Onsite visit/ Request for further information	Visual impression of staff employed onsite Review of HR record of staff concerned
A2	Discrimination in employment	Document review	HR policy document
A3	Unreasonable terms of employment	Document review	HR employment terms & remuneration (in the context of the average remuneration locally)
A4	Safe & satisfactory work environment	Onsite visit/ Request for further information	Physical environment of workplace (E.G. hygiene, ventilation, lighting) Use of safety gear for handling hazardous materials
		Document review	Reference any local country government policy or legislation

[B] On ethics

	Checklist items	*Method*	*Things to look at*
B1	Company policies to guide business operation	Document review	Money laundering prevention policies Insider trading prevention policies Conflict of interest handling approach Bribery and corruption handling approach Staff guidelines & codes of conduct

[C] On environment

	Checklist items	*Method*	*Things to look at*
C1	Company policies, objectives & targets	Document review	Documented policies Published objectives
C2	Regular practice to audit and review environmental performance	Document review	Track record of past review
C3	Intention towards accreditation	Document review	Records of such effort or certificate of environmental management standard such as ISO14001
C4	Potential environmental risk in production process	Onsite visit/ Request for further information	Explanation by relevant personnel
C5	Control measures in place to minimise environmental risk	Onsite visit/ Request for further information	Physical set up in workplace to minimise environmental hazards Work practices & procedures in line with environmental objectives
C6	Product features	Onsite visit/ Request for further information	Capability to be recycled Eco label or energy star standards of products

Transfer pricing

The transfer-pricing system is a technique that is primarily used in international business as practiced by multinational corporations. Under this method the price of goods and services is not determined by the local market structure, but by a highly sophisticated internal sales system within subsidiaries of an MNC. The system offers opportunities to manipulate the market prices according to the changing demands in various countries. MNCs can thus maximise their global profits by reducing income taxes, tariffs and foreign currency exchange rate risks. The economic dependency of third-world nations on advanced industrialised countries leaves them highly vulnerable to international transfer pricing. These practices have an adverse impact on the balance-of-payments of less developed nations, and subsequently the poor people of these nations suffer unfairly.

In this case the economic impact of the transfer-pricing system by Standard Chartered was also examined from the humanities' perspective. In this regard, the study contends that the burden of moral responsibility is on the MNCs rather than on the poor people in developing countries. The legal issues of the transfer-pricing system are reviewed. These are not heavily emphasised, because the legal issues remain a grey area in many advanced industrial countries.

CASE 7—Prayas: An NGO in Trying

Background note

Prayas was started as an initiative by a group of young men who wanted to bring about a change for the poorest of the poor in urban localities in the country. As a beginning, they targeted the food and shelter program for the poorest of the poor in the country.

The poor were classified as those who had earning of less than Rs. 20/- a day in a family of four members. Once that was decided, the next point was to identify how to fund the project to start the shelter and food program.

A standard answer to the question was by approaching the government under the several poverty elevation programs that the government has started. The only difficulty under this method would be that, they would have to reach out to the poor only through financial intermediaries designated to channelise such government funds. This in turn meant implementing programs that are acceptable to the financial intermediaries and institutions which will channelise these funds and therefore may or may not meet the specific needs of the program which Prayas was to start.

Teething problems

Designing an appropriate structure for the organisation as a part of the delivery system was of primary concern. Though there were no needs internally, the external pressure was high so that the organisational structure had to be put in place.

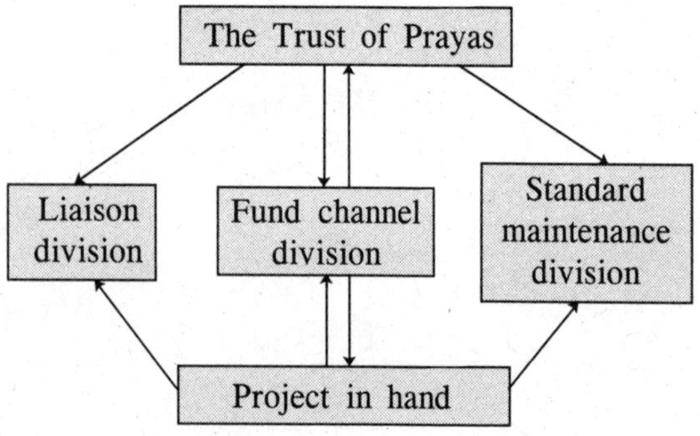

Fig. 4: The organisational structure of Prayas

After a lot of deliberation, a matrix structure was designed. The structure included one functional line and a few staff functions, which were to be carried out linearly, in order to keep the reporting simple. The organisational structure is given below for a general understanding.

The independent divisions of the organisation, i.e., liaison, fund channel and standard maintenance divisions were to maintain mutually exclusive, yet common objectives i.e., to maintain the standards required by the fund provider to the organisation and to maintain the internal standards set by the organisations towards the community at large. This organisational structure was in response to two different needs of the organisation.

i. The external needs of the project. This was due to the fact that the organisation had to interface with several levels of ministerial and administrative personnel.
ii. The internal requirements of the organisation, which needed high specialisation in respect to liaison and fund management.

The organisation had to create a space for interlinking the projects in hand with all the respective organisational departments and hence the matrix form of the organisation.

Besides the organisation had to develop the knowhow to erect low cost houses from a Dutch Company and translate it into action. The problem was that the raw material required by the Dutch prototype was not available locally. Hence it was necessary to search for equivalent material, keeping in mind that the quality of the prototype should not be compromised.

The other project that the organisation took up was to provide food to the children as a part of mid-day meal for the street children. In this too, hygiene, quality of food and the place where it can be served needed to be identified.

Target group identification and land acquisition for the purpose was a challenge in itself as land under the free distribution was available only far from the cities. This was a constraint as the income of the replaced poor in their new homes could invariably make them lose their livelihood.

Besides the above, the organisation had to identify a mechanism to monitor the development of their projects. Initially they created a system where a weekly report of the progress was to be submitted in a standard format to the Prayas trust by each of the project divisions. This turned out to be cumbersome as repetitive reports with no value addition piled up. The 'action taken' column would often contain 'ditto' of the earlier reports.

Besides, there slipped into the system an ad hoc process of identifying the beneficiaries. This would be guided either by the government or by other groups working on similar lines. This became the order of the day as there were very few definitions, other than the one developed by the organisation, to guide them regarding the urban poor at large.

Questions

1. What do you think is the real problem with this NGO?
2. Do you agree with the organisational structure that is proposed?
3. What is the best mechanism that can be set up to develop a monitoring system for the organisation?

CASE 8—Birla Sun Life Insurance Company Ltd.—Insuring Peace of Mind

"We are the first insurance company to launch investment linked insurance plans and others followed suit. Even now, our products are distinctly superior to the ones available from others in the market."

—**Mr. Nandgopal, Associate Director, BSLI Co. Ltd.**

The Insurance Market

Contribution of the life insurance sector to economic development is growing as the market is maturing over time. The insurance market has experienced many ups and downs. It was often felt that it would stabilise, but this did not happen, and the industry is still going through more or less the same kind of situation. One critical question in this environment for advisors and brokers is what can be done to hold on to existing clients and generate new business? One obvious answer to this question is to stay informed of industry happenings; know and understand the risk; be involved in claim settlement and maintain professionalism.

There are about fourteen companies in the life insurance business that cater to the needs of individuals as well as groups. LIC dominates the industry with almost 80% of the market share; the rest (20%) is shared by the remaining private players. These private companies are trying to maximise their market by offering various innovative products. Despite competition from an insurance giant such as LIC, the companies are trying to maximise their market share because there is a huge untapped market in India.

An Innovator is Born

Until the late 1990s there was only one life insurer (LIC)[1] in India, which had a monopoly in the market. In the year 2000, the Insurance Regulatory & Development Authority (IRDA) of India took a decision to allow the foreign players into the insurance industry with a 26% FDI stake (Exhibit I). This decision was taken after it was observed that there was a huge untapped market for the insurance industry which LIC was unable to explore due to various reasons. Moreover, it was found that people were under- or over-insured.

One of the new players to enter the insurance market was Birla Sun Life Insurance (BSLI), which pioneered in bringing innovations in insurance products. It was the first insurer in India to bring in the concept of Unit Linked Insurance Plans (ULIP)[2] and also the first to sell insurance through a website. In the past few years it has emerged as a major player in life insurance business.

Within four years of its launch, BSLI cemented its position as a leading player in the private life insurance industry and was the first to have an operational business continuity plan. It focuses on investment linked insurance products, supported with protection products to maintain leadership in product innovation. It has multi distribution channels - a direct sales force, alternate channels and groups, offering convenient channels of purchase to customers. BSLI has successfully distinguished itself from the other private players through its corporate governance and a high degree of transparency in all business practices and procedures.

Background Note

Birla Sun Life Insurance is a merger between the Aditya Birla Group (India) and Sun Life Financial (Canada).

The Aditya Birla Group (Refer to Exhibit II) has more than 72,000 employees all over the world and a market capital of Rs 33,000 crore. It is headed by Mr. Kumarmangalam Birla who is the chairman of the company. Currently it has Asset Under Management (AUM) of US$ 298 billion. On the other hand, Sun Life Insurance Co.

1. Life Insurance Corporation of India was created on 1st September, 1956.
2. Unit Linked Insurance Plans: Premium collected from the customer is invested in the mutual funds chosen by the holder.

was in India before 1956 but due to political reasons it had to close down its operations. In the year 2001 a liberal economic policy was announced and Sun Life came back to India and formed a joint venture with the Aditya Birla Group for carrying out insurance business (Refer to Exhibit III for mission and vision). The capital contribution is 74% (Birla) to 26% (Sun Life) which is expected to increase to 49% in the future.

Pioneered by Birla Sun Life Insurance, unit linked solutions bring together the best of life insurance and investment. They are aimed at the corporate sector as well as individuals. Introduced in line with the latest global trends, these plans put a customer in total control of their money. They are simple, transparent and flexible while offering a minimum of 3% guaranteed overall returns on the premium.

Management Control at Birla Sun Life

The organisational structure of BSLI was so designed that in any branch there are only three levels of hierarchies. The top authority of a particular branch is the branch head who has 15 - 25 agency managers. Again, each agency manager is allowed to recruit 25 - 30 advisors[3] under him. These advisors, who are the direct sales force for the company, go to the market and convince prospects to do business with the company.

At Birla Sun Life, everything is flexible. It offers policies that are highly flexible and can be customised to a certain extent. The flexibility reflects in the HR policies of the company also. There are no fixed office hours for the Agency Managers (AM) or agents, who are allowed to log-in 24 × 7. The branch head receives a target from headquarters, which he distributes among the AMs who again distribute them to the agents assigned to them.

Agents of Birla Sun Life Insurance enjoy three types of commission:

- Basic commission
- Productivity bonus
- Renewal commission

The percentage of commission depends upon the insurance plans and long term business relationships are awarded accordingly. For example if the plan requires the customer to pay a single premium, the agent gets 2% of the premium. As the paying period increases, the percentage of commission increases. They are given their commission after Tax Deduction at Source (TDS).

Commission structure for insurance cum investment plan*

No of premium payments	*Percentage of commission on premium*
Single premium payment	2%
5 Pay	11.5%
10 Pay	21%
15 Pay onwards	25%

Extra commission on 2nd and 3rd year: 7.5%

Extra commission 5th year onwards: 5%

Commission structure for investment cum insurance plan*

No. of premium payments	*1st year's commission*	*Subsequent commissions*
3 Pay	10%	4%
5 Pay	12%	4%

Percentage on pension plans is 7.5% for the first year and 5% for the subsequent years.

Further, the slabs are divided if the premium is paid by the customer on a half-yearly or quarterly basis. These divisions are based upon two policies known as Net Annual Agency Credit (NAAC) and Net Agency Credit (NAC).

To boost the performance of the agents and the agency managers, the company conducts tours which can be enjoyed after fulfilment of certain targets.

3. IRDA approved insurance agents

* In insurance cum investment plans the investment portfolio has a low risk and low return. On the other hand, the investment portfolio in investment cum insurance plans has a higher return.

According to an agency manager, the work culture at BSLI is excellent when compared to other private life insurance companies, "*Our company does not have a hire and fire policy, it gives an employee ample opportunities for improvement and growth*". BSLI maintains high ethical standards and the employees are constantly reminded of the values associated with the company. It does not believe in aggressive marketing and sells a policy after assessing the correct worth of one's life.

On the other hand some employees say that the flexibility offered to its employees enable many agents to escape without meeting their targets, which has led to a decrease in the sales volume and subsequently decreased the market share (Refer to Exhibit IV).

Advertisements and Promotions

Previously, people were put off by insurance advertising, as it reminded them of the demise or accidents of their loved ones. Today, that has changed. Marked by the entry of private players post 2000, Indian insurance industry has moved into exciting and thrilling times. Over a dozen life insurers are fighting it out to win that special position in the hearts of the customers. The huge untapped potential is pushing insurance majors to think of innovative ways to rope in more customers.

BSLI relies mostly on the print media such as newspapers and magazines to communicate with the public (Refer to Exhibit V). It has largely ignored the benefits of the electronic media such as T.V. and the internet. BSLI had a very small budget apportioned for advertisements and promotions as the company wanted to break even by the end of 2006.

What Lies Ahead

In this highly regulated industry there are a few differences among the products. Analysts say that in face of competition from giants like LIC, making loss or minimal profit is normal. As the country develops, people will be more aware about the need for insurance, besides the market tapped is hardly 80%.

EXHIBIT I

Capital composition of the private life insurers

Company	Indian promoter/ partner	Foreign insurer	Total capital (Rs. Cr)	FDI(%)	Foreign capital (Rs. Cr)	Market share* (Based on premium)
AMP Sanmar+	Reliance	None Group	217	0	0	0.54
Aviva Life	Dabur	Aviva, UK	459	26	119.34	1.12
Bajaj Allianz	Bajaj Auto	Allianz, Germany	368	26	96	6.12
Birla Sun Life	Aditya Birla Group	Sun Life, Canada	400	26	104	1.84
HDFC Standard	HDFC	Standard Life, UK	250	.9	47	2.96
ICICI Prudential	ICICI Bank	Prudential, UK	1085	26	282	7.11
ING Vysya	Vysya Bank	ING Insurance, Netherlands	440	26	68	0:63
Kotak Mahindra Old Mutual	Kotak Mahindra Bank	Old Mutual, South Africa	260	26	68	0.71
Max New York	Max India	New York Life, US	500	26	130	1.32
MetLife	Jammu &	MetLife, US Kashmir Bank	355	26	92	0.4
Sahara Life	Sahara India	None	100	0	0	0.06
SBI Life	SBI	Cardiff, France	350	26	91	1.52
Tata AIG	Tata Group	AIG, US	381	26	99	1.78

+ Reliance Capital is in the progress of merging with the operations of AMP Sanmar with Reliance Life Insurance

Source: Ernst & Young, Businessworld 13th February 2006 ***Source: IRDA**

EXHIBIT II

The Aditya Birla Group

Industry	Company
Cement & fibre	Grasim, Ultratech
Aluminium	Hindalco
Power	Bina Power
Telecom	Idea Cellular
Garments	Indian Rayon
Fertilizer	Indo Gulf
Chemicals	AV Cell Inc.
Financial services	BGFL

EXHIBIT III
Mission and vision statement

Mission

To be a world class provider of financial security to individuals and corporates and to be amongst the top three private sector life insurance companies in India.

Vision

To be the first preference of our customers by providing innovative, need based life insurance and retirement solutions to individuals as well as corporates. These solutions will be made available by well-trained professionals through a multi channel distribution network and superior technology.

Source: www.birlasunlife.com/insurance/aboutus

EXHIBIT IV

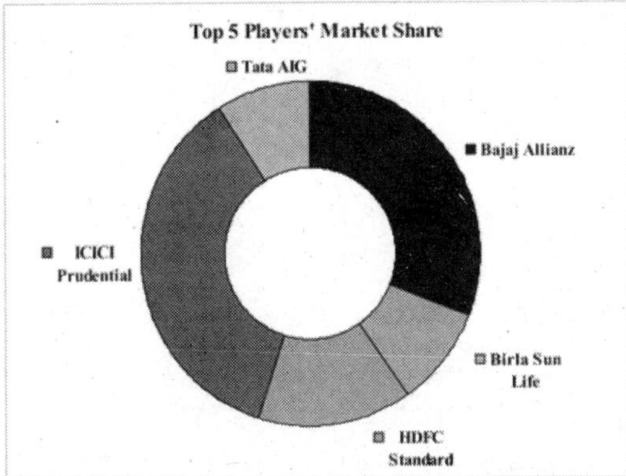

Source: *IRDA Journal March*, 2006. According to premium collected till January 2005

EXHIBIT V

Press advertisements of BSLI's life insurance plans

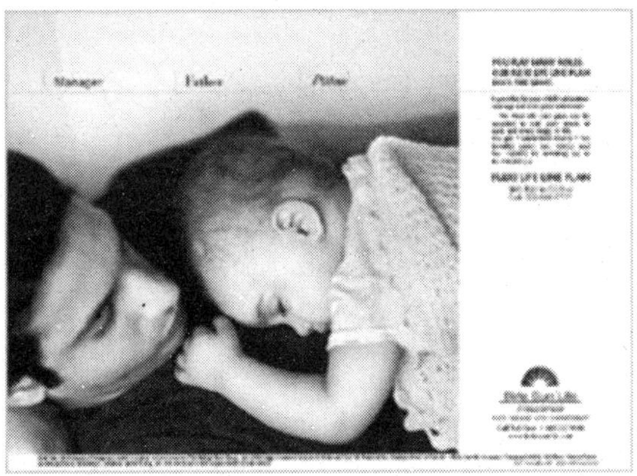

Additional Readings and References

1. www.birlasunlife.com
2. www.irdaindia.org.
3. www.bajajallianz.com
4. www.licindia.com

5. www.rediff.com/business
6. www.peakalpha.com
7. www.way2wealth.com
8. www.domain-b.com
9. www.wiaaindia.com
10. www.s-m-a-r-t.com
11. www.outlookmoney.com
12. "Gasping for Capital," *Businessworld*, 13th February 2006, 34-38
13. Philip Kotler, *Marketing Management*, 11th Ed, Princeton-Hall India 2003
14. "How can you Gain from Policy Riders," *Outlook Money*, 15th February 2006, 46-48
15. ICMR Text Book, *Life Insurance*, ICFAI University Press
16. "Insurance Operations," *Insurance Chronicle*, June 2005, 43-45
17. "Branding Insurance," *Insurance Chronicle*, February 2006

Short Cases

CASE 1—Praga Tools Private Ltd.: Motivating the Sales Force

Background

Praga Tools was established as a unit to act as an ancillary industry to tractor manufacturing companies, which were spread across the country. Established in Hyderabad, Andhra Pradesh in the year 1972, Praga became a subsidiary of another public sector company, which was producing machine tools in India, in the year 1979.

Praga tools became a market leader during its initial years as there were hardly any competitors in the market. Praga's main industrial buyers were HMT and Gujarat Tractors Ltd. In the small tool segment, there were local companies and some major public sector companies such as NMDC, HCL and IPCL to name a few.

Product profile

Praga Tools had a huge range of products, which ranged from furrows to small hand-held tools. It also produced tilling machines, winnowing machines, etc., which were used in the agricultural sector and which were sold through independent sales efforts.

Table 1: Product profile of Praga Tools

Name of the product	Name of the industry to which the product was ancillary	Sold to which sector/ company*
1. Furrow	Tractor industry	GTL and HMT
2. Bearings	Tractor industry	GTL, HMT, NMDC, CONCOR
3. Winnow machine	Agricultural market	Self effort to sell in the market
4. Tilling machine	Tractor industry	GTL, HMT besides self effort to sell in the market
5. Sowing machine	Tractor industry	GTL and HMT
6. Hand-held power tools like drills etc	Defence companies, tractor industries, railways, state transport companies and retail market	Self effort to sell in the market.

Note: ***The name of a company, means that there was a buy-back agreement with that company.***

Competitors' profiles

Praga had a handful of competitors which included companies like Willmar in hand tools, HMT (a major buyer in the tools market), and some foreign companies whose products were at a disadvantage of price.

The Indian competitors were large and had widespread distribution systems. Willmar had an exclusive store pattern of distribution besides every big city had sole distribution rights of the company. It operated in the replacement market of the entire product range that Praga produced. HMT on the other hand had a buyback arrangement of Praga's agrarian tools, which it sold through its own outlet under its own name. Praga acted as a stop gap arrangement for the company. Though, Praga bought most of its technology from Russia, the foreign tools were in great demand for their superior quality and long lasting performance despite their price being slightly higher than that of Praga's products.

Table 2: Sales figures of Praga

Name of the product	1978	1980	1990
1. Furrow	Rs. 2.8 cr.	Rs. 2.3 cr.	Rs. 1.65 cr.
2. Bearings	Rs. 3 cr.	Rs. 2.8 cr.	Rs. 2.72 cr.
3. Winnow machine	Rs. 1.80 cr.	Rs. 2.22 cr.	Rs. 2.86 cr.
4. Tilling machine	Rs. 1.78 cr.	Rs. 2.30 cr.	Rs. 1.85 cr.
5. Sowing machine	Rs. 1.72 cr.	Rs. 2.00 cr.	Rs. 75 lakh.
6. Hand-held power tools like drills, etc.	Rs. 1.35 cr.	Rs. 1.50 cr.	Stopped production

Sales distribution problems

Praga had a dedicated sales force whose role was to liaise between the major buyback companies and act as an independent sales team in the market. The organisation of the sales division was as follows. There was a general manager of sales and marketing. Under him were the territory managers of sales. There were five territories, which included north, south, central, west and east. Each of the sales territory managers had four to five sales officers working for them. The sales team comprised mechanical engineers as this was an industrial product and it required technical know-how in the matter of sales. Besides, there was an agriculture officer in each territory who directly reported to the general manager of the sales and marketing division. The role of the agriculture officer was to create market awareness for Praga's products and help the retail purchaser making the right decision in purchasing Praga's products in the agriculture market.

Praga's sales were continuously declining. The sales figures for the company in the product range are given in Table 2.

The sales team met in the year 1991 in order to understand the basic problem in the sales.

The following emerged from this:

1. The market was fragmented and the sales force was not large enough to meet the required sales demand.
2. New entrants in the market were more efficient.
3. It was necessary to enhance the salary of the sales force as trained manpower was leaving the company and moving to competitors for more money.
4. There was no coordination between the sales divisions of each zone. As a result short supply in one zone could not be met by another zone, since this was against company rules.
5. The reporting system required the sales force to report on a daily basis whereas the territory managers reported on a fortnightly basis.
6. There was over reliance on buyback arrangements with other companies.
7. Competition in certain segments came from the companies that bought its products.
8. The old technology gave the company a cost disadvantage.
9. There was no motivation as there were rumours of the company being sold off to a private company.

Following this meeting, it was decided by the company that it would re-look at the pricing and it signed a major contract to upgrade its technology at a huge cost. Salaries were revised as per the fourth pay commission report.

Concluding remarks

The total sales of the company dropped despite the efforts made by the company.

Questions

1. How can Praga improve its sales and keep its sales force motivated?
2. What are the various issues you would keep in mind in designing a control system?

CASE 2—Bengal Lamps: Issues in Quality Control

Bengal Lamps Ltd. was established with a motive to provide cheap and durable dome bulbs to the urban and rural masses of eastern India. Tracing its way back to 1952, the company was unique in its own way as it was amongst the first indigenous companies to be established in this industry.

Bengal Lamps Ltd. had three main products to begin with, 100 watt, 200 watt and a zero watt (15 watt) bulb with a tungsten filament. Later it added some more products, such as neon lamps (bar tube), and starters and capacitors for the use of the neon tube lamp.

It had three works establishments, all in and around the city of Kolkata. The first work establishment produced only 100 watt bulbs, the second work establishment produced all three kinds of dome-tungsten filament bulbs and the third establishment produced only bar tube neon lamps.

The technology for the dome bulb was developed indigenously, with the design bought from General Electrics of USA. The market for the product was to begin with in Bengal, Orissa and Assam. Later, Bihar and Uttar Pradesh was also included. The size of the market kept on rising and the market spread into western India. The penetration in the south was low as Mysore Lamps, a state level public enterprise, provided competitive prices. In terms of the market share, Bengal Lamps was fourth after the major players like Philips, Crompton Greaves and Bajaj Bulbs.

During the early eighties, the company started to face major problems, amongst others was the labour unrest, which was prevalent in Bengal at that time due to the influence of the left front government. Due to this, schedules were delayed and major orders were cancelled. Tungsten, which was used as a raw material was often oxidised and as a result could not be used. This led to loss of the market share.

After the labour problems were sorted out, the operations of the company improved, but the market share kept on falling. The feedback from the market was that the products in the dome category of bulbs had decreased in quality.

It should be kept in mind that the glowing life of a bulb (the maximum period through which the bulb glowed without fusing) is the benchmark of the quality of a bulb. The general standard of the tungsten bulb is 1000 hours of glow life. Bengal Lamps conducted a quick quality test of the bulbs in the production line for 15 days, whose results showed the following (normal lot 1,00,000):

Days	Number of bulbs produced in the lot (After deduction of the bulbs broken)	Defect per lot (of the size tested)
1	60,000	1.8
2	1,00,000	3.1
3	80,000	2.6
4	1,00,000	3.0
5	96,000	0.6
6	78,000	5.6
7	98,000	1.2
8	97,000	1.8
9	1,00,000	1.3
10	1,00,000	1.2
11	98,000	1.4
12	98,000	1.7
13	96,000	4.1
15	89,000	3.0

The test did not include broken bulbs. From the lot of non-broken bulbs a random of 60 lamps were chosen for testing. The bulbs were switched on for 500 hours constantly and the defects were decided on the basis of the bulbs, which continued to glow after the duration of 500 hours and the ones which fused before that. It was found that 80% of the bulbs (declared defective) worked for 400 hours, 10% for 450 hours and the remaining for an average of 490 hours.

The quality department was very clear on the result. They wanted to study the production process immediately by stopping the production at least for a month. However, this was not possible from a business point of view. Since the market share had already been lost due to the earlier problems of labour, the company was not very keen on this suggestion. Alternatives had to be found, but what they were, was not clear.

Questions

1. What should be done in order to improve the quality of the product and how does one interpret the data given above in this context?
2. How does one implement control without stopping the production process but at the same time addressing the concerns of the quality department?

CASE 3—Paperback Books: Reporting System in the Sales Team

Paperback Books, mostly publishes works of fiction of leading authors in the English language. They have an enviable list of publications, which include 30 top-rated writers of the world and an equal number of bestsellers of the world.

The company has an arrangement with three major publishers of the world, who have given the rights to publish paperback versions of several original books that these companies publish. However, the right to sell these titles is restricted to India, Bangladesh, Pakistan and Sri Lanka. The company also had to agree to fight against any piracy cases in this region.

The companies, which gave Paperback Books the right to publish the books, retained the right to publish hard bound editions and e-mode editions in India, Pakistan, Bangladesh and Sri Lanka.

However, in order to reduce the marketing costs of Paperback Books, these companies agreed to include the name of Paperback Books in their website, which gave an active link to the home page of Paperback Books. They also agreed to put up a note that Paperback Books have the sole distribution right of the titles in the South Asian region.

The sales effort of Paperback Books involved the following:

1. Exclusive store arrangements in each state of the country.
2. Arrangement with Crossword Ltd., to display books in a particular corner of the retail chain.
3. Arrangement with Future Stores to put up books for sale.
4. Keeping stocks of books in railway station book kiosks.
5. Attending major book fairs in the state, where they could actively sell their books.
6. Maintaining a sales team, which could visit prospective buyers such as public libraries and clubs.
7. Facilitate, through dedicated stores, the supply of the books for the demand created by the sales team

The company had a sales force on the payroll of the company in all the major states of India, besides a tie-up with other companies in Bangladesh, Pakistan and Sri Lanka.

All members of the sales team sent a written monthly report of the books which were given as complimentary copies and the demand raised in the market. The sales team was coordinated at New Delhi through a central monitoring marketing department.

Problems faced by the company

The company was facing cross selling by the original company as many readers and libraries were interested in hard bound books rather than paperback books. The books which were sold fell short of the demand created by the representative. Complimentary copies were given, which did not generate any referral sale later on. The company suspected that representatives were selling some of the complimentary copies in the open market and making money.

Questions

1. Recommend a control system for Paperback Books.
2. How should a reporting system for representatives be designed, so that it takes all the problems, both direct and indirect, into consideration?

CASE 4—Rolta Motors: Ethical Issues in Trying to Retain Employees

Rolta Motors, a dealer in Maruti Udyog Limited (MUL) (a Government of India enterprise in collaboration with Suzuki Motors of Japan) had its operations in three district cities of Odisha, an eastern province of India. It managed showrooms for all categories of Maruti cars, which were largely present in the domestic car segment.

In addition, the company had three other workshops to provide after sales services to customers. It had a specially trained workforce for each of the car produced by MUL.

The company had a centrally located administrative department which had a human resource department, a general administration department and an accounting department which included an internal audit.

It was found in due course that the workshop workers were leaving their jobs and joining a private garage, who paid them a larger salary. This garage privately catered to Maruti cars once the company's sales warranty was over. This garage was also big enough to draw some of the administrative staff of the company. Besides, Maruti showrooms of other neighbouring states also provided lucrative jobs for the employees of Rolta Motors.

The company was desperate to retain its employees. The general manager of the company suggested a two stage plan to the board of directors. In the first stage, the employees would be selected as trainees. The salary paid to him/her will be 30% less than the negotiated salary. This will not be disclosed to the fresh recruits and they will be promised the payment of the balance 30% once their jobs were confirmed. On confirmation, the employees will be asked to deposit their original educational certificate with the company and only then will they be paid the salary along with their 30% dues. This will ensure that the trainees will not leave the job on training, since their original education certificate will be in the custody of the company, which would mean that they will not be able to leave the company without prior permission of the management.

In reality, it was found that while the first part of the program was working, however, when the new employees were asked to keep their original educational certificate in the custody of the company, they refused as they felt that the company was not trustworthy enough for such a deal. Most of them stopped coming to work within seven days of being asked to deposit their educational certificate.

Questions

1. What do you think about the employee retention program?
2. What went wrong with the program?

CASE 5—Sujata Bakery: Issues in Managing the Transfer Prices of an Organisation

Sujata Bakery had three divisions, (i) the bakery, which produced bread and confectionery items, (ii) the cake and pastry division and (iii) Indian confectionery. It worked in a small way and catered to the twin cities of Cuttack and Bhubaneswar. Largely a family business, the bakery had a simple organisation where, three brothers from the same family looked after the business.

All the three divisions sold products on the open market, besides selling through the outlet of Hot Chips (an Indian confectionery store, which sold various kinds of vegetable chips), Sujata Bakery (general confectionery) and Venus Hotel Chain (a south Indian specialty hotel). The divisions had the option of selling through general retail outlets in the market.

The open market gave the division 15% profit, whereas the internal transfer gave 13% profit. However, the transfer ensured that the firm got an overall profit of 22% over the total cost.

Sale in the open market by Division (i) and Division (iii) increased the overall profit marginally by 3%, but together all the divisions' open market operations reduced the overall profit by 2%.

However, the firm found it difficult not to sell in the open market as there was a huge demand. After a lot of deliberation the firm decided to sell 23% of the products of Division (i), 8% of the products of Division (ii) and 35% of Division (iii) in the open market.

Question

Comment on the decision of the firm to sell on the open market.

CASE 6—Viswal Steel: Land and Project Management

Viswal Steel was set up in order to promote the iron ore mines of the eastern India in the year 1999. It was a Rs. 500 crore project, which ensured a total capacity of 1000 metric tons of steel in a year at its full capacity. It was an integrated iron and steel plant set up with German technology.

The project had a total investment, in terms of land and capital, of Rs. 350 crore. Funded through a consortium of financers, the project was to be set up in the joint sector (government and private sector together).

The land was to come from the respective state government, as it required about 500 acres of land for the establishment of the plant. It was decided that the state should give land to the extent of Rs. 150 crore and not bring in any equity in cash.

As such, the land was bought in by the state. The project site was chosen near a local port town and about 70 kms away from the iron ore mines. The land was partly agricultural and partly arid. The government started procurement at a declared rate from the local farmers through the district administration. The arid land was already available as it belonged to the government. The proportion of arid land to agricultural land was 1:3.

In the meantime, a few local farmers started to oppose the land acquisition, which soon took a political turn. Members of the opposition started an agitation and the land procurement became murky.

However, the government stepped in with appropriate measures and after several rounds of protracted negotiations, it was decided that the land would be procured at a slightly higher price plus a job in the plant for each displaced agricultural family. The land procurement went on smoothly thereafter.

However, the project was delayed by a year and a half. By the time the project was completed it was felt that the number of persons employed, as a part of the job for land scheme, was much too high and it was adversely affecting the project's break even costs. Sooner or later, this would put the company in trouble, making it a losing proposition.

Question

In the light of the above, discuss what went wrong and what should have been done in order to implement the project correctly.

CASE 7—Pumul: Problems of a Milk Union

Phulbani Milk Union Limited (PUMUL) was established in the year 1986, as a part of "Operation Flood" of the Government of India in the Phulbani district of Orissa and the integrated movement under the Orissa Milk Federation Limited (OMFED).

PUMUL was to cater to three basic needs of the movement, "Operation Flood" which was to ensure milk sufficiency in the country.

1. Provide a collection point for locally produced milk in the Phulbani district and ensure its delivery to the local plant of OMFED for pasteurisation.
2. Provide veterinary services for the care of the cow and buffalo herds of the district, besides providing for quality breeding of cows and buffalos.
3. Provide financial help as well as cooperative banking facilities for the members of the union.

PUMUL had a total number of 3000 individual members and six dairy firms. It covered about 186 villages and collected about 2,000 litres of milk each day. It had a profit of Rs. 7,20,000 each year and its beneficiaries received a total of 58% of the amount as loan. Twenty percent was invested as term loans in OMFED, and the remaining was ploughed back as capital each year.

PUMUL, in the meantime had procured 3 vehicles, to transport the collected milk. This cost the company about Rs. 15,00,000.

In 1997, the beneficiaries wanted a bonus from their profit. This could mean a decrease in the plough back of the profits in the capital.

The board of governors was not in favour of this, but this led to complex issues, as some members were ready to leave the union and work as independent sellers in the market. The resistance was so high that PUMUL had to agree to its members' demands. However, successively, this eroded the capital in ten years.

Question

What was the actual problem in PUMUL? How does one design a control system for a cooperative business?

CASE 8—SHG: Helping the Way to Weave

Swamsidhaya Housing Group (SHG) was essentially a group of housewives who lived in an apartment of Mumbai by the same name. These were highly educated women, who had given up job opportunities to cater to their families' and children's needs. The members of the group were between 43 to 60 years in age. Most of them were well to do and had completed their basic responsibilities in life.

They were looking for meaningful work and struck upon the idea to help some local weavers in the Pune region who were reported to be in heavy debt to the local money lenders and had even sought the government's help to redress their problems.

Mrs. Wadia, who lived in the housing society, but was not a member of the group, had been working with a women's self-help group earlier in Delhi where her husband worked. Her neighbour, Mrs. Kulkarni, came to know that there were chances to help the poorer sections of society through a micro finance scheme, in which some financial institutions were interested. She put this idea to the group, which was immediately interested. They invited Mrs. Wadia to a subsequent meeting, and discussed the method in which the self-help group worked, in detail. They also discussed, the way in which the Pune based weavers could be helped by the group.

It emerged from the discussion, that the Pune based weavers could be helped by forming a self-help group, which could take up skilled jobs, and sell and market the products themselves.

Swamsidhaya was prompt to act on this. Three or four visits saw them forming the self-help group, consisting of both men and women. The self-help group was designed in such a way that it provided an end to end integration of the activities of the weavers. They tied up with few spinning mills at one end and few sari showrooms at the other end. In addition some activity based tie ups were made. The self-help group also participated in trade fairs organised by the state governments in various parts of the country.

The self-help group also had a common bank account, which could be operated through four signatories (any two signatories at a time). There were only six members in the group who were literate enough to operate a bank account.

The group was operative for six months and was able to pay off most of the debts, one by one. By now Swamsidhaya's efforts were well known to the government and they wanted them to be involved in some other similar cases, which the government thought it could handle better through the group.

Due to the increased work, Swamsidhaya made weavers' group self-reliant, so that they could work on their own.

Questions

1. How do you think Swamsidhaya helped in making the weavers self-reliant?
2. What should be the organisational structure to enable the weavers to continue to work in the same way and grow?
3. What are the factors that should be kept in mind in designing a control system for the weavers group?

CASE 9—Bioappliences: Issues in Managing the Culture of an Organisation that has been Taken Over

Anita Sood started her entrepreneurial drive Bioappliences by setting up a small handheld equipment firm for biotechnology driven R&D centres in India after she completed her graduation in biotechnology, at the age of 24. She came from a business family, which had a distribution firm of medicine in Bangaluru and few other southern states of India.

The firm did well from day one as it had very few competitors and the family business had a strong network of retail outlets in that part of the country. Anita soon decided to expand the business and started to look for avenues that could possibly lead to the acquisition of a similar firm in the northern part of India so that she had a wider coverage of the market. She was able to identify one such company, Lohia Equipment, in Ludhiana, Punjab which was for sale. The firm was similar to Anita's business in many ways. In the first place, it was a family held business and in the second, it was supported by a medical retail business. The products were also distributed through retail medical stores in Delhi, Lucknow, Chandigarh and few other large cities of the northern part of India.

The deal was settled for Rs.50 crore, which gave Bioappliences the total rights of the company. It took over an asset based inventory of Rs.36 crore and the rest was settled for liabilities. The company absorbed the current employees, both in the production and sales units. Their total number was about 112 persons.

Aftermath of the takeover

Bioappliences had standard rules of employment, which were put into force once the company was taken over. Salaries were increased by 30% over the current structure and sales incentive was made on a point basis; where Rs. 10,000 to Rs. 30,000 equalled 1 point, Rs.31,000 to Rs. 50,000 equalled 2 points, Rs.50,001 to Rs.1,00,000 equalled 3 points, and sales above Rs.1,00,000 equalled 5 points. The points were cumulative in nature and each sales team had to collectively get 10 points and individually at least 3 points. There was no hard and fast rule of how the team could get the points.

After the takeover, work timings were increased from 5 to 6 days. Soon there was resistance from the employees of company taken over. They started complaining that they were bullied and that the culture of the new company was insensitive to culture of northern part of the country. Bioappliences on the other hand found that the personnel were not hard working enough and were unnecessarily critical about the new set up.

Question

Discuss the problems that emerged in this issue and how a management control system is relevant in this discussion.

CASE 10—Signature Breweries: Financial Dilemma

Signature Breweries started with the idea of using locally available, low grade sugarcane produced in Chhattisgarh to manufacture alcohol for industrial use and human consumption, to be sold in the local market. It remained a single product company, producing seasonal and year round beers with smaller production volumes and slightly higher prices.

Signature used to outsource most of its brewing activities. The company was financially conservative and went through cost cutting initiatives to counterbalance the recent surge in packaging and freight costs. However, in recent times the company shifted its strategic focus and mass marketed its product under a variety of names. It adopted an extensive network of breweries and distribution systems. The company also got involved in a number of businesses related to its core business such as snacks, retail stores and theme parks, in order to give its products a strong foothold in the market.

The financial details of the company before and after the strategic changes are given below along with the major financial ratios.

The before and after conditions are camouflaged as A and B.

Table 1: Common sized balance sheet and income and expenses statement of the Company

Particulars	*A*	*B*
Assets		
Cash and term loans	1.4	55.6
Receivables	4.3	11.9
Inventories	4.3	11.7
Current asset (others)	1.3	2.4
Current asset Total	11.2	81.7
Net fixed assets	54.7	16
Assets - others	7.2	1
Intangibles	7.4	1.3
Investments & advances	2.9	0
Assets - total	**100**	**100**
Liabilities		
Account payable	7.4	9.1
Debt in current liabilities	0	0
Income tax payable	0.9	1.7
Current liabilities - others	3.8	13.7
Current liabilities - total	12.2	24.4
Long term debt	51.2	0
Deferred taxes	10.7	1.9
Liabilities - others	9.5	0.7
Liabilities - total	83.5	27.1
Stockholders' equity	16.5	72.9
Total liabilities and equity	**100**	**100**

Table 2: Common sized financial data and ratios

Particulars	*A*	*B*
Market data		
Beta	0.55	0.6
Price/Earning ratio	16.85	19.73
Price to book value	13.99	2.56
Dividend payout ratio	33.16	0
Liquidity		
Current ratio	0.92	3.35
Quick ratio	0.47	2.77
Asset management		
Inventory turnover	12.6	7.44
Receivables turnover	21.87	18.68
Fixed asset turnover	1.72	12.67
Debt management		
Total debt/Total assets ratio	51.19	0
Long term debt/ Shareholders equity	310.28	0
Interest coverage after tax	6.25	0
DuPont analysis		
Net profit margin	15	5.76
Asset turnover ratio	0.97	2.33
Return on equity	83.97	15.95

Questions

1. Which one is the 'before' and which one is the 'after' situation i.e., the earlier condition and the one after the strategic change of the company?
2. How do you think, these data help in financial reporting leading to control in the above case?

Bibliography

Aaker, Jennifer. "Dimensions of Brand Personality", *Journal of Marketing Research*, Vol 34 Issue 3, August 1997, p. 347.

Alles, M. and Datar, S. "Strategic Transfer Pricing", *Management Science*, Vol 44 No.4, April 1998.

Anthony, R.N. and Govindarajan, V. *Management Control Systems*, 10th ed., Tata McGraw-Hill Publishing Company, New Delhi.

Atkinson, Anthony A. "Organization Control System for Nineties", *CMA Magazine*, Vol 66, June 1992.

Barton, K.M. and Martin C.D. *Management*, New York, Irwin, McGraw Hill, 3rd ed., 1998.

Bhattacharyya, S.K. "Management Control Systems and Conflict – Framework for Analysis and Resolution", *International Studies of Management & Organization*, Winter 73/74, Vol 3 Issue 4.

Burns, W.J. and McFarlan. F.W. Information Technology Puts Power in Control Systems, *Harvard Business Review*, Sep/Oct 1987, Vol 65 No.5, p. 89.

Cecily, A. et al. *Managerial Accounting*, 1st ed, West Publishing Company, Minneapolis, 1993.

Daniel, S.J. and Reitsperger, W.D. "Management Control System for J.I.T: An Empirical Comparison of Japan and the US", *Journal of International Business Studies*, 1991, Vol. 22, No.4.

Gadiesh, Orit and Gilbert, James L. "Profit Pools: A Fresh Look at Strategy", *Harvard Business Review*, May-June 1998.

Hornegren, C.T. et al. *Cost Accounting: A Managerial Emphasis*, 10th ed., 21st Indian Reprint, PHI, 2002.

Jaworski, Bernard J. and Stakeholder, Vlasis. "Control Combinations in Marketing: Conceptual Framework and Empirical Evidence", *Journal of Marketing*, Vol.57, No. 1, January 1993.

Jaworski, Bernard J. "Towards a Theory of Marketing Control: Environmental Context Types and Consequences", *Journal of Marketing*, Vol. 52, No.1, July 1998.

Jefkins, Frank. Public Relations for Your Business, Jaico Publishing House, 2006, p. 11.

Kapferer, Jean-Noel. *The New Strategic Brand Management: Creating and Sustaining Brand Equity Long Term*, First South Asian edition, Kogan Page India Private Limited, 2004, p. 14.

Kumar, Nirmalya. "Kill a Brand, Keep a Customer", *Harvard Business Review*, Vol 81 Issue 12, December 2003, pp. 86-95.

Lebas, M.A. and Selto, F.H. Management Control: The Roles of Rules, Market and Culture, *Journal of Management Accounting Research*, 2001.

Maciariello, J.A. and Kirby, C.J. *Management Control System*, 2nd ed., PHI, New Delhi.

Merchant K.A. *Modern Management Control System: Text and Cases*, Prentice Hall, 1st ed., New Jersey, New York.

Pass, C. "Transfer Pricing in Multinational Companies", *Management Accounting*, September 1994, Vol. 26, No. 8, p. 44.

Picken, Joseph C. and Dess, G.G. "Out of (Strategic) Control", *Organizational Dynamics*, Summer 1997, Vol 26, No. 1, pp. 35-36.

Preble, John F. "Towards a Comprehensive System of Strategic Control", *Journal of Management Studies*, Vol.12 No.1, 1987, pp. 91-409.

Ramanathan, Kavasseri. A Proposed Framework for Designing Management Control System in Non-Profit Organizations, *Financial Accountability of Management*, Summer 1995.

Robbins, S.P. *Organizational Behaviour*, 10th ed., Pearson Education, 2003, New Delhi.

Ronald, W.H. *Management Accounting*, 6th ed., TMH, New Delhi.

Schreyogg, G. and Steinmann. "Strategic Control: A New Perspective", *Academy of Management Review*, Vol. 12 No.1, 1987, pp. 91-103.

Sharma, S. *Management Control System: Text and Cases*, 1st ed., 7th reprint, TMH, 1999.

Still, Richard R., Edward W. Cundiff and Norman A.P. Govoni. Sales Management Decisions, Strategies and Cases, 5th ed., Prentice Hall India, 1988.

Teall, H.D. Winning and Strategic Management Control System, *CMA Magazines*, March 1992, Vol 66 No. 2.

Williamson, D. *Cost and Management Accounting*, 1st ed., Indian Reprint 1996, PHI, New Delhi.

Wilmshurst, John. *The Fundamentals and Practices of Marketing*. 3rd ed., Butterworth-Heinemann, Oxford, 1995.

Wysocili, R.K., Beck Jr. Robert et al. *Effective Project Management*, John Wiley and Sons, New Jersey, 2000.

Yaitz, B. and Newman, W.H. *Strategy In Action: The Execution, Politics and Payoff of Business Planning*, The Free Press, New York, 1982.

Web References

1. Unilever PLC is a UK-based FMCG company founded in the 1890s. It has products in major categories including healthcare, personal care, and food products source:<http://www.unilever.com/ourcompany/aboutunilever/introducingunilever>
2. Procter & Gamble is a US-based FNCG company founded in 1837. It markets its range of products-personal care, household cleaning, laundry detergents, prescription drugs, etc. - in several countries. Source: <http://www.pg.com/company/who we are/ourhistory.jhtml>
3. KFC Corporation, based in Louisville, Kentucky, is a popular chicken restaurant chain, specializing in original Recipe®. Extra Crispy™ Twister®, and Colonel's Crispy Strips® Chicken. It was founded in 1930. http://www.kfc.com/
4. McDonald's is a leading global foodservice retailer with than 30000 local restaurants serving 52 million people in more than 100 countries. It was founded in 1955. http://www.mcdonalds.com/
5. Marks & Spencer plc is a UK-based retailer. As of September 2007, it had more than 750 stores across 30 countries. Source: <http://www.marksandspencer.com>
6. Shoppers' Stop, founded in 1991, is one of India's largest retail chains. As of September 2007, it had 22 stores in different cities of India. http://www.shoppersstop.com
7. <http://www.dmow. org/site/pp.asp?c=9fLIJWOwHE&b=274586>
8. <http://www.cipr.co.uk>
9. The systematic collection of data derived from direct observation of the everyday life of a particular society, group or subculture. This methodology requires the researcher's immersion in the culture/subculture under study and is an interactive process. Source:< members.ozemail.com.au/~mghslib/subjects/society%20culture/Glossary.htm>
10. Interbrand is a leading international branding consultancy specializing in brand services and activities, such as brand strategy, corporate identity, etc.
11. SAP AG, founded in 1792, based in Germany. It is a leading provider of collaborative business solutions for all type of industries and for every major market. Source: <http://www.sap.com/company/index.epx>

Glossary

Accounting: A process of recording business transactions in monitory terms set by the laws of book keeping

Activity: A Business transaction or any other process in the business.

Action Control: Control of activities set on standard procedures.

Administered Compensation: Compensation which does not go through collective bargaining.

Agency theory: A process of control by entering into contract with individual for incentives to motivate the individuals.

Audit: A process of financial management where recording of transactions are verified and proof of the transactions are checked. It is now broadened to other areas of management control where there is need to verify the transactions with set standards.

Audit Evidence: Information used by an auditor for checking reliability of a transaction in audit.

Benchmarks: The desirable level of business that is required to perform well in a competitive environment and by comparing the best practices in the business.

Benchmarking: The process of setting up benchmarks.

Benchtrending: A process through which the common trend in a good quality practice is assured in an industry.

Bower's Model: A model which suggest inclusion of the lower level of management to participate in the decision taking and planning of the business.

Budget: An annual financial plan which allocates resources based on the activities that are to be addressed based on the previous years experience. Budgets are incremental in nature. They consist of budget committee and budget manual.

Budget Control: It is a process of using budget to measure the actual performance against the real and calculate variance analysis in order to bring back normalcy in the business.

Ceiling: The maximum amount allowed to be spent under an incremental budget.

Closed Loop Control: The corrective actions are initiated automatically since it is assessed and affected by intelligent feedback process within the organisation.

Close-ended Questionnaire: This consist of questions which have a set of alternative answered already spelled out.

Cooperative Society: A legal entity which is generally formed between groups of common interest individual who perform a business or like activity generally for no profit motive.

Cost-based Transfer Pricing: The transfers are based on the basis of cost incurred by the other business centers.

Critical Path Method: A tool of project management where time-cost estimation is done and the optimum schedule for the project is created.

Cybernetic Control: The entire process of control and communication which has been learned from nature.

Diagnostic Control System: Use of diagnostic tool such as data analysis to find out anything unusual in the business.

DSS: Decision support system is an aid to decision making process by using a series of 'what if' questions.

Entrapment: Getting in a mode to justify wrong doing by sighting legal and moral issues without recourse to corrective action.

Expense Centre: Responsibility centers where inputs are only measured or are measurable.

Floor: The least that can be spent under a budget.

Focus Group: A method of research and information seeking where a group of people who can find relevant answer to the problem, belonging to the effected problem, are used to collect information through unstructured questions.

Formal Control System: Control system in an organisation which is laid down through and along the line of organisational structure.

Go/no go Control: Here project's team performance is primarily in control rather than results received.

Historical Standards: The actual performance of past of an organisation when used as a control tool.

Human Resource Audit: The method of adhering to set process of human resource practice in an organisation.

Incremental Budget: A budget where the current year is a percentage increased on the last year's allocation.

Informal Control System: The unwritten and self initiated control mechanics that happens in an organisation.

Information Asymmetry: The difference in information sought in a market by the investors and the firms leading to difference in price of the investment.

Input Control: A process where the input in a system is controlled in order to reach quality.

Investment Centers: A responsibility centre whose profit is evaluated in terms of cost and profit associations.

JIT: An acronym for Just in Time. A system of managing inventory where procurement is done on a need based leading to piling up cost.

Key Success Variables: The variables in an organization which if changed will affect the business as a whole.

Loose Control: A system where no external control is inflicted on the people in an organisation and it is believed that people will work properly as they know what to do without recourse to any control on them.

Management Control System: A system where inter-related part of business are coordinated and operated by use of a predetermined process and a group of information channels by the managers.

Open ended Questionnaire: Answers are sought not on pre-determined responses.

Marketing Audit: A comprehensive audit done on the marketing function in a periodic manner in order to endorse the strategies of the business.

Master Budget: A summary budget which incorporates all the functional budgets of the business.

Matrix Organisation: In this organisation the basic structure is arranged by the functions and alongside is superimposed a structure by projects.

Open Loop Control System: A system where the initiative of corrective action lies outside the scope of the system.

Post Controls: These are seen as report cards of control and are exercised at the end of the control.

Process Controls: The specification of the control lies on the process of the business.

Profit Centers: A responsibility centre where output is compared with the assets used in monetary terms.

PERT: Project evaluation and review techniques suggest a method of taking all uncertainty of a project and trying to optimise the schedule.

Responsibility Centers: A functional unit of a business which is headed by a responsible manager who is responsible for all the functions of the business.

Revenue Centers: Responsibility centers where output in measured in monetary terms.

Self Control: A process where individuals set personal goals and monitor their own activity to reach a desired result.

Shared Goal: The set of values or aspirations which the organisation stands for. It is also known as superordinate goal.

Social Accounting: It is the systematic accounting and reporting of those parts of a business that have a social impact.

Social Control: Social control refers to the prevailing social perspective and patterns of interpersonal interactions within subgroups in the firm.

Social Information System: The system which enables the organisation in an aggregate to know the social objectives.

Systematic Information System: These are used to appraise the views in the making of decision through dialectical approach.

Target Cost: The cost which the customers are willing to pay which is incorporated in the production system to reflect the aspiration of the common minimum customer.

Tight Control: The structured control intervention in an organisation which leads to reward and punishment system.

TQM: A process by which the quality of services and products is constantly improved in order to satisfy the customers.

Transfer Price: The value placed on the transfer of goods or services among two or more profit centers of the same organisation.

Value Chain: Value chain analysis is a strategic analysis tool that can be used to identify areas in which value can be enhanced for customers or cost can be reduced.

Variance Analysis: The method in which the difference between the actual performances is measured against the budgeted performance standards and correction taken.

Zero Based Budgeting: A budget in which no base year is used. It is also known as the scratch budget.

Index

J